Decision Support Systems: Theory and Application

NATO ASI Series

Advanced Science Institutes Series

A series presenting the results of activities sponsored by the NATO Science Committee, which aims at the dissemination of advanced scientific and technological knowledge, with a view to strengthening links between scientific communities.

The Series is published by an international board of publishers in conjunction with the NATO Scientific Affairs Division

A Life Sciences   Plenum Publishing Corporation
B Physics   London and New York

C Mathematical and   D. Reidel Publishing Company
    Physical Sciences   Dordrecht, Boston, Lancaster and Tokyo

D Behavioural and   Martinus Nijhoff Publishers
    Social Sciences   Boston, The Hague, Dordrecht and Lancaster
E Applied Sciences

F Computer and   Springer-Verlag
    Systems Sciences   Berlin Heidelberg New York
G Ecological Sciences   London Paris Tokyo
H Cell Biology

Series F: Computer and Systems Sciences Vol. 31

Decision Support Systems: Theory and Application

Edited by
Clyde W. Holsapple
Andrew B. Whinston
Management Information Research Center
Krannert Graduate School of Management
Purdue University, West Lafayette, IN 47907, USA

Springer-Verlag
Berlin Heidelberg New York London Paris Tokyo
Published in cooperation with NATO Scientific Affairs Divison

Proceedings of the NATO Advanced Study Institute on Decision Support Systems:
Theory and Application held at Acquafredda di Maratea, Italy, June 3–14, 1985

ISBN 3-540-17774-4 Springer-Verlag Berlin Heidelberg New York
ISBN 0-387-17774-4 Springer-Verlag New York Berlin Heidelberg

© Springer-Verlag Berlin Heidelberg 1987
Printed in Germany

Printing: Druckhaus Beltz, Hemsbach; Bookbinding: J. Schäffer GmbH & Co. KG, Grünstadt
2145/3140-543210

PREFACE

This volume contains revised versions of papers presented
at the N.A.T.O. Advanced Study Institute on Decision Support
Systems Theory and Applications. This meeting took place in
Maratea, Italy for a two week period in June 1985. The lecturers
represented an international assortment of distinguished research
centers in industry, government, and academia. Participants in
the Institute represented eleven N.A.T.O. countries. Both
participants and lecturers shared in the common goal of learning
about emerging theoretical and applied developments in the decision support system (DSS) field.

Researchers and practitioners interested in current DSS
issues and the shape of future decision support systems are the
intended audience for this book. There is a particular, recurring emphasis on the adaptation of artificial intelligence techniques for use in the DSS world. The book's chapters are organized into two major sections, the first dealing with theoretical
topics and the second with applications.

Although much progress has been made in understanding the
foundations of decision support systems, there is clearly room
for enlarging on basic concepts, frameworks, theories, and
techniques. The seven papers contained in Section I are directed
along these lines. In the initial chapter, Henk Sol identifies
several paradoxes that can be observed in the DSS field. He
argues that these are indicative of the need for a clearer delineation of the concept of DSS and, to this end, he introduces a
framework for DSS-design environments. Chapter 2 descends from
this global perspective to focus on the topic of model management.
Here, Robert Blanning discusses the principal features of a
relational theory of model management. In this view, a DSS's
models are managed as a set of virtual relations. Expanding on
this perspective, he suggests that relational data base management ideas can similarly be adapted to managing other kinds of
knowledge in the context of a DSS. Dimitris Karagiannis and
Hans-Jochen Schneider point out some limitations of relying on
traditional relational data base management to handle a DSS's

descriptive knowledge. To help overcome these, they discuss an extension that allows rules to be used in conjunction with relational tables. Under this approach, a DSS can answer user requests by a combination of deduction on the rules and retrieval from the tables.

In Chapter 4, Amilcar and Cristina Sernadas point out the need for accommodating logical, structural, and procedural kinds of knowledge representation in decision support systems. As a possible basis for DSS development, they propose a framework for unified treatment of these three modes by means of parameterized theories. Michel Klein, Jean-Eloi Dussartre, and Francois Despoux discuss DSS development with the OPTRANS tool in Chapter 5. In particular, they explore extensions to the OPTRANS problem processor that allow it to make inferences using sets of rules in addition to its data management and model management capabilities.

The final two chapters in Section I are concerned with the evaluation of DSS development tools. In the first of these, Nasir Ghiaseddin identifies nine areas that a developer should consider when assessing DSS development tools. He derives these developer needs from an analysis of end user needs. Chapter 7 takes a narrower perspective by concentrating on tool characteristics that should be considered for the construction of artificially intelligent decision support systems. It focuses on the integration, representation, and processing of reasoning knowledge within decision support systems.

Section II contains ten papers presenting an interesting assortment of DSS applications. The application areas range from office automation and accounting to the support of strategic planning. In Chapters 8, G. Bracchi and B. Pernici argue that decision support systems can facilitate a variety of office activities. In discussing these activities, they survey the behaviors of relevant decision support systems and suggest several related research topics.

Chapters 9 through 11 examine DSS applications in the area of accounting. In the first of these, Eric Denna and William

McCarthy describe the implementation of an events accounting
system that supports a variety of decisions in a manufacturing
environment. The knowledge system for this DSS involves the
integrated use of relational data bases, spreadsheets, procedural
models and graphic images. The DSS development tool used for
this system is the KnowledgeMan environment. In Chapter 10,
Andrew Bailey et al. examine the applicability of decision support systems to financial auditing and describe an ongoing
research project into DSS usage for evaluating internal accounting controls. Particular attention is given to the contributions
expert system and other artificial intelligence techniques can
make to these DSS applications. A general DSS environment
intended specifically for auditors is proposed by James Gerlach
in Chapter 11. It is conceived to provide not only a strong
basis for general auditing support, but also to allow customiza-
tion to reflect unique traits of an audit staff and audit engagements.

In Chapter 12, Leif Methlie examines the applicability of
expert system techniques to building DSSs in the realm of financial management. In this vein he describes an experimental
expert system for supporting bank loan evaluations. Three more
DSS applications are reviewed by James Gantt and Donovan Young
in Chapter 13. The three DSSs are designed to assist planners
in the allocation of resources for purposes of project management, location allocation, and mobilization planning. Chapter 14
describes a large-scale energy management DSS that operates on a
microcomputer. Norman Revell explains how this data-intensive
system has been developed to support both operational and strategic decisions of an energy manager.

Chapter 15 explores the use of expert system techniques for
supporting decisions about microeconomic systems. Elizabeth
Hoffman et al. argue that rule and information flow structures
of microeconomic systems are amenable to expert system modelling.
This is illustrated with the example of an auction bidding mechanism and participating economic agents. They further propose
an approach for testing resultant systems from a qualitative as
well as quantitative perspective.

Section II closes with two papers concerning DSS applications in the area of strategic planning. In the first of these,
Vicente Salas Fumás discusses the nature of strategic planning
and points out the implications for building DSSs that address
strategic planning problems. He emphasizes the issues of real-
time strategic decision making and the use of competitive gaming
models within the systems' modelling capabilities. In Chapter
17, Peter Mertens identifies various ways in which today's information technology can be used to enhance an organization's
strategic position. He proceeds to explain how these techniques
may improve strategic decision making.

In closing it is appropriate to acknowledge the support of
the lecturers and participants in ensuring stimulating intellec-,
tual interchange as well as creating a friendly ambiance.
Mr. Guzzardi and his staff of the Hotel Villa del Mare greatly
enhanced this atmosphere. We would also like to express our
appreciation of the N.A.T.O. Scientific Affairs Division, which
was invaluable in providing financial support for many participants. We are particularly grateful to Dr. Craig Sinclair,
Director, ASI Programme. Professors G. Bracchi, N. Revell and
H. Schneider, members of the organizing committee, provided
useful suggestions and contacts. Furthermore, the administrative
and financial assistance provided by Professors Sergio de Julio
and Manlio Gaudioso of CRAI (Consorzio per la Ricerca e le
Applicazioni di Informatica) was very helpful during the meeting.
Mrs. Barbara Kester of International Transfer of Science and
Technology was helpful in the selection of Maratea as the site
of the meeting. Finally, we are deeply indebted to Kathy Smith
whose patient and diligent efforts in producing and editing this
book's manuscript have significantly enhanced its value to all
concerned.

Clyde W. Holsapple
Andrew B. Whinston

TABLE OF CONTENTS

X

SECTION I - CONCEPTS AND THEORY

1. PARADOXES AROUND DSS

Henk G. Sol
Department of Mathematics and Informatics
Delft University of Technology
2628 BL Delft, The Netherlands

1. INTRODUCTION

Numerous researchers and practitioners have no hesitations
in putting the label Decision Support Systems (DSS) to their
work. It is remarkable that the term DSS is much used without
a very strict definition of its content. Many writers seem to
approach DSS as a philosophy to seek a useful complementarity
between technological tools and human judgement and discretion.
Klein and Hirschheim [1985] point out that 'there appears to be
an implicit assumption on the part of DSS writers that DSS are
beneficial to organizations and the DSS intervention process is
not inherently polemic'. Gintzberg and Stohr [1982] remark that
'the basis for defining DSS has been migrating from an explicit
statement of what a DSS does to some ideas about how the DSS
objective can be accomplished (i.e., what components are required?, what usage pattern is appropriate?, what development
process is necessary?)'. This migration during the years can be
shown in the following descriptions of DSS:

1. In the early 1970's DSS was described as 'a computer-based
    system to aid in decision making'. The starting point was
    found in the application of interactive technology to mana-
    gerial tasks in order to use computers for better decision
    making. There was a strong cognitive focus in this DSS-
    concept, viz. that of a single decision maker.

2. In the mid to late 1970's the DSS-movement emphasized
    'interactive computer-based systems which help decision
    makers utilize data bases and models to solve ill-structured
    problems'. The emphasis lies not so much on the decision
    process, but rather on the support for personal computing
    with tools for fast applications development and packages
    for financial planning.

3. In the later 1970's to early 1980's the DSS bandwagon

NATO ASI Series, Vol. F31
Decision Support Systems: Theory and Application
Edited by C. W. Holsapple and A. B. Whinston
© Springer-Verlag Berlin Heidelberg 1987

provides <u>systems</u> 'using suitable and available technology to improve effectiveness of managerial and professional activities'. User-friendly software is produced almost unexceptionally under the label DSS. Disciplines like operations research and psychology are jumping on the bandwagon. Concepts like information center and prototyping are put forward in the same utterance as DSS.

4. By now we face a new technical base for DSS: the convergence on intelligent workstations. Telecommunication technology puts forward the issues of organizational versus personal computing and distributed DSS. We see new technologies emerging as expert systems and document-based systems. This is expressed by Elam et al. [1985] in the need for a new vision on DSS. They propose to confine the notion DSS to 'the exploitation of intellectual and computer-related technologies to improve creativity in decisions that really matter'.

We do not want to enter a new debate on definitions of DSS. Rather, we like to explore what new insights we gained from applying the DSS concept to improve organizational efficiency and effectiveness. In general, for a comparison of research contributions dealing with organizational decision making, one might wonder
   - what problems are addressed,
   - what paradigm or 'Weltanschauung' governs the process of problem conceptualization and problem specification,
   - what construct-paradigm or model cycle is followed, expressing in broad terms the order of activities,
   - what methodology, as an actual sequence of activities in view of a problem situation, is used, telling what to do in which activity, what project control is performed, during the activities,
   - what theory is followed, contributing to the actualization of the model cycle and the methodology in terms of how the activity is to be performed, and especially, how alternative solutions are to be generated.

2. PARADOXAL OBSERVATIONS ON DSS

A useful framework for research on DSS is introduced in
Sprague [1980]. He discusses the perspective of the end-user,
the builder and the toolsmith from which a DSS can be viewed.
In accordance with this distinction the concept of a DSS-genera-
tor is put forward to bridge the gap between general tools and
specific DSS. Sprague distinguishes as the main components of
a DSS a data base, a model base, and an intermediate software
system which interfaces the DSS with the user.

Within the data base for decision support one can distinguish
between external data from public data sources, administrative
data produced by the transaction processing system, and internal
data created by personal computing. The models in the model
base as envisaged by Sprague are mostly of the 'equation' type:
great number of so called corporate models or financial models
consists of definition equations and behavioral equations. Econometric models also consist of equation models. Another category is formed by optimalization models based on linear, dynamic
or stochastic programming.

A first generation of so-called DSS-generators focuses on
equation models with data base and interactive facilities like
data-, model- and text manipulation, cf. Klein and Manteau [1983]
and Bergquist and McLean [1983]. By now, the integrated facilities are not only offered on mainframes, but also on micro-
computers together with facilities for 'down-loading from and
up-loading to central computer systems through data-communica-
tion'.

A less technological framework is put forward by Bonczek
et al. [1981]. They replace the components mentioned by the
concepts of a language system, a knowledge system and a problem
processing system. The language system is the sum of all linguistic facilities made available to the decision maker by a
DSS. A knowledge system is a DSS's body of knowledge about a
problem domain. The problem processing system is the mediating
mechanism between expressions of knowledge in the knowledge
system and expressions of problems in the language system.

The framework put forward by Bonczek et al. makes it easy to relate the work in the field of artificial intelligence to DSS. We define an expert system as 'a computer system containing organized knowledge, both factual and heuristic, that contains some specific area of human expertise, and that is able to produce inferences for the user', see Chang, Melamud and Seabrook [1983].

When one looks upon an inference system as a special kind of problem processing system and upon the knowledge base as a special kind of knowledge system, then these expert systems fit neatly into the framework. Along this line, a school of researchers focuses on the representation of knowledge for decision support, cf. Fox [1984], Bonczek et al. [1983]. The relevance of epistemology to improve decision-making processes is addressed by e.g., Lee [1983], Stamper [1984].

The process of designing DSS is as yet not much addressed. Sprague and Carlson [1982] advocate an approach 'to systems analysis which is intended to identify requirements in each of the three major capability areas of DSS. The approach is based on a set of four user-oriented entities: Representations, Operations, Memory Aids and Control Mechanisms'. Humphreys et al. [1983] report empirical research on rounds and stages in the development paths and the roles played by various participants, as analyzed in several projects. Empirical research as presented e.g., in Fick and Sprague [1980], Ginzberg et al. [1982], Bennett [1983], Sol [1983], shows the variety of approaches undertaken by various researchers and practitioners to create systems for effective decision support.

It may be dangerous to draw conclusions from the available expertise on DSS. However, following the framework for evaluation outlined above it is possible to present some conclusions in the form of several paradoxes.

1. The paradox of understanding and designing.
    DSS are directed at ill-structured problem situations. It is striking, however, how little attention is paid to the process of problem solving. There are various frames to

describe these processes. If one takes, for instance, the
phases of intelligence - design - choice - implementation,
then one might observe that a great number of DSS address
the phases of choice and implementation. Recently there is
argumentation to focus on intelligence and choice, see e.g.,
Landry et al. [1985], Sol [1982]. Before one can start
looking for a problem solution or designing a DSS or, more
generally, an information system, one has to understand the
problem situation or the actual object system. Of course,
design of an application or choice of a solution has to be
done within constraints of time and resources. But, 'thinking before doing' is also applicable to DSS-design. Therefore, more emphasis should be placed on the activities of
problem identification and specification.

2. The paradox of aggregation.
As to the paradigm or Weltanschauung applied we may conclude
that a great many of the contributions start from the premise
that decision support can be achieved through aggregation of
data. Keen [1980] presents a summary of major case studies,
all using data on an aggregated level. The same applies to
the case studies presented in Alter [1980] and Sol [1983].
A great many approaches are starting from the premise that
more and better information will also lead to better decisions. Dickson [1983] identifies as required facilities for
management support: writing, communicating, individual
processing, managing data, problem finding, making decisions
and conveying decisions. As Sprague and Carlson [1982] put
it: 'Data bases and DBMS are an important prerequisite to
DSS because building a DSS without existing data bases and
associated DBMS will be extremely difficult'. In several
organizations using DSS one may observe a logical or even
physical distinction between
  - a data base with detailed figures on primary processes,
  - a decision support data base with individual data, ex-
    ternal data and aggregated administrative and trans-
    actional data.
One can give several, mainly technical, arguments for this

distinction:
- The efficiency of existing data base management systems
  and especially of relational ones, still is a technical
  problem, if one tries to develop one physical data base.
- Personal computing demands a hardware- and software
  environment different from the one for transaction processing.
- Data in the decision support data base may be not as
  accurate as the transactional data.

The decision support data base mostly contains data aggregated from the basic figures, e.g., on time or on product
characteristics. However, it is shown in several studies
that use of this type of data may be dangerous for decision
making: One may question the validity of management information produced through aggregation, see Reuijl [1982], Sol
[1982], Sol [1985]. It is difficult to give the appropriate
degree of aggregation for various decisions. Aggregated
data do not always support equations that give a valid description of reality. Many decision support system-genera-
tors are based on the use of aggregated data, which is in
contradiction with the empirical findings.

3. The paradox of input and output.
   The model cycle behind a great many contributions in the DSS-
   field can be characterized as one, trying to integrate
   scientific, ethical and esthetic modes of thought in a syn-
   thetic, interdisciplinary way. The availability of data
   and appropriateness of decision making in organizations is
   not much questioned. Or, to put it in another way, the
   modelling paradigm is mostly the one of thinking in terms of
   relationships between variables. Most models encountered in
   DSS are of the 'equation' type: a set of definition and
   behavioral equations, possibly together with a goal function.
   Once the behavioral equations are estimated and empirically
   validated, one starts playing with the model, e.g., in an
   optimalization mode, or in a 'what-if' or 'goal-seeking'
   mode. However, these models are only applicable under the
   assumption that the equations can be filled in and that they

give a valid description of reality. This assumption that
one can describe reality based on an input-output specification of a black-box, seems to hold only in a very few
decision-making situations. A way-out can be found in the
application of models of the 'process' type, as presented in
the next paragraph.

4. The paradox of incremental design.
As to a methodology for developing DSS, it is difficult to
identify a generic framework. Keen [1980] applies the term
DSS to situations where a final system can be developed only
through an adaptive process of learning and evolution.
Henderson and Ingraham [1982] remark that 'prototyping or
adaptive design has been suggested as an effective approach
for developing and implementing DSS. Empirical research has
shown this design strategy is effective in establishing meaningful user involvement and high user satisfaction. A comparison with the information requirements generated by a
structured group process indicates that prototyping is a
convergent design method that may overlook important user
information needs'. It is clear that an evolutionary or
iterative approach is prevailing in many cases of DSS development, see e.g., Davis et al. [1980] and Sol [1982]. However, such a prototyping or incremental approach is not
necessarily converging and is no guarantee for an effective
DSS. Our experiences with prototyping in a number of practical studies lead to the conclusion, see Sol [1984b], that
  - prototyping may overemphasize the activity of solution
    finding by jumping to a dynamic model of the target
    system. The activity of understanding a problem situa-
    tion may get too little attention.
  - not every organization can bear the 'throw away' aspects
    of prototyping. In a bureaucratic organization and
    even in a traditional data processing department it may
    be difficult to set aside a prototype in which money
    and manpower is invested.
  - a prototype is easily taken away as a pilot system or
    as a final production system, before one has properly

experimented with the prototype.
- developing prototypes for various sub-systems in an
  information system may lead to isolated thinking or a
  'tunnel vision', neglecting the overview of the total
  system. This danger can be reduced if one starts prototyping from a good information system plan for an organization.

5. The paradox of personal computing management.
    DSS is closely related to phrases as end-user computing and
    personal computing. A lot of development effort and tools
    are directed at the support of individual decision making.
    An uncontrolled stimulation of this path may lead to a chaos
    of hardware and software, of personal files and of models.
    This asks for a strong management of personal computing
    resources and facilities.

6. The paradox of loosely coupling.
    As to possible theories for developing DSS we observe that
    coordination of decision-making processes is still a neglect-
    ed topic. Many DSS and DSS-environments tacitly take the
    assumption that loosely coupled systems, be it individual
    decision makers, groups, departments or DSS-environments, are
    an appropriate answer to the coordination problem in organ-
    izations. However, this is not obvious at all, cf. Bosman
    [1983]. This starting point is still much used.

3. RETHINKING THE CONCEPT

The paradoxes formulated make clear that the bandwagon of
DSS does not necessarily follow a right track. Although the
interest for DSS should be welcomed, a clearer delineation of
the concept of DSS is needed in order to make it a potentially
rich track. Rich, in the sense that it can foster the effectiveness and efficiency of organizational decision making. Keen has
questioned the role of modelling and quantitative models in
stimulating creative thinking. If the OR-discipline is taking
up the DSS-line, it should pick up this challenge and focus on
creative decision making and learning on the merge of MIS and
OR/Management Science. Some researchers try to design DSS

according to principles from cognitive psychology. Cats-Baril
and Huber [1984] point out that the generalizability of these
principles is still low. They also mention a critical factor
in decision support, viz. the presence of problem-solving heuristics. Another consideration deals with the relevance of AI-
research to DSS. Stamper [1984] remarks: 'Our growing technical
capacity to produce, store and distribute information is no
guarantee of the information's organizational and social usefulness. The trend towards intelligent, knowledge-based systems
cannot solve the problem; instead it could well make the problem
worse by disguising poor information under a cloak of logical
self-consistency'. Although DSS may provide a link on the path
from traditional information processing towards knowledge engineering, we may recall that expert systems are always based on
historical expertise. The search for expertise should not
detract attention from grasping creativity-process in new, un-
experienced problem situations. However, I would prefer to take
up the process of problem solving in a knowledge-based framework,
which may give a solution to the paradoxes formulated. Therefore,
I extended in Sol [1983] the frameworks presented by Sprague and
Bonczek into a new one, see Figure 1. I propose to direct DSS-
research to the concept of DSS-generators or, more generally,
DSS-design environments. One of the main reasons for this choice
is the lack of generalizability in dealing with specific decision
support systems. Another reason is that one has to address all
stages in the process of problem solving, not only at the empirical, problem-dependent level, but also at the conceptual level.

Especially for the solution of ill-structured problems, the
choice of a Weltanschauung and a construct-paradigm or model
cycle, as point of departure for activities of problem conceptualization and problem specification, are closely related. The
expression of a methodology and a theory, in view of a problem
under consideration, follows these choices closely. I put forward the idea that it is possible to combine a Weltanschauung
with a construct-paradigm by giving the concepts of a DSS-gener-
ator, a language system, a knowledge system and a problem processing system a concrete form in the notion of an INQUIRY

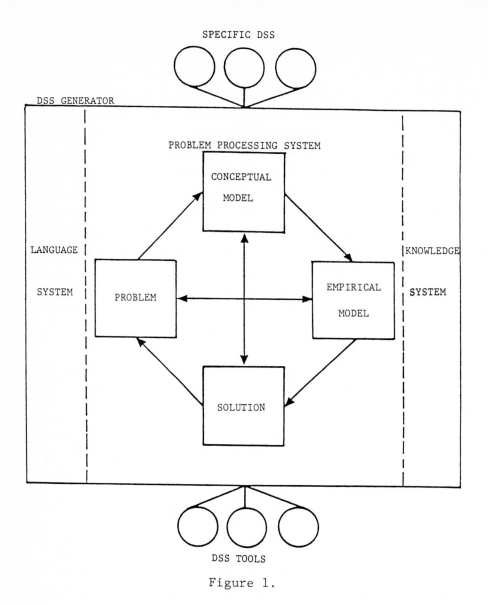

Figure 1.

SYSTEM. I define an inquiry system as a structured set of instruments which can be used as a context or modelling environment in the problem solving activities. It expresses a methodology in view of a problem area.

The inquiry system serves in the first instance as a 'context for conceptualization'. It presents in its language system and knowledge base the building blocks for the creation of a

system description. Subsequently, the inquiry system appears
as a conceptual model for the problem specification, in an
empirical model for the solution finding and in a target system
for the implementation. The notion of an inquiry system has
several important contributions.

1. By translation of a Weltanschauung and a construct-paradigm
    into a context for conceptualization one can discuss the
    premises behind theory formulation. Through its applica-
    tion in the construction of a conceptual model and a model
    system, a theory comes about.

2. The products of the various activities in the process of
    problem solving are building on each other as successive
    layers. This allows for an easy adjustment of individual
    theories and organizational theories and for an evolution-
    ary development of a target system.

3. The modelling environments in the inquiry system enable a
    flexible support of all phases in the process of problem
    solving. Problem finding can get at least as much attention
    as solution finding.

For the construction of conceptual models and empirical
models one needs a language system which does not restrict the
capabilities of inquirers and decision makers in using knowledge
to make models and to create evidence. I make a distinction
between on the one hand a description form using equations and
on the other hand process or rule-based models. The EQUATION
MODELS are frequently encountered in DSS for strategic and organizational problems, especially in corporate or financial models.
In these models one has to define functional relationships in
terms of definition equations or behavioral equations. Although
these may be specified in a non-procedural way as in several
DSS-generators, they still apply to the outside of a phenomenon,
seen as a black-box.

In the PROCESS OR RULE-BASED MODELS one does not try to summarize a process in equation form. Instead, one tries to describe the sequence of events in a system. I introduce the
notion of an ENTITY as an identifiable set of associated
ATTRIBUTES. An entity may portray behavior by applying one or

more transformation rules to change the values of some of its attributes and by interactions with other entities. I define in a SCENARIO related to an entity the possible transformation rules and the possible interaction paths of an entity, as well as the conditions under which these can be actualized. This can be done in various modes. One mode is the 'declarative' mode, as e.g., encountered in interpreted predicate logic, see Bubenko [1982], Sernadas [1982]. Another mode is the 'procedural' mode, as we know this style from a great many procedural programming languages. It is sometimes suggested that these modes are their antagonists. I prefer to see them as complementary. Depending on the application domain and the users involved, one might prefer one of the modes.

In combining within an entity a data part and an action part, I come close to the concept of object-representation in object oriented languages, see e.g., Cox [1984]. The notions of an entity and a scenario enable us to 'open the black-box' of an individual decision maker and specify the concepts and rules applied. We are able to specify their own language system, knowledge system and problem processing system. As to the construction of a conceptual model of an individual decision maker, we have to describe how scenarios of entities with their attributes are actualized. We may specify various psychological types of a decision maker in a multidisciplinary way by introducing entities with corresponding attributes and scenarios for processing data and making decisions. In a scenario for an individual we may even describe the changes in the data input mode and decision making during the process of problem solving. We observe that scenarios for portraying behavior may bring about transformation rules not previously thought of, as well as attributes and interaction paths involved. We may have to describe that a decision maker has a local scope: As an entity he only deals with a specific set of attributes and specific access-paths to other entities. He only observes a 'representative state' of an entity, i.e., those attributes and that part of the scenario which gave meaning to him. However, this representative may change dynamically during the problem solving process.

To summarize, through process-specifications of objects we can look into the dynamics of decision-making processes and the resulting behavior. In this way we may create evidence on problem solving processes in specific situations using strategic and actual knowledge in the process-specifications.

The inquiry system mentioned supports the process of problem solving, firstly by creating an epistemological specification of processes in an empirical situation. This specification is based on a conceptual model formulated against the background of knowledge of an application domain. Subsequently, the inquiry system facilitates the generation of alternatives and the choice of a solution. By keeping track of the subsequent steps in the process of problem solving we may acquire knowledge, not only on the actual problem situations, but also perhaps for future situations. The inquiry system can be seen as a problem solving environment. When it is supported on a computer, we are dealing with a DSS-environment. How can we apply these environments to create supporting inquiry systems for individual decision makers? The construction of the descriptive understanding model and the prescriptive target solutions can be facilitated by a design environment in which various expert systems and knowledge bases have their place. The process of producing the epistemological representation can be facilitated by an expert system with a knowledge base characteristic for the application domain. Further expert systems with a different knowledge base, to support the process of problem solving are dedicated at
- verification and validation of the descriptive model;
- screening and evaluating this model and setting up an experimental design;
- creating suggestions for alternative target specification.

The approach in applying these knowledge bases is then:
- choose appropriate building blocks for a system description of the existing situation
- identify decision entities and describe rules in the existing situation
- develop a simulation model and analyze the problem
- develop prototype alternatives and experiment

- transform the target prototype to a concrete DSS/IS
Pilot applications of this approach are reported in Sol [1984a, 1984b].

REFERENCES

Alter, S.L. (1980). Decision Support Systems: Current Practi-
cies and Continuing Challenges, Addison-Wesley, Reading.

Bennet, J.L. (ed.) (1983). Building Decision Support Systems,
Addison-Wesley.

Bergquist, J.W. and McLean, E.R. (1983). "Integrated Data Analy-
sis and Management Systems: An APL-Based Decision Support
System," in Processes and Tools for Decision Support, H.G.
Sol (ed.), North-Holland, Amsterdam.

Bonczek, R.H., Holsapple, C.W. and Whinston, A.B. (1981).
Foundations of Decision Support Systems, Academic Press.

Bonczek, R.H., Holsapple, C.W. and Whinston, A.B. (1983).
"Specification of Modeling Knowledge in Decision Support
Systems," in Processes and Tools for Decision Support,
H.G. Sol (ed.), North-Holland, Amsterdam.

Bosman, A. (1983). "Decision Support Systems: Problem Processing and Coordination" in Processes and Tools for Decision
Support, H.G. Sol (ed.), North-Holland, Amsterdam.

Bubenko, J.A. et al. (1982). "CIAM," in Information Systems
Design Methodologies: A Comparative Review," T.W. Olle,
H.G. Sol and A.A. Verrijn Stuart (eds.), North-Holland,
Amsterdam.

Burch, J.C. and Strater, F.R. (1974). Information Systems:
Theory and Practice, Hamilton Publishing Company, Santa
Barbara.

Cats-Baril, W.L. and Huber, G.P. (1984). "DSS for Ill-Structured
Problems: A Cognitive Approach and an Empirical Study,"
Proceedings of the IFIP 8.3 Working Conference on Knowledge
Representation for Decision Support Systems, Durham.

Chang, C., Melamud, Y. and Seabrook, D. (1983). "Expert Systems,"
The Butler Cox Foundation, Report Series no. 37.

Cox, C. (1984). "Message/Object Programming: An Evolutionary
Change in Programming Technology, IEEE Software, January.

Davis, G.B. et al. (1980). "A Contingency Method for Selection
for a Requirements Assurance Strategy," The Journal of Systems
and Software, 1.

Dickson, G. (1983). "Requisite Functions for a Management Support Facility," in Processes and Tools for Decision Support, H.G. Sol (ed.), North-Holland, Amsterdam.

Elam, J. et al. (1985). "A Vision for DSS," Proceedings DSS-85.

Fick, G. and Sprague, K.H. (eds.) (1980). Decision Support Systems: Issues and Challenges, Pergamon Press, Oxford.

Fox, M.S. (1984). "Knowledge Representation for Decision Support," Proceedings of the IFIP 8.3 Working Conference on Knowledge Representation for Decision Support Systems, Durham.

Ginzberg, M.J. and Stohr, E.A. (1982). "Decision Support Systems: Issues and Perspectives," in Decision Support Systems, M.J. Ginzberg, W. Reitman and E.A. Stohr (eds.), North-Holland, Amsterdam.

Henderson, J.C. and Ingraham, R.S. (1982). "Prototyping for DSS: A Critical Appraisal," in Decision Support Systems, M.J. Ginzberg, W. Reitman and E.A. Stohr (eds.), North-Holland, Amsterdam.

Humphreys, P., Lariche, O.I., Vari, A. and Vecseny, J. (1983). "Comparative Analysis of Use of Decision Support Systems in R&D Decisions," in Processes and Tools for Decision Support, H.G. Sol (ed.), North-Holland, Amsterdam.

Keen, P.G.W. (1980). "Adaptive Design for Decision Support Systems," Data Base, 12, 1 and 2.

Klein, H.K. and Hirschheim, R. (1985). "Consequentialist Perspective of Decision Support Systems," Decision Support Systems, 1, 1.

Klein, M. and Manteau, A. (1983). "Optrans: A Tool for Implementation of Decision Support Centers," in Processes and Tools for Decision Support, H.G. Sol (ed.), North-Holland, Amsterdam.

Landry, M., Pascot, D. and Briolat, D. (1985). "Can DSS Evolve Without Changing our View of the Concept of 'Problem'?," Decision Support Systems, 1, 1.

Lee, R.M. (1983). "Epistemological Aspects of Knowledge-Based Decision Support Systems," in Processes and Tools for Decision Support, H.G. Sol (ed.), North-Holland, Amsterdam.

Naylor, Th.H. (1982). "Decision Support Systems or What Happened to MIS?," Interfaces, 12, 4.

Olle, T.W., Sol, H.G. and Tully, C.J. (eds.) (1983). Information Systems Design Methodologies; A Feature Analysis, North-Holland, Amsterdam.

Olle, T.W., Sol, H.G. and Verrijn Stuart, A.A.(eds.) (1982).
    Information Systems Design Methodologies: A Comparative
    Review, North-Holland, Amsterdam.

Reuijl, J.C. (1982). On the Determination of Advertising
    Effectiveness, An Empirical Study of the German Cigarette
    Market, Stenfert Kroese, Leiden.

Sernadas, A. (1982). "Software Behaviour Specification with
    Triggering Logic," Infolog Research Report RR02, Lisbon.

Simon, H.A. (1960). The New Science of Management Decision,
    Harper and Brothers, New York.

Sol, H.G. (1982). "Simulation in Information Systems Develop-
    ment," Ph.D. Thesis, University of Groningen.

Sol, H.G. (1983). Processes and Tools for Decision Support:
    Inferences for Future Developments, North-Holland, Amsterdam.

Sol, H.G. (1984a). "The Emerging Role of Simulation Based
    Inquiry Systems," in Beyond Productivity, Information Systems
    Development for Organizational Effectiveness, Th.M.A.
    Bemelmans (ed.), North-Holland, Amsterdam.

Sol, H.G. (1984b). "Prototyping: A Methodological Assessment,"
    in Approaches to Prototyping, R. Budde et al. (eds.), Berlin.

Sol, H.G. (1985). "Aggregating Data for Decision Support,"
    Decision Support Systems, 1, 2.

Sprague, R.H. (1980). "A Framework for Research on Decision
    Support Systems," in Decision Support Systems: Issues and
    Challenges, G. Fick and R.H. Sprague (eds.), Pergamon Press,
    Oxford.

Sprague, R.H. and Carlson, E.D. (1982). Building Effective
    Decision Support Systems, Prentice Hall, Englewood Cliffs.

Stamper, R. (1984). "Management Epistemology: Garbage In,
    Garbage Out," Proceedings of the IFIP 8.3 Working Conference
    on Knowledge Representation for Decision Support Systems,
    Durham.

2. A RELATIONAL THEORY OF MODEL MANAGEMENT

Robert W. Blanning
Owen Graduate School of Management
Vanderbilt University
Nashville, Tennessee 37203   USA

1. INTRODUCTION

The field of DSS, which began as an investigation into the
need for tools to help managers to solve ill-structured problems
[Carlson, 1977; Keen and Morton, 1978; Keen and Wagner, 1979;
Alter, 1980], has grown to encompass a variety of approaches and
concerns, including artificial intelligence, model management,
information economics, and individual and group behavior
[Blanning, 1983b; Bonczek, Holsapple and Whinston, 1981]. This
is also reflected in the content of several recent collections
of papers on DSS [Fick and Sprague, 1980; Ginzberg, Reitman,
and Stohr, 1982; Bennett, 1983; House, 1983; Sol, 1983], and in
attempts to develop a framework for DSS that includes stored
data, data analysis procedures, and decision models [Blanning,
1982c, 1982d, 1979].

Although the DSSs used in practice incorporate a wide variety
of approaches and techniques, a major purpose of the research
currently being done on DSS is to develop a theory of information
management that is as independent as possible of the way in which
the information is stored and processed. At present, there is
no theory that encompasses the variety of information available
to decision makers: stored data, data analysis procedures,
decision models, pictorial and narrative information, and information representing the knowledge, expertise, and judgement of
experienced managers and staff specialists. However, one theory
that has proven quite useful in the restricted domain of stored
data is a relational theory, in which a data base is viewed as
a system of relations over a set of domains corresponding to the
ranges of attribute values in the data base. Relational data
base theory has led to: (1) a set of explicit criteria for the
organization of data bases, (2) a set of explicit criteria for
the design of structured data base query languages, and (3) an

NATO ASI Series, Vol. F31
Decision Support Systems: Theory and Application
Edited by C. W. Holsapple and A. B. Whinston
© Springer-Verlag Berlin Heidelberg 1987

understanding of the need to integrate information in separate
files in response to a single user query [Maier, 1983; Merrett,
1984].

During the past five years a similar theory has been developed for the management of decision models. (For general literature on model management, see Sprague and Carlson [1980],
Bonczek, Holsapple and Whinston [1982], and Konsynski [1983],
and for literature on relational model management, see Blanning
[1985b, 1985f, 1984d, 1984g, 1983a, 1983c, 1982a, 1982b, 1981a];
for a CODASYL-like view of model management, see Stohr and
Tanniru [1980] and Konsynski [1981].) In relational model
management theory a model bank is viewed as a system of virtual
relations, and the theory has led to a better understanding of
(1) model bank organization, (2) the design of model bank query
languages, and (3) the process of model bank integration. The
purpose of this paper is to summarize the principal features of
this theory and to suggest how relational theories may be developed for other important types of management information.

We begin in Section 2 by comparing the relational views of
data and of models, with an emphasis on the distinction between
stored relations and virtual relations. In the following seven
sections we examine three important topics in relational model
management: the structure of model banks (Sections 3 and 4),
languages for model bank definition and manipulation (Sections 5
and 6), and joins in model banks (Sections 7, 8 and 9). In
Section 10 we demonstrate that relational theories are not
limited to stored data and decision models by presenting a
relational theory of assertions (i.e., statements that can be
true or false). We conclude in Section 11 by discussing the
possible extension of existing relational theories to encompass
a broad range of information management.

2. THE RELATIONAL VIEWS OF DATA AND OF MODELS

In relational data base theory a file is viewed as a relation
-- that is, as a subset of the Cartesian product of a set of
domains corresponding to the key and content attributes of the

file. Each tuple is maintained in secondary storage and is retrieved as needed. In relational model management theory a model is viewed as a virtual relation -- that is, as a subset of the Cartesian product of a set of domains corresponding to the input and output attributes of the model. The tuples in the relation do not exist in stored form; rather, they are generated on demand by executing an algorithm temporarily resident in primary storage. In addition, the output of a model is functionally dependent on the input, just as the content attributes of a file are functionally dependent on the key [Blanning, 1984c, 1982b, 1981b]. (See Figure 1.)

When viewed from this logical level, the operations performed with models appear quite similar to those performed with stored data. For example, one can select model tuples either by specifying the values of the input attributes and requesting the values of the output, just as one can retrieve the content attributes of a file by specifying the value of the key. One

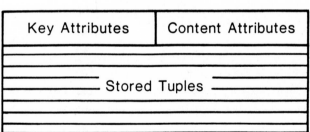

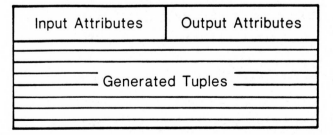

Figure 1. Files and Models as Relations

can also perform an operation with a model similar to content
retrieval by specifying an output value and requesting the
corresponding input values, as is done in breakeven analysis.
One can also specify certain attribute values for a model and
project the relation along some of the other attributes, as is
done in parametric programming. Finally, when the output of
one model is an input to another model, an operation corresponding to a relational join is performed.

Although there are similarities between the relational views
of data and of models, there are also four differences whose
importance will become apparent in the following sections.
First, since files are stored relations and models are virtual
relations, the tuples in data relations are retrieved on demand,
whereas tuples in model relations are generated on demand. It
may appear that this difference is unimportant, since relational
theories are logical theories, not physical ones, and the mechanism of tuple realization is transparent to the user. However,
we will see in Section 3 that this difference is crucial in
model bank organization. Since model tuples are not updated
individually, the storage anomalies of relational data base
theory do not exist in relational model management, and different criteria must be established for the construction of normal
forms.

The second difference concerns the definition of input in a
model relation. In relational data base theory, a key is a set
of attributes such that (1) all content (i.e., non-key) attributes are functionally dependent on the key and (2) there is at
least one content attribute that is fully functionally dependent
on the key. In other words, there are no functional dependencies involving only key attributes. In relational model management we retain the first of the first of these criteria and
discard the second. That is, the input to a model may contain
more attributes than are needed to specify the outputs.

The reason for allowing functional dependencies among inputs
is that a user may wish to perform sensitivity or "what if"
studies that make use of one set of functional dependencies but
that violate another set of functional dependencies. For

example, consider a model that predicts volume as a function of
price and another model that calculates profit as a function of
price and volume. The output of the second model is not fully
functionally dependent on the input, since price is sufficient
to determine profit. However, the user may wish to experiment
with several price-volume combinations, including ones inconsistent with the first model, to see what the resulting profit
would be, and this is possible only if functional dependencies
involving input attributes are permitted.

The third difference also concerns the functional dependencies between key and content and between input and output. In
the first (data) case, there is an entity in the real world
corresponding to each tuple in the relation (e.g., a person
with a social security number and a salary), and in the second
(model) case there is a single entity in the real world corresponding to the entire relation (e.g., a factory with a production quantity and a resulting production cost). In a data relation the functional dependency between key (social security
number) and content (salary) is assigned; it is a result of the
assignment of a key value by the user or another agent (the
Social Security Administration). In a model relation the
functional dependency between input (production quantity) and
output (production cost) is causal; it represents a causal
relationship between input and output.

Although this difference may seem obscure, it is of great
importance in the determination of criteria for the relational
completeness of model bank query languages (Section 5). There
is one operation, sensitivity analysis, that is central in
model management but unknown in data management. One would
never use a data relation to find the sensitivity of salary to
social security number, but models are commonly used to find
such sensitivities as that of production cost to production
quantity (i.e., the marginal cost of production). The reason
is that changing a social security number does not change the
pension assigned that number and hence, does not change his
salary. But changing the production quota of a factory does
change the production cost that is causally dependent on it.

The fourth and final difference is that a model relation must have at least one output attribute (whereas a file need not have any content attributes), and the outputs will generally be pairwise disjoint. For example, if one model used to respond to a user query calculates production cost, then no other model used to respond to the same query can also calculate the same production cost; there can be only one production cost. We will see in Section 4 that this greatly simplifies the problem of detecting lossy joins in model banks.

3. ANOMALIES AND NORMAL FORMS IN MODEL BANKS

The criteria for the organization of model banks are analogous, but not identical, to those used in relational data base theory. That is, a sequence of anomalies are identified and a set of normal forms are created whose purpose is to eliminate the anomalies. In relational data base theory the anomalies are storage anomalies -- anomalies that can arise as individual tuples are inserted into a relation, deleted from a relation, or changed in a relation. As was mentioned in Section 2, these anomalies do not exist in relational model management, because tuples in a model relation are not individually updated. However, there is another set of anomalies, called processing anomalies, that arise in relational model management. There are three types of processing anomalies -- called input, search, and output anomalies -- and these lead to the construction of three normal forms, called the alpha, beta, and gamma forms. We begin by presenting a rigorous definition of a model bank and then describe the anomalies and normal forms.

In order to define rigorously a model and a model bank, we must examine the nature of functional dependencies in model banks. Functional dependencies arise from calculations involving attributes (e.g., the calculation of volume from price), and these calculations correspond to causal relationships in the real world. Thus, it makes sense to begin with the notion of a calculation dependency and to define functional dependencies as the transitive closure of the calculations. Since the output attributes of any model are functionally dependent on the input attributes, we can view model bank organization as a process of allocating calculation dependencies to models. We use an arrow (→) to denote functional dependencies. (See Blanning [1984d] for examples of the definitions and a proof of the theorem.)

We now present:

DEFINITION I: A <u>model bank</u> is a triple (Ψ, θ, Λ) where:

1. Ψ is a set of <u>attributes</u>

2. θ is a set of M <u>calculation dependencies</u> $[Z_j, W_j]$ for $j = 1 \ldots M$, such that

   a. $\underset{j}{\cup}(Z_j \cup W_j) = A$

   b. $W_i \cap W_j = \emptyset$ for $i \neq j$

   c. $Z_j \cap W_j = \emptyset$ for all j

   d. Each W_j is a single element of A

3. Λ is a set of N <u>models</u> $<X_i; Y_i>$ for $i = 1 \ldots N$ such that

   a. $X_i \neq \emptyset$, $Y_i \neq \emptyset$, and $X_i \cap Y_i = \emptyset$ for all i

   b. $X_i \rightarrow Y_i$ for all i

   c. $\underset{i}{\cup}(X_i \cup Y_i) = A$,

   d. $\underset{j}{\cup}W_j = \underset{i}{\cup}Y_i$

We note that condition 3.b. means that each $<X_i, Y_i>$ pair is in the transitive closure of the $[Z_j, W_j]$ pairs of condition 2.

To define an input anomaly we must first define the concept of relevance, and to do that we must define a derived dependency.

DEFINITION II: Given a set of attributes and calculation dependencies, their <u>derived dependencies</u> are defined as follows:

1. The calculation dependencies are derived dependencies.

2. If $Z \rightarrow W$, $(Z', W) \rightarrow W'$, and $(Z, Z') \rightarrow W'$ are derived dependencies, then $(Z', Z) \rightarrow W'$ is a derived dependency.

3. There are no other derived dependencies.

DEFINITION III: Consider a model $<X; Y>$ and two attributes $X' \in X$ and $Y' \in Y$. Then X' is <u>relevant</u> to the calculation of Y'

if there is a derived dependency X'' → Y' such that
X' ∈ X'' ⊆ X.

We can now define input anomalies and the alpha form:

DEFINITION IV:
1. A model <X; Y> contains an $\underline{\text{input anomaly}}$ if there are
   two attributes X' ∈ X and Y' ∈ Y such that X' is not
   relevant to the calculation of Y'.
2. A model bank is in the $\underline{\text{alpha form}}$ if each model in the
   bank is a calculation dependency.

Before discussing the relationship between input anomalies
and the alpha form, we will define the other two anomalies and
normal forms. We assume without formal definition that a model
bank contains an input, search, or output anomaly if any model
in the bank contains such an anomaly.

DEFINITION V:
1. A model contains a $\underline{\text{search anomaly}}$ if it contains two
   sets of attributes R and R' such that R → R' and the
   user must execute the model more than once to determine
   the value of R' resulting from a particular value of R.
2. A model bank is in the $\underline{\text{beta form}}$ if for each model
   <X; Y> in the bank there are no two disjoint attribute
   sets Y' ⊆ Y, Y'' ⊆ Y such that Y' → Y''.

We now define output anomalies and the gamma form. To do
so, we must also define an acyclic model bank -- that is, one
whose models, ordered by their input and output attributes, form
a partially ordered set.

DEFINITION VI:
1. Let the models in a model bank be $<X_i; Y_i>$, i = 1...N
   and let $S = (\underset{i}{\cup} X_i) \cap (\underset{i}{\cap} \bar{Y}_i)$. The model bank contains an
   $\underline{\text{output anomaly}}$ if there is a value of S that results in
   more than one value of A ∩ S̄.

2. A model bank is in the $\underline{\text{gamma form}}$ if for any two models
   <X; Y> and <X'; Y'>, Y ∩ Y' = ∅.

3. A model bank is <u>acyclic</u> if there is no sequence of
    models $<X_i; Y_i>$, $i = 1...I$ and attributes X'_i, $i = 1...I$
    such that

    a. $X'_i \in X_i$, $i = 1...I$

    b. $X'_i \in Y_{i-1}$, $i = 2...I$

    c. $X'_1 \in Y_I$

    Otherwise, the model bank is <u>cyclic</u>.

    We now state:

THEOREM I:
1. The alpha form of a model bank is unique.
2. A model bank in the alpha form contains no input anoma-
    lies.
3. A model bank contains no search anomalies if and only if
    it is in the beta form.
4. An acyclic model bank in the gamma form contains no out-
    put anomalies.
5. A model bank in the alpha form is also in the beta and
    gamma forms.

The normal forms for relational model management are similar
in some respects to those of relational data base theory, but
there are differences. Input anomalies are similar to the
anomalies that lead to second normal form in that they result
from a relation with too much information in the input. However,
matters are complicated by the provision that the output need
not be fully functionally dependent on the input. Thus, the
need to define derived dependencies and attribute relevance.
The beta form, on the other hand, is identical to third normal
form. Hence, dependencies among the output or content attributes
of a relation create problems whether the relation is a file or
a model.

Finally, output anomalies are caused by nondeterminism in
model banks. (We assume that the individual models are deterministic.) If the model bank is cyclic, then it is necessary to
find a fixed point for the attributes in the cycles, and there

may be no fixed point (i.e., the models are inconsistent), one
fixed point (i.e., the models are deterministic), or two or more
fixed points (i.e., the models are nondeterministic). This is
discussed in Section 7. However, if the model bank is acyclic,
then it can be projected onto a deterministic normal form.

4. LOSSY AND LOSSLESS JOINS

An important problem in relational data base theory is the
lossy join problem. Consider a "universal" relation U and a set
of projections $R_1, R_2 \ldots R_N$ of U. The relations $\{U; R_i, i=1 \ldots N\}$
are said to possess the lossless join property iff the join
$J(R_i, 1=1 \ldots N) = U$. Otherwise, the relations are said to possess
the lossy join property, because projection of the universal
relation would cause information to be lost.

We now state three theorems (proven in Blanning [1985f])
that demonstrate that under reasonable conditions the lossy join
property does not arise in model management. The conditions
are (1) that the model bank be in the gamma form (so that model
outputs are pairwise disjoint) and (2) no attribute values are
lost in the projection. In the following we let X, Y, J, K,
and L be nonvoid pairwise disjoint sets of attribute values.
All joins will be across J, K, and L, as appropriate.

First, we consider the case in which the projections have
the same input:

THEOREM II: Consider the relation $U = <J,X,Y>$ with functional
dependency $J \rightarrow XY$ and its projections $R_1 = <J,X>$ and $R_2 = <J,Y>$.
Then $\{U; R_1, R_2\}$ possesses the lossless join property.

Next, we consider the case in which the output of one projection is the input to another projection:

THEOREM III: Consider the relation $U = <X,J,Y>$ with functional
dependencies $X \rightarrow J$ and $J \rightarrow Y$ and its projections $R_1 = <X,J>$ and
$R_2 = <J,Y>$. Then $\{U; R_1, R_2\}$ possesses the lossless join property.

Finally, we consider the case in which some of the output
attributes of each projection are inputs to the other:

THEOREM IV: Consider the relation $U = <J,K,L,X,Y>$ with functional dependencies $JK \rightarrow LX$ and $JL \rightarrow KY$ and its projections $R_1 = <J,K,L,X>$ and $R_2 = <J,L,K,Y>$. Then $\{U; R_1,R_2\}$ possesses the lossless join property.

We conclude by noting that this latter relation may be nondeterministic (in the attribute J), for it is cyclic (Definition VI. 3.). Therefore, there may be no fixed point, one fixed point, or more than one fixed point for the attribute set $\{K,L\}$. Thus, the nonexistence of lossy joins does not guarantee determinism, it only ensures that any determinism, nondeterminism, or nonexistence of a solution in the universal relation is preserved in its projections.

5. THE RELATIONAL COMPLETENESS OF MODEL BANK QUERY LANGUAGES

The criteria for relational completeness of structured model bank query languages differ from those of data base query languages in three respects. First, selection and projection are combined in a single operator called execution: the user specifies any constraints to be placed on the attribute values and the model relation is restricted to an appropriate subset of its tuples and attributes. Second, the join operation is not included in the criterion for relational completeness of model management languages, since joins are transparent to the user as long as outputs are pairwise disjoint. Third, there are two additional operations in the criteria for relational completeness: optimization and sensitivity analysis. In optimization one designates a nonvoid subset of the input attributes (i.e., the decision variables), a single output attribute (the objective function), and a maximum or minimum designator; the result is the values of the decision variables that optimize the objection function. A sensitivity measure is the rate of change of one attribute value with respect to another attribute value with appropriate constraints on the remaining attribute values. A common example is the rate of change of a designated output attribute with respect to a designated input attribute, all other inputs being held constant. This operation is performed by many financial planning languages [Naylor and Mann, 1982], and surveys [Naylor and Schauland, 1976] and case studies [Boulden, 1975] on the use of planning models by managers have demonstrated that the ability to perform sensitivity analyses is an important feature of these models.

Since the operations of relational data base theory can also be expressed in first order logic, we begin by asking whether first order logic is operationally complete for model management as well. That it is complete is proven in Blanning [1983a]:

THEOREM V: The criteria for relational completeness for model query languages can be expressed in the first order predicate calculus.

We now present two relationally complete model bank query languages: MQL (Model Query Language) [Blanning, 1984g], a linear language similar to SEQUEL [Chamberlin et al., 1976], and TQL (Table Query Language) [Blanning, 1983a], a graphical language similar to Query by Example [Zloof, 1975]. To illustrate these we consider a model CORP with two inputs, a sale price P and a raw material price R, and two outputs, a raw materials expense E and a net income N. We demonstrate two queries, a constrained optimization -- maximize N over P when R = 5 -- and an imbedded optimization.

An example of imbedded optimization is as follows: select R to maximize E given that P will then be selected to maximize N. This query might be formulated by a (monopoly) supplier of raw materials who wishes to select his price to maximize his revenues (and hence, his customer's raw material expense) given that his customer will select a sale price to maximize net income for that raw material price. This type of query is of special interest because of its self-referential property. In this respect it is similar to the query "Find all employees who earn more than their supervisors," used as an unofficial test query in relational data base management (for a file whose fields are employee identifier, employee salary, and identifier of employee's supervisor). Imbedded optimization may have a similar function in the testing of query languages in model management.

The MQL and TQL expressions for optimization and imbedded optimization appear in Figure 2. The reserved words in MQL are underlined. We note that in MQL imbedded optimization is accomplished by a relational mapping. Thus, relational mappings are used in model management not to implement joins (which are transparent to the user), but to implement imbedded optimization. We also note that the P designators are used in TQL not only to specify a projection (as is the case in Query by Example), but also to identify decision variables for optimization.

Optimization (MQL):

MAXIMIZE N
OVER P
WITH (R=5)
USING CORP
PUT P

Imbedded Optimization (MQL):

MAXIMIZE E
OVER R
USING
    MAXIMIZE N
    OVER P
    USING CORP
PUT R

Optimization (TQL):

CORP	P	R	E	N
	P	5		MAX

Imbedded Optimization (TQL):

CORP	P	R	E	N
	P1	P2	MAX2	MAX1

Figure 2.   MQL and TQL

A BNF syntax of MQL is found in [Blanning, 1984g], where it is proven that:

THEOREM VI: MQL is context free, is of star height one, and is not of finite order and hence, does not possess the finite power property. However, an extension of the MQL syntax to allow for unbounded repetition of MQL sentences is a first order language and hence, possesses the finite power property.

6. MODEL DEFINITION

Before a user can query a model bank, he must identify and describe the models that will be used to respond to the query -- that is, (1) to describe the inputs and outputs of the models and (2) to identify, if necessary, a set of models to be used in responding to the query so as to eliminate from consideration certain models that are not to be used. The first function must be performed for the entire model bank and the second for a particular query or sequence of queries (or perhaps, for a particular user). The reason for the latter is that a user may wish to have several models in a model bank that calculate a particular output attribute, even though only one of them will be used for any query. Thus, we will distinguish between a model bank, which is the set of all models available to an organization, and a model set, which is a subset of these models identified for a particular purpose. If the model bank is in the gamma form, then any model set will be the model bank (in the sense that there is no need to identify a model set). The models in a model bank are described by a model description language (MDL), and the models in a model set are specified with a model set specification language (MSSL). An MSL statement contains the names of the model, its inputs and outputs, and the program (or master program) that executes the model. An MSSL statement contains the name of the model set and the names of the models in the set. The set of all MSL-defined models is the model bank, which is the default model set.

We illustrate these concepts with an example, which will also be used in the following sections to illustrate important

concepts in the implementation of joins (see Blanning [1985b]).
Consider a model set (CORP) containing four models: a manufacturing model (MFG) with input volume (V) and output expense (E),
a pricing model (PRI) with inputs V and E and output price (P),
a market model (MKT) with input P and output V, and a financial
model (FIN) with inputs P, V, and E and output net income (N).
(See Figure 3.) We note that this is a cyclic model bank. The
MDL and MSSL statements appear in Figure 4.

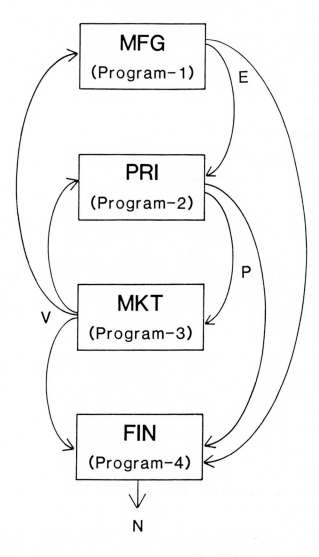

Figure 3. Diagram of CORP

MODEL NAME IS : MFG
PROGRAM NAME IS: PROGRAM-1
INPUT IS: V
OUTPUT IS: E .

MODEL NAME IS: PRI
PROGRAM NAME IS: PROGRAM-2
INPUTS ARE: V, E
OUTPUT IS: P

MODEL NAME IS: MKT
PROGRAM NAME IS: PROGRAM-3
INPUT IS: P
OUTPUT IS: V

MODEL NAME IS: FIN
PROGRAM NAME IS: PROGRAM-4
INPUTS ARE: P, V, E
OUTPUT IS: N

MODEL SET NAME IS: CORP
MODELS ARE: MFG, PRI, MKT, FIN

Figure 4.   MDL and MSSL Descriptions for CORP

For purposes of numerical illustration in the following sections, we assign functional forms for these models. Let:
1. $E = \text{fix} + \text{var} \times V$, defined for $V > 0$
2. $P = \text{mkup} \times E \div V$, defined for $E > 0$, $V > 0$
3. $V = \text{const} - \text{regr} \times P$, defined for $P \in [0, \text{const} \div \text{regr}]$
4. $N = P \times V - E$

Thus, expense is linear in volume, price is a markup of unit expense, volume is linear decreasing in price, and net income is revenue net of expense. We note that this model set is in the alpha form.

In the following three sections we will let fix = 10^6, var = 8, mkup = 1.1, and regr = 4.4 x 10^4. Values of const will be given later.

7. THE EXISTENCE AND UNIQUENESS OF EXECUTION JOINS

There are two ways in which two or more models may be integrated in response to a query. First, a consistent set of attribute values will have to be found for all of the models. This is identical to the relational concept of a join and will be called here an execution join. Second, it may be necessary to integrate sensitivity measures for the individual models to calculate a sensitivity measure for the model set. This will be called a sensitivity join. A sensitivity join cannot exist unless an execution join exists. However, a model set may have an execution join but no sensitivity join.

If a model bank is acyclic and is in the gamma form, then an execution join exists and is unique -- that is, it is possible to find a sequence of models in the model set such that the information needed to execute each model is available either in the input to the model set or in the outputs of previously executed models. On the other hand, if the model set is cyclic, then it is necessary to find a consistent set of attribute values by finding a fixed point for a subset of the attributes. (If the model set is not in the gamma form, then it should be restructured until it is in the gamma form.)

For cyclic model banks it is necessary to identify a stationary set -- a set of attributes whose elimination would render the model set acyclic -- and to experiment with it until a fixed point is found. In the example, the stationary set may be P or V. To do this it is necessary to identify the stationary set -- that is, to determine whether a directed graph forms a partially-ordered set. One way of doing this is to calculate the successive powers of the adjacency matrix for the graph, as in Blanning [1982a]:

THEOREM VII: For a model set containing N models let m be a matrix indexed over the models in the set such that m_{ij} is 1

if there is at least one attribute that is both in the output
of model i and the input to model j and is zero otherwise. Let

$$t = \text{TRACE}(\sum_{n=1}^{N} m^n).$$

Then the model set is acyclic if and only if t = 0.

If the model set is cyclic then it is necessary to determine
whether an execution join (and therefore, a fixed point for the
stationary set) exists and whether it is unique. A classical
mathematical result relevant to the existence of fixed points
is Brouwer fixed point theorem, which in a form most appropriate
to model management states that a continuous mapping from a non-
empty convex compact set into itself has at least one fixed
point [Roberts and Schultze, 1973]. Unfortunately, there are
three circumstances common to model management under which
these conditions will not be met:

1. some of the domains may be discrete,
2. some variables may be unbounded (in which case the
    domain of the stationary set will not be compact), and
3. any attempt to bound the latter variables may destroy
    the "into" character of the mapping.

A classical relevant result concerning the uniqueness of
fixed points is the contraction mapping theorem, which states
that in a nonempty complete metric space a contraction mapping
(i.e., one whose metric between any two points in the space is
reduced by the mapping) has a unique fixed point [Smart, 1974].
Unfortunately, neither the builders nor the users of the models
in the model bank will know whether the models will combine to
produce a contraction mapping from the stationary set.

Ahn and Hogan [1982] have investigated conditions for the
existence and uniqueness of equilibrium prices in supply and
demand models, the input of each of which includes a nonvoid
subset of the output of the other. They demonstrate that under
certain conditions, including opposing monotonicity conditions,
a market equilibrium, if it exists, is unique.

We present and illustrate a result that does not require
opposing monotonicity [Blanning, 1985b]:

THEOREM VIII: Consider a model set consisting of two models M_1 and M_2 with scalar inputs I_1 and I_2 and scalar outputs O_1 and O_2, with O_1 a concave strictly decreasing function of I_1 and O_2 a convex strictly decreasing function of I_2. Let at least one of these mappings be strictly convex or concave. Then there exist at most two fixed points that yield the solutions $I_1 = O_2$ and $I_2 = O_1$.

For example, it can be shown that in CORP there is a critical value for const ($C^* = 827,200$) such that: (1) there is no execution join if const $< C^*$, (2) there is one execution join if const $= C^*$, and (3) there are two execution joins if const $> C^*$ [Blanning, 1985b]. An example of the latter is that if const $= 2.1 \times 10^6$, then there are two consistent sets of attribute values, one of which leads to $N = 122,992$ and the other of which leads to $N = 1,447,248$.

One may ask how nondeterminism (of model sets containing deterministic models) can occur in the real world. If const $= 2.1 \times 10^6$, then either $N = 122,992$ or else $N = 1,447,248$; N cannot take on both values simultaneously. Certain notions from catastrophe theory may be helpful in understanding this phenomenon [Thom, 1977; Zeeman, 1977]. A real world system in which multiple states can be realized is in a state of "structural instability," in which certain factors not included in the model will bring about a realization of one -- but only one -- of the multiple states. Faced with this situation, the user of the model management system can (1) passively accept the nondeterminism of the real world, (2) augment the results of the model management system with a stochastic interpretation of the process being modelled, or (3) enhance the models in the model set to include consideration of the unknown factors, which may consist of the addition of decision rules that will force one of the possible outcomes to occur. Thus, nondeterminism in a model set is not merely a characteristic of the mathematical structure of the models, but rather is a characteristic of the real world or of management's understanding of the real world, and the purpose of a model management system is to inform managers of the existence of nondeterminism so that they can respond appropriately.

8. THE RELATIONAL IMPLEMENTATION OF EXECUTION JOINS

Since for any model bank, cyclic or acyclic, in the gamma form joins are transparent to the user, there is no need for the user to specify the procedure for performing the join (which is the model management analogue to the determination of an access path in data base management). However, for reasons of efficiency, the user may wish to identify the stationary set and specify the fixed point algorithm for cyclic model banks. This process can be given a relational interpretation. In this section we demonstrate that join algorithms can be described in relational terms and specified by a relational language [Blanning, 1985f]. This work is based on a relational theory of algorithms, in which algorithms are viewed as a binary relation with the operations of relational composition and extension (to all possible compositions of a relation with itself) and the definition in relational form of the operations (1) if-then-else, (2) while-do, and (3) repeat-until [Sanderson, 1980]. The algorithms in question are those relevant to the iterative search for an approximation to a fixed point for the stationary set.

To describe the join operation in relational terms we define four relations, as follows:

1. A mapping relation, A(X,J,K,Y), in which X is the input attributes of the model set, J is the stationary set entered at the start of an iteration, K is the stationary set at the end of the iteration, and Y is the output attributes of all models in the model set except for those in the stationary set.

2. An iteration relation, B(J,K,L), in which J and K are defined as above and L is the values of the stationary set for the following iteration.

3. A stopping signal relation, C(J,K,S), in which J and K are as above and S is a stopping signal used to determine whether the iterative search should continue.

4. A stopping rule relation, which may be in either of
    two forms: a continue relation, PC(S,Z), and a halt
    relation, PH(S,Z). In each case, S is the stopping
    signal and Z is a Boolean decision to proceed or not.

Letting ◇ represent a join, ? represent while-do, and !
represent repeat-until, we state [Blanning, 1985f]:

THEOREM IX: The search process of an execution join may be
represented to each of the following deterministic compositions:
  (1)   (C ◇ PC) ? (A ◇ B)
  (2)   (A ◇ B) ! (C ◇ PH)

Although these relations are deterministic, they need not
converge (i.e., they may be infinite). However experience with
large complex models [Hogan, 1975] as well as simpler demonstra-
tion cases [Blanning, 1985b] suggests that simple stopping
rules may lead to rapid convergence within reasonable limits of
accuracy.

We conclude by demonstrating Extended Table Query Language
(ETQL), a language similar to Query-by-Example [Zloof, 1975],
but with some of the calculation features of System for Business
Automation [Zloof and de Jong, 1977], based on the framework
given above. ETQL consists of four table skeletons, which are
similar but not identical to the four relations defined above.
We illustrate this with CORP in which (1) P is the stationary
set, (2) the starting value is P = 8, (3) the price to be
entered at a new iteration (P''') is 10% of the iteration start
price (P') plus 90% of the iteration and price (P''), (4) the
stopping signal is the absolute value of the price difference
ABS(P' - P''), and the stopping rule is to halt when the stopping signal is 0.5 or less. We assume that const is an input
to the model set and is set to 827,200. All other parameters
(fix, var, mkup, and regr) are defined within the models.

The four ETQL table skeletons, illustrated in Figure 5, are
as follows:
  1. The mapping table skeleton, which contains a column for
      each input to the model set and for the initial value of

Mapping Table Skeleton:

const	P
827200	5

Iteration Table Skeleton:

P′	P″	P‴
x	y	$(0.1 \times x) + (0.9 \times y)$

Stopping Signal Table Skeletons:

P′	P″	S
x	y	ABS(x−y)

Continue Table Skeleton:

S	Z
> 0.5	t
≤ 0.5	f

Halt Table Skeleton:

S	Z
≤ 0.5	t
> 0.5	f

Output:

P	V	E	N
12.15	292582	3340653	334065

Figure 5.   ETQL Statements for CORP

each attribute in the stationary set.

2. The <u>iteration table skeleton</u> uses example elements to describe the calculation of the stationary set.

3. The <u>stopping signal table skeleton</u>, which also uses example elements.

4. The <u>stopping rule table skeleton</u>, which appears either as a <u>continue table skeleton</u> or a <u>halt table skeleton</u>.

The output of the iterative process also appears in Figure 5.

9. SENSITIVITY JOINS

A <u>sensitivity measure</u> was defined in Section 5 as the rate of change of one attribute in a model with respect to another attribute, with certain constraints being placed on some of the other attributes. In this section we will assume that each output attribute of a model is a differentiable function of each input attribute and define a sensitivity measure for an input-output attribute pair as the first partial derivative of the output attribute with respect to the input attribute. We examine here the problem of calculating the sensitivity measure for a model set given the sensitivity measures of the models in the set. The operation that maps the sensitivity measures for the individual models into sensitivity measures for the model set will be called a <u>sensitivity join</u>, and the technique presented below for accomplishing the mapping will be called <u>sensitivity mapping</u>.

There are four methods of calculating sensitivity measures for a model in a model set. The first, which applies when the model is a closed-form function, is to calculate the derivative directly. The second is to increment the appropriate input, and to divide this increment into the observed increment in output. The third, which applies to optimization models, is to use the appropriate Lagrange multipliers (or dual variables, adjoint variables, etc.). The fourth method is to construct a model of the sensitivity properties of the decision model -- that is, a repromodel [Meisel and Collins, 1973], metamodel [Blanning, 1975; Kleijnen, 1979], or heuristic model [Blanning and Crandall, 1978, 1979]. These latter models can be used not only for sensitivity mapping, but also to search for appropriate policies related to the individual decision model, such as breakeven or optimal policies [Blanning and Crandall, 1978; Kalymon, 1975].

Let q be an input attribute to a model set, $\{a_i\}$ be the set of all attributes except for the input attributes, and s be a matrix indexed on the latter attributes with

$$S_{ij} = \begin{cases} \partial a_i / \partial a_j & \text{when } i \neq j \\ 0 & \text{when } i = j \end{cases}$$

Then by the chain rule

$$\frac{da_j}{dq} = \frac{\partial a_j}{\partial a_i} \times \frac{da_i}{dq} + \frac{\partial a_j}{\partial q}$$

In matrix form this is written

$$\frac{da'}{dq} = S' \frac{da'}{dq} + \frac{\partial a'}{\partial q}$$

where prime denotes transposition. This is solved to give the sensitivity mapping formula

$$\frac{da'}{dq} = (I - S')^{-1} \frac{\partial a'}{\partial q}$$

where I is the identity matrix. If this is calculated for each input attribute q, the resulting matrix of sensitivity measures is a sensitivity join.

For example, in CORP we let a = (E,P,V) and q = const = 2×10^6. Then

$$S = \begin{cases} 0 & \text{mkup}/V & 0 \\ 0 & 0 & -\text{regr} \\ 0 & -\text{mkup} \times E^2/V & 0 \end{cases}$$

and

$$(I - S')^{-1} = \left(\begin{array}{ccc} V^2 - \text{mkup} \times \text{regr} \times E & -\text{var} \times \text{regr} \times V^2 & \text{var} \times V^2 \\ \text{mkup} \times V & V^2 & \text{mkup} \times \text{var} \times V - \text{mkup} \times E \\ -\text{regr} \times \text{mkup} \times V & -\text{regr} \times V^2 & V^2 \end{array} \right) \div r$$

where r = V^2 + mkup × regr × var × V - mkup × regr × E.   To calculate da/dq we first calculate $\partial a/\partial q = (0,0,1)$ and obtain

$$\frac{dE}{d(const)} = \frac{var \times V^2}{r}$$

$$\frac{dP}{d(const)} = \frac{mkup \times var \times V - mkup \times E}{r}$$

$$\frac{dV}{d(const)} = \frac{V^2}{r}$$

and

$$\frac{dN}{d(const)} = P \times \frac{dV}{d(const)} + V \times \frac{dP}{d(const)} - \frac{dE}{d(const)}$$

$$= \frac{(P - mkup \times var - var) \times V^2 - mkup \times E \times V}{r}$$

It is clear that a sensitivity join can be implemented if and only if (I - S') is non-singular -- that is, if its determinant is nonzero. Consider the model set consisting of two models for which

$$S = \begin{pmatrix} 0 & x \\ x^{-1} & 0 \end{pmatrix}$$

for some $x \neq 0$. In this case, a sensitivity mapping cannot be performed, and no sensitivity join exists. It is shown in Blanning [1985b] that CORP does not have a sensitivity join when const = C* = 827,200 -- even though a unique execution join exists at that point.

We present an extension of this result to a more general case (also given in Blanning [1985b]). We first state:

DEFINITION VII: An s-cyclic model set of order N is a set of models $\{M_n, n=1...N\}$ with scalar inputs I_n and vector outputs O_n containing scalar elements $O_n' \in O_n$ such that

$$I_n = \begin{cases} O_{n-1}' & \text{for } n = 2,3...N \\ O_N' & \text{for } n = 1 \end{cases}$$

A theta function defined for all integers $N \geq 2$ is defined as

$$\theta(N) = \begin{cases} +1 \text{ for N odd or N=2; i.e., } N = 2,3,5,7,9... \\ -1 \text{ for N even and N>2; i.e., } N = 4,6,8,10... \end{cases}$$

We now present

THEOREM X: Consider an s-cyclic model set of order N with
individual sensitivity measures $\partial O_n'/\partial I_n$ for n = 1...N.   Then for
any execution join in the set, a sensitivity join exists if and
only if

$$\prod_{n=1}^{N} (\partial O_n'/\partial I_n) = \theta(N)$$

10.   AN EXTENSION TO RELATIONAL ASSERTION MANAGEMENT

We demonstrate here that relational theory need not be confined to stored data and decision models; it can also be applied
to logical (yes/no) information as well.   We define an assertion
as a single two-valued Boolean variable (x,y,z...) or a well-
formed expression containing such variables (x → y, y ∨ z, etc.).
We may view these assertions in intensive form, as above, or
extensively in the form of a modified truth table in which the
tuples are restricted to those for which the assertion is true
and the column containing the truth value of the assertion is
deleted.   This will be called an a-relation (assertion relation)
over the set of Boolean variables.   (See Blanning [1985d] for a
more complete development of the following material and for
proofs of the following theorems.)

We begin with two definitions:
1. An a-relation scheme, S, is a set of attributes
    {x,y,z...} each of whose domains is {0,1} (where 0 =
    false and 1 = true).
2. An a-relation, R, defined on an a-relation scheme S is
    a subset of the Cartesian product of the domains of S.
    If S contains N variables, then R is a subset of $\{0,1\}^N$.

We now define four relational operations:
1. Intension. If R is an a-relation on S, then I(R), the
    intension of R, is a predicate formula that is true for
    any variable values corresponding to a tuple in R, and
    is false otherwise.
2. Extension. If J is a predicate formula defined on S,
    then E(J), the extension of J, is an a-relation R which

contains a tuple for each set of variables for which J
is true and contains no tuple whose values would cause
J to be false.

3. <u>Projection</u>. Let R be an a-relation on S and let $S' \subseteq S$.
Then $P(R,S')$, the projection of R along S', is the
a-relation formed by deleting from R all columns in
$S \cap \bar{S}'$, and eliminating duplicate tuples.

4. <u>Join</u>. Let R and R' be a-relations on the schemes S and
S'. Then $J(R,R')$, the (natural) join of R and R', is
the a-relation on $S \cup S'$ consisting of all tuples in R
and R' for which the $S \cap S'$ tuples are identical. If
$S \cap S' = 0$, then $J(R,R')$ is the Cartesian product of R
and R'. Since the join operation is associative, we
can write $J(R,R',R'',...)$. We note that $E(I(R)) = R$,
$I(E(J)) \equiv J$, and $P(R,S) = R$.

We now state three results. The first is that extensional
join is equivalent to intensional conjunction:

THEOREM XI: Let R and R' be two a-relations. Then $J(R,R') = E(I(R) \wedge I(R'))$.

Next, we show that extensional projection is equivalent to
intensional inference:

THEOREM XII: Let R and R' be a-relations on S and S' such that
$S' \subseteq S$ and $R' = P(R,S')$. Then $I(R) \to I(R')$. Furthermore, if J
is a predicate formula on S' such that $I(R) \to J$, then
$I(P(R,S')) \to J$.

Finally, we show that the lossy join problem does not arise
in relational assertion management as long as the projections
of the universal relation are a complete set of conjunctive
components of the universal relation:

THEOREM XIII: Let $R_0,R_1,R_2...R_n$ be N+1 a-relations on $S_0,S_1,$
$S_2...S_N$ such that $S_i \in S_0$ and $R_i = P(R_0,S_i)$ for $i = 1,2...N$.
Then $J(R_1,R_2...R_N) = R_0$ iff $I(R_0) \equiv I(R_1) \wedge I(R_2) \wedge ... \wedge I(R_N)$.

We conclude by presenting AQL (Assertion Query Language), a

language similar to Query be Example [Zloof, 1975] for constructing a-relations and drawing inferences from them [Blanning, 1985d]. We assume that all assertions are in clausal form -- that is, a conjunction of an implication between (possibly null) conjunctive expressions and (possibly null) disjunctive expressions. Clauses are entered or displayed in a table skeleton by entering arrows under the appropriate attribute names: "→" for a conjunctive component of an antecedent and "←" for a disjunctive component of a consequence. Projection is accomplished by entering "P" under the appropriate attribute names.

Consider the example illustrated in Figure 6. Let
    x = product cost is low
    y = product performance is acceptable
    z = product will break even
We assume that if cost is low and performance is acceptable, then the product will break even -- that is, $(x \land y) \rightarrow z$. This is entered in Step 1 of Figure 6. We also assume that cost is low. This is entered in Step 2. We now wish to determine the relationship between acceptable performance and whether the product will break even -- that is, we request a projection along $\{y,z\}$. This is done in Step 3. The result -- that the product will break even if performance is acceptable (i.e., $y \rightarrow z$) -- is displayed in Step 4.

11. CONCLUSION

It was stated at the beginning of this paper that an important purpose of the research being done on DSS is to develop a theory of information management that is as independent as possible of the way in which the information is stored and processed. The research reported here, along with the extensive body of research on relational data base theory, suggests that a comprehensive theory of information management may have a relational foundation. Such a foundation has proven its usefulness in developing a theory of stored data, and the work reported here is evidence of its usefulness in developing a theory of decision models. We now ask whether it might be useful in developing theories concerning other types of management information.

1. The assertion (x ∧ y) ➤z:

1	0	x	y	z
		→	→	←

2. The assertion x:

1	0	x	y	z
→		←		

3. Request for projection along y,z:

1	0	x	y	z
			P	P

4. System response:

1	0	x	y	z
			→	←

Figure 6. Example of AQL

The principal type of additional information is the expertise
of experienced managers and staff analysts. Until recently,
this information was located only in the heads of the managers
and staff analysts or was occasionally recorded in memoranda,
procedures manuals, etc. However, there have been a growing
number of attempts to capture this information in concise symbolic (quantitative and qualitative) notation, to render it into
machine readable form, and to apply it to specific decision
problems. The computer-based systems that maintain and apply
the knowledge are expert systems for management, or ESMs.

The development of ESMs has been motivated by the construction during the past 20-25 years of expert systems for non-
management professionals and other specialists -- such as doctors
diagnosing infectious diseases and geologists exploring for

mineral deposits [Hayes-Roth, Waterman and Lenat, 1983; Weiss
and Kulikowski, 1984]. A number of such systems have been constructed, a few of which have successfully contributed to non-
management decision processes [Barr and Feigenbaum, 1982; Miller,
1984]. This, in turn, has led to the construction of several
ESMs in such areas as resource allocation, problem diagnosis,
and scheduling and assignment [Blanning, 1984b, 1984f]. At
present these systems are experimental -- they have been developed at universities and industrial research laboratories and
have not yet seen commercial implementation. In addition, consideration is being given to several issues concerning ESMs,
such as their construction and validation [Blanning, 1984a],
their impact on management [Blanning, 1984e], their relation to
data-based and model-based DSS [Blanning, 1985c], and their
potential applicability to the various functional areas of an
enterprise [Blanning, 1985a].

ESMs, like other expert systems, are similar to (causal)
decision models in that they attempt to predict the consequences
of a proposed decision or to identify an appropriate decision
to make. On the other hand, ESMs differ from decision models
in that (1) the source of information (expert knowledge rather
than causal data) is different and (2) their structure emphasizes
logical relationships (if-then rules, network structures, etc.)
rather than quantitative relationships. The question is whether
the existing relational theories of data management and model
management can be extended to encompass knowledge management.

The research summarized in Section 10 suggests that they
can -- or at least, that this is a promising area for research.
Of course, assertion management is only one form of knowledge
management; but the logical character of assertions is found in
many other knowledge structures (rules, nets, frames, etc.),
and it may be possible to develop relational theories for these
more general structures. Whether such theories would provide
any additional insights into the management of knowledge structures is not yet clear, and this can only be determined by
additional research.

49

ACKNOWLEDGEMENT

This research was supported by the Dean's Fund for Faculty Research of the Owen Graduate School of Management of Vanderbilt University.

REFERENCES

Ahn, Byong-hun and Hogan, William W. (1982). "On Convergence of the PIES Algorithm for Computing Equilibria," Operations Research, 30, 2, March-April, pp. 281-300.

Alter, Steven L. (1980). Decision Support Systems: Current Practice and Continuing Challenges, Addison-Wesley, Reading.

Barr, Avron and Feigenbaum, Edward A. (eds.) (1982). The Handbook of Artificial Intelligence, 2, William Kaufmann, Los Altos ("Applications-Oriented AI Research," pp. 77-294).

Bennett, John L. (ed.) (1983). Building Decision Support Systems, Addison-Wesley, Reading.

Blanning, Robert W. (ed.) (1985a). Foundations of Expert Systems for Management, to be published by Verlag Rheinland, Köln.

Blanning, Robert W. (1985b). "The Existence and Uniqueness of Joins in Relational Models Banks," International Journal on Policy and Information, 9, 1, June.

Blanning, Robert W. (1985c). "Expert Systems for Management: Research and Applications," Journal of Information Science, 9, 2, March.

Blanning, Robert W. (1985d). "A Relational Framework for Assertion Management," Decision Support Systems, 1, 2, April, pp. 167-172.

Blanning, Robert W. (1985e). "Management Applications of Expert Systems," Information & Management, forthcoming.

Blanning, Robert W. (1985f). "A Relational Framework for Join Implementation in Model Management Systems," Decision Support Systems, 1, 1, January, pp. 69-82.

Blanning, Robert W. (1984a). "Knowledge Acquisition and System Validation in Expert Systems for Management," Human Systems Management, 4, 4, Autumn, pp. 280-285.

Blanning, Robert W. (1984b). "Management Applications of Fifth Generation Computers," Business Forum, 9, 4, Fall, pp. 28-31.

Blanning, Robert W. (1984d). "A Relational Framework for Model Bank Organization," _Proceedings of the IEEE Workshop on Languages for Automation_, November, pp. 148-154.

Blanning, Robert W. (1984c). "A PROLOG-based Framework for Model Management," _Proceedings of the First International Workshop on Expert Database Systems_, October, pp. 633-642.

Blanning, Robert W. (1984e). "Issues in the Design of Expert Systems for Management," _Proceedings of the National Computer Conference_, July, pp. 489-495.

Blanning, Robert W. (1984f). "Expert Systems for Management: Possible Application Areas," _DSS-84 Transactions_, April, pp. 69-77.

Blanning, Robert W. (1984g). "Language Design for Relational Model Management," in _Management and Office Information Systems_, S-K. Chang (ed.), Plenum, New York, pp. 217-235.

Blanning, Robert W. (1983a). "TQL: A Model Query Language Based on the Domain Relational Calculus," _Proceedings of the IEEE Workshop on Languages for Automation_, November, pp. 141-146.

Blanning, Robert W. (1983b). "What is Happening in DSS?," _Interfaces_, 13, 5, October, pp. 71-80.

Blanning, Robert W. (1983c). "Issues in the Design of Relational Model Management Systems," _Proceedings of the National Computer Conference_, June, pp. 395-401.

Blanning, Robert W. (1982a). "A Relational Framework for Model Management in Decision Support Systems," _DSS-82 Transactions_, June, pp. 16-28.

Blanning, Robert W. (1982b). "Data Management and Model Management: A Relational Synthesis," _Proceedings of the Twentieth Annual Southeast Regional ACM Conference_, April, pp. 139-147.

Blanning, Robert W. (1982c). "A Decision Support Language for Corporate Planning," _International Journal of Policy Analysis and Information Systems_, 6, 4, pp. 313-323.

Blanning, Robert W. (1982d). "Ambiguity and Paraphrase in a Transformational Grammar for Decision Support Systems," _Proceedings of the Fifteenth Hawaii International Conference on System Sciences_, 1, January, pp. 765-774.

Blanning, Robert W. (1981a). "Model Structure and User Interface in Decision Support Systems," _DSS-81 Transactions_, pp. 1-7.

Blanning, Robert W. (1981b). "Model-based and Data-based Planning Systems," _Omega_, 9, 2, February, pp. 163-168.

Blanning, Robert W. (1979). "The Functions of a Decision Support System," Information & Management, 2, 3, pp. 87-93.

Blanning, Robert W. (1975). "The Construction and Implementation of Metamodels," Simulation, 24, 6, June, pp. 177-184.

Blanning, Robert W. and Crandall, Robert H. (1979). "Heuristic Modeling and Technological Impact Analysis," Technological Forecasting and Social Change, 15, 4, December, pp. 259-271.

Blanning, Robert W. and Crandall, Robert H. (1978). "Budget Planning and Heuristic Models," Urban Systems, 3, 213, pp. 101-116.

Bonczek, Robert H., Holsapple, Clyde W. and Whinston, Andrew B. (1982). "The Evolution from MIS to DSS: Extension of Data Management to Model Management," in Decision Support Systems, Michael J. Ginzberg, Walter Reitman and Edward A. Stohr (eds.), North-Holland, Amsterdam, pp. 61-78.

Bonczek, Robert H., Holsapple, Clyde W. and Whinston, Andrew B. (1981). Foundations of Decision Support Systems, Academic Press, New York.

Boulden, James B. (1975). Computer-assisted Planning Systems, McGraw-Hill, New York.

Carlson, Eric D. (1977). "Proceedings of a Conference on Decision Support Systems," Data Base, 8, 3, Winter.

Chamberlin, D.D., et al. (1976). "SEQUEL 2: A Unified Approach to Data Definition, Manipulation, and Control," IBM Journal of Research and Development, 20, 6, November, pp. 560-575.

Fick, Goran and Sprague, Ralph H., Jr. (eds.) (1980). Decision Support Systems: Issues and Challenges, Pergamon, Oxford.

Ginzberg, Michael J., Reitman, Walter and Stohr, Edward A. (eds.) (1982). Decision Support Systems, North-Holland, Amsterdam.

Hayes-Roth, Frederick, Waterman, Donald A. and Lenat, Douglas B. (eds.) (1983). Building Expert Systems, Addison-Wesley, Reading.

Hogan, William W. (1975). "Energy Policy Models for Project Independence," Computers and Operations Research, 2, 3/4, December, pp. 251-271.

House, William C. (ed.) (1983). Decision Support Systems: A Data-Based, Model-Oriented, User-Developed Discipline, Petrocelli, New York.

Kalymon, Basil A. (1975). "An Optimization Algorithm for a Linear Model of a Simulation System," Management Science, 21, 5, January, pp. 516-530.

Keen, Peter G.W. and Morton, Michael S. Scott (1978). Decision Support Systems: An Organizational Perspective, Addison-Wesley, Reading.

Keen, P.G. and Wagner, G.R. (1979). "DSS: An Executive Mind-Support System," Datamation, 25, 12, November, pp. 117-122.

Kleijnen, Jack P.C. (1979). "Regression Models for Generalizing Simulation Results," IEEE Transactions on Systems, Man, and Cybernetics, SMC-9, 2, February, pp. 93-96.

Konsynski, Benn R. (1983). "Model Management in Decision Support Systems," in Data Base Management: Theory and Applications, Clyde W. Holsapple and Andrew B. Whinston (eds.), D. Reidel, Dordrecht, pp. 131-154.

Konsynski, Benn R. (1981). "On the Structure of a Generalized Model Management System," Proceedings of the Fourteenth Hawaii International Conference on System Sciences, 1, January, pp. 630-638.

Maier, David (1983). The Theory of Relational Databases, Computer Science Press, Rockville.

Meisel, W.S. and Collins, D.C. (1973). "Repro-modeling: An Approach to Efficient Model Utilization and Implementation," IEEE Transactions on Systems, Man, and Cybernetics, SMC-3, 4, July, pp. 349-358.

Merrett, T.H. (1984). Relational Information Systems, Reston Publishing Co., Reston.

Miller, R.K. (1984). The 1984 Inventory of Expert Systems, SEAI Institute, Madison, 1984.

Naylor, Thomas H. and Mann, Michele H. (1982). Computer Based Planning System, Planning Executives Institute, Oxford.

Naylor, Thomas H. and Schauland, Horst (1976). "A Survey of Users of Corporate Planning Models," Management Science, 22, 9, May, pp. 927-937.

Roberts, Blaine and Schultze, David L. (1973). Modern Mathematics and Economic Analysis, W.W. Norton, New York (Chapter 9: "Existence and Stability of Solutions to Static Models," pp. 273-317).

Smart, D.R. (1974). Fixed Point Theorems, Cambridge University Press, Cambridge (Chapter 1: "Contraction Mappings," pp. 1-8.

Sol, Henk G. (ed.) (1983). Processes and Tools for Decision Support, North-Holland, Amsterdam.

Sprague, Ralph H., Jr. and Carlson, Eric D. (1982). Building Effective Decision Support Systems, Prentice-Hall, Englewood Cliffs.

Stohr, Edward A. and Tanniru, Mohan R. (1980). "A Database for Operations Research Models," International Journal of Policy Analysis and Information Systems, 4, 1, pp. 105-121.

Thom, Rene (1977). Structural Stability and Morphogenesis, W.A. Benjamin, Reading.

Weiss, S.M. and Kulikowski, C.A. (1984). A Practical Guide to Designing Expert Systems, Rowman & Allenheld, Totowa.

Zeeman, E.C. (1977). Catastrophe Theory, Addison-Wesley, Reading.

Zloof, Moshe M. (1975). "Query by Example," Proceedings of the National Computer Conference, pp. 431-438.

Zloof, Moshe M. and de Jong, S. Peter (1977). "The System for Business Automation (SBA): Programming Language," Communications of the ACM, 20, 6, June, pp. 385-394.

3. DATA- AND KNOWLEDGE- BASE MANAGEMENT SYSTEMS FOR DECISION SUPPORT

Dimitris Karagiannis and Hans-Jochen Schneider
Technical University of Berlin
Franklinstr. 28/29, FR 5-8
D-1000 Berlin 10
Federal Republic of Germany

ABSTRACT

In this paper we would like to present a survey of one main basic component for a Decision Support System, namely the Knowledge System. For components of this kind we describe a design with a 3-level architecture of a relational deductive data base management system. The three main components of this system are the user interface, deduction processor and data base interface. A very comfortable user interface with xx-languages is available to the user. Within it he can describe a model - a subpart of the real world - through facts and rules, based on a relational data base. The deduction processor operates on this knowledge base. The data base interface supports the knowledge transformation between the external data base and the system. The realization of a system - such as the one suggested here - seems to be very useful for solving the difficult problem of a Knowledge System component in the Decision Support System subject area.

1. INTRODUCTION

Minker and Gallaire were the first to present results in the deductive data base area at the 'Logic and Database' Congress in Toulouse [Gallaire and Minker, 1978; Minker and Nicolas, 1983]. Deductive data bases are extended relational data base systems and consist of relations defined extensionally by tuples and intensionally by rules. These relations can be defined recursively. This is not possible in conventional relational data base systems [Nicolas and Gallaire, 1978]. The rules are presented in Horn definite clauses, i.e., clauses with exactly one positive literal [Henschen and Naguvi, 1984]. In relational data bases it is not possible to represent negative

NATO ASI Series, Vol. F31
Decision Support Systems: Theory and Application
Edited by C. W. Holsapple and A. B. Whinston
© Springer-Verlag Berlin Heidelberg 1987

literals explicitly. The assumption that the set of all literals cannot be derived from the intensional data base is false.
This theory is presented in deductive data bases and is developed
and studied by Reiter [1978]. We have two major methods to
answer all queries concerning these relations. First, the method
'rule interpretation' would be particularly inefficient in
practice if the user query includes recursive rules. The rule
interpreter deals with the deduction and the data base access
at query time [Minker, 1978, 1982]. The termination of the
program is not guaranteed. Secondly, the method 'rule compiling'
is very efficient for recursive rules. The rule compiler deals
with the deduction and data base access separately (at different
times). A query should be transformed into an iterative data
base program which gives all correct answers. The termination
of the program is guaranteed [Chang, 1981; Henschen and Naguvi,
1984]. For user-friendliness and efficiency reasons, we used
both the methods which are independent from the user query.

This paper is organized as follows: in Section 2 we present
general definitions of data- and knowledge bases, Section 3
describes an example that illustrates the handling of a simple
case study about a 'room planning' model. The appendix contains
a protocol with examples of the 'room planning' model derived
from our system REPRO.

2. FROM DATA TO KNOWLEDGE PROCESSING

The historical development from data base to knowledge base
processing is described in this chapter. The basic concepts
are compared and the analogies are shown.

Definitions/analogies

DBMS	KBMS
data	knowledge
input	knowledge acquisition
storage structure	knowledge representation
data manipulation	inference/deduction
data item	knowledge unit
data base system	knowledge base system

Assuming that the area of information systems is split into
the two sub areas of (classical) conventional data processing
systems and knowledge based AI (Artificial Intelligence) systems,
one can imagine a unique interface from both systems to a knowledge base. The interface to the 5th generation AI-systems
consists of expressions built with frames, semantic nets and
semantic representation languages. In contrast, the interfaces
to the 4th generation software systems are built with tuples/
relations and/or records/files.

Architecture of a data/knowledge base management system

The requirements of fifth generation systems which can also
run conventional software imply that new techniques and tools
for KBMS and DDBMS development are needed. In Figure 1 the
main components of a suggested KBMS are shown. This list can
by no means be considered complete, but these are prerequisites
for a conceptual basis and the corresponding languages.

Conventional DBMS can only handle facts in the form of
relations and tuples or in the form of files and records. The
main characteristics of applications well-suited for these
systems are applications with a huge number of data having the
same structure described in a schema. The number of data types
is very limited. The applications utilizing these systems are
in most cases in the commercial field.

New application areas require data base management systems
fulfilling other characteristics. The number of data types
are now very huge, the number of each data type is no longer
not as high as in conventional DBMSs. The knowledge to be
represented cannot be described only with facts anymore, and
deduction and inference rules are becoming more and more important. These facts and rules are now stored as tuples/relations
or records/files in conventional DBMS, building a new layer in
the system architecture. Knowledge manipulation procedures
work on these facts and rules.

The architecture of our data/knowledge base management
system allows the conventional software systems as well as the

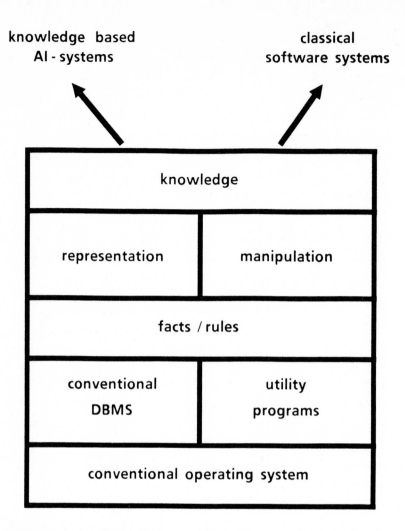

Figure 1.   Interface to AI-Systems and Classical
             Software Systems

knowledge-based AI-systems to work on these data.

In Figure 2 the architecture with a natural language query
interface is presented. The casual user utters a natural language expression (NLE). This NLE is analyzed according to
general language knowledge stored in a lexicon, in a grammar,
in dialog memories and dialog knowledge components. But the
NLE is also analyzed according to application and expert knowledge stored in a conceptual knowledge box.

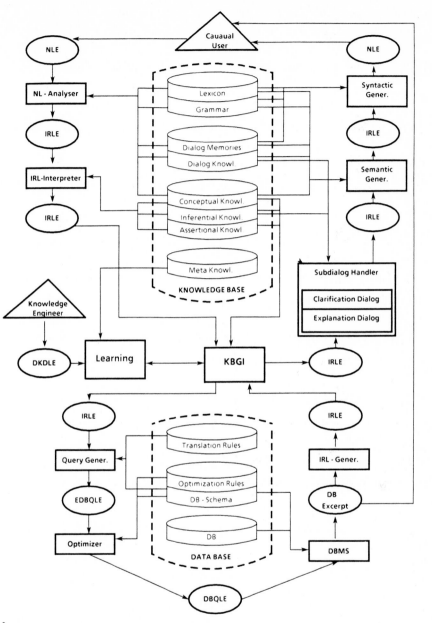

Figure 2. Architecture of a Suggested Data and
Knowledge Management System

Legend

NLE	:	Natural Language Expression
IRLE	:	Internal Representation Language Expression
EDBQLE:		Extended DB Query Language Expression
DKDLE	:	Declarative Knowledge Definition Language Expression
KBQI	:	Knowledge Base Query Interpreter
DBQLE	:	DB Query Language Expression

Natural language (NL)

The NL analyzer delivers an internal representation language expression (IRLE) to the IRL-interpreter which itself is driven by knowledge stored in the inferential and assertional knowledge component. The supplemented IRLE is then sent to the knowledge base query interpreter, which decides whether something has to be explained to the casual user, whether a clarification dialog has to be initiated or whether the IRLE has to be sent to the DBMS. In the latter case the query generator component translates the IRLE according to the translation rules into an extended DB query language expression (EDBQLE). This expression will be given to an optimizer, which will deliver a conventional DBQLE to the DBMS. The DBMS runs the DBQLE against its DB giving a DB excerpt. This result is either given directly to the casual user or handled by the knowledge base component delivering the result in the form of a natural language expression (NLE) to the user. A knowledge engineer instructs the system through a learning component using metarules.

The architecture of future systems should be supplemented with components dealing with methods and models knowledge, graphics and speech knowledge. Generalized components for problem understanding and solving should further support the casual user in his problem solution process. The system should be expanded by a software development environment.

3. THE 3-LEVEL ARCHITECTURE OF A RELATIONAL DEDUCTIVE DBMS (DDBMS)

The pure AI approach is too expensive, because knowledge acquisition is very time consuming. Only applications in which a large number of users are involved can be shown to be economical. There are two so-called strategies for developing very large knowledge-based projects, the top-down and the bottom-up strategy. Both of them have the same goal but:

a) With the first strategy one starts from the NL-interface and the application domain. In this case we talk about knowledge-based management systems.

b) With the second strategy one starts from the conventional
    DBMS and expands it. In this case we talk of deductive
    data based management systems (DDBMS).

A survey of a 3-level architecture for developing a DDBMS based
on the botton-up strategy is given in what follows. The system
support for the user's decision making will be explained in
this paper. A common framework used to describe the structure
of our system is shown in Figure 3.

3.1. xx-Languages

The essential difference between the relational model and
other data base systems (hierarchical, network) lies in the fact
that no difference is made between objects and their mutual
relations during the forming of a model. The representation for
a relational model occurs in an integrated concept: the relation. A number of descriptive languages have been developed,
for example, relational algebra [Codd, 1970], Query by Example
[Zloof, 1977] and Sequel [Astrahan and Chamberlin, 1975], since
the relational data model was introduced. Important goals for
the design of such languages were that they be easy to learn and
simple to understand, so that nonprofessionals could also use
them easily. It has to be noted that the distinction between
Data Definition Language (DDL) and Data Manipulation Language
(DML) is not applicable to descriptive languages. The main components of the xx-languages are:
a) Editor commands for rules
b) Editor commands for metarules
c) Deductive DBMS command
d) Individual user-interface commands
e) User application commands
f) Interface commands to external systems (e.g., graphical
    system).

We present query management with simple query statements
(like in SQL) and an adjustable layout. Orders in the form of
DBMS queries as well as rule entries and calls are managed by
the user programs. The data manipulation component offers
query possibilities to the user which are easy to learn. A

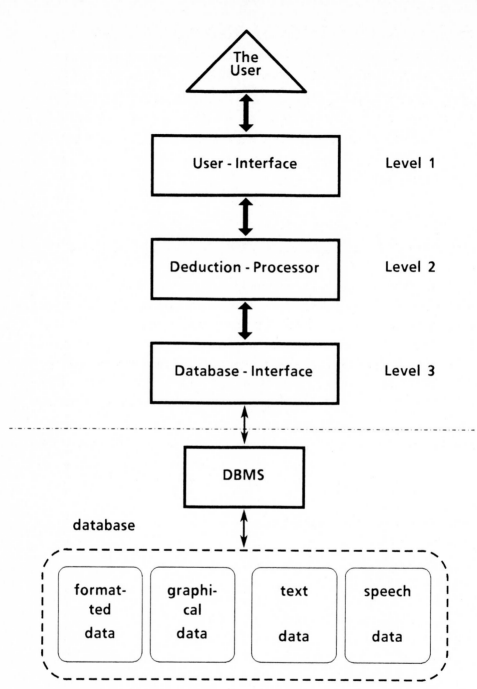

Figure 3.   The 3-Level Architecture of a DDBMS

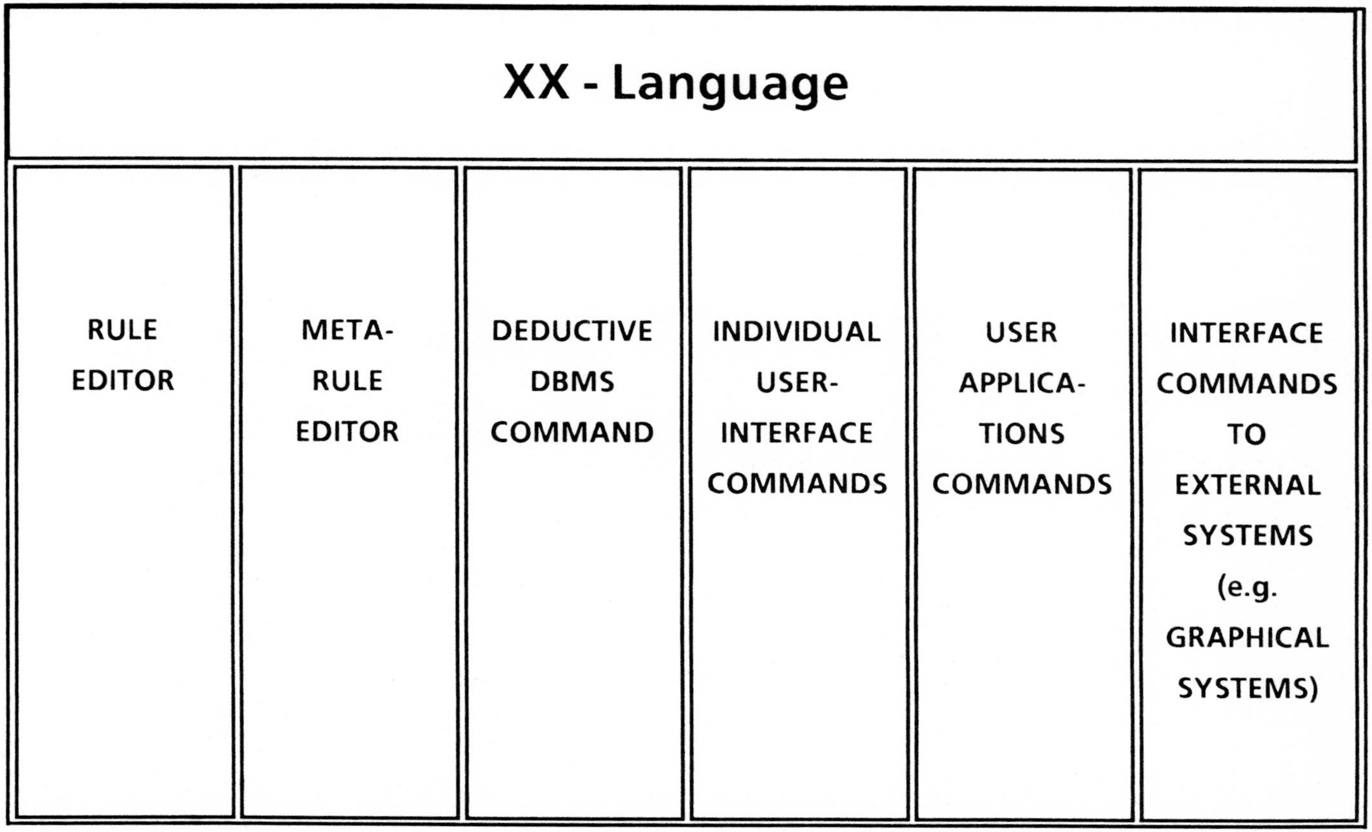

Figure 4. Component of the User Interface

subset of the language includes the data definition component.
In addition, a dynamic layout was introduced. During the
queries SELECT and QUERY the user can choose between different
types of layout. Furthermore, the system offers two message
modes:

    1st short system messages and
    2nd system messages with guidance for the user.

Deductive DBMS Commands

    While inserting, erasing and changing relations (tuples),
basic integrity conditions of the relational model as well as
user-defined restrictions have to be differentiated. The basic
integrity conditions in the relational model are:
    - All tuples of a relation have a one-valued key
    - If a tuple t of the relation R refers to a relation R' with
      a key, then an entry t' with a primary key fi in R' has to
      exist for each tuple from R.

    These two key conditions result in the following restrictions
of the change operations:

1. Insertion of a tuple t in a relation R is done only if its
    primary key is uniquely in R. A tuple which refers to a
    relation R' with a key is only inserted if a tuple with
    this key exists already in R'.

2. Updating a tuple t will not be executed if its primary key
    is affected. A key of t will only be updated if the cor-
    responding tuple in R', to which it refers, exists already.

3. Deletion of a tuple can only be done if its primary key does
    not exist in other tuples.

Apart from these basic conditions, further user-defined integrity
conditions restrict the status of the miniworld, as for example:
    ranges for attributes
    relations between attributes
    (family status - tax group)
    the changing of an attribute can result in
    improvements of other tuples (marriage), among others

The xx-language offers the commands create, drop, insert, delete, and update. Create and drop affect not only tuples but whole relations.

The Rule and Metarule Editor

The editor of a deductive DBMS must make the 'system-user' communication possible as well as the management of the rules and metarules. For interaction a 'human-computer communication' [Fischer and Schneider, 1984] must be put at the disposal of the user (e.g., multiple windows, menus, pointing devices). The manipulation should be realized with an 'intelligent' dialog between the system and the user. In addition, through the editor efficient consistency checks should be made possible; this can be done during the entry of these rules. These checks can be realized with a special editor production system, and they should be activated by the entry of new rules and metarules. The rule/metarule editor has to transcribe the generated knowledge automatically into the following points of entry: rules data base and corresponding interfaces. It should be required generally that the user need not have a survey of the internal system structure and the representation form of rules and metarules in order to describe his model.

Rule Languages

If R is an n-attribute relation with attributes A_1 to A_n and if each attribute A_i belongs to a domain D_i then R is a subset of the 'cartesian' product of the domain D_i.

$$R \subseteq D_1 \times \ldots \times D_n$$

The domains may be equal, while the attribute names of a relation have to be different.

The atomic formula
$$R(A_1 : t_1 ,\ldots, A_n : t_n)$$

is now assigned to the relation R, i.e., formulas in a many sorted logic are assigned to the relations. Each term t_i is either a variable or a constant with the sort D_i. As a constant, t_i has to be an element of the domain D_i. If the

constants of the corresponding domain are assigned to all the
variables in R (variable assignment), then the atomic formula
is true according to the variable assignment, if the tuple
$(t\_1,...,t\_n)$ is an element of the relation R. For each subset
$A\_k,...,A\_m$ of the attribute set, further atomic formulas can
be assigned to the relation R. These have the form

   $R(A\_k : t\_k,...,A\_m : t\_m)$

These atomic formulas are true in terms of a variable assignment
if the tuple $(t\_k,...,t\_m)$ is an element of a projection of R
concerning A_k to A_m.

   For simplicity all formulas have the same name. They are
only distinguished by the attributes specified at the time.

   With the help of quantifiers and propositional connectives
optional formulas can now be constructed from the atomic formulas defined above.

   The AND operation of two atomic formulas

       $R1(A\_11 : t\_11,...,A\_1n : t\_1n)$
   AND $R2(A\_21 : t\_21,...,A\_2n : t\_2n)$

has a close connection with the join of the relations R1 and
R2. The join has to be formed over attributes with the same
variables. Then the expression is true in terms of a variable
assignment if the tuple

   $(t\_11,...,t\_1n,t\_21,...,t\_2n)$

is an element of the join. The integrity rules of the data base
can also be expressed in this logic. In this case the formulas
shall be used for defining new relations. We restrict ourselves to the formulas of the form:

   $\forall x\_1,...,x\_n$ R IF R_1 AND ... AND R_n .

R and R_i are atomic formulas and x_i are the variables which
appear in the formula. All variables of R have to appear in
R_1 to R_n. The atomic formula R is true if a variable assignment for R and R_1 to R_n exists, so that the atomic formulas

   $R\_1,...,R\_n$

are true.

If R is equivalent to

R_name (A_1 : t_1,...,A_n : t_n),

then the formula above defines a relation R_name with the attributes A_1 to A_n. It includes all tuples for which the atomic
formula R is true. Relations which are defined through rules
are called virtual relations. Relations which define the data
base schema are called basic relations. We expand the rule
language by atomic formulas given by the system. They define
built-in relations. The following example refers to the 'room
planning' data base.

Basic relation:

lecturer (lecture_no:*lec_no, conference_no:*con_no)

Built-in relation:

count_participants (lecture_no:*lec_no, capacity:*capac).

Rules with a basic relation and a built-in relation:

number_of_lecture_participants

(lecture_no:*lec_no, conference_no:*con_no,

capacity:*capac)

IF

lecturer

(lecture_no:*lec_no, conference_no:*con_no)

AND

count_participants

(lecture_no:*lec_no, capacity:*capac) .

The virtual relation 'information_flow' can be realized
through the SQL-commands 'join' and 'select' according to the
relation between AND operation and join-instruction described
above. Virtual relations can also be defined recursively.

Explain: At a conference it is possible that a lecturer who
has listened to a lecture is himself going to give a lecture
later. The rule 'information_flow' should realize information
flow at a conference and select all participants who at the same
time are lecturers, too.

```
information_flow
            ( lecture_no      :*lec_no,  date :*date,
              participant_no:*part_no, info_flow_step:'1' )
IF
lecture
            ( lecture_no      :*lec_no,  date :*date          )
AND
visit_lecture
            ( participant_no:*part_no, lecture_no:*lec_no )
AND
participant
            ( participant_no:*part_no, status:'speaker'    )
AND
later_lecture
            ( lecture_no      :*lec_no,  date :*date          )
AND
information_flow
            ( lecture_no      :*lec_no,  date :*date,
              participant_no:*part_no, info_flow_step:*old)
AND
add_info_flow_step
            ( old_step   :*old, step   :'1', new_step :*new ).
```

Recurrence step

```
information_flow
            ( lecture_no      :*lec_no,  date :*date,
              participant_no:*part_no, info_flow_step:'1' )
IF
lecture
            ( lecture_no      :*lec_no,  date :*date          )
AND
visit_lecture
            ( participant_no:*part_no, lecture_no:*lec_no )
AND
participant
            ( participant_no:*part_no, status:'speaker'    )
```

Recurrence connection

A virtual relation which is defined recursively is only put into the internal relation after the recurrence connection has been entered. This allows a direct and indirect recursion. For example, computations in the virtual relations give us the rule 'information_flow' with the literal 'add_info_flow_step'. Recursive relations and computations are not possible in relational query languages. A metarule language is under development. It should have the same syntax as the rule language. It defines control strategies and manipulates knowledge/metaknowledge of the search tree of each model.

3.2. Deduction Processor

Deductive data bases originate from the close relation between relational data base concepts and logic-based deduction; furthermore there exists a close connection between a relational data model and predicate logic. A relational data base can be regarded as a logic theory by interpreting every tuple of an n-digit relation R as an atomic formula of an n-digit predicate R. The world described through the relational data base is at the same time a model of this logical theory [Gallaire and Minker, 1978]. Another possibility is to interpret every relation as an extension of a predicate. Then the relational data base is an interpretation of this logical theory (see Gallaire). The logic is even a logic with sorts, since every component of a tuple and therefore every term of a predicate belongs to a domain. The domains of the RDB are then to be equated with the sorts of the logic. Our generic description views a deduction processor as having four principal components:

a user request analyzer
a rules compiler
a rules interpreter and
knowledge and rules for inference components.

3.2.1. The Inference Mechanism

The inference mechanism deduces all tuples of a virtual relation from the rules and atomic formulas of the RDB. In this

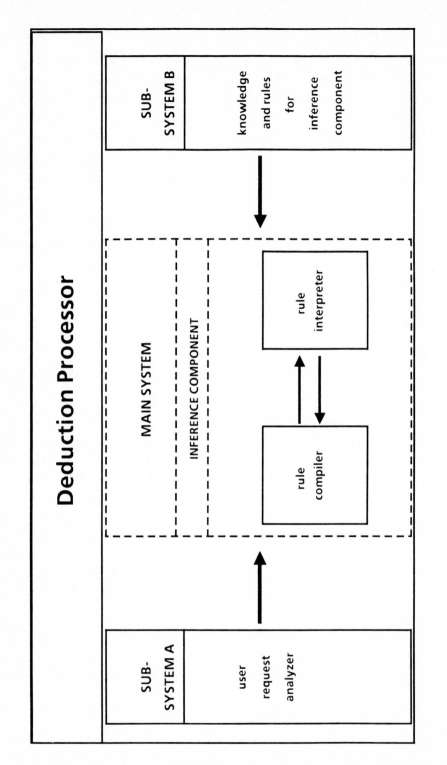

Figure 5. Components of the Deduction Processor

case only the syntactic form of the rules should be used. The
system deduces the knowledge in the following way:

(1)   Interpretation of the rules

(2)   Compiling of the rules

During the interpretation all the needed rules and atomic formulas are searched for and deduced at query time. In contrast to
the rule interpreter, the rule compiler compiles the rules during
the input into DB-programs and processes them at query time.

3.2.1.1. Rule interpreter

For each user query the rule interpreter is called (activated)
by the DBMS over a virtual relation. It tries to find all possible deductions for all the rules which the virtual relation
defines.

A rule

$$\forall\, x\_1,\ldots,x\_n \quad R \;\; IF \;\; R\_1 \;\; AND \;\; \ldots \;\; AND \;\; R\_n$$

is deduced according to the following steps:

(1)   a formula R_i of the rule body is chosen
   (a)   if R_i defines a basic relation or a built-in relation,
       a matching variable assignment is searched for. R_i
       is recorded as having been deduced,
   (b)   if R_i is defined through a rule, the rule is deduced.

(2)   Step (1) is executed as long as all formulas of the rule
   body have been deduced.

The variable assignment for R delivers a tuple of the virtual
relation. There are several (different) search strategies.
They determine (define) which predicate should be evaluated
next.

   (a)   Depth-First   = evaluate from left to right
   (b)   Breadth-First = equivalent evaluation from top to bottom

Rigid strategies have the disadvantage of minor flexibility.
Therefore, the possibility is offered of controlling the deductive strategy through metarules.

It is appropriate, for example, always to analyze the predicate next which contains the least variables. This reduces the

search space for a query. Furthermore, the search space for
queries is also limited by integrity rules.

The rule interpreter can only process using knowledge represented in main memory; storage problems occur in large knowledge
bases. In addition to the currently processed relations, the
present state of proof is located in the main memory during the
proof. These are the intermediate results determined during a
proof. In the PROLOG system this is realized through a stack
mechanism.

3.2.1.2. Rules compiler

During the rule compilation all rules are derived independent of the user query. Thus so, the focal point lies on the
treatment of the recursive rules. A query is transformed into
an iterative data base program, whose execution supplies all the
correct answers. The termination of the programs is guaranteed
while the derivation of the atomic formulas can only occur at
the time of user query. Therefore, they are compiled in DB-
queries. Thus, the program corresponding to a rule consists of
a number of DB-queries. In view of the recursive rules it cannot be determined completely at the time of compilation. The
number of the DB-queries depends on the actual state of the
RDB. Therefore, the recursion is transferred into an iteration.
The cut off criterion is then tested at query time. Not all
the rules can be compiled. These are only rules in which the
defined relation appears within the rule body, directly or indirectly (i.e., within further rules). The memory problems
which appear during rule interpretation are solved through the
use of the RDBS as a memory. Aside from the base relations,
all results and intermediate results as well are stored in relations. In doing so, it is also possible to guarantee the termination of cyclic relations.

3.2.2. The Subsystems

The two subsystems A and B provide the 'main system' of the
deduction processor with the knowledge needed for the processing
of the rules. The implementation environment has to be

considered for the specification and realization of the 'user request analyzer' as well as the 'knowledge and rules for the main system'.

3.3. Data Base Interface

The deductive system is developed as a supplement to an existing data base system, so software problems have to be clarified. First, the possibility of calling external systems from PROLOG - and at the same time from the deductive systems - represents an important problem. Secondly, there is no mechanism for the displacement of the temporary relations deduced and buffered by the 'theorem prover'. Apart from the validity of the derivations, the necessary memory capacity is of great importance for memory management strategies. The memory management as well as the displacement strategies resulting from this are dealt with in [Vassiliou et al., 1985].

Memory management strategies for a deductive system

The link to a relational data base system (for example RDS) implies a new layer. Since the returned results are transcribed into main memory at run time, a memory management system is desirable to avoid an interrupt of the system caused by the transcription of the results into the main memory.

The following difficulties can be encountered:

1) It is not at all possible to determine the actually needed memory capacity of the system at an instant.

2) The operating system indeed allows one demand resp. release (through GETMAIN and FREEMAIN, see IBM Supervisor Services and Macro- instructions) of main memory capacity dynamically during the run time of the system, but the PROLOG interpreter is not able to use this storage capacity (see WPROLOG). Hence it follows that only the memory capacity, which was demanded by call of the interpreter, is available.

This means that at the beginning of the system run the memory capacity of the PROLOG interpreter and the system files

are calculated in order to generate the memory capacity which
has to be controlled. Furthermore, the necessary memory capacity
has to be generated and controlled for each change of the main
memory if a new fact or a new rule is added. For each entry it
also has to be verified whether there actually is enough memory
capacity available in order to protect the system from unnecessary complications. A control of memory has also to take place
after interrupts and the delete commands. For this reason it
is desirable that all relations, especially the capacity system
relations, be stored in the RDS. Moreover, the user should not
have access to all PROLOG data base predicates like ADDAX,
DELAX. As many facts as memory capacity permits are entered.
Control needs at least:
1) A list of the existing temporary result relations,
2) A list of the result relations entered partially as facts.
These lists, and the size of the still available memory capacity
as well, can be stored as relations. During the start of the
system, the system relations are picked up by the RDS, entered
as facts and marked as being nonerasable. Only a system admin-
istrator is allowed to process changing, inserting and erasing.
Temporary files are only valid as long as the corresponding
relations in the RDS are being locked by the user. Result
relations are detected as being invalid if at least one of the
relations involved in their formation has changed. For each
resulting relation, therefore, the relations which they originated from are recorded on the list of result relations. If
there is not enough memory capacity available, facts have to be
erased from temporary result relations. If in this case not
enough memory capacity is released, the system terminates with
the corresponding error message. The interpreter can have access
to the rules represented internally (IDB), to the entries in
the extensional data base (EDB) and to the external data bases.
The access authority is realized through pattern entries which
were generated by the rule and metarule editor during the compilation.

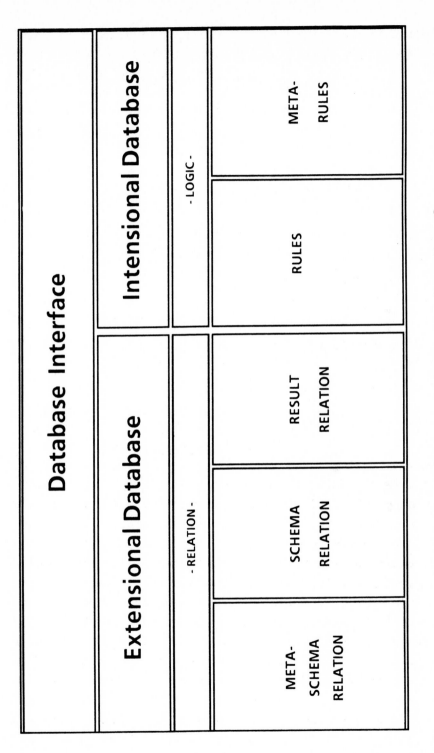

Figure 6. Component of the Data Base Interface

Coupling between the deduction system and external data bases

The interaction between the data base and the deductive system should be realized with the following relations:

Schema of the relation 'axiom'.

```
axiom
    ( axiomname          : < string >,
      number_of_arguments : < number >,
      number_of_axioms    : < number >,
      type                : < string >     ).
```

Schema of the relation 'representation'.

```
representation
    ( axiomname          : < string >,
      number_of_args     : < number >,
      predicate          : < prologpredicate > ).
```

Schema of the relation 'basescheme'.

```
basescheme
    ( relationname       : < string >,
      prologname         : < string >,
      list_of_variables  : < list >,
      basegoal           : < prologgoal >,
      type               : < string >         ).
```

For each relation included in a rule there exists an entry in the relation 'axiom'. The rules which belong to a virtual relation should run under the control of the interpreter. They are stored in the relation 'representation'. For the interpreter the base and built-in relations have a special interpretation at run time. It is different from the interpretation strategy for virtual relations. The access to the base and built-in relations takes place during the entry in the relation 'base-scheme'. The attribute 'type' includes the description of the type of the relation. With the relation 'axiom' through 'type' simple relations will be distinguished from complicated ones at run time. The rule interpreter takes a built-in relation as a set of facts. The PROLOG predicate 'basegoal' which defines the relation will be sequentially processed from the PROLOG

interpreter and the result will be given to the rules interpreter as a fact at its disposal. The tuples of base relations
can be got through the matching of 'basegoal' with the extensional data base. In the complicated case, a translated rule
in the form of a data base command or an external data base
'call' includes 'basegoal'. In this case the rule interpreter
runs with the complicated (complex) data base command. The
tuples which we have got will be loaded in the extensional data
base. The following procedure will be handled just like the
simple case. The translated virtual relations and external
data base 'calls' will be processed in the form of commands
only once. The rule interpreter deals with their results as
base relations. This corresponds with the 'metaevaluate' that
was suggested by Vassiliou [1983].

3.3.1. Extensional Data Base

The extensional data base includes three different types of
relations.
a) schema relations
b) meta relations (relations for the representation of each
relation schema)
c) result relations.

Schema relations

With the schema representation the existing relations should
be entered into the relation 'relation'. The relations are
shown as follows:

    relation
            (relation_name   : < string >
             attributes   : < list   >
             key_attributes   : < list   >
             type   : < string >
             comments   : < string >   ).

Metaschema relations

All relations which are used in order to create a schema

are indicated as metaschema relations (e.g., the metaschema
relation 'relation'. The relations 'attribut' and 'domain' are
created in a similar way.

```
relation
        (relation
        rel_name.attributes.key_attributes.type.comments.nil
        rel_name.nil
        'system relation'
        'non'                                              ).
```

Result relations

These are the relations which are derived by the rules. By
their activation and running we get the extension of the created
relation. For example, the rule 'information_flow' and the
derived relation.

```
relation (information_flow,
        lectno.date.participant_no.level.nil,
        lectno.participant_no.nil,
        'intensional db'
        'non'                                              ).
```

3.3.2. Intensional Data Base

The intensional data base includes the internal representation of the rules and metarules. The internal representation of
the rules from the rule editor will be automatically entered in
the intensional data base with the production of rules. The
metarules will be generated with the support of the metarule
editor.

Rules

The input form of the rules is shown as follows:

ruleheader IF rulebody1 AND rulebody2 AND ...... rulebodyN.

Example:

```
quantity_of_lecture_participant
        (lecture_no:*lec_no, conference_no:*con_no,
         capacity:*capac)
IF
lecturer
        (lecture_no:*lec_no, conference_no:*con_no)
AND
count_participant
        (lecture_no:*lec_no, capacity:*capac).
```

Metarules

The development of metarules has to be realized in two phases: In the first phase the search control strategy of the production system must influence the metarules, which are usually indicated as 'flow control rules'. In the second phase it will be possible to create metarules (resp. metarules strategies which will use the existing knowledge).

Strategy

At first the interpreter tries to prove the predicate which has the most instantiated arguments.

```
before
 (literal_1:*pos_1, literal_2:*pos_2)
IF
literal (*position_1, *name_1, *property_1)
AND
literal (*position_2, *name_2, *property_2)
AND
condition.
```

The condition could be shown as:

```
gt (*property_1, *property_2)
```

4. AN EXAMPLE

This simple study of conference 'room planning' shall give a better understanding of our approach to DDBMS and their new

concepts. It is realized by an experimental deductive DBMS, named REPRO (RElation and PROLOG). The basic depth-first search strategy of the logic programming language PROLOG (PROgramming in LOGic) and the strategies, which were defined through the metarules, were used in REPRO. The problem descriptions appear as follows:
- 'Room planning' should be made for a future conference.
- A casual user should describe his problem, and the system presents an answer.

The following components should be considered:
- 'room planning' of the buildings
- expected number of participants
- occupation time of rooms
- planned lectures.

The rule system could be extended very easily with new concepts like costs, parallel sessions and ideal buildings.

The following EDB-Relations are specified:

relation: conference
```
--------------------------------------------------------------
/ conf_no /  title  / area_code / building_no / from / until /
--------------------------------------------------------------
```

relation: visit_lecture
```
----------------------------------------
/ participant_no / lecture_no / conf_no /
----------------------------------------
```

relation: lecturer
```
------------------------------------
/ lecture_no / conf_no / begin / date /
------------------------------------
```

relation: lecture
```
--------------------------------------------------------------
/ lecture_no / participant_no / short_title / time-of-session /
--------------------------------------------------------------
```

```
relation: conference_room
-----------------------------------------------
/ room_no / building_no / area_code / capacity /
-----------------------------------------------
```

The 'room_planning' rule should realize the following conditions:
1. Modify the room-list according to the date
2. Give the best room for each lecture with the criteria
    capacity and time.
For this purpose we need some new virtual relations. One of
these is the relation 'room_planning', which includes the attributes:

```
    relation: 'room_planning'
    -----------------------------------------------
    / lecture_no / room_no / date / begin / end /
    -----------------------------------------------
```

A simple rule system for room_planning is as follows:

```
    room_planning     ( conference_number :  conf_no,
                        lecture_number     : *lecture_no,
                        room_number        : *room_no,
                        date_of_lecture    : *date,
                        time_of_lecture    : *time )

  IF
     lecture          ( conference_number :  conf_no,
                        lecture_number     : *lecture_no_list )
```

comment:
make a list of lecture numbers

prolog notation:
head   (lecture_no_item.lecture_no_list)

```
AND
    visit_lecture      ( conference_number : conf_no,
                         lecture_number    : lecture_no,
                         number_of_members : *num_member )

AND
    conference_room    ( count_participant : count_participant,
                         available_rooms   : *room_list )

AND
    conference         ( conference_number : conf_no,
                         start_time        : *from,
                         end_time          : *until )

AND
    lecture            ( lecture_number    : lecture_no,
                         session_length    : *min )

AND
    distribution_of_rooms
                       ( start_time        :  from,
                         end_time          :  until,
                         room_list         :  room_list,
                         session_length    :  min,
                         room_number       : *room,
                         date_of_lecture   : *date
                         time_of_lecture   : *time ).
```

A suggested rule for room planning

```
DEDUCTIVE DATABASE SYSTEM START
room_planning
Welcome to Waterloo Prolog 1.4
Copyright 1983 Intralogic Inc
load(BASIS)<-
load(BUILT13)<-
load(NTRACE)<-
DBMS is loaded.
<-
rules interpreter is loaded !
<-
rules editor      is loaded !
<-
extensional database of conference is loaded !
<-
system management is loaded !


/***************** comment
For the system-layout the following table is
available to the user      ***************/
```

password	select	query	message	.
--------	------	-----	-------	.
tys	tuple	yes/no	short	.
mms	match	match	short	.
mme	match	match	example	.
vvs	variation	variation	short	.
qqs	quantity	quantity	short	.
xxx	*select	*query	*message	.

```
Identification:?                               .
qqs.

Quantity of tuples for SELECT:?                .
10.

Query-layout  for command  SELECT             .
10    result tuples                            .
```

```
01    matching line                        .

Quantity of tuples for QUERY:?             .
10.

Query-layout for command QUERY            .

10    result tuples                       .
01    matching line                        .

short message                             .

/****************** comment
At this point the user wants to see the number
of lectures and rooms that are available ***********/

command:.
========.

count lecture.      :

   matchings       :   41.

command:.
========.

count conference_room.

   matchings       :   4.

command:.
========.

select * from conference_room.

Relation:  temporary.
```

room_no	building	area_code	capacity
r1	TU - building	d-1000	100
r2	TU - building	d-1000	7
r3	TU - building	d-1000	20
r4	TU - building	d-1000	20

matchings : 4.


```
/****************** comment
Check if any extension for the virtual relation
'room_planning' exists            **********/
```

command:.
=======.

count room_planning.

   matchings   :   0.

command:.
=======.

select * into plan from room_planning.

extension 1 to 10.

```
/****************** comment
A subset of the extension which was derived through
the rules 'room_planning'          **********/
```

Relation: plan.

lecture_no	room_no	date	begin	end
v58	r3	25-03-85	09.00	09.45
v59	r4	25-03-85	09.00	09.45
v60	r1	25-03-85	09.00	09.45

v61	r3	25-03-85	10.00	10.45
v62	r4	25-03-85	10.00	10.30
v63	r1	25-03-85	10.30	11.00
v64	r3	25-03-85	14.30	15.00
v65	r4	25-03-85	15.00	15.30
v66	r3	25-03-85	15.30	16.00
v67	r4	25-03-85	16.00	16.30

matchings   :   41.

```
/****************** comment
The lectures which take place in the
'conference_room "r1"'              **********/

command:.
========.

select * from plan where room_no=r1.
```

Relation: temporary.

lecture_no	room_no	date	begin	end
v60	r1	25-03-85	09.00	09.45
v63	r1	25-03-85	10.30	11.00
v73	r1	26-03-85	09.00	09.15
v78	r1	26-03-85	11.00	11.45
v84	r1	27-03-85	12.00	14.00
v86	r1	27-03-85	16.00	16.20

matchings   :   6.

```
/****************** comment
The reason for matching 0 is that all the
lectures have more than 7 participants
(room capacity for r2 = 7)          ******/
```

```
command:.
========.


count plan where room_no=r2.


    matchings        :    0.

/***************** comment
The lectures which begin
at 10:00 o'clock                         ******/
command:.
========.


select * from plan where beginning='10.00'.


Relation:   temporary.


  lecture_no     room_no        date         begin        end

      v61            r3       25-03-85       10.00       10.45
      v62            r4       25-03-85       10.00       10.30
      v75            r3       26-03-85       10.00       10.45
      v83            r4       27-03-85       10.00       12.00
      v92            r3       28-03-85       10.00       10.45

matchings    :    5.


/***************** comment
Delete the conference room r3
                                         ******/
command:.
========.


delete conference_room where room_no=r3.


    conference_room (r3, TU - building, d-1000, 20).


    matchings        :    1.
```

```
/****************** comment
Draw up the new room_planning
with  3 conference_rooms            ******/


command:.
========.


select * from room_planning.


extension  1  to  10.


Relation:  tmp.


lecture_no  room_no     date        begin        end


    v58      r4      25-03-85      09.00      09.45
    v59      r1      25-03-85      09.00      09.45
    v61      r4      25-03-85      10.00      10.45
    v62      r1      25-03-85      10.00      10.30
    v64      r4      25-03-85      14.30      15.00
    v65      r1      25-03-85      15.00      15.30
    v66      r4      25-03-85      15.30      16.00
    v67      r1      25-03-85      16.00      16.30
    v68      r4      26-03-85      09.00      09.15
    v69      r4      26-03-85      17.00      17.15


matchings    :    35.


/****************** comment
The room configuration does not match the
quantity of lectures
(lecture quantity 41) **************/


command:.
========.


stop.
```

ACKNOWLEDGEMENTS

The authors would like to thank the researchers of the group 'deductive Data Base System / Artificial Intelligence' (dDBS/AI) at our institute for helpful discussions as well as Mrs. Manuela Weitkamp-Smith, who helped with the translation and put the finishing touches on the manuscript.

REFERENCES

Astrahan, M.M. and Chamberlin, D.D. (1975). "Implementation of Structured English Query Language," Comm. of ACM, 18, 10, October, pp. 580-588.

Chang, C.L. (1981). "On Evaluation of Queries Containing Derived Relations in a Relational Data Base," in Advances in Data Base Theory - Volume 1, H. Gallaire et al. (eds.), Plenum Press, New York, pp. 235-260.

Codd, E.F. (1970). "A Relational Model of Database for Large Shared Data Banks, CACM, 13, pp. 377-387.

Fischer, G. and Schneider, M. (1984). "Knowledge-Based Communication Processes in Software Engineering," in Proc. of the 7th International Conference on Software Engineering, Orlando, Florida.

Henschen, L.J. and Naguvi, S.A. (1984). "On Compiling Queries in Recursive First-Order Databases," Journal of the ACM, 31, pp. 47-85.

Minker, J. (1978). "An Experimental Relational Database System Based on Logic," in Logic and Data Bases, H. Gallaire and J. Minker (eds.), Plenum Press, New York, pp. 104-147.

Minker, J. (1982). "Interfacing Predicate Logic Languages and Relational Databases," in Proceedings of the First International Congress of Logic Programming, Marseille, pp. 91-98.

Minker, J. and Nicolas, J.M. (1983). "On Recursive Axioms in Deductive Databases," Information Science, 1, pp. 1-13.

Nicolas, J.M. and Gallaire, H. (1978). "Data Bases: Theory vs. Interpretation," in Logic and Data Bases, H. Gallaire and J. Minker (eds.), Plenum Press, New York, pp. 33-54.

Reiter, R. (1978). "Deductive Question - Answering on Relational Databases," in Logic and Data Bases, H. Gallaire and J. Minker (eds.), Plenum Press, New York, pp. 149-177.

Vassiliou, Y., Clifford, J. and Jarke, M. (1983). "How Does an Expert System Get its Data?," in Proceedings of the VLDB, IEEE, Florence, Italy.

Vassiliou, Y., Clifford, J. and Jarke, M. (1985). "Access to Specific Declarative Knowledge by Expert Systems: The Impact of Logic Programming," Decision Support Systems, 1, 1, North-Holland.

Zloof, M.M. (1977). "Query-By-Example: A Data Base Language," IBM Systems Journal, 16, 4, pp. 324-343.

4. CONCEPTUAL MODELLING FOR KNOWLEDGE-BASED DSS DEVELOPMENT

Amilcar Sernadas and Cristina Sernadas
Departamento de Informática e Ciencias da Computacao
Faculdade de Ciencias da Universidade de Lisboa
Lisboa, Portugal

ABSTRACT

The role of conceptual modelling in the development of knowledge-based DSSs is discussed. Arguments are given in favor of identifying conceptual modelling approaches with knowledge representation schemes. A brief overview is made of the three current paradigms in conceptual modelling and knowledge representation. The need for an integration of the logical and structure-oriented paradigms is pointed out. The use of the clausal institution for structuring and using knowledge is advocated on the basis that it leads to the envisaged integration. The knowledge base is identified with a theory in this institution. Knowledge representation approaches are defined as collections of parameterized theories (abstractions) which can be used for building knowledge bases, as well as new abstractions. The resulting knowledge base is shown to have an explicit structure established according to the adopted knowledge representation approach and to be accessible through clausal logic general purpose inference machanisms. Implementation issues in a PROLOG environment are also discussed.

1. INTRODUCTION

It is now clear that the next generation of Decision Support Systems (DSSs) will be designed around the concept of Intelligent Knowledge-Based Systems (IKBSs), as pointed out, for instance, in [Coelho et al., 1985] and [De et al., 1985]. An IKBS has basically two components: the knowledge base, a repository of facts, and the inference engine, a module for reasoning on those facts.

In order to be able to assess the impact of the knowledge base technology on the design of DSSs, it seems worthwhile to overview the multitude of knowledge representation approaches (KRAs)

NATO ASI Series, Vol. F31
Decision Support Systems: Theory and Application
Edited by C. W. Holsapple and A. B. Whinston
© Springer-Verlag Berlin Heidelberg 1987

which have been proposed and experimented. Indeed, different knowledge representation approaches tend to assume and provide a wide range of facilities for knowledge organization. Furthermore, one should not forget the related conceptual modelling approaches (CMA) which have been used for similar purposes in the data base field. To the extent that both conceptual modelling approaches and knowledge representation approaches are used for structuring knowledge, there is no need to distinguish them. A strong practical argument in favor of this view is put forward in this paper - an almost classical conceptual modelling approach is used for organizing clausal knowledge bases. Another example can be found in [Sernadas and Sernadas, 1985c].

Adapting from [Mylopoulos and Brodie, 1985], three knowledge representation (or conceptual modelling) paradigms are recognized:

Logical: Borrowing the basic tools from Mathematical Logic, it identifies the knowledge base with a theory (e.g., within the first order calculus). Thus, the knowledge base is the set of theorems in the theory. From a computational point of view, these theorems are obtained from a (varying) set of stored axioms using a set of (fixed) general purpose inference mechanisms.

Structural: The emphasis is on the organization of the facts composing the knowledge base. Several semantic primitives are provided for building the knowledge base. From a computational point of view, the facts are obtained from the instanced semantic constructs (units) using predefined rules. As examples, consider semantic nets and frames, as well as most of the conceptual modelling approaches used for data base conceptual schema design (e.g., the E-R approach [Ng and Paul, 1980] or the Infolog approach discussed in this paper).

Procedural: The knowledge base is composed of active agents with definable reaction patterns. Thus, from a computational point of view, the use of the knowledge is achieved by reacting to a given situation and obtaining the relevant results. For examples see Mylopoulos and Brodie [1985].

Naturally, each of these paradigms has some advantages as

well as some clear drawbacks compared to the others. From the discussion included in [Mylopoulos and Brodie, 1985], it seems that the unifying view of the knowledge base as a theory (a set of theorems which can be obtained on demand from a varying set of axioms using a fixed implementable inference mechanism) is the major contribution of the logical paradigm. Its weak points are a lack of structuring principles and no specific control of the inference procedures.

On the other hand, the structural approaches do provide some of the required organizational principles by imposing the use of a fixed set of semantic primitives or abstractions. However, these approaches use inference mechanisms which are closely linked to their semantic constructs. For this reason it is not possible to find a common inference engine unless one adopts first a common framework (e.g., logic) and defines them on top of it.

The procedural approaches in general have direct implementations for accessing the knowledge base, but this advantage is achieved with a lower degree of understandability (they bring search control issues into the knowledge structure level).

An important step towards putting together the logical and the procedural paradigms has been given with the development of PROLOG [Kowalski, 1979] and its use in the design of knowledge bases (e.g., [Coelho et al., 1985]). Moreover, from a computational point of view, the so-called fifth generation systems should provide the necessary implementation environment [Kunifuji and Yokota, 1982].

However, no serious effort has been reported in the literature for putting together in the same framework the logical tools (e.g., of clausal logic) and the structuring constructs, barring the very recent work described in [Sernadas and Sernadas, 1985c, 1985e, 1985f]. Herein, that work is presented keeping the design of knowledge-based DSSs in view.

In [Sernadas and Sernadas, 1985a] the institutional framework (first developed in the context of the theory of abstract data types [Goguen and Burstall, 1984]) is used for establishing a general theory of conceptual modelling approaches (and knowledge representation approaches). In that framework, it is possible to identify a knowledge base with a theory in the relevant institution (e.g., the equational institution). Moreover, a knowledge representation approach is identified with a collection of shared parameterized theories (theory mappings) which can be used to build other theories (e.g., the knowledge bases structured according to that approach). Thus, in general, each semantic primitive of a knowledge representation approach corresponds to a theory mapping.

In other words, by introducing the notion of theory mapping (which, given some argument theories, returns a new theory), it is possible to bring into the logical viewpoint structuring tools. Indeed, the structure of the resulting theory is established by the theory mappings (semantic primitives) which are used in its construction.

As a preliminary example, consider, in the semantic net approaches, the theory mapping IS-A which returns a new theory IS-A(X) given the argument theory X. Naturally, when defining the theory mapping IS-A it is necessary to indicate the relationship between the resulting theory and the argument theory. Note that a theory is defined by its language and set of theorems. Thus, it is necessary to relate the resulting language and theorems with the language and theorems of the argument theory.

Moreover, since it is also possible to define new theory mappings, there is no restriction to use only the basic semantic constructs of the adopted knowledge representation approach. It is possible to define new, more complex parameterized structures (user-defined abstractions) which can be used again and again (on different argument theories). That is to say, it is possible to organize a library of theory mappings for the modular construction of knowledge bases.

Taking into account these possibilities, it seems to be worthwhile to adopt the proposed unifying framework. Indeed, it is then possible to envisage an IKBS working with clauses and supporting effective structuring tools. The basic goal of this paper is the presentation of such a system as the most suitable kernel for the next generation DSSs.

In Section 2 the notion of institution is reviewed, namely the clausal institution. In Section 3, the Knowlog tools for building new theories from given theories (all of them in the clausal institution) are presented. In Section 4, an interesting fragment of the Infolog modelling approach is introduced and illustrated within the setting of a decision support problem. In Section 5, the Knowlog tools are used for defining some of the Infolog semantic primitives as clausal theory mappings. In Section 6, the envisaged architecture of the extensible IKBS for DSSs is outlined.

Part of the results included in this paper, namely those in Sections 2 and 3, have already been presented in [Sernadas and Sernadas, 1985f]. The overview of the Infolog approach included in Section 4 is a summary of the relevant parts of [Sernadas et al., 1985b].

2. THE CLAUSAL INSTITUTION

Before formalizing the notion of theory mapping, it is necessary to choose the family of theories which are used as domains and codomains of the mappings. Since each theory is characterized by a language (the vocabulary plus the associated set of well formed formulae) and the set of its theorems, that family should include theories with different languages, besides different sets of theorems.

Thus, the proposed institution should define the family of allowed vocabularies and the associated collection of vocabulary changes. Moreover, it should establish the language (set of well formed formulae) generated with each of the allowed vocabularies, as well as the changes implied on the language by each vocabulary change.

The envisaged institution should also associate to each language a collection of possible models,[1] as well as a way to reduce every model of a changed language into a model of the argument language. Finally, it should include, for each language,

the satisfaction relation between the models and the formulae
of that language. Naturally, these satisfaction relations should
respect the translation mechanism.

Within this context, given a vocabulary (which defines a
language as a set of formulae), a theory is a subset of that
language. Changing the vocabulary leads to the indicated change
of the language and, as a by-product, of the theory (as a set of
formulae). As usual, any element of a theory (a formula) is
said to be a theorem.

The concept of institution was first introduced in [Goguen
and Burstall, 1984] following some related results on abstract
model theory [Barwise, 1974]. For illustrations of its usefulness in software engineering see Burstall and Goguen [1981].
In [Sernadas and Sernadas, 1985a, 1985b] the concept is used in
the development of the theory of conceptual modelling.

There are several institutions which are widely used, such
as the equational institution and the first order logic institution. A certain institution is characterized by the specific
set of allowed vocabularies, as well as the particular methods
for building the formulae and identifying the allowed models
(for each of the vocabularies). In [Goguen and Burstall, 1984]
several institutions are defined or outlined, all of them assuming
a many-sorted vocabulary.

In Section 3.1, the problem of defining theories from other
theories is discussed within the setting of a particular institution. Some of the most important operations for modular theory
development are introduced, as well as some of the requirements
that they impose on the underlying institution. Naturally,
vocabulary enrichments and addition of theorems are two of the
most useful kinds of theory operations.

The many-sorted equational institution has been extensively
studied and used for the specification of abstract data types.
It has been proved [Goguen and Burstall, 1984] that it satisfies

---

[1]Model in the sense of Mathematical Logic (interpretation
structure). It should not be confused with model in the sense
of Database Theory (e.g., as in "data model").

all the requirements necessary to guarantee the existence of all of the most useful theory building constructs. In that equational framework, the basic objects are functions and the axioms are equations.

Herein, a quite different institution is adopted because it is much closer to the envisaged PROLOG implementation environment although one has to pay the price of proving that it is well behaved concerning the existence of those constructs.

In the proposed uni-sorted pure clausal institution, the basic objects are predicates and the axioms are Horn clauses. No function symbols are allowed.

The uni-sorted nature of the institution is easily overcome by introducing sort predicates which are used extensively in Section 3. The choice of a pure predicative (without function symbols) institution was made both on simplification and method-ological grounds. In this context, one must express with clauses what otherwise would probably be stated with the extensive use of function symbols and equality.

However, even in this pure predicative framework, it is possible to specify functions when they are needed by imposing functional restrictions on predicates. Thus, the inclusion of function symbols is only a matter of convenience, since the clausal calculus has the same expressibility power with and without them. It should also be stressed that it is straight-forward to extend the proposed institution in order to include function symbols. The problem is further discussed in Section 3.3.

The proposed <u>uni-sorted</u> <u>pure</u> <u>clausal</u> <u>institution</u> consists of:

VOC - A category of vocabularies whose objects are clausal vocabularies and whose morphisms are vocabulary changes.

clau - A functor VOC → SET[2] which assigns to each vocabulary the set of well formed clauses and to each vocabulary change the corresponding language translation.

---

[2]SET is the category of sets whose objects are sets and whose morphisms are functions. SETop is similar to SET but its morphisms are reversed.

mod - A functor VOC → SETop[2] which assigns to each vocabulary
       the set of possible clausal models and to each vocabulary
       change the corresponding model reducing morphism.

:=v - For each vocabulary v, a binary relation in
           mod(v) * clau(v)
       such that, for each vocabulary change c from v into v',
           m' :=v' clau(c)(f) iff mod(c)(m') :=v f
       for every m' in mod(v') and f in clau(v).

Note that formulae translate in the same direction as a
change of vocabulary. However, models should translate in the
opposite direction which was achieved by defining the functor
mod into SETop, instead of into SET. Indeed, when translating
from a vocabulary v into a vocabulary v', given a v'-model it is
trivial to find a v-model but not the other way around.

It remains to define the category VOC, the functors clau and
mod, as well as the satisfaction relations. These definitions
are presented below adapting from [Lloyd, 1984].

A clausal vocabulary v (an object of VOC) is a sequence such
that v(n) is the set of n-ary predicate symbols. A vocabulary
change c (a morphism of VOC) from v into v' is a sequence of
mappings such that c(n) maps elements of v(n) into elements of
v'(n).

Given a clausal vocabulary v, a v-clause is a pair <a,sa>,
usually written as a ← sa, such that a is a v-literal and sa is
a (possibly empty) finite sequence of v-literals. A v-literal
is of the general form p(t1,...,tn) provided that p belongs to
v(n), where t1,...,tn belong to X (the set of variables).

The set clau(v) is the set of all v-clauses built with v as
indicated above. Moreover, for each vocabulary change c from
v into v', clau(c) maps clauses of clau(v) into clauses of
clau(v'), as follows:
     clau(c) (a0 ← a1,...,ak) is a0' ← a1',...,ak'
where
     p(t1,...,tn)' is c(n)(p)(t1,...,tn).

Given a clausal vocabulary v, a v-model is a pair <D,I> such

that D is a non-empty set (the <u>domain</u>) and I is a sequence of
mappings such that I(n) maps each p of v(n) into a n-ary relation in D.

The set mod(v) is the set of all <u>v-models</u> associated with v
as indicated above. On the other hand, for each vocabulary
change c from v into v', mod(c) reduces models of mod(v') into
models of mod(v), as follows:
    mod(c)(<D',I'>) is <D,I>
where
    D is D'
and
    I(n)(p) is I'(n)(c(n)(p)).

Finally, for each vocabulary v, the satisfaction relation
is defined as follows:
    m :=v a0 ← a1,...,ak
iff, for every m-assignment s, either a0 is true in m for s or
at least one of the a1,...,ak is not true in m for s. An m-
assignment maps each variable into a value in the domain of m.
A literal p(t1,...,tn) is said to be true in m = <D,I> for an
m-assignment s iff <s(t1),...,s(tn)> belongs to the n-ary relation I(p).

It is straightforward to verify that clau and mod are indeed
functors as indicated above, as well as that the satisfaction
relations do respect the translation mechanism.

Given a vocabulary v, a <u>v-theory</u> is a set T of v-clauses
(the theorems of T) such that T** is identical to T, where, in
general, given a set F of v-clauses,
    F* = {m in mod(v): m :=v f for every f in F}
and, in general, given a set M of v-models,
    M* = {f in clau(v): m :=v f for every m in M}.
Thus, a theory is closed for semantic entailment as expected.

Given a v-theory T and a v'-theory T', a <u>theory morphism</u>
from T into T' is a vocabulary change c (a morphism in VOC) from
v to v' such that clau(c)(f) belongs to T', for every f in T.

It is worthwhile to introduce the category THE whose objects
are the theories of the clausal institution above and whose

morphisms are the associated theory morphisms.

Note that the envisaged notion of theory mapping is introduced only in the next section and it should not be confused
with the underlying concept of theory morphism.

3.   BUILDING THEORIES

3.1.   Operations on Theories

There are four basic ways of building new theories with
previously defined theories: combination, enrichment, derivation and application [Burstall and Goguen, 1980].   The latter is
discussed in the next paragraph of this section.

Roughly, a combination of two theories is a theory which
includes both argument theories.   That is to say, its vocabulary
is the union of the vocabularies of the operands and its theorems
are those of the arguments plus their semantic entailments.
Actually, the operation is a bit more complex because one wants
to share any part common to both arguments.   For details see
[Burstall and Goguen, 1980].   Ignoring the sharing of common
parts, given two theories T and T' in THE, their combination is
the coproduct of T and T' [MacLane, 1971].

An enrichment of a given theory T (with vocabulary v) can be
achieved by extending the vocabulary and/or by including new
theorems.   An extension of the vocabulary is a vocabulary change
from v to v' such that, for every n, v(n) is included in v'(n).
Extending only the vocabulary, one obtains a theory with the same
set of theorems.   If one wants to include more theorems, say a
set of clauses F, without changing the vocabulary, the theorems
of the resulting theory are obtained by adding F to T and ensuring the semantic entailment closure.   Thus, the new theory is
$$(T \cup F)^{**}$$
which in general is larger than $T \cup F$.

Sometimes it is useful to enrich a given theory both by extending the vocabulary and introducing new theorems.   The resulting theory has the new vocabulary and is the closure of the union
of the previous theorems with the new theorems.

Note that the set of theorems never decreases. If one wants
to add a clause which contradicts the given theory one obtains
the rather useless theory where every formula is a theorem.

The derivation from the theory T through the theory morphism
c, denoted by T:c, is obtained by identifying in T the symbols
which are brought into the resulting theory. Thus c is a morphism from T:c into T. For details see Burstall and Goguen
[1980]. Derivations are useful, for instance, to extract from a
given theory what is necessary, hiding the rest.

All these operations are useful for building theories from
other theories. Naturally, one has to start somewhere. The
only basic theory which is necessary is the void theory whose
vocabulary is empty.

3.2. Theory Mappings

The tools introduced so far do not allow user-defined operations on theories. For this purpose, it is necessary to introduce the notion of theory mapping (parameterized theory).

A theory mapping is a pair <c,T> where c is a theory morphism
and T is a theory (in the category THE). Making an analogy with
procedures in sequential programming, c corresponds to the body
of the procedure and T to the declaration of the formal parameters.

Assuming that c' is a theory morphism from T to T', the
application of <c,T> to T' through c' is denoted by c(T')c'.
The resulting theory is obtained by using the theory morphism c'
from T to T' (called the fitting morphism of the application)
in order to identify the symbols of v' (the vocabulary of T')
which are made to correspond to the symbols of v (the vocabulary
of T). Technically, the application is the pushout of T, T',
c and c' [MacLane, 1971]. Returning to the analogy above, the
fitting morphism states how the actual parameter replaces the
formal one.

In general, it is necessary to consider several arguments.
The multi-argument situation is reduced to the simple case by
using the combination of the argument theories [Burstall and

Goguen, 1980].

Note that, given <c,T> and T', it may not be possible to make an application. There must exist a fitting theory morphism c' from T to T' (a vocabulary change such that clau(c)(f) belongs to T' for every f in T). If, for instance, in v(2) there is a predicate symbol p, but v'(2) is empty, no such vocabulary change exists. Moreover, even if the vocabulary change is possible (there is a p' in v'(2) which can be made to correspond to p), the fitting may still not be possible. Indeed, for instance, assume that

    p(t1,t2) ←

belongs to T, but T' is empty (it has no theorems). Then, it would not be possible to find a fitting theory morphism.

The existence of pushouts (as well as coproducts) imposes certain restrictions on the category THE and, consequently, on the adopted institution [Goguen and Burstall, 1984]. It remains to be proved that the clausal institution does satisfy those restrictions, although some preliminary results have already been established [Mayr and Makowsky, 1982a, 1982b]. Further restrictions on the category THE should be imposed in order to allow the possibility of canonical constructions. These are illustrated in the next section.

3.3. The Knowlog Language

Having introduced the tools for building clausal theories and theory mappings, it remains to bring them together into a practical language. Knowlog (KNOWledge LOGic) is similar to Clear [Burstall and Goguen, 1981], but it is adapted to the proposed clausal institution. For details on Knowlog see Sernadas et al. [1985a]. In this section, the language is outlined on a by example basis. The chosen examples are widely known so that the reader can concentrate on understanding the language itself.

As an example of a theory definition consider Specification K1. It introduces a theory of the Boolean objects with some of their operations.

```
    theory boolean =

      let auxiliary =
          void enriched by canonical
              spreds bool
              fpreds
                  1-ary true, false
              clauses
                  bool(X) ← true(X)
                  bool(X) ← false(X)
      end

          in auxiliary enriched by
              fpreds
                  2-ary not
                  3-ary and
              clauses
                  not(X,Y) ← true(X), false(Y)
                  not(X,Y) ← false(X), true(Y)
                  and(X,Y,Z) ← false(X), false(Z)
                  and(X,Y,Y) ← true(X)

      end
```
--------------------------------------- Specification K1 ---

   This specification of the theory boolean is made in two
stages. First, a canonical construction is made of the boolean
objects. Then, this theory is enriched by the introduction of
two additional predicate symbols (corresponding to negation and
conjunction), as well as new clauses which state their intended
interpretation. For instance, the clause
    and(X,Y,Z) ← false(X), false(Z)
states that the conjunction of X and Y is Z whenever X is false
and Z is also false (no matter the truth value of Y).

   The theory auxiliary is local to the specification of the
theory boolean. That is to say, it cannot be referenced from
outside the definition of boolean. This auxiliary theory makes
the canonical construction of the objects of sort bool using

the operations true and false. Note that both true and false
are introduced as fpreds (functional predicates), since they
correspond to functions (actually, 0-ary functions, also called
constants). This simple canonical construction imposes the
existence of two distinct values of sort bool, one corresponding
to true and the other to false. Furthermore, it imposes that
no other value is included in the sort bool.

   Whenever a <u>fpred</u> p is introduced, it is assumed that the
necessary clause for expressing its functional nature is included in the theory. For instance, if p is binary it corresponds to a unary function and the following functional dependency is imposed:

   eq(Y1,Y2) ← p(X,Y1), p(X,Y2)

Clearly, one is assuming the implicit declaration of the equality
predicate <u>eq</u> with the usual semantics. Note that, if desired,
the introduction of the function symbol f corresponding to p
is straightforward and their relationship is easily established
as follows:

   p(X,f(X)) ←

   Another implicit declaration is also rather useful: the
unary fpred symbol <u>error</u> is assumed whenever a spred is introduced. It serves to identify the error element of that sort.
A <u>spred</u> (sort predicate) is introduced for identifying each
relevant class of objects. A <u>gpred</u> (general predicate) is used
for any predicate which does not correspond to a sort or a function (e.g., the eq predicate is a gpred).

   As an illustration of a theory mapping definition consider
<u>Specification</u> K3. As indicated above, a theory mapping is a
pair composed of a theory morphism (its body) and a theory (its
parameter declaration). In Specification K3, the latter is the
theory sort defined in <u>Specification</u> K2. The theory sort is
very simple. It contains the unary predicate so (besides the
implicit error predicate).

   The theory mapping stack-map accepts arguments which can be
fitted into the theory sort. Note that the body of the mapping
corresponds to the definition of the theory which is obtained

from T through the stack-map morphism. Thus, one avoids introducing constructs for defining theory morphisms.

```
-------------------------------------------------------------

    theory sort =

       void enriched by
           spreds so

    end
-------------------------------------- Specification K2 ---


-------------------------------------------------------------

    mapping stack-map (T : sort)
       using so, error of T
       introducing stk, new, push, pop, top
       =

       let auxiliary =
           T enriched by canonical
               spreds stk
               fpreds
                   1-ary new
                   3-ary push
               clauses
                   stk(X) ← new(X)
                   stk(X) ← push(Y,Z,X), stk(Y), so(Z)

       end

           in auxiliary enriched by
               fpreds
                   2-ary pop, top
               clauses
                   pop(X,Y) ← new(X), new(Y)
                   pop(X,Y) ← push(Y,Z,X), stk(Y), so(Z)
                   top(X,Z) ← new(X), error(Z)
                   top(X,Z) ← push(Y,Z,X), stk(Y), so(Z)

       end
-------------------------------------- Specification K3 ---
```

As in the case of the theory boolean, it was helpful to write the body of the stack-map in two parts. The first corresponds to the parameterized (depending on the argument theory of the mapping) <u>canonical construction</u> of the objects of sort stk with the generation operations new and push. For instance, note that the clause

    stk(X) ← push(Y,Z,X), stk(Y), so(Z)

states that X is a stack if it is obtained by pushing an element Z of sort so into a stack Y. The other unique way of building stacks is by using the operation new, as stated in the clause

    stk(X) ← new(X)

The second part of the body of the mapping extends the parameterized theory of stacks by introducing the additional operations pop and top (as functional predicates), including clauses imposing their intended semantics. For example, the clause

    pop(X,Y) ← push(Y,Z,X), stk(Y), so(Z)

states that Y is obtained by popping X if X is obtained by pushing an element Z of sort so into a stack Y. Note that the antecedent

    stk(X)

is not necessary since it can be derived from the other antecedents.

Given a theory mapping, such as stack-map above, it is possible to apply it to a specific argument theory, as long as it can be fitted into the formal parameter theory (sort in the example). Indeed, one can obtain a stack of Booleans as indicated in <u>Specification K4</u>.

The theory stack-of-bools is obtained by applying the theory mapping stack-map to the argument theory boolean through the fitting morphism defined by the vocabulary change

    so is bool

which indicates the symbol in boolean replacing the symbol so in the theory sort. The implicit predicates are fitted as expected.

Moreover, the vocabulary introduced by the application is

changed so that no confusion arises between the vocabularies of
the parameterized theory and those of the resulting theories.
This was achieved in <u>Specification</u> <u>K4</u> using the <u>with</u> construct.
This construct has the semantics of a derivation morphism which
substitutes stkb for stk and so on.

<u>theory</u> stack-of-bools =

    stack-map (boolean)

        <u>through</u>

           so <u>is</u> bool

           error <u>is</u> error

      <u>with</u>

           stkb <u>is</u> stk

           newb <u>is</u> new

           pushb <u>is</u> push

           popb <u>is</u> pop

           topb <u>is</u> top

  <u>end</u>

-- Specification K4 ---

4. <u>INFOLOG MODELLING CONCEPTS</u>

The Infolog approach to conceptual modelling has been extensively used in the area of data base design (see Sernadas et al.
[1985b]). Lately, the Infolog abstractions have also been used
for structuring clausal knowledge bases (see Sernadas and
Sernadas [1985e]). Infolog is a rather heavy modelling approach
which includes tools for structuring knowledge on both static
and dynamic aspects of the real world. Herein, only the semantic
primitives useful for organizing static knowledge are discussed.
Those interested in dynamic modelling should read Sernadas and
Sernadas [1985d] and some of the papers on the Infolog logic of
events, namely Carmo [1985]. The Infolog tools for static modelling are extensions of some of the most popular constructs in
conceptual modelling and knowledge representation (see ISO
[1982]). In Sernadas et al. [1985b], a comparison is made to

other approaches. Herein, it is sufficient to say that Infolog
is an extended version of the so-called entity-relationship
approach (see, for instance, Ng and Paul [1980]).

In the subsequent paragraphs of this section, the IFIP test
case (see Olle et al. [1982]) is used for illustration purposes.
Assume that it is necessary to organize a knowledge base for a
DSS supporting the activity of the Program Committee of an IFIP
Working Conference. The envisaged system is called CSS (Confer-
ence Support System). The basic goal is to illustrate the
Infolog semantic primitives in the design of the CSS knowledge
base.

4.1. Archetypes, Designators and Properties

An archetype is a class of similar objects which are called
archetype occurrences. An archetype occurrence aggregates the
information kept in the knowledge base about some real-world
entity or association between entities. Thus, occurrences that
keep the same kind of information are grouped in the same archetype.

The knowledge associated to each archetype is organized in
attributes of that archetype. Every occurrence of an archetype
has the same properties and designators possibly with different
values. There are two kinds of attributes: properties and
designators.

A property is a data-valued attribute of an archetype. A
designator is an archetype-valued attribute of an archetype.
Both kinds of attributes are functions whose domains are archetypes. However, the codomain of a property is a data type and
the codomain of a designator is an archetype.

IFIP Examples of archetypes are PERSON, AUTHOR and PAPER. These
archetypes have several occurrences.

As an example of a designator consider:
SPOKESMAN: PAPER → AUTHOR
The above designator maps each occurrence of the archetype
PAPER into an occurrence of the archetype AUTHOR.

As an example of a property consider:

    TITLE: PAPER → STRING

The property TITLE maps each occurrence of PAPER into a string (of characters).

It is assumed that the Boolean-valued property THERE-IS is defined for every archetype. This property indicates if information about each archetype occurrence is present or not in the knowledge base.

There are several kinds of archetypes: surrogate, relation, particularization, generalization, characteristic, aggregation, condition, location, clock and fact. Herein, only the first three are discussed (see Sernadas [1984] and Sernadas et al. [1985b] for information on the other kinds of archetypes).

4.2. Surrogates

A surrogate archetype is an archetype whose occurrences denote real-world entities for which there is a naming mechanism (key mechanism) independent of the rest of the knowledge base.

IFIP An example of a surrogate archetype is PAPER. Indeed, the occurrences of PAPER are identified through a serial number. This naming mechanism is independent of the other information to be kept in the CSS knowledge base.

Another relevant surrogate archetype is PERSON, although it is not further analyzed herein.

The naming mechanism of a surrogate type has the following components: the key data type, the key property and the key map. The key property is a property that indicates for each surrogate occurrence the respective name (which is a value of the key data type). The key map is a function that maps names into occurrences of the respective surrogate archetype. The key property and the key map are the reverse of each other.

IFIP The naming mechanism for the surrogate archetype PAPER can be defined as follows:

```
Key data type ---------- INTEGER
Key property ----------- CODE
Key map ---------------- PAP
```

where

```
CODE: PAPER → INTEGER
PAP: INTEGER → PAPER
```

The key property assigns to each paper an integer (its code) and the key map assigns to each integer the occurrence of PAPER whose value of the key property CODE is that integer.

4.3. Relations

A relation archetype is an archetype whose occurrences aggregate the information about some association between archetypes. The archetypes involved in the association are called the arguments of the relation and their number is called the arity of the relation. The arity of a relation can be greater than or equal to one. No restrictions are imposed on the kinds of the argument archetypes. Each occurrence of the relation is associated to an occurrence (only one) of each of the relation arguments. Moreover, for each tuple of occurrences of the argument archetypes, there is at most one occurrence of the relation.

IFIP An example of a binary relation is AUTHORSHIP which associates the archetypes AUTHOR and PAPER. Thus, AUTHOR is the first archetype argument of AUTHORSHIP and PAPER is the second archetype argument of the relation.

Intuitively, the existence of a certain occurrence of AUTHORSHIP implies that the corresponding occurrence of AUTHOR is an author of the corresponding occurrence of PAPER.

Note that it is not possible to refer to the occurrences of the relation without referring to the respective occurrences of the argument archetypes. Moreover, given an occurrence of PAPER and an occurrence of AUTHOR there is at most a unique occurrence of AUTHORSHIP linked to the pair.

The example above indicates the need for some compulsory designators which are essential to the concept of relation. A (relation) <u>argument designator</u> is a designator which identifies an argument of each relation occurrence. For n-ary relations, n argument designators must be defined (one for each of the argument archetypes). The (relation) <u>reverse designator</u> returns an occurrence of the relation archetype, given a tuple of occurrences of the argument archetypes. These designators are related as illustrated in the following example.

IFIP In the case of the AUTHORSHIP relation archetype the following compulsory designators must be defined:

    Argument designator 1 ---------- AU
    Argument designator 2 ---------- PA
    Reverse designator ------------ AUPA

The designators above have the domains and codomains indicated below:

    AU: AUTHORSHIP → AUTHOR
    PA: AUTHORSHIP → PAPER
    AUPA: AUTHOR * PAPER → AUTHORSHIP

The argument designators AU and PA, when applied to a certain occurrence of AUTHORSHIP, return, respectively, the paper occurrence and the author occurrence corresponding to that authorship occurrence. For each occurrence of PAPER there will be as many occurrences of AUTHORSHIP as authors of the paper. For each occurrence of AUTHOR there will be as many occurrences of AUTHORSHIP as papers written by that author.

The following integrity constraints are assumed:

    AUPA (AU(ap),PA(ap)) = ap
    AU (AUPA(a,p)) = a
    PA (AUPA(a,p)) = p

where ap is a variable of type AUTHORSHIP, p is a variable of type PAPER and a is a variable of type AUTHOR. These integrity constraints state that the argument designators

and the reverse designator are in a sense reverse of each
other (hence the name of reverse designator). They are
essential to the concept of relation archetype, like those
relating the key map and the key property are essential
to the concept of surrogate.

Note that the designer of the knowledge base is able to
impose additional integrity constraints which are application dependent. For instance,

THERE-IS (AUPA (SPOKESMAN(p),p)) for every p in PAPER

states that the spokesman of every paper is one of its
authors.

4.4. Particularizations

A particularization archetype is an archetype whose occurrences correspond to the occurrences of the argument archetype
which satisfy a discriminant condition. A particularization has
always arity one (that is to say, it has only one argument archetype).

IFIP An example of a particularization of PERSON is AUTHOR.
      Assuming that the archetype PERSON has the Boolean property
      IS-AUT, then the discriminant condition for the archetype
      AUTHOR can be the following:

          IS-AUT (person) = TRUE

      Thus, every occurrence of AUTHOR corresponds to some occur-
      rence of PERSON where the IS-AUT property has the value
      TRUE.

There are several compulsory elements in a particularization
archetype: the argument designator, the reverse designator and
the discriminant property, constant and condition. The argument
designator maps occurrences of the particularization archetype
into occurrences of the argument archetype. The reverse designator returns an occurrence of a particularization archetype,
given an occurrence of the argument archetype satisfying the
discriminant condition. The discriminant property is a property

of the argument archetype of a particularization which is used for identifying the occurrences which are relevant. The <u>discriminant constant</u> is a value belonging to the codomain of the discriminant property. The <u>discriminant condition</u> is the Boolean expression obtained by identifying the value of the discriminant property with the discriminant constant.

IFIP   The particularization AUTHOR is defined with the following compulsory elements:

> Argument designator ------------ PER
> Reverse designator ------------- ATH
> Discriminant property ---------- IS-AUT
> Discriminant constant ---------- TRUE
> Discriminant condition -------- IS-AUT (PERSON) = TRUE

where

> PER: AUTHOR → PERSON
> ATH: PERSON → AUTHOR
> IS-AUT: PERSON → BOOLEAN

Note that the particularization can be seen as a refinement of the unary relation. At most an occurrence of the particularization is linked to a given occurrence of the argument archetype. Thus, every occurrence of the particularization can be identified through its corresponding argument occurrence.

4.5.   The CSS Knowledge Base

Consider the fragment of the CSS knowledge base which was developed in the previous paragraphs. Its Infolog structure is neatly depicted in Diagram 1. Therein, it is easy to identify the archetypes PERSON, AUTHOR, PAPER and AUTHORSHIP, as well as some additional information on how they relate to each other.

In such Infolog diagrams, boxes denote archetypes. Their kinds are indicated on the right down corner, as follows:

X - Surrogate
R - Relation
P - Particularization
...

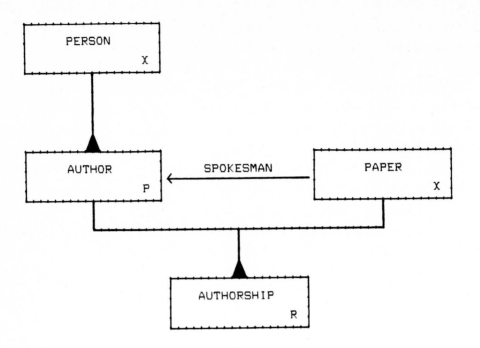

Diagram 1

Moreover, the argument archetypes are indicated through directed
branching edges in the graph. Finally, standard arrows denote
(non-compulsory) designators.

In these diagrams it is better to leave out the details of
the archetypes (e.g., compulsory designators), since they are
useful only when defining navigation operations in the knowledge
base (see Sernadas et al. [1985b]).

5. DEFINING AND USING THE INFOLOG APPROACH

As indicated in the Introduction, a knowledge base is identified with a structured theory. Its structure is obtained by
using a certain collection of theory mappings corresponding to
the adopted semantic primitives. Thus, a knowledge representation
approach is seen as a library of theory mappings. These mappings
are repeatedly used for building the successive states of the
knowledge base. That is to say, they return the new knowledge
base upon acting on the previous knowledge base.

In this section, the definition of the Infolog knowledge representation approach is outlined. The use of theory mappings in the modular construction of Infolog knowledge bases is also briefly discussed.

5.1. Some Infolog Theory Mappings

Recall that an archetype is a class of relevant objects (archetype occurrences) which have a similar structure. Herein, only the surrogate and the relation archetypes will be discussed and formally defined as clausal theory mappings. The concept of attribute (property and designator) will also be formalized, as well as the notion of surrogate insertion. The rest of the Infolog semantic primitives can be easily defined following these examples, since they do not raise any new problem.

```
    theory numbers = void enriched by canonical

        spreds int
        fpreds
            1-ary integer, zero
            2-ary suc
        clauses
            int(X) ← zero(X)
            int(Y) ← suc(X,Y), int(X)

    end
```
--------------------------------------- Specification I1 ---

In Specification I1, the theory of non-negative integer numbers is introduced. This theory is necessary for naming the different arguments of a relation archetype. The predicate integer is used subsequently for denoting the new data type. The predicates zero and suc have the usual semantics. The sort predicate int, when applied to an argument, is true if and only if that argument is an integer.

The theory kernel-kb outlined in Specification I2, is a meta or "data-dictionary" theory. For instance, the predicate

```
-------------------------------------------------------------------
theory kernel-kb =

    numbers enriched by
        spreds archclass, surclass, relclass, dtclass, kmapclass,
               attclass, propclass, desclass, rvdclass, ...
        fpreds
            2-ary dom, codom, rcodom
            3-ary km, am, rdom
            4-ary rm
        gpreds
            2-ary vp, op, xp
        clauses
            dtclass(X) ← integer(X)
            archclass(X) ← surclass(X)
            archclass(X) ← relclass(X)
            attclass(X) ← propclass(X)
            attclass(X) ← desclass(X)
            archclass(Y) ← dom(X,Y), attclass(X)
            dtclass(Y) ← codom(X,Y), propclass(X)
            archclass(Y) ← codom(X,Y), desclass(X)
            dtclass(Y) ← dom(X,Y), kmapclass(X)
            surclass(Y) ← codom(X,Y), kmapclass(X)
            relclass(Y) ← rcodom(X,Y), rvdclass(X)
            archclass(Z) ← rdom(X,Y,Z), rvdclass(X), int(Y)
            dtclass(X) ← vp(X,Y)
            archclass(X) ← op(X,Y)
            archclass(X) ← xp(X,Y)
            kmapclass(X) ← km(X,Y,Z)
            attclass(X) ← am(X,Y,Z)
            rvdclass(X) ← rm(X,Y,Z,W)
            ...

end
---------------------------------------- Specification I2 ---
```

archclass is used for identifying the archetypes already introduced in the knowledge base.

For similar reasons, the requirements for starting the construction of an Infolog knowledge base include the availability
of the other sort predicates necessary for the identification
of surrogate types, relation types, data types, attributes,
properties, designators, reverse designators, key maps and so on.
Those requirements also include the mappings dom and codom which
indicate, respectively, the domain and codomain of each attribute
and key map. The mappings rdom and rcodom have similar roles
for each reverse designator. The predicate vp identifies the
values of every data type. The predicates op and xp identify,
respectively, the possible and existing occurrences of every
archetype. The predicates km and am are used, respectively, for
defining the functions corresponding to every key map and attribute. The predicate rm has a similar role for the reverse designators. Note that, for the sake of simplicity, it is assumed
herein that only binary relation types are allowed. The use of
rm will be illustrated in the definition of the theory mapping
add-binrel-type-os below.

   In <u>Specification I2</u>, the clause
      dtclass(X) ← integer(X)
states that integer is the name of a data type, that is to say,
integer is a member of the data type class. The clause
      archclass(X) ← surclass(X)
establishes that every surrogate type is an archetype. Similarly, the clause
      attclass(X) ← propclass(X)
indicates that every property is an attribute. Another trivial
axiom
      archclass(Y) ← dom(X,Y), attclass(X)
states that the domain of every attribute is an archetype. On
the other hand,
      dtclass(Y) ← codom(X,Y), propclass(X)
imposes that the codomain of a property is a data type. Finally,
it is worthwhile to analyze the clauses on the reverse designators. The clause
      relclass(Y) ← rcodom(X,Y), rvdclass(X)
indicates that the codomain of a reverse designator must be a

relation type. The clause

    archclass(Z) ← rdom(X,Y,Z), rvdclass(X), int(Y)

states that every domain of a reverse designator is an archetype. Recall that the domains of a reverse designator are the
argument archetypes of the relation type.

The theory kb-with-data-type is an enrichment of the kernel
theory, as depicted in <u>Specification</u> I3. It includes three new
predicates. The sort predicate dtvp identifies the values of
the data type. The constant predicate dtid identifies the data
type itself. The constant predicate vid identifies one value
of the data type.

    <u>theory</u> kb-with-data-type =

        kernel-kb <u>enriched</u> <u>by</u>
            <u>spreds</u> dtvp
            <u>fpreds</u>
                <u>1-ary</u> dtid, vid
            <u>clauses</u>
                dtclass(X) ← dtid(X)
                dtvp(X) ← vid(X)
                vp(X,Y) ← dtid(X), dtvp(Y)
                dtvp(Y) ← vp(X,Y), dtid(X)

    <u>end</u>

--- Specification I3 ---

The first clause in this specification establishes that dtid
must belong to the class of data types. The second clause
merely states the inclusion of the indicated value in the set
of values of the data type. The other clauses establish the
necessary binding between dtid and dtvp, stating that the latter
identifies the possible values of the former.

Given an argument theory fittable into the theory kb-with-
data-type, the application of the theory mapping add-sur-type-sq
allows the introduction of a new surrogate type schema. This
theory mapping is defined in <u>Specification</u> I4. The indicated

---

```
    mapping add-sur-type-sq (KB : kb-with-data-type)
        using surclass, propclass, kmapclass,
              dom, codom, dtid of KB
        introducing surid, kmapid, kpropid

        =

            KB enriched by
                fpreds
                    1-ary surid, kpropid, kmapid
                clauses
                    surclass(X) ← surid(X)
                    propclass(X) ← kpropid(X)
                    kmapclass(X) ← kmapid(X)
                    dom(X,Y) ← kpropid(X), surid(Y)
                    codom(X,Y) ← kpropid(X), dtid(Y)
                    dom(X,Y) ← kmapid(X), dtid(Y)
                    codom(X,Y) ← kmapid(X), surid(Y)

        end
```

--------------------------------------- Specification I4 ---

requirements for applying this theory mapping are given in
Specification I3.

In Specification I4, the constant predicate surid identifies
the surrogate type itself. The associated key map is identified
by the constant predicate kmapid. The key property is identified
by kpropid.

The first clause
surclass(X) ← surid(X)
states that the new surrogate type must be included in the
class of surrogate types. Note that according to the axioms in
the data dictionary the new surrogate type is also included in
the archetype class. The other clauses have similar purposes
related to the data dictionary information.

The set of possible occurrences of a surrogate type is introduced using the theory mapping defined in Specification I6. The
argument knowledge base must be fittable into the theory given

in <u>Specification</u> I5. Note that any theory obtained by using
the theory mapping add-sur-type-sq is fittable into the theory
kb-with-sur-type-sq.

    <u>theory</u> kb-with-sur-type-sq =

        kb-with-data-type <u>enriched by</u>
           <u>fpreds</u>
             <u>1-ary</u> surid, kpropid, kmapid
           <u>clauses</u>
             surclass(X) ← surid(X)
             attclass(X) ← kpropid(X)
             kmapclass(X) ← kmapid(X)
             dom(X,Y) ← kpropid(X), surid(Y)
             codom(X,Y) ← kpropid(X), dtid(Y)
             dom(X,Y) ← kmapid(X), dtid(Y)
             codom(X,Y) ← kmapid(X), surid(Y)

    <u>end</u>

--- Specification I5 ---

In <u>Specification</u> I6, the sort predicate surop identifies
the possible occurrences of the new surrogate type. Note that
the set of all possible occurrences is canonically generated
using the key map. That is to say, for each value of the indicated data type there is a different occurrence of the surrogate
type, according to the clause
    surop(Z) ← km(X,Y,Z), kmapid(X), dtvp(Y)
The clauses
    am(X,Y,Z) ← kpropid(X), km(W,Z,Y), kmapid(W), dtvp(Z)
    km(X,Y,Z) ← kmapid(X), am(W,Z,Y), kpropid(W), surop(Z)
state that the key property is the reverse of the key map and
vice versa, as indicated above. Note that these clauses express
universal knowledge (application independent) which could be
codified in the kernel theory using second order clauses.

The sort predicate surxp is introduced for indicating the
currently existing occurrences of the surrogate type. The clause

```
    surop(X) ← surxp(X)
simply states that an existing occurrence must be one of the
possible occurrences.


-----------------------------------------------------------------
   mapping add-sur-type-os (KB : kb-with-sur-type-sq)
      using op, xp, km, am, surid, kmapid, kpropid, dtvp of KB
      introducing surop, surxp
      =

         let aux =
            KB enriched by canonical
               spreds surop
               clauses
                  surop(Z) ← km(X,Y,Z), kmapid(X), dtvp(Y)
         end

            in aux enriched by
               spreds surxp
               clauses
                  am(X,Y,Z) ← kpropid(X), km(W,Z,Y),
                              kmapid(W), dtvp(Z)
                  km(X,Y,Z) ← kmapid(X), am(W,Z,Y),
                              kpropid(W), surop(Z)
                  surop(X) ← surxp(X)
                  op(X,Y) ← surid(X), surop(Y)
                  surop(Y) ← op(X,Y), surid(X)
                  xp(X,Y) ← surid(X), surxp(Y)
                  surxp(Y) ← xp(X,Y), surid(X)

      end
--------------------------------------- Specification I6 ---
```

The last four clauses establish the binding between surid
and surop, as well as between surid and surxp.

An occurrence of a given surrogate type is inserted into the
knowledge base using the theory mapping defined in Specification
I7. The argument knowledge base must be fittable into the
theory kb-with-sur-type-os whose definition is omitted herein,

```
--------------------------------------------------------------
    mapping insert-sur-occ (KB : kb-with-sur-type-os)
      using km, surxp, kmapid, vid of KB
        =

          KB enriched by
              clauses
                  surxp(Z) ← km(X,Y,Z), kmapid(X), vid(Y)

    end
```
-------------------------------------- Specification I7 ---

recalling only that any theory obtained by using the theory mapping add-sur-type-os should be fittable into the theory kb-with-
sur-type-os.

Given a suitable argument knowledge base, the theory mapping
insert-sur-occ allows the insertion of an occurrence of the indicated surrogate type. This occurrence is identified by a key
value (the constant predicate vid).

The clause
surxp(Z) ← km(X,Y,Z), kmapid(X), vid(Y)
simply states that the surrogate occurrence corresponding to
the key value (using the key map) exists in the resulting knowledge base.

Note that one might strengthen the requirements theory kb-
with-sur-type-os by adding the assertion
(not surxp(Z)) ← km(X,Y,Z), kmapid(X), vid(Y)
which states that the surrogate occurrence named by vid does not
exist. In that case, it would be necessary to modify the definition of the theory mapping insert-sur-occ in order to avoid an
inconsistent result.

The assertion above is a non-clausal formula which can be
verified within a PROLOG environment using the closed world
rule, that is to say, using failure as negation [Lloyd, 1984].
This kind of non-clausal pre-condition is rather common, but,
for the sake of simplicity, the issue is not further discussed
herein.

A property is a function from an archetype into a data
type. In <u>Specification</u> <u>I</u>9, the corresponding theory mapping
add-property is defined, assuming an argument knowledge base
theory with an archetype and a data type. This theory is defined
in <u>Specification</u> <u>I</u>8.

    <u>theory</u> kb-with-arch-and-data-type =

      kb-with-data-type <u>enriched</u> <u>by</u>
        <u>spreds</u> archop, archxp
        <u>fpreds</u>
          <u>1-ary</u> archid
        <u>clauses</u>
          archclass(X) ← archid(X)
          archop(X) ← archxp(X)
          op(X,Y) ← archid(X), archop(Y)
          archop(Y) ← op(X,Y), archid(X)
          xp(X,Y) ← archid(X), archxp(Y)
          archxp(Y) ← xp(X,Y), archid(X)

   <u>end</u>
--- Specification I8 ---

Given a theory fittable into kb-with-arch-and-data-type, the
theory mapping add-property allows the introduction of a new
property. The constant predicate propid is the identifier of
the new property.

In <u>Specification</u> <u>I</u>9, the clause
   propclass(X) ← propid(X)
merely states that the new property must be put in the class of
properties. The clause
   dom(X,Y) ← propid(X), archid(Y)
states that the domain of the property must be the indicated
archetype. The clause
   codom(X,Y) ← propid(X), dtid(Y)
establishes that the domain of the property must be the indicated
data type. The clause

```
---------------------------------------------------------------
    mapping add-property (KB : kb-with-arch-and-data-type)
       using propclass, am, dom, codom
              dtid, dtvp, archid, archxp of KB
       introducing propid
       =

          KB enriched by
             fpreds
                1-ary propid
             clauses
                propclass(X) ← propid(X)
                dom(X,Y) ← propid(X), archid(Y)
                codom(X,Y) ← propid(X), dtid(Y)
                dtvp(Z) ← am(X,Y,Z), propid(X), archxp(Y)

    end
---------------------------------------- Specification I9 ---
```

dtvp(Z) ← am(X,Y,Z), propid(X), archxp(Y)
states that the value Z of the property X on an existing archetype occurrence Y must be an occurrence of the codomain data
type. Recall that the map am is used for defining every attribute as a function.

Given an argument theory which can be fitted into the theory
kb-with-two-archs, the theory mapping add-binrel-type-sq allows
the creation of the schema of a binary relation type. It is
possible to define in Knowlog one theory mapping for introducing
relation types of any arity. A restricted form of that mapping
is depicted in Specification I10. In that restricted form, the
mapping is able to introduce only binary relation types. The
definition of the requirements theory kb-with-two-archs is
omitted, since it raises no difficulty.

The theory mapping add-binrel-type-sq introduces a new
relation type, including the predicates relid, darg1id, darg2id
and rvdid. The predicate relid identifies the new relation
type itself. The predicates darg1id and darg2id correspond to
the argument designators. Finally, the predicate rvdid names

the reverse designator of the relation type.

```
    mapping add-binrel-type-sq (KB : kb-with-two-archs)
        using relclass, desclass, rvdclass, dom, codom,
              rdom, rcodom, archlid, arch2id of KB
        introducing relid, darglid, darg2id, rvdid
        =

            KB enriched by
               fpreds
                  1-ary relid, darglid, darg2id, rvdid
               clauses
                  relclass(X) ← relid(X)
                  desclass(X) ← darglid(X)
                  desclass(X) ← darg2id(X)
                  rvdclass(X) ← rvdid(X)
                  dom(X,Y) ← darglid(X), relid(Y)
                  codom(X,Y) ← darglid(X), archlid(Y)
                  dom(X,Y) ← darg2id(X), relid(Y)
                  codom(X,Y) ← darg2id(X), arch2id(Y)
                  rcodom(X,Y) ← rvdid(X), relid(Y)
                  rdom(X,N,Z) ← rvdid(X), archlid(Z)
                                zero(M), suc(M,N)
                  rdom(X,N,Z) ← rvdid(X), arch2id(Z),
                                zero(L), suc(L,M), suc(M,N)

    end
```
------------------------------------ Specification I10 ---

The theory mapping add-binrel-type-os allows the definition of the set of all possible occurrences of a binary relation type. It assumes that the argument theory is fittable into the theory kb-with-binrel-type-sq whose definition is omitted herein.

In Specification I11, the set of the possible occurrences (identified by the predicate relos) is canonically generated using the reverse designator. That is to say, for each pair of possible occurrences of the argument archetypes there is a

```
---------------------------------------------------------------
   mapping add-binrel-type-os (KB : kb-with-binrel-type-sq)
      using op, xp, relid, darglid, darg2id, rvdid,
            archlos, arch2os, archlxp, arch2xp of KB
      introducing relop, relxp
      =

         let aux =
            KB enriched by canonical
               spreds relop
               clauses
                  relop(Z) ← rm(W,X,Y,Z), rvdid(W),
                               archlos(X), arch2os(Y)

         end

            in aux enriched by
               spreds relxp
               clauses
                  am(X,Y,Z) ← darglid(X), rm(W,Z,T,Y),
                               rvdid(W), archlos(Z), arch2os(T)
                  am(X,Y,T) ← darg2id(X), rm(W,Z,T,Y),
                               rvdid(W), archlos(Z), arch2os(T)
                  rm(W,Z,T,Y) ← rvdid(W), archlos(Z), arch2os(T),
                                   am(A,Y,Z), darglid(A),
                                   am(B,Y,T), darg2id(B)
                  relop(X) ← relxp(X)
                  op(X,Y) ← relid(X), relop(Y)
                  relop(Y) ← op(X,Y), relid(X)
                  xp(X,Y) ← relid(X), relxp(Y)
                  relxp(Y) ← xp(X,Y), relid(X)
                  archlxp(Z) ← relxp(Y), am(X,Y,Z), darglid(X)
                  arch2xp(Z) ← relxp(Y), am(X,Y,Z), darg2id(X)

      end
---------------------------------------- Specification I11 ---
```

different occurrence of the relation type, according to the
clause

```
      relop(Z) ← rm(W,X,Y,Z), rvdid(W), archlos(X), arch2os(Y)
```

On the other hand, the clauses

```
am(X,Y,Z) ← darglid(X), rm(W,Z,T,Y),
            rvdid(W), archlos(Z), arch2os(T)
am(X,Y,T) ← darg2id(X), rm(W,Z,T,Y)
            rvdid(W), archlos(Z), arch2os(T)
rm(W,Z,T,Y) ← rvdid(W), archlos(Z), arch2os(T),
              am(A,Y,Z), darglid(A),
              am(B,Y,T), darg2id(B)
```

state the reverse relationship between the two argument designators and the reverse designator.

The last two clauses in <u>Specification</u> <u>Ill</u> state that no occurrence of the relation may exist unless the corresponding argument
occurrences exist. For instance, the clause

```
arch1xp(Z) ← relxp(Y), am(X,Y,Z), darglid(X)
```

imposes the existence of the occurrence of the first argument
associated to each existing occurrence of the relation.

5.2. Building an Infolog Knowledge Base

As an illustration of the use of the Infolog theory mappings
introduced above, assume that one wants to build a knowledge
base on the program of a conference. One of the most important
archetypes is paper. Assuming that each paper is uniquely identified by its arrival number, one should consider the surrogate
type paper. In <u>Construction</u> <u>1</u>, the resulting knowledge base
contains the schema of the surrogate type paper (surid), with
the key map pap and the key property num, assuming that kb is a
theory fittable into kb-with-data-type. The domain of key values
is identified by the sort predicate int.

Note that, for example, the clause

```
surclass(X) ← paper(X)
```

is a theorem of the theory kb', since it is the relevant instance
of the generic clause

```
surclass(X) ← surid(X)
```

in the theory mapping add-sur-type-sq.

The construction of a useful knowledge base would go on
along these lines using the other Infolog theory mappings, in

order to introduce, for instance, relations, occurrences and
attributes.

```
------------------------------------------------------------------
    theory kb' = add-sur-type-sq (kb)

        through
            surclass is surclass
            propclass is propclass
            kmapclass is kmapclass
            dom is dom
            codom is codom
            dtid is integer
        with
            paper is surid
            kmapid is pap
            kpropid is num

    end
----------------------------------------------- Construction 1 ---
```

It is clear that Knowlog is not a practical language for the
construction of knowledge bases. Knowlog is effective for defining a knowledge representation approach library of theory
mappings. It is also effective in the formal definition of the
semantics of the knowledge base construction operations. Naturally, a more practical language should be used for the construction itself, probably a different language for each knowledge representation approach. Thus, one should not confuse
Knowlog with a knowledge representation language. Knowlog is
better seen as a meta language. The relationship between
Knowlog and the Infolog knowledge representation language will
become clear in the next section.

6. THE EXTENSIBLE IKBS

At the heart of the DSS should be an extensible IKBS. Recalling the arguments outlined in the Introduction, the envisaged
extensible IKBS should be able to support:

a) The definition and use of extensions to the adopted knowl-
    edge representation approach (KRA), e.g., Infolog, including
    the corresponding extensions to the associated knowledge
    representation language (KRL).

b) Effective tools for the modular construction of structured
    knowledge bases (KBs), allowing the definition and applica-
    tion of parametric components, that is to say, theory map-
    pings.

In order to fulfill these ambitious requirements, taking
into account the institutional framework proposed in the previous sections, the envisaged IKBS is developed according to the
following principles:

1. A fixed _inference engine_ is adopted within the clausal
    formalism. This inference engine is used for inferencing
    and explanation purposes on any knowledge base built ac-
    cording to the adopted knowledge representation approach
    and its extensions.

2. The knowledge base has two alternative representations: a
    data base representation supporting fast concurrent dumb
    access to shared data and a _clausal representation_ (probably
    generated on demand) used by the inference engine for intel-
    ligent access. The overall structure of the data base repre-
    sentation is depicted in Figure 1. Non-monotonic changes
    to a knowledge base are trivial if made on the data base
    representation. Generating on demand its clausal representa-
    tion avoids the problem of finding an efficient way of im-
    plementing those changes within the clausal setting.

3. A _definition engine_ is included in order to process the
    Knowlog definition of extensions to the adopted knowledge
    representation approach.

4. The definition engine is able to generate the _meta-schema_
    corresponding to each version of the evolving knowledge
    representation approach. Each KRA meta-schema is the schema
    of a dictionary containing the schemas of the data bases
    representing knowledge bases built according to that particu-
    lar version of the KRA. On the other hand, the meta2-schema

is the fixed schema of a higher-level dictionary containing
such meta-schemas.

5. The definition engine is able to generate a compiler for
    each version of the evolving knowledge representation lan-
    guage. Each KRL is used for building knowledge bases (KBs)
    structured according to the associated version of the knowl-
    edge representation approach. The construction of each KB
    includes the definition of its data base schema, as well as
    the addition of tuples to its data base. A KRL can also be
    used for writing queries. Those queries can be evaluated
    either against the data base representation or using the
    inference engine on the clausal representation.

```
+------------------------------------------------+
|                                                |
|   meta2-schema          (Knowlog)              |
|                                                |
+------------------------------------------------+
|                                                |
|   meta-schemas    (KRA versions)               |
|                                                |
+------------------------------------------------+
|                                                |
|   schemas                                      |
|                          (KBs)                 |
+--------------------------+                     |
|   tuples                                       |
|                                                |
+------------------------------------------------+
```

DATABASE REPRESENTATION

Figure 1.

6. The definition engine is able to generate an interactive
    build and browse module tailored for each version of the
    knowledge representation approach. Each IB2 module is used
    as an alternative way of building and browsing the data
    base representation of knowledge bases structured according
    to the associated version. It is based upon the classical
    technology of interactive concurrent access to the data
    base, in order to speed up this type of dumb access to repet-
    itive knowledge (which is kept in tuples in the data base
    representation).

7. The definition module must also generate, for each version of the knowledge representation approach, a <u>clausal gener-ator</u>, which is a collection of procedures responsible for producing the clausal representation of any knowledge base built according to that version (extracting the necessary information from its data base representation).

The overall architecture of the envisaged IKBS is depicted in Figure 2. A system organized according to these principles is under development at the University of Lisbon. A preliminary experience has been done successfully. This experience consisted of manually organizing the data base representation of the Infolog approach and producing by hand the associated clausal generator (see Fiadeiro and Sernadas [1985]). This generator was developed taking into account the definition (in Knowlog) of the Infolog theory mappings (see Sernadas and Sernadas [1985e]).

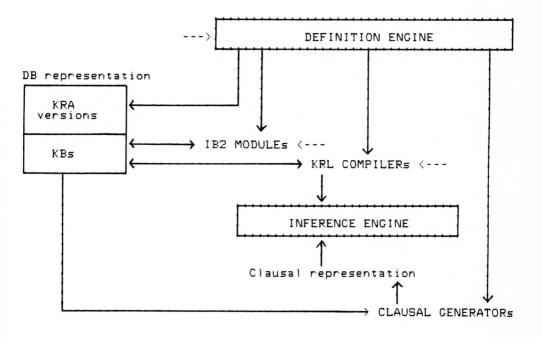

Figure 2.

Another interesting development is the design of a Knowlog compiler for the automatic production of the IKBMSs, given their respective knowledge representation approaches (assumed to be defined in Knowlog as collections of theory mappings). Such a compiler is also under intensive research at the University of Lisbon (see Sernadas and Sernadas [1985f] and Sernadas et al. [1985a].

7. CONCLUDING REMARKS

The goal of bringing together into a unique theoretical framework the three knowledge representation paradigms (logical, structural and procedural) is fulfilled within the setting of the clausal institution. Therein, it is possible to define any structural semantic primitive as a theory mapping which can be used for building structured clausal theories. Naturally, the resulting clausal theories can be accessed taking either the logical view or the procedural view, thanks to the two alternative semantics of the clausal logic.

As a by-product of this integration effort, it is possible to introduce effective tools for the modular construction of theories, that is to say, knowledge bases. Indeed, the Knowlog language may also be used for defining additional mappings (parameterized theories), besides those corresponding to the semantic primitives of the adopted knowledge representation approach (Infolog).

As a consequence of these results, it is possible to outline the architecture of an extensible IKBS, to be implemented in PROLOG, supporting the modular construction of knowledge bases structured according to the Infolog knowledge representation approach. Such a system allows the definition of the evolving knowledge representation approach as a collection of clausal theory mappings. The resulting knowledge bases, as clausal theories, are accessed using a universal clausal inference engine.

Further work is necessary on the insertion of such extensible IKBS into a practical, inference-capable DSS, taking advantage

of the proposed integration of the three paradigms of knowledge
representation.

ACKNOWLEDGEMENT

This work was partially supported by Junta Nacional de
Investigacao Científica e Tecnológica under the research contract
no. 417.82.57.

REFERENCES

Barwise, J. (1974). "Axioms for Abstract Model Theory," Annals
of Mathematical Logic, 7, pp. 221-265.

Burstall, R. and Goguen, J. (1980). "The Semantics of Clear, a
Specification Language," in Abstract Software Specifications,
D. Bjorner (ed.), Springer-Verlag LNCS 86.

Burstall, R. and Goguen, J. (1981). "An Informal Introduction
to Specifications Using Clear," in The Correctness Problem
in Computer Science, R. Boyer and J. Moore (eds.), Academic
Press.

Carmo, J. (1985). "The Infolog Branching Logic of Events," in
Information Systems - Theoretical and Formal Aspects, A.
Sernadas, J. Bubenko and A. Olive (eds.), North-Holland.

Coelho, H., Rodrigues, A. and Sernadas, A. (1985). "Towards
Knowledge-Based Infolog Specifications," Decision Support
Systems, 1, 2.

De, S., Nof, S. and Whinston, A. (1985). "Decision Support in
Computer-Integrated Manufacturing," Decision Support Systems,
1, 1.

Fiadeiro, J. and Sernadas, A. (1985). The Infolog Clausal
Generator, Infolog RR29, Faculty of Sciences of Lisbon.

Goguen, J. and Burstall, R. (1984). "Introducing Institutions,"
in Logics of Programs, Springer-Verlag LNCS 164.

ISO/TC97/SC5/WG3 (1982). Concepts and Terminology for the
Conceptual Schema and the Information Base, J. van Griethuysen
(ed.).

Kowalski, R. (1979). Logic for Problem Solving, North-Holland.

Kunifuji, S. and Yokota, H. (1982). "Prolog and Relational
Databases for Fifth-Generation Computer Systems," in Logical
Bases for Data Bases, J.-M. Nicolas (ed.), workshop pre-
prints, Toulouse.

Lloyd, J. (1984). Foundations of Logic Programming, Springer-Verlag.

MacLane, S. (1971). Categories for the Working Mathematician, Springer-Verlag.

Mayr, B. and Makowsky, J. (1982a). An Axiomatic Approach to the Semantics of Specification Languages, Technical Report, Technion, Israel Institute of Technology.

Mayr, B. and Makowsky, J. (1982b). Characterizing Specification Languages which Admit Initial Semantics, Technical Report, Technion, Israel Institute of Technology.

Mylopoulos, J. and Brodie, M. (1985). "AI and Databases: Semantic vs. Computational Theories of Information," in New Directions for Database Systems, G. Ariav and J. Clifford (eds.), Ablex Publishing Company.

Ng, P. and Paul, J. (1980). "A Formal Definition of Entity-Relationship Models," in Entity-Relationship Approach to Systems Analysis and Design, P. Chen (ed.), North-Holland.

Olle, T., Sol, H. and Verrijn-Stuart, A. (1982). Information Systems Design Methodologies: A Comparative Review, North-Holland.

Sernadas, A. (1984). Time Abstractions in the Design of Historical Databases, Infolog RR21, Faculty of Sciences, IFIP WG 8.1 Meeting, Linz, September 3-5.

Sernadas, C. and Sernadas A. (1985a). "Conceptual Modeling Abstraction Mechanisms as Parameterized Theories in Institutions," in Database Semantics, R. Meersman and T. Steel (eds.), North-Holland.

Sernadas, C. and Sernadas, A. (1985b). The Institutional Approach to Conceptual Schema Transformations, Infolog RR41, Faculty of Sciences of Lisbon.

Sernadas, A. and Sernadas, C. (1985c). "The Use of E-R Abstractions for Knowledge Representation," in Proceedings of the 4th International Conference on Entity-Relationship Approach, IEEE.

Sernadas, A. and Sernadas, C. (1985d). "Capturing Knowledge about the Organization Dynamics," in Knowledge Representation for Decision Support Systems, L. Methlie and R. Sprague (eds.), North-Holland.

Sernadas, C. and Sernadas, A. (1985e). "Conceptual Schema Abstraction Mechanisms for Knowledge Representation," Fourth Scandinavian Research Seminar on Information Modeling and Data Base Management, Tampere, June 5-7.

Sernadas, A. and Sernadas, C. (1985f). "Abstraction and Inference Mechanisms for Knowledge Representation," Knowledge
Base Management Systems, Crete, June 24-26.

Sernadas, A., Sernadas, C. and Carapuca, R. (1985a). Knowlog:
A Language for Building Modular Clausal Theories, Infolog
RR53, Faculty of Sciences of Lisbon.

Sernadas, A., Sernadas, C, Fiadeiro, J. and Granado, J. (1985b).
Information Systems Design with Infolog, Infolog RR25,
Faculty of Sciences of Lisbon.

5. INTRODUCING AI IN OPTRANS A DSS GENERATOR*

Michel R. Klein, Jean-Eloi Dussartre and Francois Despoux
Département Système d'Information et d'Aide à la Décision (SIAD)
Centre HEC-ISA
78350 Jouy-en-Josas, France

1. PRESENT STRUCTURE OF OPTRANS

OPTRANS is a DSS Generator or DSS shell. The notion of DSS will not be described here, for this notion we refer the reader to Scott Morton [1971], Klein and Tixier [1971] and to Bonczek, Holsapple and Whinston [1984] for a very good and more recent survey of developments in the field. The structure of OPTRANS was described in some detail in Klein and Manteau [1983], we shall just recall it here. The structure of OPTRANS is represented in Figure 1. It is a layered structure with a nucleus and several specialized subsystems. The nucleus is to be used in the generation of any DSS, the other subsystems can be added according to the problem area.

1.1. Description of the Nucleus

The nucleus consists of 4 integrated subsystems:
- a specialized DBMS,
- an information display subsystem,
- a modelling language,
- a monitor function (front end).

1.1.1. The DBMS Function

This subsystem includes a data definition language (DDL) and a data manipulation language (DML) for a multidimensional DBMS (using an entity-relationship data model) an entity relation. This system provides usual DBMS functions such as:
- multi-access to data and models,
- control of access to data and models,
- ability to allow concurrent update and retrieval,

---

* Work started at ENSIMAG and finished at SIG (Systèmes Informatiques de Gestion).

NATO ASI Series, Vol. F31
Decision Support Systems: Theory and Application
Edited by C. W. Holsapple and A. B. Whinston
© Springer-Verlag Berlin Heidelberg 1987

138

- no redundancy at the data base level,
- physical independence between the data base and decision models.

1.1.2. The Information Display Subsystem

This subsystem includes a report generator and simple graphical capabilities (curves, scater diagrams, histograms, bar charts...) for color-plotter. The report generator includes a non-procedural language to create, save, retrieve and modify reports and a language to define reports.

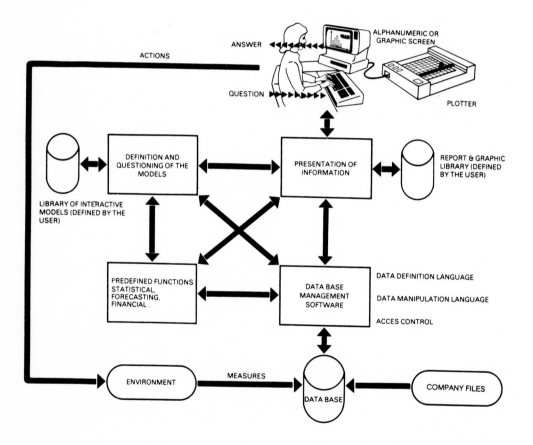

Figure 1. Initial Functional Structure of the
OPTRANS DSS Development Tool (without AI)

1.1.3. The Modelling Function

This subsystem includes a non-procedural command language
to create, save, unsave, evaluate and modify decision models,
and a language with procedural capabilities to define the relations of models. This language is particularly suited for defining decision models in the financial, marketing, management
control and production management areas.

1.1.4. The Monitor (user front end)

This is the system's executive, at this level the command
language enables the user to:
- list and select available:
    - data bases,
    - subsystems,
    - decision models libraries,
    - reports libraries,
- define the control of access to the data base and model base
  for users (when in proprietary mode),
- define the rights for updating the data base,
- run models and/or report,
  etc.

1.1.5. Specialized Subsystems

In certain domains the user expects the DSS to give him
access to analytical tools which have become standard. Such
domains are: financial and credit analysis, economic and financial planning, marketing, management control, interactive use of
large financial or economic data base (for credit scoring). It
is the goal of a specialized subsystem to provide him with an
access to these analytical tools which have to be integrated
with the data base. In OPTRANS three main subsystems are presently available: ANALYS - a statistical and data analysis subsystem,
AVNIR - a short term forecasting system, FINSIM - an interactive
financial analysis and engineering model. Also connection is
provided with some other known Data Analysis packages such as
SPSS or SAS.

2. PRESENT DEVELOPMENT

Four main areas of interest have been defined, on which work has been going on for a couple of years. These areas are:
- introduction of window management in the rapport generator,
- introduction of Artificial Intelligence (AI) in the system,
- development of a version of OPTRANS for the IBM-PC and IBM AT and compatible computers,
- introducing connection capabilities between the micro and mainframe versions of OPTRANS to enable the user to define and develop decentralized DSS.

We shall, in this paper, mainly give some information on the work done on the introduction of AI in the system.

3. INTRODUCTION OF AI IN THE SYSTEM

We are going first to give an idea of our research goal. Then we give an example of the interaction between the user and the system, the structure of the system and its integration within OPTRANS, the principle of the inference engine and rule compilation.

3.1. General Objective

The objective can be defined by saying that we wish to integrate a (Knowledge-Based) management system and a library of inference engines to OPTRANS in such a way that users can develop a DSS with an expert component which can be used at several levels:
- the data base and knowledge base level,
- the modelling level,
- the analytical subsystem level,
- the command language level.

To take an example let's examine the case of credit analysis. We wish to let the user be able to define the data base[1] and the decision models and reports he needs for financial and credit analysis. Such a system is described in PARNET [PARNET, 1985]

---

[1]In our case composed of several hundred or thousand balance sheets and income statements (we are presently facing a case with some tens of thousands of companies).

for a DSS used for credit analysis of the clients of a large
industrial company or in Klein [1985] or Klein and Tixier
[1971] for a system used for teaching and research in
financial and credit analysis at HEC. In [Klein, 1977] is described a decision model which can be connected to OPTRANS and
is used for the simulation and projection of financial statements in a credit analysis department. OPTRANS enables the user
to compute any kind of financial fact he wishes, or define most
kinds of financial models. However, OPTRANS does not enable the
user to:
- get assistance such as a financial diagnosis (the system
  does not give any advice, as an expert would, letting the
  user make his final decision),
- introduce his own set of rules[2] for financial analysis.

3.2. Example of a Conversation

The interaction between the knowledge-based DSS (KB DSS) and
the user will be of the following type:

MONITOR ? BASE *> DAFSA (the user loads the DAFSA[3] Data base)
          <password>
MONITOR ? PRINT BS   (balance sheet)
          company name ? carrefour

              printing of the BS

          PRINT IS (Income statement)
          company name ? carrefour

              printing of the IS

---

[2]Which is, for anybody aware of the problem, not an easy job
in financial analysis (knowledge engineering aspect).
[3]DAFSA is a French company providing a tape of financial data
from the balance sheets and income statements of companies on the
Paris and European stock exchanges.

```
MONITOR ? BASE            (the user switches to the DB level)
BASE ? contexte company carrefour (the user selects the data of
                                   the company carrefour)
BASE ? context time year79-year80  the user selects a period of
                                   time

                    the user works with the data (printing financial
                    data, defining new aggregates, plotting curves...)

BASE ? END        (the user switches to the front-end level)
MONITOR ? Diagnosis company carrefour
```

We have 5 fiscal years in the DB for company carrefour.
Would you like to use all the historical period?

yes
the expert diagnosis is : conditional approval

explain conclusion
liquidity is good
return is good
structure is bad

explain liquidity

explain liquidity
the liquidity is measured by the ratio : (cash+
receivable+clients)/(short.term debt+suppliers)>1.2
(distribution
industry)

NB : We have underlined what is typed by the user.

explain structure

the structure is measured by the ratio : debt/equity > 2.

comment : in the distribution industry a debt/equity ratio over
2 is considered bad

what are conditions ?

increase in capital of 80 KF combined with the loan.

do you wish to evaluate reimbursement capacity?

yes

amount of credit (KF), duration (years) ?

160,5

depreciation method (straight line, accelerated)

straight

interest rate for the loan (%)

9.5

sales and expense variation due to the investment

sales : 85, 0, 50, 100, 120, 150

expenses : 85, 10, 30, 30, 30

do you wish to see the reimbursement capacity ?

no

sufficient capacity to reimburse the loan.

approval confirmed

end

3.3. Problems Involved

3.3.1. Relation between the Knowledge Base and the Data Base

As it can be seen, financial rules use variables, the variables can be complex to evaluate[4] (the more so if we use aggregates computed over an industry such as the mean return on
assets in the road transport industry). In other words, we need
to use rules, which use variables to deduce facts such as
"financial structure = bad." These variables being themselves
facts which are presently in the OPTRANS data base.

3.3.2. Relation between the Modelling Part and the Knowledge Base

In the above example, the capacity to reimburse the loan is
computed by a simple financial model using a uses and sources
of funds equation. In other words, the rules can also use variables computed by a model to deduce facts such as "capacity to
reimburse = good." In OPTRANS a decision model can update the
data base, so the computed variable can be accessed in the data
base itself or in the working space of the decision model.

4. PRESENT STATE OF INTEGRATION OF AI IN OPTRANS

The present state of integration was developed using a problem oriented approach. The domain which was chosen is the domain
of financial and credit analysis which was identified already in
1977 [Klein, 1978] as being a good one for the application of
artificial intelligence techniques in DSS. We shall give first
some information on the structure of the KB in such a domain,
then on the reasoning process which is simulated in OPTRANS.

---

[4]Some of them are elementary variables, others are aggregates
(or virtual data) using OPTRANS terminology.

4.1. Structure of the KB

An analysis of the knowledge used by a credit analyst points out that the KB is made of facts and rules.

4.1.1. Definition of the Different Kinds of Facts at the KB Level

Three kinds of facts were identified:

- facts which the credit analyst can <u>observe</u> when comparing certain aggregates (indicators) with values considered as limits (threshold)

    ex : liquidity.ratio > 1.2

    these facts we shall call <u>observed facts</u>[5]

- facts which are <u>deduced</u> by the credit analyst

    These more empirical facts, correspond to grades the analyst will give, according to his experience,[6] to variables considered the measure of important points of view in credit analysis such as: liquidity, return, structure, etc... These facts we shall call: <u>deduced facts</u>. Some examples are:

    return on assets = good

    financial structure = bad

    etc...

- facts which are of the <u>common sense</u> type

    Very often nonnumerical in nature. Examples of such facts are:

    - The industry to which the company we study belongs is presently undergoing a crisis.
    - The quality or the business practice of the management is not considered very good.
    - The products which the company produces are fashion items, etc...

---

[5] In the vocabulary of logic they are predicates.
[6] These "deduced" facts vary with the industry which is studied.

4.1.2. Evaluation of These Facts

The evaluation of these facts has led us to make a distinction between two kinds of facts from the computer science point of view: facts which are internal to the Expert System (ES) Module and facts which are external to the Expert Systems. The facts internal to the ES are kept in the Internal Fact Base, they are made of the deduced facts and common sense facts (non-numerical). The facts external to the ES are kept in the OPTRANS data base. They are the observed facts. The syntax of the facts in the internal fact base is:

(<attribute> (<val1><val2>...<valn>)<source>)

with

<attribute> = name of a fact

<val1>
<val2>
.
.   the set of values that the fact can take
.   within the corresponding scale
<valn>

- val1 will be the lowest value on the scale
- valn will be the highest value on the scale.

<source> list of rule numbers from which the fact can be
        deduced

ex : (advice (x1,x2,x3) <source>)

where x1, x2, x3 are indicators giving information on the following terms:

- approval
- conditional approval
- not approved.

Remark: these indicators[7] will be allowed to take three values:

- possible: possible value for the attribute
- thrue   : value of the attribute
- false   : value impossible for the attribute

These indicators will represent possibility links between terms and attributes. At the beginning in the internal fact base, these links will be (except otherwise decided by the user) stated

---

[7]Vi $\in$ (1,n)<vali>

as "possible." As new deduced facts will be obtained from the
reasoning process these links will evolve. The important
advantage of such a structure is that we are able to gain information from all backward chaining. (If we do not have this
structure, in searches which are guided through backward chaining
on hypotheses-facts, we do not take into account the impossibil-
ity to affect a given value to an attribute.) With such a
structure, several cases can be taken into account:
- the search guided by a value sends back "thrue," then the
  link between the considered value and the attribute is put
  to "thrue," and the other links to "false" (this is also
  valid for forward chaining),
- the guided search sends back the value "false," then the
  link between the considered value and the attribute is put
  to "false,"
- the guided search sends back the value "false" for a whole
  region (set of contiguous terms) then the links between the
  considered value and the attribute is put to "false."
This structure will allow optimization at the level of the evaluation of conditions. The search algorithm will not try to
deduce a fact corresponding to an impossible (false) link. Also
this method allows for the evaluation of a fact by stepwise
refinement, as an expert can refine his solution set by getting
rid of the impossible hypotheses to spend more time on possible
cases. So, this structure will avoid making unneeded backward
chaining. It could be shown that this structure can be used to
detect incoherence in the KB.[8]

The facts which are external to the ES are present in the
OPTRANS DB under a numerical form. These facts will never be
stored in the internal fact base of the ES, we have called them
observed facts. These facts are evaluated by calling OPTRANS
access functions. This is where lies the link between the DB
and KB.

---

[8]When all links for a hypotheses-fact will be impossible,
the algorithm will detect incoherence in the KB.

4.1.3. Link between the DB and KB

We had first imagined the following solution: when the expert system (ES) needs a fact, it looks in the fact base. If the fact is not there the ES looks in the OPTRANS DB and updates the ES fact base. In other words, the fact base would contain the deduced facts and the observed facts together.

The consequence was that it was needed to find a structure for the fact base which could have a very large size and should be very fast to access. Also, the data coming from OPTRANS are indexed by time, which is not the case of concluded facts (presently). For these two reasons we have dropped the dynamic link for a solution with a systematic call to OPTRANS for the research of a fact and even for the computation of functions with arguments on numerical facts coming from OPTRANS (for example: maximum, standard error, ...). As a consequence, we do not memorize the observed fact in the KB. On the contrary, the internal facts are in constant number, whatever the expertise. We recall that the internal facts (or deduced facts) are criteria which the expert uses to guide himself in the reasoning. For example:

IF (WORKING-CAPITAL > 1.5 * SHORT.TERM DEBT)
Then (short-term-risk = weak)

4.1.4. Rules

4.1.4.1. Structuring the rules

Some examination of the reasoning process of a credit or financial analyst will show that the analyst will first attempt to study the historical financial statements of a company from different points of view such as:
- return
- financial structure
- liquidity.

Within each of these points of view he will usually refine his analysis. For example, he will compute several ratios to measure liquidity, several measures of return (on equity, on assets, before financing...). As a consequence, we have decided to

segment rules by subset. Each rule subset is a family of rules
which studies a given point of view or criteria or sub-problem.
This organization allows for extensive evolution of the rules
and will be used in the analysis or the problem to reach the
conclusion.

4.1.4.2. Rule syntax

The present syntax is the following:

(<rule-subset>, <conditional-expression>, <deduced-fact>,
<comment>, <deduced-rule-subset>, <link-level>)

where:

<rule-subset> denoted the rule-subset to which the rule belongs.
This rule-subset is a subset of rules used to study a point
of view or criteria such as in our example: short term
risk, financial structure, return on assets, return on
equity, ...

<conditional-expression> is a predicate as in:
IF financial structure > 2
    then

<deduced-fact> is a new fact such as "liquidity = good"

<comment> is a text which can be printed or is there to help
the knowledge engineer when working on the rules

<concluded-rule-subset> is a subset of rules which has to be
examined as a whole

<link-level> is the strength of the link of the rule with the
concluded-rule-subset.
Three levels of priority exist.

As a consequence, the examination of the rule will lead in certain cases to the examination of another subset of rules (point
of view or criteria or sub-problem) (see Section 4.2.2). There
is a rule number which is given automatically by the system.

4.2. Reasoning Process Within the System

This reasoning process can be subdivided in 3 parts from
the analytical point of view. The choice of rules-subset (control), the sequencing and the inference itself.

4.2.1. Choice of Rule-Subset (control)

Figure 2 gives the algorithm for guiding the reasoning process: the algorithm starts with one criteria (rule-subset). As soon as a rule is activated, the algorithm puts the new criteria (rule-subset) in the stack using the "field" <concluded-rule-subset>.

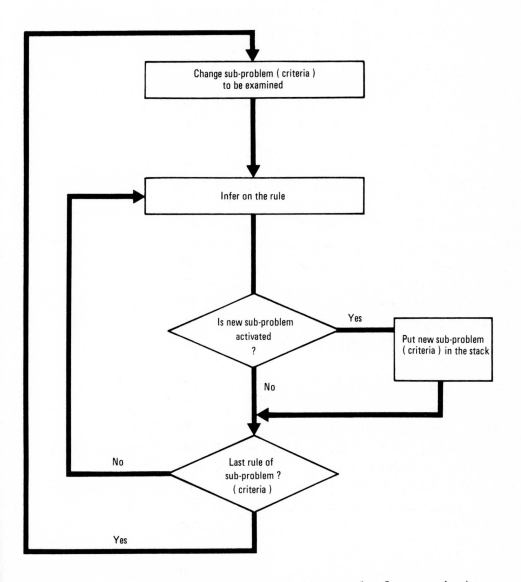

Figure 2.   Choice of Rule-Subset (control of reasoning)

4.2.2. Sequencing

The sequencing is done at two levels:
- when a rule-subset (criteria) is called by an activated rule,
- at the end of each rule-subset (criteria).

The <link-level> will be used according to the following priority:

first level: (immediate)	stop the examination of the present rule subset and switch immediately to the deduced-rule-subset
second level: (equal)	finish the examination of the present rule subset and then switch to the deduced rule subset which will be put on top of the stack
third level: (inferior)	finish the examination of the present rule subset and put deduced rule subset at the bottom of the stack

- at the end of each rule-subset, reorganization of the stack can occur due to the meta-rules.

4.2.3. Inference

The inference will be mainly done using forward chaining according to Figure 3. However, there is a backward chaining engine which will be used to look for unknown facts. It is also through this backward chaining that it will be possible to ask the user questions on unknown facts.

4.2.4. Structure of the ES Part of OPTRANS

This structure is best explained through Figure 4.

5. NEW STRUCTURE OF THE DSS DEVELOPMENT TOOL (GENERATOR OR SHELL)

This structure is best explained by Figure 5.

We just wish to point out that as we had a library of statistical or mathematical routines to work on the data base, we now have also a library of inference engines to work on the KB, DB, model library and data processing routines... A typical demarche for a DSS developer being:

a. find out elementary entities (variables) and entity types
    used in the problem,
b. define aggregates,   ⎫
c. define relations between entity types,   ⎬ DB definition
d. feed data in the DB,   ⎭
e. define needed decision models,
f. define needed reports and graphical representation,
g. define KB in relation with the DB   ⎫
h. select suited inference engine for   ⎬ ES definition
    working with the KB,   ⎭
i. use the system and iterate on any of the above points.

6. <u>NEXT STEP</u>

A certain number of improvements are being planned, the main
ones are the following.

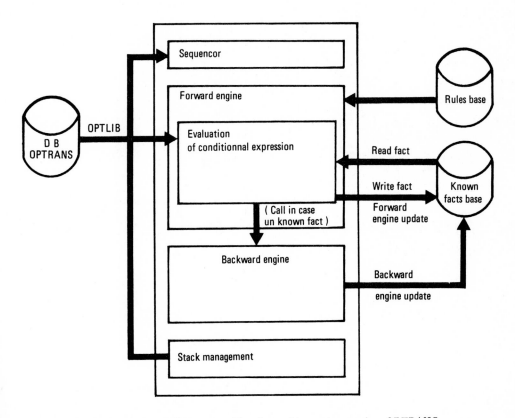

Figure 3. Inference Engine Structure in OPTRANS

152

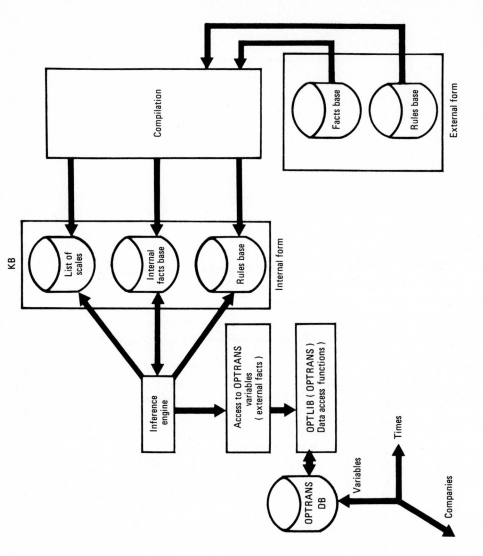

Figure 4. General Structure of the Expert System Integrated within OPTRANS

153

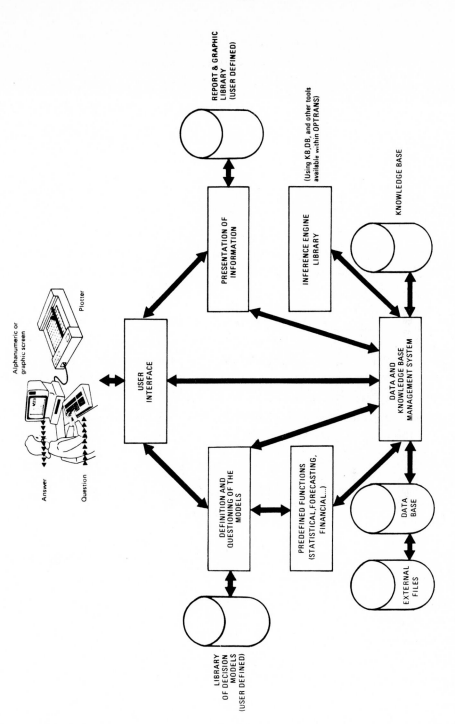

Figure 5. Functional Structure of OPTRANS: A DSS Development Tool

6.1. Improving the Set of Rules for Financial Analysis

The present set of rules for financial analysis is of 120
rules. It is forecasted that a set of rules to give an assistance of an average quality will be at least of several hundred
rules.

6.2. Improving the Integration with OPTRANS

This improvement is obtained by enabling the user to write
any sequence of OPTRANS commands in a rule. As a consequence
the extension of a rule will be the following:

(<rule-subset>, <conditional-expression>, <deduced-fact>,
<comment>, <sequence of OPTRANS commands>, <deduced-rule-
subset>, <link-level>)

With this capacity the user will be able to call a model within
a rule, and use the model output in another rule... We remind
the reader that in OPTRANS a model can update the data base.
For example, the knowledge engineer will use, in a rule, a model
computing the capacity to reimburse a loan. Then the capacity
to reimburse and the repayment of the loan will be compared in
a rule. With this extension the inference engine becomes
procedural.

6.3. Extending the System to Other Domains

The system which is proposed being a development tool must
accommodate the kind of knowledge found in other fields of management such as:
  - control,
  - marketing,
  - planning,
  - production management.
We plan to study if the present syntax and inference engine is
suited for these other domains and if needed we shall extend this
syntax.

6.4. Developing a Library of Inference Engines

Presently we have developed an inference engine working with rules which do not include uncertainty coefficients. In other domains this might not be possible. As a consequence, a new type of inference engine will be needed. Also the present inference engine is procedural, we shall for other domains need a non-procedural inference engine. So we think the evolution of the system will be toward a library of inference engines as new domains will be studied.

6.5. Introduction of AI at the Modelling Level

One usually difficult task for end users is the definition of models. In certain domains (finance, marketing...) it is possible to:
- check that certain needed relations are not missing given a list of variables,
- suggest certain relations,
- explain underlying causal relationships of models...

6.6. Introduction of AI at the Data Processing Level

Most DSS development tools integrated analytical tools such as: statistical models, short term forecasting models, ... These models rely on a certain number of hypotheses. AI can be used to remind the user of appropriate conditions of use of these models and so the system can behave as a statistics consultant or expert.

7. IMPLEMENTATION

- A prototype system has been implemented in Franz Lisp and is presently running on a Digital VAX computer on which OPTRANS is available. The Lisp version is calling FORTRAN procedures (Data Access and Evaluation functions of OPTRANS).

- The prototype has been converted to PASCAL to be integrated in the PC XT and AT versions of OPTRANS and is being converted to FORTRAN 77 to be integrated in the multi-users version (which includes the multidimensional DB).

ACKNOWLEDGEMENT

We would like to thank, Professor A. Lux from LIFIA ENSIMAG for his help in the design of the ES, Mrs. Rico for typing the manuscript, and the company SIG for financing this research, Mr. Veillon, Director of ENSIMAG, for his encouragement.

REFERENCES

Abel, J., Menu, J. and Probst, A.R. "Un Prototype de Système Expert pour la Finance," Université de Lausanne, H.E.C., Ecole Polytechnique Fédérale de Lausanne.

Aucoin, Marcel and Pham-Hi, Duc (1985). "Système Expert à l'Institut de Formation de la Banque de France," Bancatique n° 2, Février.

Bonczek, Robert H., Holsapple, Clyde W. and Whinston, Andrew B. (1984). "Developments in DSS," Advances in Computers, 23, Academic Press.

Cordier, Marie-Odile (1984). "Les Systèmes Experts," La Recherche n° 151, Janiver.

De Langle, Claude and Sall, Michel (1985). "Systèmes Experts de Placements Bancaires pour les Particuliers," Bancatique n° 5, Mai.

Demians D'Archimbaud, L. (1982). "Une Introduction aux Systèmes Experts," Revue Technique Thomson-CSF, 14, 4, Décembre.

Klein, Michel (1977). "FINSIM A Decision Support System for Financial Planning and Engineering," in Information Processing, Gilghrist (ed.), North Holland.

Klein, Michel (1978). "Systèmes Questions-Réponses et aide à la Décision en Analyse Financière," International Seminar on Intelligent Question-Answering and Database Systems, Bonas, June 1977, IRIA.

Klein, Michel (1985). Manuel d'utilisation de la Base de Données DAFSA Exploitée sous OPTRANS, Centre HEC-ISA, 1, rue de la libération 78350 Jouy-en-Josas.

Klein, Michel and Manteau, Alain (1983). "OPTRANS: A Tool for Implementation of Decision Support Systems," in Processes and Tools for Decision Support, H.G. Sol (ed.), North Holland.

Klein, Michel and Tixier, Vincent (1971). "SCARABEE, A Data and Model Base for Financial Engineering and Research," IFIP-Congress, North Holland.

Lux, Augustin. "Vers une Présentation Axiomatique de l'IA, " Note interne, LIFIA, Grenoble.

"Parnet, Un Système de'aide à la Décision pour l'analyse de Crédit," (1985), Actes du Colloque SIAD-1984 (Deauville). Agence pour la Développement de l'Informatique.

Rapport Interne SIG. 4 bis, rue de la libération 78350 Juoy-en-Josas.

Scott Morton, M.S. (1971). "Management Decision Systems: Computer Based Support for Decision Making," Division of Research, Graduate School of BA, Harvard University, Cambridge, Massachusetts.

6. CHARACTERISTICS OF A SUCCESSFUL DSS USER'S NEEDS vs. BUILDER'S NEEDS

Nasir Ghiaseddin
Department of Management
College of Business Administration
University of Notre Dame
Notre Dame, IN 46556, U.S.A.

ABSTRACT

As decision support systems become more popular, the need for the development of such systems becomes more obvious. This paper takes an in-depth look at the decision support systems and studies their purpose and properties. By investigating the user's needs, a set of desirable characteristics for a successful DSS are identified. These characteristics are then used to identify a set of essential tools for the builder of the decision support system in order to help him/her to develop a successful decision support system.

1. INTRODUCTION

The subject of decision support systems (DSSs) is concerned with improving the productivity of the decision maker through exploitation of an information processing system.

A decision support system may be a human information processor, an electronic information processor, or a human-machine information processing system embedded within an organizational decision-making system [Bonczek et al., 1981]. Although according to the above definition it is possible that a DSS only consist of human information processor(s), this possibility is of no interest to us. Rather, our interest is in computer-assisted tools which can assist decision makers in their decision-making activities and enhance the effectiveness of their decisions. More specifically, we define a DSS to be a computer-based support system which can enhance the productivity and effectiveness of the decision maker, especially in unstructured or semi-structured problems.

Research in the field of decision support systems began in

NATO ASI Series, Vol. F31
Decision Support Systems: Theory and Application
Edited by C. W. Holsapple and A. B. Whinston
© Springer-Verlag Berlin Heidelberg 1987

the early 70's, first under the term "management decision systems," and subsequently under the title "decision support systems." This area grew slowly at the beginning, but recently the growth of this subject area has accelerated. This is mainly due to the following reasons: a) management is realizing that better decisions mean more profit, and even a small improvement in decision making sometimes adds considerable value to the final outcome of the decision, b) rapid technological improvements in micro electronics, which have resulted in drastic reduction in hardware costs and faster processing capabilities, has made it feasible to use computers in semi-structured and non-structured problem solving activities, c) due to advances in management and computer-related sciences, it has been made possible to produce more analytical models to support management decision-making activities, and d) decision support systems have been shown to increase management's effectiveness and productivity. The above reasons plus knowledgeability of the managers about computers have stimulated the interest of the managers in acquiring computer support for decision making.

2. DSS vs. MANAGEMENT INFORMATION SYSTEM vs. OPERATIONAL DATA PROCESSING SYSTEM

A formal definition of a complex subject like decision support systems is a challenge. The term "decision support system" is used by various authors, vendors, and users to represent a wide range of products (or ideas) from an interactive computer-based system to a genuine DSS, that is an extensible system with capability to support both recurring and ad hoc data management, analysis, and reduction as well as modelling activities. The DSS literature often attempts to distinguish between Management Information System (MIS) and DSS. The earlier DSS literature distinguishes between MIS vs. DSS on the basis of structuredness vs. unstructuredness of the decision problem. However, the difference between MIS and DSS is more than the structuredness vs. unstructuredness of the problem for which it is used. Instead, we use a three-way taxonomy similar to the ones used by Moore and Chang [1980] and Sprague [1980]. Business data processing activities can be categorized into three categories: Operational Data Processing Systems (ODPSs), Management Information Systems (MISs), and Decision Support Systems (DSSs).

1. Operational Data Processing System (ODPS) consists of a set of preprogrammed routines for capturing, storage, retrieval, updating, performing computation, etc. necessary for an operational data processing task. Example includes an accounts receivable system.

2. Management Information System (MIS) is often built on top of an ODPS by adding a set of preprogrammed routines to provide managerial reports for control purposes, as well as the capability for inquiry. However, the MIS does not effectively support decision making at top management level, nor does it provide extensive modelling capability, especially on an ad hoc basis. An example includes an accounts receivable system with summary reports for managers, exception reports, as well as query capability.

3. Decision Support System (DSS) is a computer-based system to assist the decision maker in his/her decision-making activities. The system provides capabilities for data management, data analysis, model building and analytical computations on recurring as well as on an ad hoc basis.

In regard to the foregoing categorization schemes, ODPS is concerned with routine data processing activities of relatively large volumes of data with high accuracy and efficiency. Management Information Systems are somewhat report-oriented, that is, providing managers with summary reports and exception reports, and usually on a periodic basis. ODPS and MIS support a set of specific and predefined activities. On the other hand, DSS can support decision-making activities on an ad hoc basis. Although the limits of support of a DSS are generally well-defined, the specific activities that can be supported by the DSS are not usually predefined. Another distinction between the DSS and the other two systems is that the DSS is somewhat future-oriented, due to the fact that a viable DSS should support modelling and data analysis activities on an ad hoc basis to be used for planning, whereas MIS and ODPS are more concerned with operational activities and management control, and therefore deal with factual data of the present and the past.

Since planning is considered to be mostly unstructured in nature, it is hardly prespecifiable and consequently the ad hoc capability of DSS is considered to be essential. Moore and Chang [1980] argue that in regard to the planning capability of DSS, there tends to be less emphasis on currency or accuracy of the data incorporated into the DSS on the grounds that planning activities should not be sensitive to minor discrepancies in data. The author does not share Moore and Chang's view since planning is not the only activity supported by the DSS, and the data gathered in the knowledge base of a DSS may be used in various other activities as well as planning.

The boundaries between ODPS, MIS, and DSS are not always clear. Both ODPS and DSS have activities common with MIS (Figure 1).

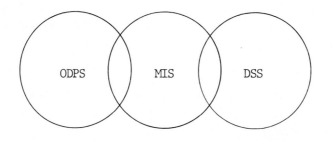

Figure 1. The Three Way Categorization of
Business Data Processing Systems

Some authors view the DSS as an extension of the MIS, the DSS has also been viewed as a subset of the MIS by some authors (e.g., Carlson [1979]). In our view the DSS is not an extension of ODPS or MIS and will not replace them either. The aim of the DSS is to improve the productivity and effectiveness of decision makers by helping them to use the knowledge more effectively.

3. THE PRINCIPAL COMPONENTS OF A DSS

The generic description as described by Bonczek et al. [1981], views a DSS as having three principal components: a language system (LS), a knowledge system (KS), and a problem processing system (PPS).

The language system (LS) is used by the user to state his/her problem to the DSS. A language system encompasses retrieval and/or computational languages. The syntactic and semantic rules of a LS determine what kind of problems can be posed to a DSS and what kind of problems cannot be presented to it for solving. With problem solving, our intention is not the problem solving in a mathematical sense, rather we think in general terms of creating a plan of action in order to produce an acceptable answer to users' questions.

The Knowledge System (KS) consists of the knowledge about the decision maker's problem domain. Indeed, a good deal of the power of a decision support system derives from its knowledgeability about a problem domain [Bonczek et al., 1981]. The knowledge system consists of application-specific data and models as well as knowledge about how to use procedural and environmental knowledge.

The Problem Processing System (PPS) is the interfacing mechanism between expressions of knowledge in the KS, and expressions of problems in the LS in order to produce the answer to decision makers' problems.

The LS and KS are representation systems. The PPS is the dynamic component of the DSS. The PPS is the component that determines the DSS's behavior pattern. Obviously the internal structure of the PPS is not independent of associated LS and KS. The PPS should be capable of explicitly recognizing the syntactically correct problem and transforming it into appropriate executable plans of action. Bonczek et al. [1981], state that "a PPS has explicitly recognized a problem when problem statement has been converted into a detailed procedural specification which, when executed, yields an answer to the problem."

The LS system of a DSS could have many different forms. At

one extreme the language could be procedural, that is, the user
of the DSS explicitly states the detail of the procedure that
should be followed in order to arrive at the desired answer.
This approach, although it offers a great deal of flexibility,
requires the user to know a sophisticated programming language,
and it also requires a considerable time for programming. On
the other extreme the language could be nonprocedural, that is,
the user only states what is desired and is not concerned with
the question of how it should be achieved. The system is responsible to work out a solution to the question posed to it.
It is the task of the PPS to figure out a plan of action which,
when executed, brings about an answer to the user's question.
If this latter approach is taken, clearly the PPS must be very
sophisticated. However, the former approach requires a less
sophisticated PPS. In other words, there is a trade-off between
the user's comfort in presenting the problem and the sophistication level of the PPS. It is obvious that if the user does
not explicitly state the required procedure for achieving the
desired answer, this task is not going to simply disappear, it
is only passed to the system, and this is the reason for the
need of a more sophisticated PPS. Here the PPS should work out
a plan of action.

When a problem is solved by a problem processor, by means
of an automatically generated program, this program usually
(not necessarily always) is not as efficient as the program
which is coded by a human programmer. However, this does not
generate a serious concern, since as computers plunge in cost,
there would be less and less concern about computer time, plus
the savings in programming time would compensate for a loss in
efficiency, especially for the programs which are not repetitive
in nature.

The existing decision support systems are all in between
the two extremes of procedural by means of a high level language
and nonprocedural through an easy-to-use query language. The
movement toward nonprocedurality is a desirable trend. This is
especially true for decision support systems, for the nature of
decision-making problems calls for an easy-to-learn nonprocedural

language. This is due to many reasons, including the following:

1. The DSS is often used by managers or people who do not have the time or desire to learn a programming language.
2. The DSS user is often under time pressure and wants to reach an answer very quickly.
3. The DSS user often reaches an answer after trying a few things (e.g., reaches an optimal price increase level after trying several figures and examining the consequences).
4. Many decision problems are one time problems and instantaneous, and the decision maker is not very concerned with efficiency as long as there is a reliable way of achieving the answer quickly.

Another characteristic of the LS, which by many is considered essential, is the interactiveness of the language.

4. DSS CHARACTERISTICS -- USER'S NEEDS vs. BUILDER'S NEEDS

The term "decision support system" has recently become very popular among managers, practitioners, and researchers. Hardware and software vendors, realizing the potential appeal of the term, have begun to adopt the term decision support system to label their new products. Some have even renamed some modified version of their old products to DSS. We tried to define the term "decision support system" in the earlier sections, but there is also a confusion between the DSS and the DSS Development System (DSSDS). That is, the tools for building the DSS and between the user of the DSS and the developer of the DSS. The DSS is designed and implemented by the DSS developer. The developer is a data processing professional who knows programming languages, data structuring, data base management, file management and other computer-related aspects of the development process. His/her function is similar to the programmer/analyst in MIS development. The DSS developer acquires all task-related information through a system analysis process. The DSS development system (DSSDS) is referred to the facilities used to implement a DSS, similar to a data base management system which is a tool for MIS development. The user of the DSS is the person who is actually using the DSS in his/her decision-making

activities. A banker is the user of the DSS for banking problems. The user is not necessarily knowledgeable in programming,
data structuring, or model building activities. But this person,
through the DSS pertinent to his/her application area, will be
able to store, modify, retrieve data, analyze data, run models,
and even initiate fairly complicated queries requiring a combination of data manipulation and model execution. Although the
DSS is an end product for the consumer, it also could be considered as a tool for the end user to develop new personalized
applications on an ad hoc basis.

A decision support system is generally tailor-made to suit
a particular user's (or class of users) needs. The end user of
the DSS is not particularly concerned about the tools used to
build the DSS. The main concern of the user is how well the
DSS can help him/her in his/her decision-making activities. In
other words, how well the product can enhance his/her productivity in making good decisions and, of course, how much the product
costs.

It is important to understand the end user's needs, since
they will impact upon the needs of the DSS developer. A study
of user's needs vs. builder's needs in the context of MIS
development appears in [Holsapple and Whinston, 1986]. The
needs of the user of a DSS are somewhat different from the user
of an MIS. The DSS should satisfy many different needs of the
decision maker and consequently the DSS developer needs a larger
collection of tools to build such a DSS. The decision maker
would like to have a decision support system with the following
features:

1. Data Management - The decision maker wants to be able to
    carry out all his/her data management needs in an easy man-
    ner without any concern about programming or data structuring.
2. Modelling - The user wants an easy method to use (or build
    and use) analytical models throughout his/her decision-making
    activities.
3. Supporting All Decision-Making Activities - The user wants
    to use the DSS in ad hoc as well as recurring decision-
    making activities.

4. <u>Personalized DSS</u> - The user would like to be able to get support in making decisions in his/her own style. In other words, the user does not want to change his/her style in order to be able to get support from the DSS.

5. <u>An Evolving DSS</u> - The user would like for the DSS to grow with jobs that it provides support to, and become more powerful.

6. <u>Learning</u> - It would be valuable if the system can learn from its experience and advance its skills in the area that it has been used the most. (This is not considered as an essential feature, however, as we will see, it would be profitable to have such a feature.)

7. <u>Security and Integrity</u> - The user wants the system to provide security for data, models, programs, etc., and be able to control the integrity of the knowledge.

8. <u>Transferability</u> - The user would like to be able to take the DSS with him/her, should he/she decide to move to a different computer.

9. <u>Other Requirements</u> - The user wants the system to be reliable, forward looking, provide timely support and be produced with a reasonable cost.

In the following sections we take a deeper look at each of the above needs of the user and examine how they could be provided. Namely, we investigate what kind of tools the developer needs in order to facilitate the development process.

5. DATA MANAGEMENT

The two most important aids that a decision support system provides to the decision maker are analytical capability and data management. The user of the DSS would like to be able to carry out all of his/her data manipulation needs in an easy and straightforward way. The user does not want to do any programming in a procedural sense and he/she does not want to be concerned with data structuring and handling. However, the user of a DSS, like the user of an MIS, would like to be able to store, retrieve, and update the data in the knowledge base through an easy to use nonprocedural means. In addition, the user of a DSS would like to be able to do inferential retrieval [Bonczek et al., 1981], where the answer is not directly stored in the data base, but it could be inferred through a series of logical steps. The user of a DSS would also like to be able to access and use data from a variety of sources other than the knowledge base of the DSS (for example, the data about the stock market's trade condition or the nation's statistical information).

The user's needs have direct impact on application of developer's needs. Let us see how the DSS developer can fulfill the above needs. For recurring needs of the user an effective approach is that the user be provided with menus about the existing possibilities. A hierarchy of menus can contain description and the requirements of each available option, and can effectively guide the user to invoking the right model for his/her needs. From the developer's standpoint, he/she would need an effective facility to specify the menu logic. A facility similar to SPF [Joslin, 1981], would greatly enhance the developer's productivity. To satisfy the user's needs the developer also needs a powerful and flexible data manipulation language for organizing and manipulating the data. The developer needs an effective facility to specify computations and other procedures to be used by the user. Means for reporting formatting, visual output generation, and producing graphical outputs also help the developer to produce a successful decision support system. For the nonrecurring problems, the user should be provided with an easy-to-use nonprocedural language for data retrieval, storage and update. Facilities like a report generator and a graphics system for easy production of graphs are a definite plus to the overall usefulness of the system and increases the chances of the success of the DSS.

The user of the DSS is likely to want to use data from outside sources, external to the DSS knowledge base. Since many of these data elements exist under different and perhaps incompatible data bases at different locations, the need for facilities for integrating data from diverse external sources into a single data base available to the user of the DSS has been pointed out by some authors [Donovan, 1976; Methlie, 1980]. A

data transfer facility for accessing the data from one data
base or file and transferring it to another data base or file
should be provided as a tool for the DSS developer and as a
utility for the user.

6. MODELLING CAPABILITY

A crucial aspect of the DSS is its capability of providing
analytical models to the end user. Effective decision making
often requires sophisticated computational facilities for analysis, projection, simulation and even optimization. The user
would like to have available a pool of modules pertinent to
his/her application area. Within an organization it is not
generally practical to develop a personalized DSS for each decision maker, instead a single DSS is used by many users in
the same general application area. In this situation the knowledge base of the DSS should contain a wide range of models,
supporting various decision-making activities in all levels of
the organization. Availability of a wide range of models is
also necessary in order to help the decision maker to conduct
the modelling activities according to his/her preferred cognitive style.

The end user of a DSS could be a person with no programming
skills, or a person with some programming knowledge. The DSS
should provide an appropriate level of support to both users.

The end user with some programming knowledge may want to
explicitly formulate a model based on his/her experience and
perception of the true requirements of the problem. The user
may use a procedural language to formulate his/her model or
he/she may use some nonprocedural means of programming available
to him/her. In either case, the user wants to have some facilities to add a new model to the system and incorporate this
option into the list of available models and even update menu
screens. Here the user is actually playing the role of the
developer, so it may be appropriate to make some of the tools
which are available to the DSS developer, available to this
knowledgeable user also. Namely, the user should be provided
with tools to create new models and add them to the system and

be allowed to modify them later on. But the user should not
be allowed to modify or delete existing models in the system.

An end user of the DSS with no knowledge of programming
would like to use the modelling capability without programming
in a procedural sense. He/she is not concerned about how the
model is built, stored, and is going to be retrieved, all he/she
is concerned with is an easy way of submitting some data to the
model and receiving some results in a useable format. The DSS
should provide the modelling capability to this user by letting
him/her invoke a model and provide him with the facilities to
interface the model with data and present the results to the
user in a useable format. In order to facilitate the task of
model invocation, it is better if the system helps and guides
the user in selecting the appropriate model. This is possible
by a series of prompts through a menu-driven interactive system.
Here the user need not remember the names of existing models
and the way they are used. The system will guide the user to
select the right model for his/her needs and will assist him/her
in how to use it. To increase the modelling capability of the
DSS, the system can assist the user in building more comprehensive models by integrating some of the existing modules. By a
module we mean a model that can be used as a stand-alone model,
or it could be used in conjunction with other modules to create
a more complex model. The task of creating more comprehensive
models could be facilitated by providing the user with information about each model and its input requirements and the nature
of the output produced by it, and of course a language for the
user to conduct his/her modelling activities. These facilities
greatly improve the useability of the system, especially among
nonprogramming users.

The DSS developer, in order to develop such a system, needs
some tools for model creation, modification, storage and access.
We call this a Model Management Language (MML). In addition,
the DSS developer needs tools for facilitating the creation and
modification of screens, that is, a Screen Management Language
(SML). The MML and SML, plus a convenient and powerful Data
Manipulation Language (DML), will greatly improve the productivity

of the DSS developer in creating a user-friendly decision support system.

Another facility that could further simplify the model usage by the end user is to provide the user with a nonprocedural Decision Support Language, through which the user can state his/her needs in a nonprocedural sense, and the system would assume the task of model invocation or creation (if necessary), data extraction, linkage handling, and all other necessary steps in order to provide the answer to the user's request. This is a further automatization of the decision support activities, and it requires a powerful problem processing system. A completely automated decision support system is obviously a very desirable goal to achieve. Reaching this goal is unlikely to happen through a revolutionary step, rather a completely automatic system will evolve over time, from semi-automated system towards complete automation. Development of tools for the developer and user is certainly a positive step toward this ultimate goal.

7. SUPPORTING ALL DECISION-MAKING ACTIVITIES

The user would want to use the DSS for ad hoc decision making as well as decisions of recurring nature. For recurring problems, the user would like a reasonably efficient system that could eventually be tuned to his/her true needs. For the ad hoc decision making the user is more concerned with a quick and reliable answer than the efficiency of the programs. Here the user needs the help of the system for a one-time decision which may or may not recur again. For example, if the user wants to decide about a major investment, he/she may want to study the impact of the new investment on various aspects of the organization for the next 10 years. More specifically, the user may want to study the effects of the new investment on cash flow, overall profit, stock prices, distribution of dividend, etc. The decision maker may also want to evaluate several options, each one under several possible conditions. For example, the user may want to study the following aspects of each option under several conditions; fixed costs versus variable costs, present value of the project, etc.

From the foregoing discussion we can summarize that in order for the user to be able to reach a decision, he/she needs to be able to access data of various kinds, process the data by means of some computational models, store the results of various options under different conditions, and finally, present all the results in a convenient form so he/she can easily compare them and arrive at a final conclusion. The first and second needs, namely the data management and modelling capability, have been discussed in earlier sections in some detail, hence we discuss the other two needs, that is, a work space for the user and a presentation facility. The user often considers several options and conditions and based on each situation, he/she does a series of data retrieval and computations, therefore he/she needs some work space to store the results of each option so they can be compared at the end. For example, the user may want to calculate the present value of a project based on several discount rates and tabulate the results so he/she will be able to study them thoroughly and perhaps find the break-even point. Tabulating in the form of a decision table greatly facilitates comparison among several options. Tables could be used by the decision maker both for storing results of computations and as a means of presentation. Another presentational facility would be an easy way of producing graphs (e.g., sales vs. time, or present value vs. discount rate). This capability, although it is not considered essential, is a great help toward the understanding of internal relationship between variables.

The foregoing discussion suggests that in addition to modelling and data management capabilities, the following facilities will also greatly improve the productivity of the decision maker in relation with the DSS:

1. A work space for the user so he/she can store temporary results so they can easily be accessed later.
2. A mechanism to allow the user to tabulate the results of his/her findings.
3. A mechanism to manipulate tables, i.e., add new rows, new columns, add or subtract two rows or columns and store the results in a new one, sum up the elements of one row or

column, etc.

4. A facility to store and retrieve user-defined tables and variables from one session to another.

5. An easy language to produce graphical outputs on CRT terminals as well as on a hard copy device.

The above facilities could also be used by the DSS developer for designing the outputs of recurring nature. These facilities could be incorporated as a part of a comprehensive language system for the user and as a part of the DSS developing system for the DSS developer.

8. A PERSONALIZED DECISION SUPPORT SYSTEM

The aim of a Decision Support System is to help the decision maker in his/her decision-making activities. The decision-making process of different individuals is not the same. Each person makes decisions according to his/her preferred cognitive style. Zmud [1979] defines cognitive behavior as:

> "Cognition refers to the activities involved in attempts by individuals to resolve inconsistencies between an internalized conceptualization of the environment and what is perceived to be actually transpiring in the environment."

Each individual is believed to have a specific (and unique, to some extent) cognitive style. The cognitive style could be defined as the constant pattern of functioning that one shows in his/her perceptual and intellectual activities over an extended period of time. There are various models for the nature of cognitive styles [Keen, 1973; Huysmans, 1970; Driver and Mock, 1975] and [Schroeder et al., 1967]. Keen categorizes decision makers as systematics versus intuitives in problem solving dimension and preceptives versus receptives in the data gathering dimension [Keen, 1973]. Others distinguish between analytics versus heuristics [Huysmans, 1970], or distinguish between abstracts who can handle more information versus concretes who can handle more complex problem situations [Schroeder et al., 1967]. The results of various studies tend to support the hypothesis that different individuals have different informational and/or computational needs for making decisions within the same problem

situation. Based on the work of Benbasat [1977] and Botkin
[1973], the decision-making needs of an individual can be summarized as follows:

Analytical decision makers prefer a quantitative approach
based on analytical models in their decision-making process.
So they should be provided with quantitative tools and perhaps
with a library of various analytical models. Heuristics, on
the other hand, rely more on information (of various kinds).
They would like to be able to generate many different alternative
solutions. They want flexible I/O capabilities, so they can
easily control the format and content of their input/output, and
they should be able to shift between levels of generality and
detail. The concept of work space and decision table discussed
in the previous section would be beneficial to this group.
Perceptive individuals would like to use summarized and filtered
data, so they would need tools to summarize and filter data,
that is, sum columns, rows, calculate totals, subtotals, select
a subgroup, etc. Receptives, on the other hand, would like to
work with the entire data, so they would need tools for quick
search and data retrieval on large data bases and files.

The foregoing discussion suggests that the cognitive style
of the decision maker should be considered in building a successful decision support system. This consideration becomes more
important when we realize the fact that many users of the DSS
are from groups and ranks that can elect not to use the system
if they decide they are uncomfortable in making decisions according to their own preferred style.

Now the question is how the DSS developer should develop a
DSS so that the cognitive style is accounted for. There are
two basic approaches that we can follow. The advocates of the
first approach [Benbasat, 1977], suggest that before we build a
decision support system we should study the cognitive style of
the user through a series of psychological tests, and then build
a very personalized system for the decision maker based on
his/her true needs. This approach may not be a practical one
because of the following reasons:

1. Study of cognitive behavior is not a simple task and requires a considerable amount of time and effort.
2. The user of the DSS is not usually one person, rather a
   group of people (sometimes as many as 100 or more people)
   will use the DSS in their decision-making activities. Study
   of the cognitive style of a large group of people obviously
   requires more time and effort, and incorporation of all the
   needs of individuals into the system may not be feasible.
3. The system will become more people-oriented rather than
   task-oriented. If the user of the DSS leaves the company,
   the system has to be rebuilt (i.e., possibly major changes
   are required) for the next user.
4. The study of cognitive styles is at best incomplete. Many
   more cognitive styles are yet to be identified and their
   informational and computational needs should be explored.

Here we offer a second approach which does not have the
disadvantages of the first approach. The idea is to build the
DSS so flexible that users with different cognitive styles will
be able to direct their problem solving and decision-making
activities according to their own preferred cognitive style. In
other words, the DSS should be adaptable to any user's needs,
provided the user stays within the general application area
framework of the DSS. Such a DSS can become personalized and
support an individual according to his/her cognitive style.

Now the main question is how such a decision support system
should be built. The general guideline for building this DSS
is that it should be very flexible. By flexibility we mean
flexible I/O, flexible modelling capability, flexible screen
formatting, etc. Flexible outputs could be provided by means
of a report generator. Flexible screen formatting could also
be embedded through a screen management language (SML). Here
there is also the need for a large pool of modules (perhaps
more primitive modules) so the user can build his/her models
according to his/her own taste. Alternative modules for a
given problem should also be provided. Search and data extraction features which were discussed in the earlier sections are
also necessary. In addition to all the features discussed so

far, we define a new feature that we call the skill acquisition
capability or learning feature through which the system can
customize its behavior to a particular user's needs. This feature is further studied in the later sections.

9. AN EVOLVING DSS

The history of data processing contains a considerable
amount of unsuccessful cases. The basic cause of most of these
failures has been found to be that the system could not fulfill
the essential needs of their users. User dissatisfaction could
be attributed to many reasons, including the following:

1. The builder did not understand the true needs of the user,
    perhaps due to lack of communication.
2. The user did not fully understand his/her own true needs
    until he/she actually started to use the system.
3. The human factor in general and/or the personality and cog-
    nitive style of some key users in particular were not con-
    sidered in the design and implementation of the system.
4. The nature of the user's job changed over time, causing a
    change in informational needs of the user, but the system
    could not be adjusted to the new changes.
5. Environmental changes, that is, changes in hardware or soft-
    ware, happened, requiring substantial changes to the system,
    but it was economically advantageous to abandon the old
    system and develop a new one from scratch.
6. The organization expanded but the system did not have any
    room for expansion.

A good design should account for all of the above factors in
order to be successful. The first factor in the above calls
for a mutual understanding between the user and the developer.
Mutual understanding can be increased by establishing a proper
channel for continuous communication between the user and the
builder throughout the design and implementation process. The
mutual understanding can be enhanced even more if the builder
is provided with a collection of development tools which would
facilitate a speedy development process with quick modification
capacity. Here the developer throughout the development process

can present the results of his/her design and implementation to the user, and use the user's feedback to adjust the system to the user's preference. That is the development tools could be used for speedy development of prototypes. The second reason for the failure states that sometimes the users themselves are confused about their true needs. Martin [1982] states, "It is often the case that the end user does not know what he wants until he gets it. When he gets it he wants something different." This is especially true for decision support systems because the decision maker does not know what kind of decisions he/she will make in the future, and therefore he/she does not know what his/her needs will be. Prediction of future needs and possible changes, and incorporation of these needs into the system is close to impossible. Instead, we propose that the system should be capable of evolving over time and with inherent flexibility to future changes. With this we have also eliminated most of the other causes of failure that were stated earlier. Because if the system is built flexible by design, then the system could be adapted to any changes.

The foregoing discussion supports the idea that the DSS should be flexible by design and capable of evolving over time. In other words, as the user's views, needs, and decision-making style changes, the system should be capable of adjusting itself (or being adjusted) to the new requirements. There are a number of empirical studies to support this line of argument. Keen [1980], after examination of several empirical studies on a collection of actually installed decision support systems, among his observations states:

1. The actual uses of DSS are almost invariably different from the intended ones: indeed, many of the most valued and innovated uses could not have been predicted when the system was designed.
2. DSS evolve; case studies frequently state that key factors explaining successful developments are flexible design architecture that permit fast modification and phased approach to implementation.
3. The functions DSS provide are generally not elaborate;

complex systems evolve from simple components.

In relation to the first observation, Keen does not elaborate on the reasons behind this behavior, but it is very likely that this behavior is caused by one or more of the following reasons.

1. The system was not well designed with the intended user in mind. The DSS was perhaps too difficult to be used by the intended user, or not well human factored, etc.
2. The user did not have a clear idea about what his/her true needs were until he/she started to use the system. At that time the user begins to learn about his/her actual needs and shifts the usage of the DSS to this new direction.
3. Having the system in hand and learning about its capabilities, the user thought of new ways for effectively using the system, some of them more important than the intended ones.

If the first reason is true, this is considered to be a weakness on the part of the system, but the other two reasons show the positive aspects of the design since the system could be adapted to the new and more essential needs. Keen's second and third observations are in support of an evolving DSS.

Now the question is how a DSS should be built so it can evolve. The basic requirement of an evolving system is a flexible design architecture; that is, the system should permit quick modification and should be extensible. The kinds of tools we have discussed so far, that is, a Data Manipulation Language (DML), a Model Management Language (MML), a Screen Management Language (SML), and programming aids will facilitate quick modification [Bonczek et al., 1983]. Extensibility, on the other hand, means that the system should be capable of growing over time. For example, if the user decides to add new models, data, reports, screens, etc. to the system, these extensions should be readily possible. This again calls for procedural and non-procedural tools to alter the structure of the knowledge base as well as modules, screens, programs, etc. Another feature that increases the usefulness of the system and facilitates the evolution process is the learning feature to be discussed in the next section.

10. THE LEARNING FEATURE

In the earlier sections we have argued that the DSS should
be capable of being customized to the individual user's needs
and his/her cognitive style, and at the same time transition
of decision-making tasks from one individual to another should
not require major changes to the system. We have also discussed
the value of an evolving DSS and a decision support system that
can handle changes to the problem or to the decision maker's
conception of the problem. One way of achieving these goals is
to incorporate a learning mechanism into the system so the
system would learn from its users and the way the system has
been used. Through this feature the system can sharpen its
skills in the direction of a particular task environment and
become customized to the cognitive style of its users. By
learning, we mean that if the user has gone through some major
steps to solve a sophisticated problem (e.g., creating a complex
model by using several smaller models), and especially if there
is a good chance that this problem will recur again, then the
system should learn from this experience; namely this user
(or even another user) should not be required to go through the
same experience in future recurrence of the same problem. If
this feature is built into the decision support system, then
the DSS can evolve over time, and grow with the job it supports.
Within this framework, the more the system is used by the
decision maker, the more support it can provide to the user,
and the user's productivity will increase by time. If a new
individual starts to use the system (in order to replace an old
one or otherwise), as the system is used over time it will adjust
itself to the needs of this new individual.

The discussion of the nature of the learning mechanism is
outside the scope of the present paper, however, we should
mention that in order for the user to be able to take advantage
of the learning feature, the system should be equipped with the
tools we discussed in earlier sections which are required for
quick development of a decision support application. The DSS

should also consist of a large pool of modules which could be used by the system itself or the user to create more complex modules based upon the need of the decision maker [Bonczek et al., 1983].

11. THE SECURITY AND INTEGRITY OF THE DSS

In the context of decision support systems, the security refers to the security of the entirety of the DSS, not only the data. In other words, security of models, expert knowledge, the meta knowledge, programs and applications, as well as the security of the data should be preserved. Due to the dynamic nature of the DSS, the data, programs, models, etc. are continually changing and causing a continuous change on the security status of the various elements of the DSS. The DSS developer needs a set of tools that he/she can define the access restrictions and other security requirements for each element in the DSS, perhaps as a part of a more comprehensive decision support development system. These tools would be used at the time of development to specify the security of various elements of the DSS as well as the time when security requirements change for any reason, to modify, add or eliminate the security requirements. A set of more restricted tools for defining security rules and access restrictions should be provided to the user as well. User's tools should be more restricted in the sense that the user should be able to define restrictions only to the portion of the DSS which is under his/her control.

The integrity of the knowledge should also be enforced by the system automatically. Tools to define the integrity rules should be provided to the DSS developer as well as to the user. When new knowledge is defined, the integrity rule will be defined as well, but the tools should also provide an easy way of changing the existing integrity rules as well as adding new restrictions or eliminating old ones as the condition changes.

12. TRANSFERABILITY

The user would like the system to be portable, that is, he/she be able to use the system should he/she decide to move

to another computer. This is especially important to the user
of an evolving DSS, because the user has built on top of the
system and would like to preserve the results of his/her efforts.
Portability is possible if the system is developed through a
set of machine-independent tools, and also the tools themselves
are defined on the new computer. Under the current situation
this is unlikely to happen. However, if the DSS development
tools become standardized so the same set of tools become available on different computers, then the portability of the DSS is
possible. But until that happens, to be able to transfer from
one computer to a different computer in which the tools are non-
existent, either the system should be redeveloped with the new
existing tools (if any) or the system should be developed with
more primitive tools like standard programming languages in
the first place.

13. OTHER REQUIREMENTS

One other requirement of the user is that he/she can rely
on the support provided by the DSS. The reliability of the
system is related to the development system, the developer, and
developing process. Good and reliable tools are essential to
a reliable DSS. Organized and structured approach to development
process as well as selecting the right development team will
increase the chances of producing a reliable system.

The user also wants the system to be forward-looking rather
than backward-looking. This means that the system should be
developed with the future in mind. One consequence of this
line of thinking is to take advantage of new technological
developments in order to increase the effectiveness of the
system, as well as designing the system so that the future
technological innovations could be added to the system as they
become available, in order to upgrade the current technology.

Since the timeliness of the decision support is very important to the decision maker, we consider the interactiveness of
the DSS as an important requirement. Although it could be
argued that a batch DSS could function also, it would be very
hard to argue that it would be successful and eventually

survive. Another serious consideration is the use of graphical
capability to provide graphical support to the decision maker.

A last but very serious concern of the user is the cost of
the DSS. If the cost of the DSS is not affordable to the user,
its features are going to be irrelevant to him/her. An evolving
DSS which is built through the use of the tools discussed in
the earlier sections is likely to be less expensive than the one
which is built directly through a procedural language.

14. OTHER TOOLS FOR THE DSS DEVELOPER

We have investigated the DSS development tools which stem
from the user's needs. In addition to the tools discussed in
the foregoing sections, there are also some tools that stem
from the needs of the developer himself (herself). Namely, since
the developer normally does most of his/her programming through
a procedural language, a program development facility will
greatly improve his/her productivity. These facilities could
be described as a powerful command language, interactive programming capabilities, tools for easy modification, easy debugging,
easy adding and deleting lines of code, moving a block of code
from one part of the program to another, etc. Some of these
capabilities are readily available in most computer systems.
The integration of these general purpose programming aids with
other tools we discussed in previous sections will create an
ideal environment for DSS development.

15. SUMMARY

The Decision Support System was defined to be a computer-
based system to assist the decision maker in his/her decision-
making activities. DSS provides capabilities for data management, data analysis, model building and analytical computations
on a recurring as well as on an ad hoc basis. DSS is capable
of supporting the decision maker on his/her unstructured or
semi-structured decision problems. The business data processing
systems were categorized into three types: ODPS, MIS, and DSS.
ODPS is concerned with routine data processing activities, MIS
is usually built on top of an ODPS and provides additional

reports for management control. The functions of ODPS and MIS
are prespecifiable by nature, while this is not normally true
for the DSS. The DSS was described as having three components:
a Language System (LS), a Problem Processing System (PPS) and a
Knowledge System (KS). The LS is used by the user to state the
problem. We emphasized the need for a nonprocedural means of
communication between the decision maker and the DSS. The KS
contains the knowledge about the decision maker's problem domain.
The PPS is the interfacing mechanism between the LS and the KS.

We looked at the characteristics of a DSS from the user's
point of view, namely, we studied the needs of the user, and
from these needs we identified a set of characteristics for a
successful DSS. These characteristics were defined as capabilities for data management, modelling, supporting all decision
making activities, decision support on personalized basis,
evolving over time, learning over time, control of security and
integrity, transferability, reliability, forward looking and
reasonable cost.

The characteristics of the DSS were used to identify characteristics of tools for the DSS developer in order to facilitate
the development process. The essential elements of the DSS
development system were identified as: a powerful data manipulation language (DML), a model management language (MML), a screen
management language (SML), tools to define security and integrity
rules, programming aids, and tools to facilitate graphic output
generation, and report formatting. These tools will increase
the productivity of the developer during the DSS development
process and help to reduce the cost of the DSS.

REFERENCES

Benbasat, B. (1977). "Cognitive Style Considerations in DSS
    Design," Data Base, 8, 3, Winter.

Bonczek, R., Holsapple, C. and Whinston, A. (1981). Foundations
    of Decision Support Systems, Academic Press.

Bonczek, R., Ghiaseddin, N., Holsapple, C. and Whinston, A.
    (1983). "The DSS Development System," Proceedings to 1983
    National Computer Conference, pp. 421-435.

Botkin, G.W. (1973). "An Intuitive Computer System: A Cognitive Approach to the Management Learning Process," doctoral dissertation, Harvard Business School.

Carlson, E. (1979). "An Approach for Designing Decision Support Systems," Data Base, Winter.

Donovan, J. (1976). "Data Base System Approach to Management Decision Support," ACM Transactions on Data Base Systems, 1, 4, December, pp. 344-369.

Driver, M. and Mock, T. (1975). "Human Information Processing, Decision Style Theory and Accounting Information Systems," The Accounting Review, 1, 3.

Holsapple, C. and Whinston, A. (1982). "Guidelines for DBMS Evaluation," in Data Base Theory and Applications, C. Holsapple and A. Whinston (eds.), Reidel, Dordrecht.

Huymans, J.H.B.M. (1970). The Implementation of Operation Research, New York, Wiley-Interscience.

Joslin (1981). "System Productivity Facility," IBM Systems Journal, 20, 4.

Keen, P. (1980). "Adaptive Design for Decision Support Systems," Data Base, 12, 1 and 2, Fall, pp. 15-25.

Keen, P.W.G. (1973). "The Implications of Cognitive Style for Individual Decision Making," D.B.A. Thesis, Harvard University.

Martin, J. (1982). Application Development Without Programmers, Prentice-Hall, Englewood Cliffs, New Jersey.

Methlie, L. (1980). "Data Management for Decision Support Systems," Data Base, 12, 1 and 2, Fall, pp. 40-46.

Moore, J.H. and Chang, M.G. (1980). "Design of Decision Support Systems," Data Base, 12, 1 and 2, Fall, pp. 8-14.

Schroeder, H.M., Driver, N.J. and Streufert, S. (1967). Human Information Processing, Holt, Rinehart and Winston, Inc., New York.

Sprague, R.H., Jr. (1980). "Guest Editors Introduction," Data Base, 12, 1 and 2, Fall, pp. 2-7.

Zmud, R.W. (1979). "Individual Differences and MIS Success: A Review of the Empirical Literature," Management Science, 25, 10, October, pp. 966-979.

7. ARTIFICIALLY INTELLIGENT DECISION SUPPORT SYSTEMS - CRITERIA FOR TOOL SELECTION

Clyde W. Holsapple and Andrew B. Whinston
Management Information Research Center
Krannert Graduate School of Management
Purdue University
West Lafayette, IN 47907, U.S.A.

ABSTRACT

The use of artificial intelligence techniques within decision support systems adds an important new dimension to these systems, giving them the ability to reason for internal purposes and for offering external advice to users. This reasoning ability is a natural extension to past kinds of decision support systems. It necessitates the inclusion of inference capabilities in a decision support system's problem processor and of reasoning knowledge (e.g., rules) in the decision support system's knowledge system. A tool for building artificially intelligent decision support systems must accommodate the representation and processing of reasoning knowledge. Criteria for assessing such a tool are discussed.

1. INTRODUCTION

Knowledge is the raw material of decision making. The central purpose of a decision support system (DSS) is to facilitate the knowledge management activities involved in decision making, allowing decisions to be made in a more effective and efficient manner. There has been a tendency in the DSS field to emphasize computer-aided management of two specific types of knowledge: descriptive knowledge about the decision-making environment and procedural knowledge about how to carry out analyses. While these two types of knowledge are very important, others have been identified as being relevant subjects for DSS treatment. Of these other kinds of knowledge, one stands out with a potential for revolutionizing the nature of decision support systems. It is reasoning knowledge concerning what conclusions are valid when certain situations exist.

NATO ASI Series, Vol. F31
Decision Support Systems: Theory and Application
Edited by C. W. Holsapple and A. B. Whinston
© Springer-Verlag Berlin Heidelberg 1987

Techniques for managing reasoning knowledge constitute a
major topic of study within the discipline of artificial intelligence. To the extent that a DSS is able to employ such techniques (e.g., expert system techniques), it is able to exhibit
artificially intelligent behavior. Not only can it retrieve
descriptive knowledge and execute procedural knowledge, but such
a DSS can actually offer advice based on its reasoning knowledge.
As it works on a stated problem, an artificially intelligent DSS
is able to process all three types of knowledge in a coordinated,
integrated fashion.

The construction of artificially intelligent decision support systems is very much dependent on the existence of tools
that support appropriate knowledge management facilities. Ideally, the needed facilities should all be available as innate,
inseparable aspects of a single DSS development tool. A developer should not be forced to coordinate separate tools, but
rather should be able to build a DSS by working within a single
software environment.

Here, we propose criteria for evaluating and selecting a
tool to be used in the creation of artificially intelligent
decision support systems. As a prelude, various practical methods of knowledge representation and processing are examined
within the generic DSS framework. The merits and significance
of a tool that synergistically blends these knowledge management
capabilities are discussed. Desirable characteristics of those
capabilities that relate to the representation and processing
of reasoning knowledge are closely scrutinized. We close with
some observations about the impacts that will be made by tools
exhibiting such characteristics.

2. ARTIFICIALLY INTELLIGENT DECISION SUPPORT SYSTEMS

A decision support system consists of a language system,
knowledge system, and problem processing system [Bonczek et al.,
1981]. The problem processing system is the active software
component of a DSS. It accepts problem statements specified
according to some language system, draws on relevant knowledge
held in a knowledge system, and proceeds to generate appropriate

responses that can be used to support a decision-making process.
Unlike the problem processor, the language system and knowledge
system are not software. They are systems of representation.
The former is a system for representing problems. It determines
what can and cannot be requested of a problem processor. The
latter is a system for representing knowledge in various guises.
The knowledge held in a DSS's knowledge system limits what can
and cannot be known by a problem processor, without relying on
a knowledge source (e.g., the user) beyond the DSS boundaries.
All three DSS subsystems can benefit from artificial intelligence
techniques.

2.1. The Language System

The language system that a DSS provides to users could furnish one or more interface styles for stating problems. As
Figure 1 suggests, these include menu guided (e.g., icon or
English options), command oriented (e.g., structured, English-
like imperatives), conversational (i.e., natural language), and
various customized methods for problem specification. The ability of a DSS to handle natural language requests might be said
to make that decision support system artificially intelligent.
This topic [Bonczek et al., 1981] is an interesting one and
deserves further research. However, it is not the focal point
here.

Depending on the interface style, various mechanisms may
exist for actually making a request. These include a keyboard,
mouse, touch screen, light pen, and voice recognition device.
In the event that a user request is unclear or incomplete, the
problem processor responds by issuing a diagnostic or by asking
the user to complete the request (via the language system). It
is not unusual for the language system of a DSS to allow requests
that are not intended to solve external problems. These are
requests for addressing problems that are internal to the DSS.
Such requests deal with the incorporation of new knowledge into
the knowledge system. In solving these update problems, the
problem processor alters the state of the knowledge system in
preparation for later requests to solve problems that directly

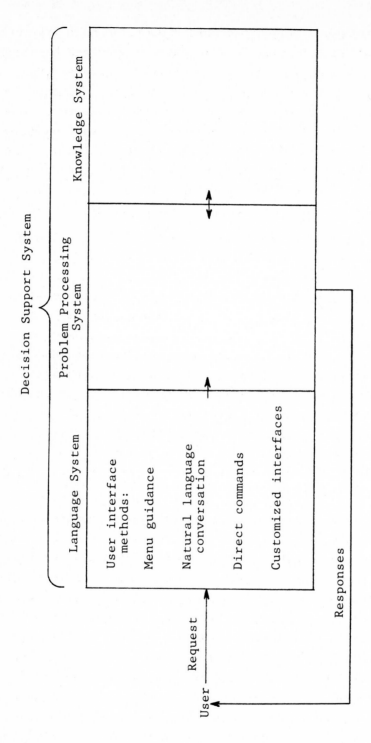

Figure 1. Language System Details

support users' decision-making activities.

2.2. The Knowledge System

A knowledge system can hold knowledge of different types, each represented in multiple ways. It is important to understand the distinction between knowledge types and knowledge representation techniques. Major types of knowledge include descriptive (also called environmental), procedural (also called modelling), linguistic, presentation, assimilative, and reasoning knowledge [Holsapple, 1977]. As Figure 2 suggests, major knowledge representation techniques include portrayals as textual passages, spreadsheets, data bases (in all their variations, from relational and network to postrelational), programs, forms, templates, grammars, lexicons, graphical images, rules, and so forth. Because of its nature and intended use, one piece of descriptive knowledge may best be represented in a data base; another piece of descriptive knowledge may be represented as text and yet another as cells in a spreadsheet. Similarly, one piece of procedural knowledge may be represented as a program, another in terms of spreadsheet cells, and another as text.

Reasoning knowledge could be represented textually or in a program. However, rules provide a particularly convenient method for representing this kind of knowledge [Holsapple and Whinston, 1986]. In its simplest form a rule consists of a premise and a conclusion. The premise characterizes some situation, while the conclusion indicates what actions are valid if the premise can be determined to be true. A collection of rules pertaining to reasoning about the same problem domain is called a rule set. One rule set in a knowledge system may contain rules to be used when reasoning about the interpretation of user requests. Another might deal with the proper interfacing of descriptive and procedural knowledge. In addition to such sub rosa rule sets, there may be others that directly pertain to reasoning about external problems (e.g., rules that capture the reasoning involved in making credit recommendations).

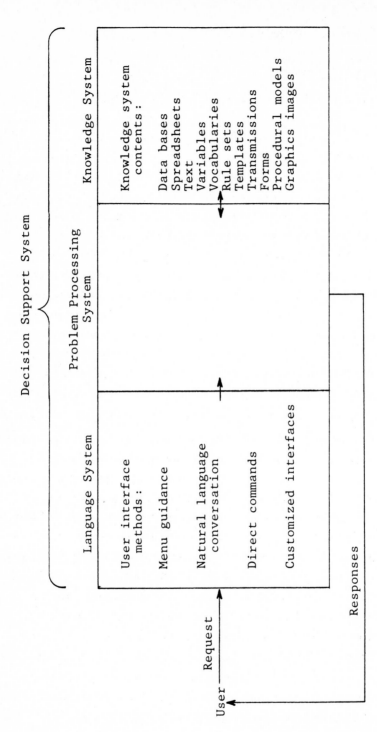

Figure 2.   Knowledge System Details

2.3. The Problem Processing System

The flexibility and power of a decision support system are
directly proportional to the breadth and depth of knowledge
representation methods permitted in its knowledge system. If
data bases are not permitted or are limited in some significant
way, the DSS's ability to handle descriptive knowledge is severely handicapped. The inability of a knowledge system to accommodate knowledge represented in the guise of programs drastically
limits a DSS's treatment of procedural knowledge. Similarly,
if rule sets are not permitted or are significantly constrained,
the DSS's ability to handle reasoning knowledge is correspondingly reduced. That is, alternative representation approaches
(e.g., text, program) are not generally adequate substitutes
for the rule approach to representing reasoning knowledge. They
are, at most, complements to the use of rules. Nevertheless,
they are much more important for representing other kinds of
knowledge.

For every representation method allowed in a knowledge
system, corresponding knowledge processing abilities must exist
in the problem processing system. Thus, if a knowledge system
can contain data bases, spreadsheets, programs, and text, the
problem processor software must be capable of data base management, spreadsheet analysis, program execution, and text processing (see Figure 3). When a knowledge system is allowed to
contain rule sets, the problem processor must be able to both
maintain and make inferences with the reasoning knowledge they
contain. In a stand-alone shell for developing expert systems
these activities are accomplished with two software tools: a
rule set manager and an inference engine [Holsapple and Whinston,
1986]. In the context of a decision support system, the problem
processor must possess comparable capabilities.

There are at least three distinct styles for incorporating
such traditionally separate capabilities into a single problem
processor [Holsapple and Whinston, 1984]. One involves the
confederation of separate, but compatible, software tools within
an operating environment. Another integration style involves
the nesting of all components within a dominant component (e.g.,

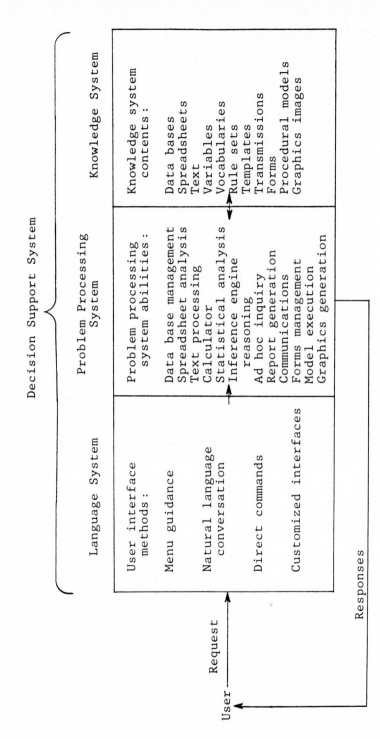

Figure 3. Problem Processing Details

a spreadsheet) to yield a single tool. Each of these styles
has certain strengths and weaknesses [Holsapple and Whinston,
1984]. The third integration style retains the respective
strengths of the other two and at the same time overcomes many
of their weaknesses. Referred to as synergistic integration,
it effectively fuses the capabilities of traditionally separate
tools into a single environment in such a way that there are no
barriers among the capabilities [Holsapple and Whinston, 1983].
For instance, there is no clear dividing line between spreadsheet analysis and data base management capabilities (e.g., a
data base may be accessed in the midst of automatic spreadsheet
evaluation and a record may be altered by spreadsheet results).
The total effect achieved with this kind of integration is much
greater than what is possible with either of the others. It
allows the entire problem processor to be viewed as an inference
engine with innate data base management, spreadsheet, and other
capabilities. But because there is no strict nesting involved,
the problem processor's inference capabilities are actually on
an even footing with all the other capabilities.

Problem processors may be more or less general. On the
one hand, there are those that are specifically designed for
a particular DSS. Relaxing this restriction somewhat yields a
problem processor that can be used in any DSS belonging to a
particular application class (e.g., financial modelling class).
At the opposite extreme is the notion of a generalized problem
processor that can serve as the software component for any DSS
[Bonczek et al., 1981]. As a practical matter, such a problem
processing system must possess an extensive repertoire of knowledge processing capabilities. Each DSS may use a different subset of the capabilities, namely those pertinent to the application being addressed.

A generalized problem processor serves as an important tool
for DSS construction. Regardless of the application area, a
DSS can be constructed by "filling in" its knowledge system,
using any knowledge representation methods for which there are
corresponding knowledge processing capabilities in the problem
processor. The positive implications for developer productivity

are obvious. Generalized problem processors with synergistically integrated capabilities, including facilities for rule processing, will play a major role in the rise of artificially intelligent decision support systems. Evaluating such a tool is
not a matter to be taken lightly.

3. CRITERIA FOR TOOL EVALUATION

Here, we introduce a fairly comprehensive set of criteria
for evaluating the rule processing capabilities of these tools.
Of course, other capabilities (e.g., data base management, programming, spreadsheet processing) also deserve careful consideration. Because these other kinds of processing are more familiar
to DSS developers than rule processing, they do not receive a
detailed treatment here. Criteria for assessing a tool's rule
processing capabilities fall into four basic categories. First,
there are rule set characteristics. What kinds of rules can a
problem processor process for the purpose of making inferences?
Second, are the rule set development and maintenance aids provided by the tool? A third category of criteria is concerned
with the actual inference activities that a problem processor
is able to perform during a consultation. Fourth, there is the
issue of performance.

3.1. Rule Set Characteristics

Though often overlooked, the flexibility and power a tool
provides for capturing reasoning knowledge within a rule set
are of crucial importance. Flexibility is concerned with the
breadth of features available for characterizing reasoning
knowledge in a rule set. Are they extensive or does a tool
support only a narrow assortment of features for specifying
knowledge in a rule set? Power is concerned with how much
leverage a tool gives to a developer. Can a complex or extensive piece of reasoning knowledge be represented in a straightforward manner -- with minimal effort? Together, flexibility
and power determine how natural and convenient a tool is to
use. Not only do these impact a developer's productivity, they
govern how intelligent the DSSs built with a development tool

can be.

Limited flexibility and power may be sufficient for a developer's first attempts at constructing intelligent DSSs. However, tool limitations are ill-advised for the long run. As developer experience expands and more ambitious decision support systems are undertaken, a limited tool becomes increasingly difficult to use -- until a cul-de-sac is reached. At such a point, the developer needs to begin again -- learning the conventions of a more powerful and flexible tool. Thus, it is vital that a tool provide developers with a growth path, allowing them to start out simply and progress at their own paces. It should be possible to ignore advanced features until they are needed. Some of the rule set features identified may not be of immediate applicability to beginners, but all are of interest for developing heavy-duty decision support systems that are able to reason.

3.1.1. Rules

Ideally, a problem processor should avoid placing an arbitrary limit on the number of rules it is able to work with when making inferences during a rule set consultation. This is an important consideration if a developer intends to build large rule sets or expand rule set sizes over the lifetimes of DSSs. The ability of a problem processor to consult one rule set in the midst of consulting another rule set can help overcome limitations in the number of rules per rule set. The ability to pack a large amount of reasoning knowledge into a single rule, rather than multiple rules, can also help overcome such limitations. This latter ability depends on what is allowed in the premise and conclusion of a rule.

The number of conditions permitted in a rule's premise should not be limited by a DSS development tool. A particular fragment of reasoning knowledge may require many conditions. Placing an arbitrary cap on the number of conditions (or characters) that can exist in a premise results in a dead end of the developer. Furthermore, all the basic conditional operators (EQ, NE, GT, LT, GE, LE, IN) should be allowed in a premise's conditions. The operands of a condition might be logical, string or numeric expressions. The nature of these expressions greatly influences a tool's value.

Beyond constants and literals, a good tool will allow expressions to directly reference a broad variety of variables including working variables (both single-valued and fuzzy), data base fields, spreadsheet cells, program variables, array elements, statistical variables, environment variables, and utility variables. Within expressions, the usual numeric (+, -, *, **, /), string (+), and logical (OR, XOR, AND, NOT) operators should be allowed. Furthermore, a healthy assortment of numeric, string, and logical functions is very desirable.

The problem processor should be able to fire (i.e., execute the conclusion of) a rule with multiple actions in its conclusion. Placing an arbitrary cap on the number of actions (or characters) that can exist in a conclusion can be unwieldy and cause an increase in the number of rules required to represent a piece of reasoning knowledge.

Another criterion is the wealth of actions that can be included in the conclusion of a rule. The variety and extent of possible actions is perhaps the most telling factor in assessing a development tool's flexibility and power. The most significant kinds of actions for constructing rules in artificially intelligent decision support systems include assignment commands, line-oriented input, line-oriented output, expert system consultation, spreadsheet processing, relational data manipulation, SQL inquiries, customized report generation, statistical analysis, business graphics generation, remote communications, dynamic function key redefinition, forms management, menu processing, execution of external programs, postrelational data base access, text processing, general-purpose procedural modelling, simulation, financial planning, and optimization. Ideally, a tool should allow any of these kinds of actions in a rule's conclusion.

The ability to include macro references in the premise or conclusion of a rule can be quite useful. Each macro allows a

single word to be used in place of a lengthy sequence of symbols.
Not only does this save many keystrokes for frequently needed
symbol sequences, it allows rules to be readily altered without
requiring editing or recompilation of a rule set.

A tool should allow rules to have pre-actions in addition
to post-actions (i.e., conclusions). A rule's pre-actions allow
the developer to prescribe actions that will be taken as soon
as the rule is selected for consideration -- prior to testing
its premise. This is a convenient localized way to establish
the value of some variable that is referenced in the premise.
In general, every kind of action that is allowed in a rule's
conclusion should also be allowed in its pre-actions.

It should be possible to designate priorities and costs for
individual rules. The ability to give rules different priorities allows a developer to prioritize the order in which the
problem processor will consider candidate rules during a consultation.

The ability to ascribe different costs to the actions of
rules allows a developer to cause the problem processor to consider least-cost candidate rules before those having more expensive actions. It is also useful to be able to specify different premise testing strategies for different rules. A strategy that is appropriate for testing one rule's premise may not
be desirable for other premises. The ability to specify a
testing strategy for each rule allows a developer to tune the
consultation performance that can be achieved with the rule set.

Allowing a developer to preserve comments on each rule is a
valuable convenience for ongoing maintenance of a rule set. A
tool should be able to display a rule's documentation as a developer views or modifies that rule. Reasonably lengthy comments should be accommodated. Similarly, a rule's reason (which
the problem processor can present to users) should not be overly constrained. An arbitrary cap on how long a reason can be
restricts the explanation ability [Holsapple and Whinston, 1986]
of decision support systems built with the tool. Furthermore,
the ability to parameterize rule reasons can be very handy.

3.1.2. Variables

Ideally, a problem processor should avoid placing arbitrary limits on the number of variables a rule set can reference. Even if an unlimited number of rules is allowed in a rule set, a cap on the number of variables can place major restrictions on rule set development. Some of the variables in a rule set are goal variables. Their values are unknown at the outset of a consultation. The problem processor uses inference techniques to try to establish values for at least some of them during any particular consultation. A tool should allow the developer to specify various characteristics of each such variable in a rule set.

As an alternative or complement to determining an unknown variable's value via inference, the tool should allow the developer to specify a sequence of actions. The ability to specify multiple actions gives a developer more flexibility and can result in expert system behavior that is not possible if only a single action is allowed per variable. The degree to which a tool goes beyond line-oriented input actions greatly influences the sophistication of resultant decision support systems. The capacities to find a value through a series of user interactions or without any user interaction at all are definite plusses. Some of the basic kinds of (non-inference) actions that a tool might support for helping to find a variable's value include line-oriented input, menu processing, forms management, assignment commands, numeric calculations, text string manipulations, spreadsheet processing, data base retrieval, statistical analyses, procedural modelling, remote communications, graphics generation, and execution of external programs. For each variable, the developer should be allowed to specify whether its find actions are to occur before or after inference is attempted.

The ability to specify different certainty factor computations for different variables is an instance of highly refined control over reasoning behavior. In some applications it may be acceptable for all variable certainty factor computations to be based on the same algebra. In others, acceptable DSS behavior may require the simultaneous use of different certainty factor algebras for different variables. Tools that do not allow a developer to select such algebras on a variable by variable basis are quite inflexible -- providing only one rigid way for trying to handle reasoning about uncertainty. On the other hand, if a tool providing, say, 10 algebras is used to build a rule set involving 40 variables, then 10^{40} different possibilities are available for reasoning about uncertain variable values.

For each variable, a tool should allow the developer to specify how rigorous the problem processor should be when attempting to infer the variable's value. Here is another example of very refined control over decision support system reasoning behavior. Within a consultation, it may be desirable for the problem processor to consider all candidate rules for one variable. However, a minimal consideration of candidate rules may be desired when trying to infer the value of another variable. For yet another variable, some compromise between these two extremes may be preferred. By specifying the rigor choices for individual variables, a developer can control the behavior that occurs during a consultation.

3.1.3. Initialization and Completion

A reasonable tool will allow the developer to specify a sequence of initialization actions and a sequence of completion actions for a rule set. At the outset of a consultation the initialization sequence's actions are executed before inference begins. Similarly, after inference ends, the problem processor carries out all actions in the completion sequence in order to gracefully terminate the consultation. The developer of a rule set should be free to declare or expand a sequence of actions that the inference engine will carry out at the start of a consultation. Similarly, there should be no arbitrary cap on the number of completion actions in a rule set.

A rich assortment of actions should be allowed in an initialization or completion sequence. These may or may not involve user interaction. Some kinds of actions that might be expected include line-oriented input and output, menu processing, forms management, assignment commands, procedural modelling,

spreadsheet processing, data base retrieval, expert system consultation, statistical analysis, remote communications, graphics
generation, execution of external programs, customized report
generation, and text processing.

3.2. Rule Set Development

Beyond the rule set characteristics that can be employed in
developing a DSS, a tool's support of the development process
itself should not be overlooked. There are two aspects to this
development process. One involves the activity of managing the
rule set -- specifying and revising it. This is accomplished
with a development tool's rule set management capabilities.
Second is the activity of testing a rule set to determine whether
the expert system behaves as desired. This is accomplished with
the tool's inference capabilities.

The problem processor's rule set management capabilities
should facilitate rapid, convenient rule set construction and
revision. In addition to its consultation role, a tool's inference capabilities should also furnish facilities to assist developers as they test rule sets. The biggest payoff in developer
productivity comes from flexible, powerful, natural methods for
representing reasoning knowledge in a rule set. A problem processor with good rule set development facilities adds to this
productivity. Weak problem processor facilities for rule set
construction and testing can severely detract from even the most
advanced rule set characteristics.

3.2.1. Rule Set Management

Rule set management capabilities are preferably an integral
part of the consultation environment rather than a separate
program. Integration means that the developer does not have to
switch among separate programs during the development and testing of a rule set. Rule set management may be accomplished via
a text processing approach or a menu-guided approach. Each has
certain advantages. Text processing requires a knowledge of
rule set syntax, but should allow very flexible rule set viewing
and editing. Menu-guidance may offer less viewing or editing

flexibility, but does not require as great a knowledge of rule set syntax. It is a plus when a tool allows a developer to choose the approach that is individually most suitable. In either case, on-line help should be available during the management of a rule set. On-line help increases developer productivity by reducing the dependency on paper reference documentation.

While working on a rule set, a tool should allow the developer to freely intermix the activities of adding, deleting, modifying and viewing rule set contents as needed. It should provide a broad assortment of control functions for working on rule set contents, each of which can be accomplished with a single keystroke. This is true regardless of whether a text processor or menu-guided approach is being used. Often times a developer may need to view or modify all occurrences of some particular pattern of characters in the rule set. The ability to focus exclusively on the pattern of interest is valuable.

The tool should be able to print out the current rule set contents after any change and then immediately carry out further changes, allowing the developer to keep a paper record of variations of a rule set. In addition the tool should be able to save the current rule set contents on a disk file after any change, immediately make further changes, save the revised rule set on disk, and so forth. This ability gives the developer a convenient way of generating multiple variations of the same rule set.

In the interest of faster consultations and increased rule set security, a good tool will be able to compile a source version of a rule set. During compilation, it will analyze the rule set for correctness, consistency and completeness. Such analysis can be a big time-saver for the developer by highlighting potential flaws in a rule set before it is even tested. Informative warning messages should be displayed as potential problems are encountered. The number of different warning messages that a rule set manager can produce is a fair indicator of how extensive the analysis is.

3.2.2. Rule Set Testing

As noted earlier, a developer should not have to switch among different programs for rule set construction, revision and testing. Furthermore, the ability to directly execute any action in an interactive way, independently of a consultation session, speeds up the rule set testing. The effects of any action can be isolated and examined before it is incorporated into a rule set -- without involving revision or recompilation of the rule set.

In order to fully test a rule set, it may be worthwhile to observe and compare the effects of different reasoning assumptions (e.g., consultation rigor, selection order, etc.) for the same collection of rules. This kind of testing activity is much more rapid if such assumptions can be altered by simply changing an environment setting outside of the rule set itself. Basic environment settings for testing include the choice of a rule selection order, a premise testing strategy, consultation rigor, certainty factor algebras for conjunctions, for disjunctions, and for variables, and an unknown threshold.

A built-in inference tracing facility allows the developer to see a step-by-step account of the reasoning as it happens. Such a facility is indispensable when the developer wants to see the sequence of inference engine actions and assess the relative speed of each action. The level of detail presented during a trace should be developer controllable. This may range from no tracing to very elaborate tracing that reports on the progress of finding each unknown variable, the selection of each rule for consideration, and each rule firing.

Moreover, the tool should allow a developer to build his or her own tracing behavior into a rule set. In this way, a developer can cause a specialized trace to occur, presenting developer-prescribed trace messages at any desired junctures in a consultation test. These junctures include any point in an initialization sequence, immediately prior to any premise evaluation attempt, before or after any action that occurs during a rule's firing, during the attempt to find an unknown variable's value, and any point in a completion sequence.

The tool should permit a developer to "comment out" (i.e., disable) any undesired portion of a rule set for a given consultation test. For instance, a developer may want to study the effects of having the inference engine temporarily ignore a particular rule, a certain condition in some premise, or a certain action in some conclusion during a consultation test. It should be possible to isolate testing to any desired variable. This expedites the testing activity by allowing a developer to focus on the treatment of a particular variable, without requiring a comprehensive consultation. In addition, any rule can be chosen as the starting point for a test. This expedites the testing activity by allowing a developer to focus on the potential firing of a particular rule, without requiring a comprehensive consultation.

A tool should provide facilities that help automate the testing of a rule set, enabling a single command to cause repeated consultations -- each solving one of a group of previously saved problem descriptions. This ability can help speed up and standardize rule set testing. Finally, the problem processor should be able to produce a printed record of all interaction that occurs during a consultation test. This helps the developer assess the effects of the test particularly for lengthy consultations.

3.3. Consultation Activities

The power and flexibility that a tool offers for representing reasoning knowledge are primary determiners of what is possible during DSS inference. Of equal importance are the inference capabilities it has for operating on a rule set. A rudimentary problem processor is capable of processing a given rule set in only one way. The technique it uses for reasoning is always the same, regardless of the rule set being processed. At the opposite extreme are sophisticated problem processors, capable of many different reasoning techniques. These adaptable tools can be set, tuned, or directed to reason with rule sets in any of many different ways. Such flexibility is a contributor

to problem processor generality, because all applications are
not the same and all reasoning does not necessarily occur in the
same way.

In addition to the versatility of inference characteristics,
the invocation method and environment should be examined when
evaluating a tool's consultation capabilities. A variety of
methods for starting consultations is advantageous to both the
users and developers of artificially intelligent decision support
systems. Similarly, a rich consultation environment is generally
preferable to a bare bones environment.

3.3.1. Inference Characteristics

The ability to reason in many different ways is an important
criterion for tool selection. In broadest terms this means the
problem processor is capable of both forward and reverse reasoning, each of which is advantageous in certain situations. Forward reasoning ("forward chaining") is generally preferable in
situations where all (or most) of a rule set's rules must be
considered, where there are few unknown variables, or where
there is no single goal. In the latter case, the consultation
determines all the implications of a problem, rather than pursuing a specific goal. An example would be a consultation that
aims to determine a broad financial plan rather than determining
how much to invest in a specific stock. Reverse reasoning
("backward chaining") is generally preferable in situations where
a substantial portion of rules may be irrelevant to the problem
at hand, where there are relatively large numbers of unknown
variables, or where there is a specific goal to be pursued.

At a more detailed level, the problem processor could support
many variants of both reasoning approaches. That is, it should
be possible to easily customize either the reverse or forward
reasoning process, without programming or altering the problem
processor itself. Built-in inference adaptability is a definite
asset for a problem processor -- allowing it to be more general
in terms of the breadth of problems handled. The problem processor should provide various "switches" that can be set to
tailor its reasoning behavior during either forward or reverse

reasoning.

Sometimes it may be desirable to limit a consultation to a certain subset of a rule set's rules. The specific rules to be fired and the order of their firing may even be known in advance. A user may want to repeat the reasoning steps employed in a previous consultation. In each case, consultation speed is increased if the problem processor is able to make use of such pre-knowledge. For instance, it may allow forward reasoning to be requested for a prescribed sequence of rules.

A good problem processor is able to accept any unknown variable in a rule set as its goal, for purposes of reverse reasoning. This kind of inference engine flexibility means that very focused consultations are possible. Any consultation can be restricted to any variable of interest, rather than using a rule set's default goal. The ability of a problem processor to permit one consultation to be nested within another is also valuable. It is one way to overcome a practical limit on the number of rules per rule set. It also provides an easy way to accomplish mixed reasoning, where some portions of a consultation proceed in a forward fashion while others proceed in a reverse manner. The maximum levels of consultation nesting should not be overly restrictive.

The inference capabilities of a problem processor should be designed to handle the same kinds of uncertainties as humans. A developer does not have to program it to accommodate uncertainties. A problem processor should be expected to handle certainty measurements from a variety of sources, including the DSS user, initialization actions, rule pre-actions, actions in the conclusions of fired rules, and variable description actions. There should be sufficient distinct levels of certainty for representing and modelling uncertainties. If there are only a few (e.g., ten) gradations between the highest and lowest levels of certainty, the problem processor's ability to reason about uncertainty is impaired.

The uncertainty threshold used during a consultation indicates the point at which a certainty factor becomes too low to allow a variable's value to be considered as being known. Depending on the nature of a problem, a low or medium or high threshold may be desired. A problem processor should be able to work with any one of many possible threshold settings.

As it executes procedural models, analyzes spreadsheets, or makes inferences, a sophisticated problem processor is able to automatically compute certainty factors for numeric expressions, string expressions, logical expressions (e.g., a premise), numeric variables, string variables, logical variables, and each value of a fuzzy variable. Versatility of this kind is important for developing extensive, artificially intelligent DSSs.

Values of numeric expressions, string expressions, and conjunctive logical expressions will have certainty factors if terms in those expressions have certainty factors. A flexible problem processor will provide a "switch" for choosing the algebra to be used for such joint certainty factor computations. Typical choices include the minimum, product, and average methods [Holsapple and Whinston, 1986]. Similarly, a tool should give a choice of the algebra to be used for computing the confirmative certainty factors of disjunctive expressions. Typical choices include the maximum, probability sum, and average methods.

As noted earlier a problem processor may support different [Holsapple and Whinston, 1986] certainty algebras for different variables in a rule set. Alternatively, a developer may not choose to prescribe certainty algebras for individual variables. Nevertheless, there should still be a "switch" for choosing a default certainty algebra for variables in a consultation. A problem processor whose inference capabilities provide several built-in methods offers more latitude in producing the desired reasoning behavior than one that does not. If a variable's value is set by the action of some rule, then its certainty factor should be based on certainties in the rule's premise and relevant action. If multiple rules resulting in the same value have fired, then the problem processor should be able to base the value's certainty factor on its derived certainties for all of those rules.

A fuzzy variable is a variable that can simultaneously have more than one value -- each with its own certainty factor. A problem processor should be able to handle a reasonably large number of values for each fuzzy variable in a procedural model or rule set. Beyond allowing constant values to be assigned to a fuzzy variable, a versatile problem processor will be able to evaluate expressions involving fuzzy variables. For instance, the problem processor is able to calculate the fuzzy sum of two fuzzy variables in the course of a consultation or procedure execution. This is a powerful feature to have in situations that involve fuzzy variable manipulation.

A problem processor should refuse to reason if a user attempts to consult a rule set without having proper access privileges. Advice offered by an artificially intelligent DSS can be very valuable and should be protected from disclosure to unauthorized persons. Once an authorized user has begun a consultation, the problem processor may prompt the user for additional input. Before responding, the user should have an opportunity to get an explanation of why this input is needed. This temporary interruption should be easy to make (e.g., by pressing a single key). After a consultation ends, the problem processor should be able to explain how and why it reasoned as it did.

If the problem processor automatically remembers the entire sequence of rule firings that occur during the reasoning portion of a consultation, then a consultation can be rapidly re-run. This trait also enables a developer to design the completion actions to make use of this remembered sequence (e.g., to produce a customized explanation of reasoning behavior).

3.3.2. Inference Engine Invocation

Versatility in the manner in which the problem processor's inference capabilities can be invoked must not be overlooked when evaluating a tool. Potential DSS users span a spectrum from computer novices and casual users to experienced and frequent users. Different modes of interaction are particularly well-suited to different segments along this spectrum. DSS accessibility is enhanced to the extent that its inference

capabilities can be invoked in various modes including the selection of menu options, natural language requests, command
language statements, and customized interfaces built by a developer (and stored in the knowledge system).

A problem processor's inference capabilities should be in-
vokable in a noninteractive manner. This allows a consultation
to be started without any direct initiative by a human user. It
may be that there is no human user of the consultation results
(i.e., the generated advice is used internally by the DSS to
control some other activity). Or, if there is a user who will
receive the results, then he or she may be unaware that rule
set consultations are taking place [Bonczek et al., 1981]. These
effects can be accomplished to the extent that a consultation
command can be embedded in a rule set's initialization actions,
rule's conclusion actions, variable description's find actions,
rule set's completion actions, procedural model, spreadsheet
cell's definition, piece of text for print-time execution, macro
definition, function key definition, and data base for subsequent
retrieval and execution.

3.3.3. Inference Environment

Unlike expert system shells, the inference capabilities of
a generalized problem processor do not exist in a vacuum. They
are blended into a rich environment for decision support. When
evaluating a tool, the qualities of this inference environment
should be examined. For instance, what kind and how many environment controls ("switches") are provided for customizing
the realm within which reasoning occurs? A rich assortment of
these controls allows the environment to be easily tailored to
a particular user's needs. No programming effort is required
and the problem processor software is itself unaffected. A
sampling of possibilities includes environment controls for
screen foreground and background colors, direction of spreadsheet
computation, baud rate used during remote communications, date
format assumed for date processing, suppressing background grids
for graphics displays, getting automatic context-sensitive
help, ignoring case differences when comparing string values,

synchronous cell movements within windows, and so forth.

A user should be able to alter such environment controls prior to requesting a consultation. The user might directly switch a control from its default setting to another setting. Alternatively, the tool may allow a developer to build a custom interface that asks a user about what environmental character- istics are desired. The corresponding settings are then made by the customized interface software. Moreover, a good tool will allow environment control settings to be established within a rule set. Such an ability allows the developer to fully con- trol the nature of the environment for consultations involving a rule set. The desired settings are made in the initialization actions and can be restored to their former states in the rule set's completion actions.

Not all decision support requires the use of inference. Thus the environment furnished by a tool should allow consulta- tion requests to be freely intermixed with other requests of interest to a DSS user. This allows consultation to be treated as a standard decision support activity. It can be exercised at any time, without having to leave one program (e.g, for spreadsheet or data base processing) and entering another before a consultation can occur. The convenience of a single program that provides a unified artificially intelligent environment for decision support should not be overlooked. Though not examined here, the breadth and extent of the other, non-inference capa- bilities in the environment are important criteria for tool selection [Holsapple and Whinston, 1986].

All else being equal, a tool that furnishes an open environ- ment is preferable to one that does not. This includes the ability to run external programs from within the environment. It also means the tool can import data from external sources for use within the environment. Data values existing on some other computer or produced by some other software could be useful for DSS processing. The tool should allow contents of ASCII, DIF and other kinds of files to be easily imported into a DSS knowl- edge system. Conversely, the tool should allow knowledge system contents to be exported out of the DSS environment in a variety of common file formats.

3.4. Performance

The foregoing criteria can help in assessing whether a tool
is technically capable of building the kinds of artificially
intelligent DSSs that are desired or anticipated. When multiple
tools meet the criteria reasonably well, their respective performance traits deserve some study. In particular, performance
of the tool's inference capability depends on a wide variety of
factors. First, there is the machine and operating system that
hosts the problem processor. A second factor is the programming
language used to implement the problem processor. In general,
a non-compiled language yields a slower problem processor than
a compiled language. Among compiled languages there are also
differences. For instance, implementing a problem processor
with the C language should result in faster consultation processing than a FORTRAN implementation.

A third factor affecting the tool's inference performance
is the quality of rule set design. Two different formulations
of the same reasoning knowledge can result in significant performance differences for the same problem processor. For instance, a rule set design that consists of 300 rules is very
likely to require more processing time than an equivalent rule
set of 100 rules. What is or is not a good rule set design from
a performance viewpoint depends on the nature of the problem
processor's inference capabilities. A rule set design that
yields acceptable performance for one problem processor may be
suboptimal or even unacceptable for another problem processor
-- even though the two pieces of software are implemented with
the same programming language and are running with the same hardware and operating systems.

The rule set characteristics discussed earlier can have a
very large impact on a problem processor's inference performance,
because they determine what rule set design alternatives are
available to a developer. As the flexibility, power, and natu-
ralness offered for representing reasoning knowledge increase,
they tend to result in rule sets that are more concise and

streamlined. Patchwork, contorted rule sets involving round-
about ways to specify knowledge can be avoided. A problem
processor's inference performance is enhanced if it does not
need to take numerous, lengthy detours to accomplish various
reasoning tasks during a consultation.

Another important factor related to performance involves the
reasoning controls that a tool provides. Many such controls
have been identified earlier. These controls allow a developer
to govern the problem processor's strategy for reasoning about
a particular problem. Depending on the nature of the problem
and the design of the rule set, one strategy may result in a
faster consultation than another strategy. By giving a developer
easily modifiable controls, a tool lets the developer assess the
relative performances of alternative strategies. Thus, the
developer can tune the inference performance of a problem processor for a specific rule set or a specific problem. If versatile tuning controls are absent from a tool, then the developer's influence over inference speed is correspondingly limited.

Performance is also affected by the quality of the rule set
compiler provided in the development tool. If there is no
compiler, then it is unrealistic to expect top inference performance from a problem processor. All compilers are not created equal. Some may generate compiled rule sets that can be
processed very efficiently, while others' compiled rule sets
may lead to relatively slow inference processing.

As the foregoing factors suggest, making sweeping generalizations about the inference performance of one problem processor relative to another may not always be possible. One should
be wary about drawing unwarranted generalizations from comparative benchmark testing. Benchmark results should always be accompanied by a clear explanation of the situation used for testing, the rule set designs employed, and the host hardware/oper-
ating system. Provided rule sets are designed fairly and tuning
controls are set fairly, the benchmark tests will give a good
idea of which tool performs fastest in a <u>specific</u> situation.
In another situation a different tool may be faster. One of the
best ways to get a quick feel for a problem processor's inference

speed is to turn on its inference tracing mechanism during a consultation. By providing an on-screen, blow-by-blow account of the inference processing activities, a tool lets the developer see how fast it can select a rule, process a rule, or find the value of an unknown variable.

In addition to inference performance, the speed of rule set management should be considered. Overly slow processing during the development and maintenance of a rule set can be very disconcerting to a developer. Rule set compilation should also be a reasonably fast activity. By segmenting reasoning knowledge into distinct rule set modules during initial development work, developers may be able to reduce rule set maintenance and compilation times. This is because they are able to focus on a small collection of rules at any given time.

4. CONCLUSION

Here we have identified a fairly detailed set of criteria to consider when selecting a tool for developing artificially intelligent DSSs. The selected tool should give a developer extensive flexibility and power for representing reasoning knowledge within a rule set. It should provide facile facilities for rule set development. The problem processor should be sufficiently general, offer a reasonable array of reasoning controls, and operate within a rich artificially intelligent environment for decision support. The traditional computing capabilities synergistically integrated into this environment should be reasonably extensive.

With the advent of new kinds of software tools that synergistically integrate traditional computing capabilities with reasoning capabilities, decision support systems that can display artificially intelligent behavior emerge from the conceptual plane [Bonczek et al., 1981] into reality [Holsapple and Whinston, 1986]. The new dimension that this adds to decision support systems is only just beginning to be appreciated. An artificially intelligent environment for decision support allows developers to create DSSs that offer expert advice. By creating computer-based "experts," expertise about using knowledge is embodied in a DSS's knowledge system. An artificially intelligent environment for decision support also allows users to both consult "experts" and be experts. By <u>consulting</u> an "expert," a user can actively employ the reasoning expertise of others to process various kinds of knowledge -- for the purpose of deriving new knowledge (i.e., advice). By <u>being</u> an expert, a user directly exercises his or her own reasoning capabilities in the course of working with knowledge held in the knowledge system's data bases, spreadsheets, models, text, graphic images and so forth. Such artificially intelligent environments for decision support can form the basis for tomorrow's knowledge-based organizations [Holsapple and Whinston, 1986].

REFERENCES

Bonczek, R.H., Holsapple, C.W. and Whinston, A.B. (1981). <u>Foundations of Decision Support Systems</u>, Academic Press, New York.

Holsapple, C.W. (1977). "The Knowledge System for a Generalized Problem Processor," Working Paper, Department of Business Administration, University of Illinois.

Holsapple, C.W. and Whinston, A.B. (1983). "Software Tools for Knowledge Fusion," <u>ComputerWorld</u> (In Depth), <u>17</u>, 15.

Holsapple, C.W. and Whinston, A.B. (1984). "Aspects of Integrated Software," <u>Proceedings of the National Computer Conference</u>, Las Vegas.

Holsapple, C.W. and Whinston, A.B. (1986). <u>Manager's Guide to Expert Systems Using Guru</u>, Dow Jones-Irwin, Homewood.

SECTION II - APPLICATIONS

8. DECISION SUPPORT IN OFFICE INFORMATION SYSTEMS

G. Bracchi and B. Pernici
Dipartimento di Elettronica
Politecnico di Milano
I-20133 Milano, Italy

1. INTRODUCTION

Office work integrates routine activities and decision-making activities. Its main goal is to handle office automation according to the organizational goals. The activities which are performed, even if routine activities, often have to take into account past experience, new organizational or legal requirements, parallel activities to be performed, new documents entering the office. The result is that office activities are globally complex, but forms of automatic support are offered only for simple or very repetitive activities. The potential applications of decision support techniques are very broad, but up to now they have been limited to very narrow domains or to prototype systems [Chang, 1984].

Office systems may offer decision support to office workers in several ways:

- In analyzing office data.

  Office data can be searched and aggregated in summary documents; information retrieval techniques may be used to provide the user with a manageable amount of information, consisting of a selection of all available items including all information needed for decision-making activities.

- Control the state of the system.

  The office work may present problems due for instance to delayed activities and unavailable information; the office system could be instructed to check the system state, periodically or on verification of particular events, in order to perform correction actions or to alert users about potential problems. On-going activities and document flows can be monitored also in a normal system state, providing office workers with information needed to continue on-going procedures (e.g., reminding of things to do next).

NATO ASI Series, Vol. F31
Decision Support Systems: Theory and Application
Edited by C. W. Holsapple and A. B. Whinston
© Springer-Verlag Berlin Heidelberg 1987

- Support decision making.

  In addition to ad hoc decision support packages specific
  to some applications, an office system can provide the user
  with a support in choosing among alternative paths, and in
  verifying preconditions to perform some activities; the
  alternative paths and conditions may be unknown to the
  user but embedded in system knowledge; the user is then
  provided by the system with explanations about its behavior
  and with suggestions.

- Support office systems design.

  As office systems are highly complex, it is useful to provide office designers with tools for supporting the design
  process, in order to make it easier and less time consuming,
  and to verify incomplete and inconsistent specifications.

The purpose of this paper is to describe systems for decision
support in the office environment proposed in the literature,
and to classify possible applications of decision support.

In Section 2, systems for control of office activities based
on triggering conditions will be examined. An alternative
approach to the control of office activities, based on the specification of office goals, will be provided in Section 3.

In Section 4 and in Section 5 office support tools will be
presented; Section 4 will discuss systems that are mainly
oriented to project management and cooperative decision making,
while Section 5 will illustrate systems that are more specific
to certain technologies available in the office environment.

In Section 6 some office systems design support tools will
be discussed. In Section 7 some possible new applications of
decision support in the office environment will finally be presented and discussed.

2. OFFICE CONTROLS BASED ON TRIGGERING CONDITIONS

Several systems have been developed to support user's definition of office activities to be triggered on the verification
of certain conditions on data or events during system operation.
Activities are started, halted, or continued on the basis of

these conditions, and warning and reminding messages are automatically sent to the office users. These facilities can be used to monitor on-going activities, to automatically control abnormal or special situations in the office, provide support in reminding deadlines and activities to be performed to keep these deadlines.

A system which supports these facilities is Office By Example (OBE) [Zloof, 1982]. OBE is an office system which uses an office data base, text editing functions and electronic mail. The user interface is based on the one provided by the system Query By Example (QBE), [Zloof, 1981], for querying a relational data base; the description of data is based on the concept of table. In OBE data are forms, which are generalizations of tables. Forms also permit conversion of numerical data inside tables into a graphical form, so that they provide manager oriented productivity tools (for instance, as a support for report generation) as well. In OBE it is possible to specify an office procedure, based on values of data in the office data base and on temporal conditions.

For instance, in Figure 1, a letter is sent to workers performing well in the sales department. In this example, the triggering condition on data is tested monthly, and the appropriate values for sending the letters are selected.

These procedures can be easily prepared by individual office workers according to their needs, so that they can automate some of their procedures. Hence these facilities can be used by office workers at all levels in the organization, for defining the procedures without the need for an analyst to prepare applications. Since OBE is a simple to use language, which requires minimum training, and yet is powerful enough to cover a large spectrum of office tools, the result is a flexible system for specifying office activities, based on general office tools such as DBMS, electronic mail, and word processing with graphics facilities.

Systems performing in the same way could be obtained by ad hoc programs prepared for office workers by system developers,

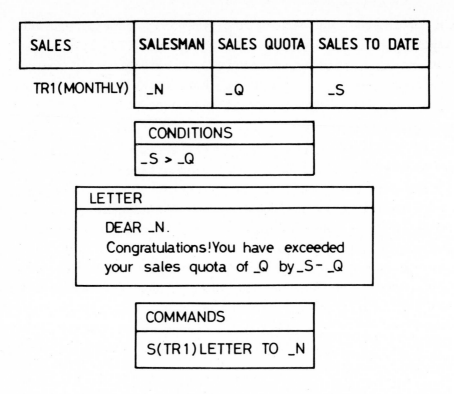

SALES	SALESMAN	SALES QUOTA	SALES TO DATE
TR1(MONTHLY)	_N	_Q	_S

CONDITIONS
_S > _Q

LETTER
DEAR _N. Congratulations! You have exceeded your sales quota of _Q by _S - _Q

COMMANDS
S(TR1) LETTER TO _N

Figure 1. OBE Commands [Zloof, 1982]

and could be based on menus selections to provide support to
various activities. The advantage of using OBE is that its
interface is more flexible than the use of prespecified menus,
which are hard to modify. Each triggering program, and each
object in the office data base, is linked directly only to other
objects used in the same environment, so that there are no complex relationships among office objects. So new applications
and new objects may be added independently by different users.

There are other systems which are based on the concept of
activity triggering. These systems differ from each other due
to the complexity of the conditions that can be specified, the
user interface they provide, and the goal of the use of the
system. The idea of specifying triggering of activities was
first used in the SCOOP system [Zisman, 1978], which is one of
the early models used for office systems design. In SCOOP procedures are described using Petri Nets and are then detailed

through production rules for each activity. An example of an
operational system has been developed based on these concepts,
to support the procedure of preparation of a journal based on
referage of papers.

A more sophisticated version of an office model based on
similar ideas is provided by the Officetalk family of models.
These models [Ellis and Bernal, 1982] describe procedures with
decision points in a formal way and in addition take into account
also the data which are used in the office system. Officetalk
has been used more to support design rather than as an operational system. It is possible to use it to simulate office
activities in order to evaluate bottlenecks in the system and
inconsistencies. Besides, it can be used to monitor the actual
operation of the office, thus providing support at the managerial
level in decision-making processes.

Other systems focus on specification of triggering rules
with complex conditions.

A sort of rule editor is provided by the system developed
at the University of Turin [Cortese and Sirovich, 1984], in
which the user can specify control rules (daemons) in input
mode using a syntax very close to that used in command mode.

Alerters can be defined in the system developed by Chang
and Chang [1982], which is mainly used to issue warning and
reminding messages to the users. Their work, moreover, is concerned with avoiding cycles of messages.

In SOS [Bracchi and Pernici, 1985], control rules can be
specified on the basis of complex conditions on office data and
on time. A semantic office model provides in SOS a hierarchical
description of office elements, so that control rules can specify control conditions at different levels of detail in the
hierarchy. General guidelines for office activities control
can thus be provided, and more detailed specifications can then
be introduced through additional rules.

3. OFFICE SUPPORT BASED ON OFFICE GOALS

Some office systems have been developed, which provide

decision support to office workers with reasoning mechanisms about the office information, based on techniques derived from the expert systems area. These systems provide the users with explanations and suggestions on modes of operating to perform their work, supporting problem solving activities of office workers in complex tasks.

The main characteristic of these systems is that goals of office tasks are represented, so that appropriate procedures can be invoked accordingly to accomplish these goals. The ability of approaching office tasks from a goal oriented perspective means that a task is not bound to a fixed series of actions, as for instance in SCOOP, where the steps to perform a certain activity are redefined at system design time.

The POISE system, developed at the University of Massachusetts at Amherst [Croft and Lefkowitz, 1984], can be used both to automate routine tasks and to provide assistance in more complex situations, following the pattern of work being performed. In POISE tasks are represented both in a procedural and a goal oriented way; the tasks considered are high level office tasks performed using generic office tools, such as electronic mail, calendar, text editors, and form management tools. The system uses an office procedure formalism to describe the tasks and their implementation using these tools. POISE is useful in environments where the same task is repeated, rather than offering support in completely new situations.

The support which is provided to the user is that of automating some tasks, and keeping an agenda of activities, the status of which can be examined using a natural language interface.

In POISE a user can specify that a particular task step is not appropriate in certain situations; this is instead hard to achieve in systems based on triggering conditions.

Tasks in POISE are specified in a hierarchical way. Procedure descriptions specify the steps typical to the task, the tool invocations which correspond to those steps, and their goals. It acts as an intelligent interface between the user and

the tools available in an office system. In Figure 2 the architecture of the system is illustrated.

The semantic data base contains the descriptions of the
objects used in the procedures and of the available tools.

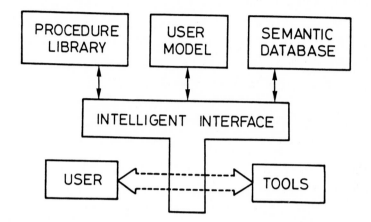

Figure 2.   POISE Architecture [Croft and Lefkowitz, 1984]

The user model represents instances of procedures and of
data elements in the system through users' states; the users'
state contains parameters the values of which account for instantiations of procedures described in the procedure library;
these instantiations are derived from users' actions. The user
model contains also the instantiations of semantic data base
objects.

A procedure in the procedure library can be specified as in
the example presented in Figure 3.

The procedure description contains a (high level) algorithm
for the procedure, a list of its parameters, a list of conditions to be met to have a valid instantiation of the algorithm,
and preconditions and goals. These goals can be used to automatically start procedure instances.

The POISE system can be used in two different modes of
operation: interpretation and planning. In the interpretation
mode the user invokes tools directly, and POISE attempts to

```
PROC       Purchase_Items
DESC       (Procedure for puchasing items with nonstate funds.)
IS         (Receive_purchase_request)
           '(Process_purchase_order | Process_purchase_requisition)
           '(Complete_purchase)
WITH       ((Purchaser  = Receive_purchase_request. Form.Purchaser)
           (Items       = Receive_purchase_request. Form.Items)
           (Vendor_name = Receive_purchase_request. Form.Vendor_name))
COND       (for_values {Purchaser Items Vendor_name }
               (eq Receive_purchase_request. Form
                  Process_purchase_order. Form
                  Process_purchase_requisition. Form
                  Complete_purchase. Form))
PRECONDITIONS-
SATISFACTION    (for_values | Purchaser Items Vendor}
                (exist Complete_purchase. Form))
```

Figure 3. POISE Procedure Specification
[Croft and Lefkowitz, 1984]

recognize the user's goals in the context of the procedure library (goals are used in this context to identify completion of procedures). In the planning mode, the user invokes a procedure and the system must then carry out as much of that procedure as possible, based on procedure's goals.

In the interpretation mode, the user is presented at the top level of the POISE system with a menu of tasks (e.g., filling out a particular form); all access to tools must be done through POISE menu choices, thus enabling the system to monitor tool usage. Every command to and response from a general tool is intercepted by POISE, though it appears as if the user is interacting directly with the tool. Intercepting messages, POISE can check whether the message is relevant to any activity in progress and, if one is found, verify if it is appropriate (error conditions and exceptional ways of carrying out a task are both considered; accordingly, messages are sent to the user performing the task). If more than one interpretation is possible, all interpretations are maintained, but there are some heuristics

criteria to determine the most plausible interpretation: if
this selection turns out to be incorrect, backtracking is performed and the next most likely interpretation is selected. If
a procedure is invoked instead of a similar one (for instance,
writing Full_Purchase_Requisition instead of Full_Purchase_Order),
the user is advised with the possible alternative action, and
an explanation of the possible error in selecting the form is
given. This can be used also to monitor data entry, with possible corrections.

POISE's natural language help facility may be invoked to
make inquiries about the state of active, completed, or expected
activities.

The planner enables tasks to be automatically carried out
or completed by the system; it can also be used to start tasks
up to the point in which the intervention of a worker is needed.

A goal oriented representation can be very useful in supporting decision making. The deduction mechanism may be used,
not only in controlling tasks sequences like in POISE, but also
in reasoning about change and contradiction, like in the system
OMEGA [Barber, 1983].

In OMEGA, the office workers' activities are supported as
the system provides a way of analyzing the reasons for contradictions when they are reached, with a deduction mechanism.
Viewpoints are used to limit the effect of contradictions, and
in the reasoning process the system explicitly keeps track of
what it believes to be true (assertions), and why they are
believed to be true (justifications). An example of use of such
a system is provided in [Barber, 1983]; the system is used to
control whether a certain employee can be assigned to a certain
job. The global goal of establishing whether the proposal is
reasonable is decomposed into several goals.

Systems based on the concepts used in POISE and OMEGA are
likely to be useful in the future to support office work as a
problem solving activity.

The range of problems which can be considered in this way
is very broad. The applications which seem more interesting

are related to the control of validity of several types of
office states (or substates): the case of POISE is an example
of such an application, concentrating mainly on states determined by the activities that are being performed in the system.

4.   PROJECT MANAGEMENT AND SCHEDULING

Systems to support office workers at the managerial level
to make decisions about on-going projects and to organize their
work have been developed. They offer querying facilities on the
available resources and ways of coordinating office activities.

A significant example of such a system is ENSEMBLE, developed
at MIT [Sarin and Greif, 1984] for supporting interactive on-
line conferences. In this system, users cooperate in a problem
solving task in real-time, being at their own workstations.
Generic facilities are provided for sharing objects and activities, and for dynamically adding and removing participants in a
conference; these functions can be used in several types of
applications. An example of application in [Sarin and Greif,
1984] illustrates the system RTCAL (Real Time CALendar) for
real-time scheduling of a meeting.

In RTCAL a meeting is scheduled in real-time by participants.
The private calendars of the participants are automatically
merged by the system to get available free times for the meeting.
Each participant sees this shared information together with the
private calendar information (Figure 4).

The shared space can be "scrolled" to show different date
and time ranges (which causes the participants' private windows
to scroll in unison). Specific times for the planned meeting
can be proposed (by one person at a time, called the controller
of the conference), and the system collects participants' votes;
several alternative proposals can be generated and reviewed,
until a meeting time is committed. Participants may leave the
conference temporarily and receive an up-to-date display when
they return.

This system can be used for other applications, such as joint
computer-aided design, joint authorship of documents, financial

```
+--------------------------------------------------------------------------+
|RTCAL 3.2 ctrl-↑ for control commands 12-4-82 11:52:07 Load=8.7    SARIN|
+--------------------------------------------------------------------------+
|scheduling meeting "thesis"    uncommitted    (2hrs. 12-25-82 to 12-31-82)|
|With SARIN       LICKLIDER      GREIF          HAMMER                      |
|    IN-Session   IN-Session     IN-Session     Absent                      |
|session Running  chairperson: SARIN    controller: SARIN                  |
+--------------------------------------------------------------------------+
|LICKLIDER joined session - all replies received                           |
+--------------------------------------------------------------------------+
|Monday 27 December 1982      |Private calendar: 27 December 1982          |
|Merge of SARIN LICKLIDER GREIF| Joe's birthday                            |
| 9:00 XXX                    | 9:00                                        |
| 9:30 XXX                    | 9:30                                        |
|10:00                        |10:00                                        |
|10:30                        |10:30                                        |
|11:00                        |11:00                                        |
|11:30                        |11:30                                        |
|12:00                        |12:00                                        |
|12:30 XXX                    |12:30 lunch                                  |
|13:00                        |13:00                                        |
|13:30                        |13:30                                        |
|14:00 XXX                    |14:00 Arpa meeting                           |
|14:30 XXX                    |14:30 xx                                     |
|15:00 XXX                    |15:00                                        |
+--------------------------------------------------------------------------+
|COMMAND> propose 10:30_                                                    |
+--------------------------------------------------------------------------+
```

Figure 4. RTCAL Interface [Sarin and Greif, 1984]

planning using spreadsheets, on-line tutorials and instruction, as well as for different types of conferences. Simultaneous interaction can also be extremely useful in rapid decision making in a crisis situation.

The structure and meaning of the objects and activities in a conference are specific to the given application (for instance, RTCAL), but the functions performed for sharing objects and performing activities are provided by the ENSEMBLE common software utility.

Other systems to support office workers in making decisions on on-going projects offer querying facilities for controlling the resources available for the project and for checking its state.

The manager's assistant [Kogan, 1984], though not specifically developed as an office system, is a decision aid for administrators of large development projects. It supports queries concerning funding and personnel issues; these queries are resolved either via direct data base search or with the aid of a deductive mechanism, which mediates data base access. It can be used to find overloaded persons in a project, to investigate whether a person is much too critical to the project, so that his absence can cause the project failure, and so on.

A system specifically designed for the office environment is XCP [Cashman, 1985]. It is designed also for managing large projects, but rather than to be oriented to the manager of the project, it is a tool for assisting office workers in coordinating their actions. Workers can ask questions about their present role in the project (what objects are they working on), about work loads, about activities to be completed and activities to be done next.

Other systems have been designed for supporting planning of use of resources in factories, like IMS [Fox, 1981], and the same ideas could be used to plan office work organization taking into consideration deadlines, resources, and relative importance of activities to be performed.

5. SPECIFIC OFFICE SUPPORT TOOLS

A few self-contained support tools have been created for some office activities. Basic support tools have been implemented (productivity tools), for instance, electronic spreadsheets; systems like word processing packages and mail systems can be considered as basic office support tools, too.

Some systems have been developed specifically for office applications: there are several form management systems [Tsichritzis, 1982; Ferrans, 1982; Barbic et al., 1984], where the main goal is to handle (retrieve, fill out, send) office forms; information retrieval tools have been studied for particular office environments [Barbic and Illuzzi, 1985]; retrieval techniques include both techniques for filtering data (according to keywords typical of the domain of the office considered), and systems which are able to deduct new information, using the available information and some inference rules; systems to enhance the communication functions provided by electronic mail, such as in Imail [Hogg et al., 1983], have also been proposed.

Imail, developed at the University of Toronto, is based on the concept of intelligent messages. Messages are used not only to deliver information, but also to collect it, and may dynamically route themselves to additional stations depending upon responses that they receive.

The system may be used to build mailing lists of workers interested in particular topics and to deliver messages to other systems and networks that the user is unaware of. They can be used to collect and summarize data on questionnaires, so they are not pure text messages, but they can be considered programs. The creator of an intelligent message (imessage) actually writes a program in the specification language used: in the message rules can be incorporated which will govern the interaction of the imessage itself with its recipients; an imessage can collect responses generated by the recipients, store them appropriately, and eventually make them available to its sender. A state is attached to the imessage, which describes its recipients, its path history, and so on. The sender can specify termination conditions to determine automatically when a message has completed its tour, and prepare the results in the form chosen by its sender.

An example of use of Imail has been prepared for a Delphi experiment. This is an iterative survey of experts to obtain a consensus answer. The results of the survey are tabulated and sent back to the experts, who can revise their answers according to the other experts' answers. This process is iterated until some criterion is satisfied, for instance, the range or variance of replies. An example of imessage for a Delphi experiment about next year inflation rate is shown in Figure 5.

```
          subject A Delphi survey of inflation rates
          set number   ?n = 0
          set number   ?sum = 0
          set number   ?sqsum = 0
          set number   ?maxvar = 0.1
          set number   ?itresps = 10
          set number   ?avg = 8.0
     >
     What do you think the inflation rate for next year will be ?
     The last average prediction was ?avg.
          get  1 number
          set   ?sum = ?sum +  #1
          set   ?sqsum = ?sqsum + #1 *#1
          set   ?n   =   ?n + 1
          ?n == ?itresps
               set ?avg = ?sum / ?n
               set !var = ?sqsum / ?n - ?avg  * ?avg
               set ?n = 0
               set ?sum = 0
               set ?sqsum = 0
               reship
          ?var < ?maxvar
               terminate
```

Figure 5.   An Example of Imessage [Hogg et al., 1983]

Different office support tools, now isolated from each other, could be integrated to form an office work environment which offers a coordinated support in several activities. The specification of automatic and semiautomatic office activities could use these tools, in addition to the basic ones that are already commonly provided by most office systems.

6. DESIGN SUPPORT TOOLS

Another area in which decision support could be useful is that of designing office systems. The designer can be supported in the requirements collection and analysis phase by development systems that are specifically designed for the office environment.

Several methods are presently being developed to support designers of office systems. Some of these methods provide guidelines for manual analysis of requirements and design, allowing a formalization of the office description with an office model. A survey of existing methodologies and models can be found in [Bracchi and Pernici, 1984]. A few methods offer computer-based support to the designer to collect and analyze data about office elements.

For example, the OFFIS system, developed at the University of Arizona, [Konsynski et al., 1982] is a support to collect office requirements and to analyze them checking consistency and completeness. An overview of OFFIS is provided in Figure 6.

The analyst can specify office requirements in terms of objects, attributes, and relationships between objects. These requirements are collected in the OFFIS data base, and they are used for producing documentation about the system. The analyst can query this data base from various perspectives, and functions to change, add, or delete selected OFFIS statements are provided. OFFIS can be used by managers to document the real organizational activities. In addition, it can be used as an analysis tool in the evaluation of the completeness and consistency of documented procedures. In this way, proposed changes may be evaluated and their impact assessed. Thus, OFFIS can serve as a tool in evaluating 'what if' questions related to

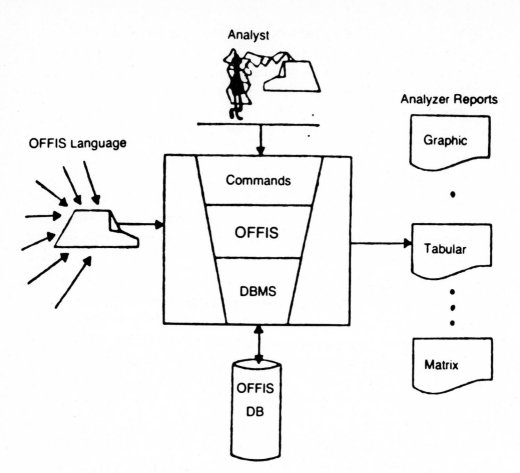

Figure 6. OFFIS System [Konsynski et al., 1982]

assessment of the impact of alternative design decisions. The
OFFIS analyzer produces reports which provide management with an
overall view of the system design, describing the organization's
functions, interfaces, and data flows. The reports show incom-
pleteness and inconsistencies in the design as well as the classification of processes in which each person participates. Various designs may be specified and evaluated using the reports,
thus making the design process iterative, converging to an
'optimal design'.

The OFFIS command language allows the analyst to produce
reports about the office data specified in OFFIS language.
Examples of such reports are data items tracking reports,

organizational hierarchy matrices, and systems interaction reports, as shown in Figure 7.

Examples of consistency and completeness checks are: to determine whether all data items (letters, data files, forms, calendars, mailboxes) have definitions specifying their creation; to identify data items created but never used; to detect if data items are sent to persons unidentified in the organization; to detect inconsistencies in the hierarchical structure of the organization (for instance, a person who, directly or indirectly, is reporting to himself; lower level employees with security levels higher than their superiors); the tasks performed by each group are listed with their frequencies, in order to determine overloaded units and bottlenecks. The OFFIS system is a useful tool for the first phases of a design methodology, mainly for requirements collection and analysis; it also provides a way to get the conceptual model of the office directly from the requirements' specifications.

How procedures are implemented is not a concern in OFFIS. Presently, the problem of automation of procedures implementation is being studied in several environments, mainly with the goal of supporting rapid prototyping.

A system that provides some form of automatic program generation is MACROS [Kumano et al., 1982]. Office data can be defined and the system offers some complex retrieval facilities, mainly in the form of summarizing forms and menus. The resulting application programs provide an extremely simplified and standardized user interface, through which even casual users can retrieve table/graphs from a large amount of table/graphs, easily, in a short time, and with few operations.

Design support tools both in the requirements collection, analysis, and specification phases and in program generation are very interesting in the office environment, since office systems implementation needs to be rapid and such tools would allow end users to take active part in the design.

```
DATA ITEM: DISPATCHERS-MAILBOX
      CREATED BY: EXECUTIVE-SECRETARY
      UPDATED BY: DIAPATCHER
      ACCESSED BY: OWNER-ONLY
      DELETED BY: DISPATCHER
      USED TO SCHEDULE OR UPDATE: .....
      OWNED BY: DISPATCHER
      ROUTED BY: .............
      SENT TO: ...............
      RECEIVED BY: ............

.......................................
```

Data item tracking report

TITLE	ROW & COL NUMBER
BOOKKEEPER	1
DISPATCHER	2
PILOT	3
EXECUTIVE-SECRETARY	4
RECEPTIONIST	5
GENL-OFFICE-MGR	6
OFFICE-MANAGERS	7
PRESIDENT	8

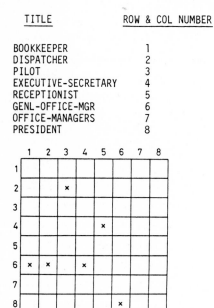

JOB TITLE	INTERACTIONS	WEIGHTED AVERAGE
BOOKKEEPER	16	3.60
DISPATCHER	3	3.50
EXECUTIVE-SECRETARY	40	3.17
GENL-OFFICE-MGR	18	3.11
OFFICE-MANAGERS	15	3.26
PILOT	1	3.50
PRESIDENT	17	3.27
RECEPTIONIST	1	2.00

Systems interaction report

OFFICE-MANAGERS   REPORTS TO ** NULL **
PRESIDENT   REPORTS TO ** NULL **

Organizational hierarchy matrix

Figure 7. OFFIS Reports [Konsynski et al., 1982]

7. NEXT STEPS AND CONCLUSIONS

In this paper a variety of systems for decision support in
the office environment have been presented. They provide different types of support (activities monitoring, sophisticated
tools, reasoning about office tasks), using a number of different techniques, the most important being based on ideas from the
data base and artificial intelligence areas.

Other types of support and techniques are likely to be
applied to the office environment in the future. A valid type
of support would be offered by learning systems; these systems
could learn automatically from experience which sequences of
activities are usually performed in the office, so that they can
offer support in doing them when they are repeated; other learning systems could maintain office workers' profiles related to
which kind of information is requested by each user and in which
form, so that they can offer adequate filtering to each user
according to his usual activities [Croft and Thompson, 1984].

As advocated by Lochovsky [1983], future office systems
should integrate different types of support to office activity,
and should be active. In most present systems, the knowledge
needed to perform office tasks resides entirely with the office
worker: he initiates and controls office tasks and knows what
are the goals to be achieved and what steps are required to
achieve them. Knowledge about office work should instead be
included directly in office systems, considering its peculiar
characteristics: office knowledge is open-ended, evolves over
time, it is often non-uniform and depends on special situations
and on who is handling them; an office activity is very often a
problem solving activity, rather than a routine processing
activity, so it should be described accordingly, not only with
automatic procedures to perform some tasks, but also as a strategy selection and/or definition activity. Activity planning
should be seen as an appropriate way to describe office work at
different levels of detail, and should be used to provide a
guideline in office work and to communicate with office workers
for capturing information about office tasks.

Office systems should be <u>flexible</u> and allow manipulation of <u>unstructured data</u>, and the presentation of the same data in different forms (tables, figures, charts, and so on), at different levels of aggregation, on different output devices: new office technologies for handling <u>vocal information</u> and <u>images</u> are to be used and integrated in existing office systems.

Another issue to be considered is providing a user friendly interface to let the user define independently its objects, procedures, goals and rules, so that office evolution is supported directly through users' specifications. Such a specification <u>interface</u> should be able to include all office tools and to handle specification of work performed by more than one office worker, considering cooperation and concurrency features and problems. An interesting application of decision support systems techniques would be in the area of organization and planning of office work. Office specific support could be offered taking into account available resources and criteria to evaluate satisfaction about the work performed. Optional strategies could then be selected according to those criteria.

These proposals do not certainly exhaust the list of possible applications of decision support systems developed for other domains to the office environment, since office work constitutes a highly varied and composite activity.

REFERENCES

Barber, G. (1983). "Supporting Organizational Problem Solving with a Work Station," <u>ACM Trans. on Office Information Systems</u>, <u>1</u>, 1, January, pp. 45-67.

Barbic, F., Carli, M., Pernici, B. and Bracchi, G. (1984). "A Tool for Form Definition in Office Information Systems Specification," in <u>New Applications of Data Bases</u>, G. Gardarin and E. Gelenbe (eds.), pp. 141-158.

Barbic, F. and Illuzzi, S. (1985). "An Office Message System," <u>Proc. RIAO '85</u>.

Bracchi, G. and Pernici, B. (1984). "The Design Requirements of Office Systems," <u>ACM Trans. on Office Information Systems</u>, <u>2</u>, 2, April, pp. 151-170.

Bracchi, G. and Pernici, B. (1985). "Specification of Control Aspects in Office Information Systems," Proc. Conference on Theoretical and Formal Aspects of Information Systems, Sitges, Spain, April.

Cashman, P.M. (1985). "An Overview of XCP: A System for Supporting Coordinated Work," Office Automation Conference, AFIPS, Atlanta, Georgia, February, pp. 69-73.

Chang, J.-M. and Chang, S.-K. (1982). "Database Alerting Techniques for Office Activities Management," IEEE Transactions on Communications, COM-30, 1, January.

Chang, S.-K. (ed.) (1984). Management and Office Information Systems, Plenum Press, New York and London.

Cortese, G. and Sirovich, F. (1984). "A Daemon-Based Programming System for Office Procedures," Conf. on Office Information Systems, Toronto, June, pp. 203-211.

Croft, W.B. and Lefkowitz, L.S. (1984). "Task Support in an Office System," ACM Trans. on Office Information Systems, 2, 3, July, pp. 197-212.

Croft, W.B. and Thompson, R.H. (1984). "The Use of Adaptive Search Strategies in Document Retrieval Systems," in Research and Development in Information Retrieval, C.J. van Rijsbergen (ed.), pp. 95-111.

Ellis, C.A. and Bernal, M. (1982). "OFFICETALK-D: An Experimental Office Information System," Conf. on Office Information Systems, Philadelphia, PA, June, pp. 131-141.

Ferrans, J.C. (1982). "SEDL - A Language for Specifying Integrity Constraints on Office Forms," Proc. ACM Conf. on Office Information Systems, Philadelphia, pp. 123-130.

Fox, M.S. (1981). "The Intelligent Management System. An Overview," Intelligent Systems Laboratory, The Robotics Institute, Carnegie-Mellon University, Pittsburgh, PA.

Hogg, J., Mazer, M., Gamvrouls, S. and Tsichritzis, D. (1983). "Imail - An Intelligent Mail System," in Data Base Engineering, W. Kim, D. Ries, F.H. Lochovsky (eds.), 2, IEEE Computer Society Press, pp. 167-182.

Kogan, D. (1984). "The Manager's Assistant, an Application of Knowledge Management," IEEE Conf. on Database Engineering, Los Angeles, CA, April.

Konsynski, B.R., Bracker, L.C. and Bracker, W.E. Jr. (1982). "A Model for Specification of Office Communications," IEEE Transactions on Communications, COM-30, 1, January.

Kumano, K., Nagai, Y. and Hattori, M. (1982). "MACROS: An Office Application Generator," in Management and Office Information Systems, S.-K. Chang (ed.), Plenum Press, New York and London, pp. 369-384.

Lochovsky, F.H. (1983). "A Knowledge-Based Approach to Support Office Work," in Data Base Engineering, W. Kim, D. Ries, and F.H. Lochovsky (eds.), 2, IEEE Computer Society Press, pp. 43-51.

Sarin, S. and Greif, I. (1984). "Software for Interactive On-Line Conferences," Conf. on Office Information Systems, Toronto, June, pp. 46-58.

Tsichritzis, D.C. (1982). "Form Management," Communications of the ACM, 25, 7.

Zisman, M.D. (1978). "Use of Production Systems for Modeling Asynchronous, Concurrent Processes," Pattern Directed Inference Systems, Academic Press.

Zloof, M.M. (1981). "QBE/OBE: A Language for Office and Business Automation," Computer, May.

Zloof, M.M. (1982). "Office-By-Example: A Business Language that Unifies Data and Word Processing and Electronic Mail," IBM Systems Journal, 21, 3.

9. AN EVENTS ACCOUNTING FOUNDATION FOR DSS IMPLEMENTATION*

Eric L. Denna and William E. McCarthy
Department of Accounting
Michigan State University
East Lansing, Mich. 48824, U.S.A.

ABSTRACT

This paper describes an implementation of an events accounting system which was specifically designed to facilitate the use
of its disaggregated data in support of various intelligence,
design, and choice decisions in a manufacturing environment.
The system also models the processing of normal accounting data
and reports, but it does so by materializing chart of account
classifications exclusively with procedures (as opposed to conventional general ledger systems which rely primarily on declarative features). The particular implementation described herein
uses a relational data base foundation, and its decision support
is effected with a variety of microcomputer facilities, such as
spreadsheets and graphics. The paper concentrates first on
describing the derivation of data-modelled relations in accordance with an REA accounting framework. It then proceeds with
a description of the DSS framework used and the correspondence
of various components of this implementation with elements of
that framework. The paper concludes with an assessment of
problems encountered and an enumeration of future plans for more
complete integration of accounting systems with marketing,
materials, and logistics planning systems.

1. INTRODUCTION

According to Keen [1976], the concept of <u>decision support
systems</u> (DSS) is based on several assumptions about the role of
the computer in effective decision making [Davis and Olson,
1985, pp. 368-369]:

---

*Support for the computer implementation described in this
paper was provided by The Touche Ross Foundation through its
Aid to Accounting Education Program.

1. The computer must <u>support</u> the manager but not replace his or her judgement. It should therefore neither try to provide the "answers" nor impose a predefined sequence of analysis.

2. The main payoff of computer support is for <u>semi-structured</u> problems, where parts of the analysis can be systematized for the computer, but where the decision maker's insight and judgement are needed to control the process.

3. Effective problem solving is <u>interactive</u> and is enhanced by a dialog between the user and the system. The user explores the problem situation using the analytic and information-providing capabilities of the system as well as human experience and insights.

The DSS idea of <u>interactive</u> <u>support</u> for <u>semistructured</u> decision makers is in sharp contrast to what most managers would consider the orientation of computerized <u>accounting</u> systems where the emphasis traditionally has been on the provision of narrow, historical data for precisely defined needs. However, much of the information accountants gather does provide at least partial support for unstructured decisions, and we intend to propose in this paper that the extent of that support could be broadened if the accounting systems in question could be designed differently. More specifically, we will present a small prototype of a <u>semantically modelled</u> accounting information system which presently is being implemented with the relational data base system Knowledge Manager [Holsapple and Whinston, 1984]. Knowledge Manager (or KMAN as we will refer to it from this point on) is actually much more comprehensive in scope than most data base systems, because it contains integrated capabilities for spreadsheet processing, text editing, graphics, and forms management as well as capabilities for a complete range of both navigational and specificational [Tsichritzis and Lochovsky, 1982] data base language operations. Holsapple and Whinston [1984] have proposed KMAN as an ideal candidate for the problem processing system (PPS) component of a generalized DSS, and we will be looking at those capabilities in this paper in the context of a wide-ranging accounting example.

The remainder of this paper is organized as follows. In the next section, we will be looking at the conceptual structure of an accounting information system implemented on KMAN. Following that, we will explain how the set of base relations used in this prototype was derived with the REA model [McCarthy, 1982] as a guide and how those relations were used to materialize a normal set of financial statement accounts. At that point, we will have explained a working accounting system, and we will proceed by exploring the use of this small prototype in the development of some sample DSS. In our conclusion, we will comment on the future directions of this implementation.

2. CONCEPTUAL STRUCTURE OF AN ACCOUNTING INFORMATION SYSTEM

In their book on management information systems, Davis and Olson define the conceptual structure of an information system (see, for example, Figure 1) as follows:

> ... a federation of functional subsystems, each of which is divided into four major information processing components: transaction processing, operational control information system support, managerial control information system support, and strategic planning information system support. Each of the functional subsystems of the information system has some unique data files which are used only by that subsystem. There are also files which need to be accessed by more than one application and need to be available for general retrieval. These files are organized into a general database managed by a database management system.
>
> A further amplification of the structure is the introduction of common software. In addition to application programs written especially for each subsystem, there are common applications which serve multiple functions. Each subsystem has linkages to those common applications. There are also many analytical and decision models that can be used by many applications. These form the model base for the information system. [Davis and Olson, 1985, pp. 45-47]

The prototype accounting information system and decision support facility which we are building with KMAN can be explained well with the terms of the Figure 1 structure. Applicable components are outlined below.

The application software for each subsystem consisted of programs written in both procedural and relational languages. In contrast to most batch oriented accounting systems, our transaction processing programs were written for on-line entry using the forms definition facility of KMAN. The

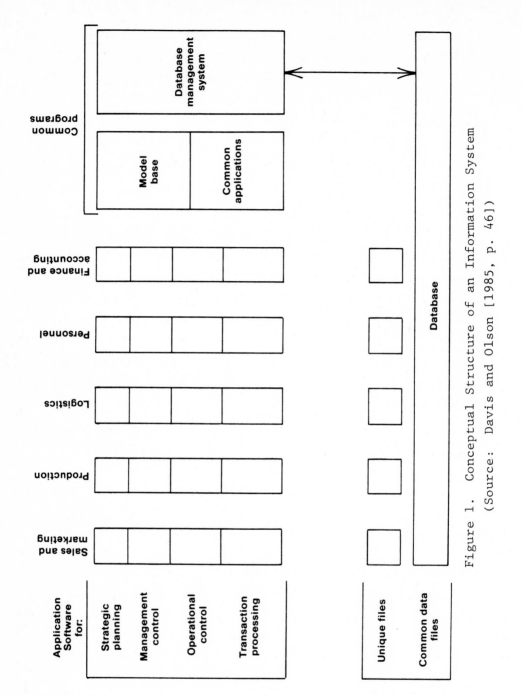

Figure 1. Conceptual Structure of an Information System
(Source: Davis and Olson [1985, p. 46])

operational control, management control, and strategic planning software consisted of spreadsheets, report generators, graphics generators, and ad hoc retrievals written for each area.

The model base consisted of spreadsheet programs or data generation programs (such as time series analysis and correlation or extrapolation techniques) which are used by more than one subsystem.

The common applications were the programs which ranged across the separate subsystems to gather the general ledger data and produce the financial statements.

The data base management system was Knowledge Manager.

The common data files were the relations generated using conceptual data modelling and the REA [McCarthy, 1982, 1984] framework. These are referred to as base tables.

The unique files were the views or "virtual relations" which we derived from the base relations procedurally whenever required.

With the major exception of the base tables, views, and application software needed to materialize the general ledger, we have implemented only part of some of the components mentioned above. We plan to implement everything, but time constraints dictate that the more novel features be addressed first. For example, having once demonstrated KMAN's facility with form-driven input, we simply filled in the rest of the accounting events.

The feature that differentiates the information system prototype illustrated in Figure 1 from a conventional accounting system is the integrated nature of its transaction processing capabilities and its decision support capabilities -- a feature due both to the integrated software used and to the method of data base design employed. The nature of that design process and the closely allied concept of events accounting are explained next.

3. EVENTS ACCOUNTING AND DATA BASE DESIGN WITH THE REA ACCOUNTING MODEL

3.1. Events Accounting

In very general terms, the concept of events accounting [Sorter, 1969; McCarthy, 1981] indicates a movement:

- away from the idea of an accountant as a person who observes the economic activities of an enterprise, records those observations as data, and then summarizes and interprets that data for interested parties, and
- toward the idea of an accountant as a person who observes and records economic activity and then simply leaves the resulting data to be interpreted by interested users.

As many computer scientists will realize, this events approach corresponds very closely to a movement in fields such as artificial intelligence and data base management called conceptual modelling [Sowa, 1984; Brodie et al., 1984; Kent, 1978]. Conceptual modelling has as its fundamental tenet the realization that the closer one can make the machine conceptualization of reality to the human conceptualization, the more useful and stable will be any information system built on that machine conceptualization. In data base management, the growing importance of conceptual modelling is reflected in the increasing attention given to semantic and infological data models [Tsichritzis and Lochovsky, 1982].

Semantic data models and events accounting systems have the same overall objective in that they both endeavor to construct man-made representations of real world phenomena. That portion of the real world that a particular designer is trying to capture is normally called the object system, and in accounting, this object system is usually a business enterprise. It is very natural then to use data-modelled concepts as the basis for user-interpreted accounting information systems. The most recent and comprehensive of these conceptual accounting frameworks is McCarthy's REA accounting model, and it was this particular framework which we used in our KMAN implementation for derivation of the common data file component of the information system prototype.

3.2. The REA Accounting Model

The declarative structure of the REA accounting model is
shown in Figure 2. The individual elements of this structure
were derived by McCarthy [1982] via a semantic analysis of
chart of account structures in a typical general ledger and via
an overall analysis of the writings of accounting theorists
such as Ijiri [1975] and Mattessich [1964]. REA components are
characterized with Chen's [1976], McCarthy's [1979] Entity-
Relationship (E-R) semantic data model. Roles of each entity
within a relationship are illustrated also.

Figure 2 represents a prototypical instance [Borgida et al.,
1984] of the concept of an accounting transaction or event. As
the reader can see, each of these events normally requires both
an inside and outside agent to act as parties to the transaction,
and the event itself normally results in either an inflow or an
outflow of resources into an enterprise. If the concept of
economic event was instantiated in a retail company with sale,
the outside and inside parties could be customer and salesperson
respectively. The economic resource involved (in this case an
outflow) would be some kind of inventory. Each event which
results in an outflow of resources to the enterprise is required
to be coupled to an event which results in an inflow and vice-
versa. The matching event in the case of the sale transaction
would be a cash receipt which the customer would normally remit
at a later date. The constraint and procedural aspects of the
REA framework are explored in other papers [Gal and McCarthy,
1983, 1985b, 1985c; McCarthy, 1984].

3.3. The Enterprise Modelling Process

For our KMAN implementation, we chose a simple manufacturing
enterprise as the object system. This enterprise buys raw
materials from various vendors and then converts those raw materials into finished goods in a manufacturing process which uses
extensive amounts of employee labor and which needs certain
machines and other factory facilities. The finished goods are
sold to customers by salespeople. This particular enterprise
has a number of other employees, and it incurs a number of other

246

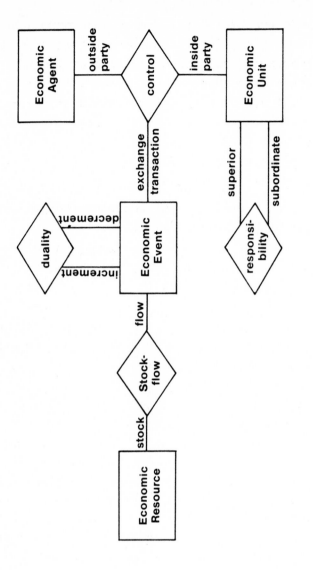

Figure 2. The REA Accounting Model
(Source: Adapted from McCarthy [1982, p. 564])

operating expenses such as rent and advertising.

The process of designing a data base begins with requirements analysis [Lum et al., 1979]. In our events system, this was a relatively uncomplicated step because we deliberately circumscribed the set of economic phenomena to be modelled in an effort to get the prototype implemented. The set of transactions which we used as a test case are given in Appendix 1 of [Denna and McCarthy, 1985].

After requirements analysis, data base design proceeds with the conceptual modelling of the enterprise. This process can be divided into the two steps explained below: view modelling and view integration.

View modelling takes the list of data elements which either an individual program or an individual decision maker needs for a particular task, and it then characterizes those data elements in terms of a particular semantic model. This list of data elements could come from documentation of the existing system (such as a data store on a data flow diagram [Demarco, 1979]), or it could be derived using other requirements elicitation techniques (such as business systems planning or critical success factor identification [Martin, 1982]).

In an REA-modelled environment, the list of data elements in a view is interpreted semantically in terms of the prototypical event instance illustrated in Figure 2. We have included an example of such an interpretation in Figure 3 for a view of labor operation processing. The economic events, agents, and resources along with their accompanying attributes are recast in an entity-relationship diagram. We have augmented in Figure 3 the basic E-R diagramming methods with conventions introduced by Atzeni et al. [1983] and Howe [1983] which illustrate attributes of entities as circles (filled-in circles are keys) and participation by entities in a relationship as either obligatory (dot inside the box) or non-obligatory (dot outside the box).

View integration takes all of the individual E-R diagrams derived above and combines them into one enterprise model. This is a very complicated step which necessitates much detailed work

248

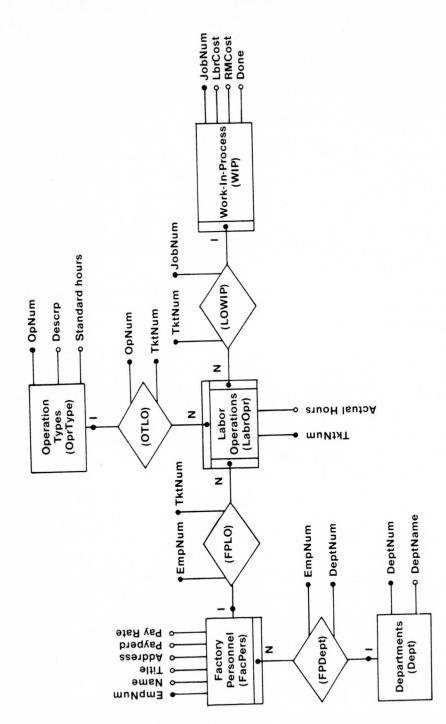

Figure 3.   Instantiation of REA Template

such as the resolution of naming and ownership inconsistencies.
However, for our purposes in this paper, we can describe it at
a more abstract level as a process of linking individual event
templates together. For example, the outflow event sale could
be linked to the inflow event received as economic compensation
for it: cash receipt. Additionally, since sale is an outflow
of finished goods inventory, it would become linked to the inflow
event for that resource which in this case would be a job operation that transfers work-in-process to finished goods. An
example E-R model which illustrates some of this integration is
given as Figure 4. After much of this linking is finished, an
additional step is performed which constructs generalization
hierarchies for those separate entity sets which need to be considered collectively for some type of information processing.
For example in our manufacturing object system, we kept separate
classes of employees and inventory as different base tables,
but we combined them together into one superset for processing
such as payroll [Smith and Smith, 1977].

View modelling and integration are much more complex operations than the brief descriptions given above would indicate,
but the discussions do give an appreciation for the use of the
REA framework in these processes. Formulation of the data base
system proceeds from this point with implementation design and
physical data base design, two additional steps for which we
also will limit our discussions to germane features of our particular KMAN implementation.

Implementation design entails tailoring the semantic model
derived in view integration to the particular data base system
to be used. In our case, this meant deriving relations from
E-R models. This was very straightforward for us, because we
were dealing with a limited quantity of data. In a more realistic events setting however, complex issues such as temporal
aggregation of data and non-implementation of certain entities
and relationships would have to be addressed. Additional organizational implementation issues such as the division of the
enterprise model into subject data bases would also have to be
considered [Martin, 1982]. A list of the relations used in our

250

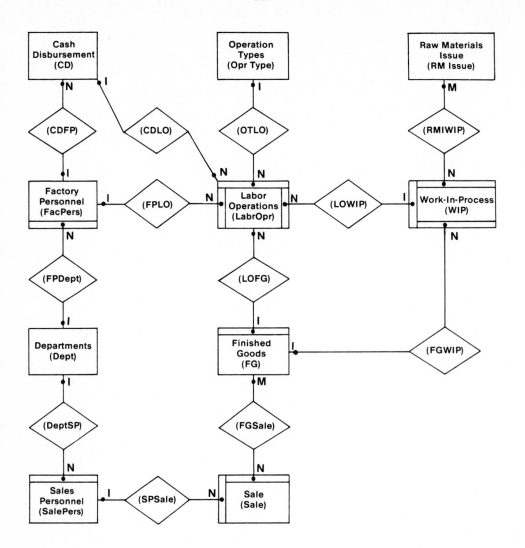

Figure 4.   Integration of REA Views in Manufacturing

implementation is included in Appendix 2 of [Denna and McCarthy, 1985].

Physical data base design involves choices such as the selection of access paths and indices. Most of the issues here are not relevant to our discussion.

At this point, we are finished describing our enterprise modelling process. We are reminded again that a much more thorough data modelling effort would be needed to deal with the complexity of an actual enterprise [Martin, 1983, p. 688], but the descriptions here sufficiently characterize our prototype.

3.4. Materialization of Account Balances and Statements

In terms of the conceptual structure of an information system illustrated in Figure 1, the data base design process described above would produce the common data files or the base tables implemented in KMAN. In this section of the paper, we will explain our use of the unique files (which were views or virtual relations) and our use of the common applications (which were the programs to gather the general ledger and produce the financial statements).

The concept of events accounting requires that the corporate store of accounting data be kept in a conceptually modelled data base which captures as naturally as possible the essence of the enterprise being tracked. Therefore predefined aggregations of data are to be avoided as much as possible, because they are biased toward the perspective of the designer or decision maker doing the aggregation. Again, this is a philosophy that events accounting shares with semantic modelling, although it is certainly true that some interpretations and representation trade-off decisions will always have to be made.

In our accounting prototype system, we decided to operationalize this philosophy by relegating (as much as possible) any processed data to views [Date, 1981] or virtual relations. Thus, we tried to define base tables only for those objects which seemed to model directly some aspect of the real world. We realize that this is an impossible objective given the problems of "relativism" [Hammer and McLeod, 1981; Winograd, 1975] (i.e., one person's entity is another's relationship is another's attribute is another's procedure ... etc.). However, as a philosophy of design, we believe that this approach has merit because it always causes a designer to look for the solution which has the closest correspondence to the underlying object system.

KMAN does not provide a view definition facility explicitly (neither do most other data base systems), so we had to implement our views with a technique that invoked a procedure which first deleted the view's extension (that is, the occurrence data or the actual rows in a data base table) and then repopulated that extension with another procedure. This same technique was used by Gal and McCarthy in a QBE data base implementation, and readers interested in more detail can refer to [Gal and McCarthy, 1985a].

The structure chart or procedure hierarchy which we used for the one application which ranged across all of our functional areas is shown in Figure 5. This application materialized the chart of accounts for our sample enterprise, and its final output was a view (or virtual table) which listed all of our account balances. The structure of this procedure hierarchy was based on one developed by McCarthy [1984] from the conceptual accounting framework project of the Financial Accounting Standards Board [1980]. With the events accounting emphasis on disaggregate and uninterpreted data, all of the account balances used for our general ledger were always current as of the last transaction occurrence, because they were materialized only as needed. After materialization, they were either displayed or passed to KMAN's form facility to be printed in the form of financial statements such as an income statement or a balance sheet. Some of the programs used in the general ledger derivation are reproduced in Appendix 3 of [Denna and McCarthy, 1985].

In addition to the general ledger materialization programs, there were other KMAN procedures written to perform accounting functions. There were form-oriented transaction entry procedures, and there were programs written to materialize generalization

253

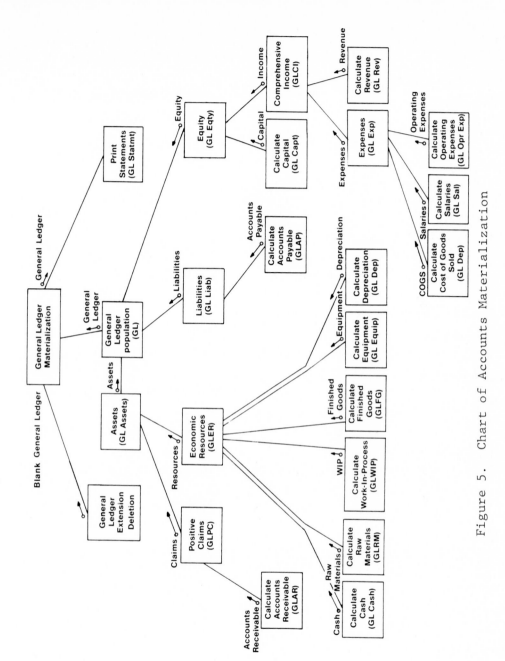

Figure 5. Chart of Accounts Materialization

hierarchies for processing (such as employees for payroll). We also found it necessary to program some data base triggers [Eswaran, 1976] to account for items such as an increase in quantity on hand for finished goods upon the completion of a factory job in process.

This discussion of account materialization concludes our treatment of the events accounting aspects of our data base design. In the next section of the paper, we will discuss the implications of this type of structure on DSS development, especially as it relates to the capabilities of a generalized problem processing system like KMAN.

4. DSS USE OF AN EVENTS MODEL

4.1. Introduction

Although there are certainly many different ways of looking at decision support systems, we will confine ourselves to the type of situation illustrated in Figure 6 where a decision maker is using an interactive computer facility to support judgement in an environment characterized by semistructured problems. These three DSS assumptions were the same ones made at the out-set of the paper, and it is our intent at this point to discuss how such a system might work in an REA-modelled environment. As we go through these discussions, we will be pointing out implemented or planned features of our KMAN information system.

4.2. Critical Role of the Internal Data Base and the Need for an Events Approach to its Development

Simon's model of the decision-making process [Simon, 1960] consists of the three phases of intelligence, design, and choice. Although the flow of activities indicated by this model has been questioned by some, it does provide a useful means for identi-fying decision-making activities in managers. Textbook presen-tations (such as [Davis and Olson, 1985; Sprague and Carlson, 1982; Bonczek et al., 1981]) and other review discussions of DSS construction and evaluation [Lerch and Mantei, 1983] rou-tinely demonstrate the general nature of computerized decision support by first of all listing example activities (such as

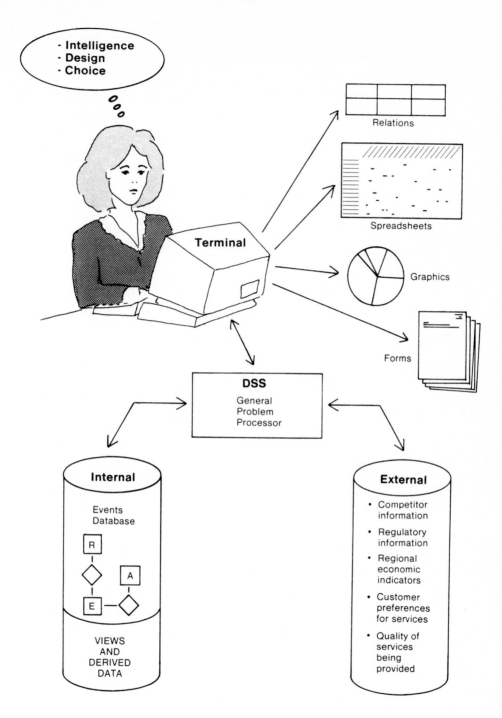

Figure 6. Events Accounting Foundation for DSS Environment

structured search and the generation of solutions) for each of these three phases and by then conjecturing on what type of computer facilities would be needed to support these activities. In all three phases, but especially in intelligence and design, the internal data base provides an essential starting point for a significant percentage of decision activity [Holsapple and Whinston, 1983]. These DSS presentations and discussions certainly point out that this support must be augmented by a data base of external information (including items such as those listed in Figure 6 [Davis and Olson, 1985, p. 44]) and by a collection of modelling techniques (such as statistical analysis and simulation). However, the necessity of these other components does not diminish the significance of a well-developed computerized store of past economic activity (such as sales, production, and financial transactions).

Although conventional accounting systems do capture data concerning economic phenomena which would be of interest to non-accounting decision makers, it is not uncommon to see discussions [Kotler, 1984; Shapiro and Kirpalani, 1984; Armitage, 1983] of these non-accounting decision activities mention the difficulties caused by accounting aggregation, classification, and allocation practices [American Accounting Association, 1969, 1971]. Suggested solutions to these problems can vary from (1) cultivation of alternative outside data sources to (2) complete reprocessing of source transactions to (3) minor manipulation of the final accounting numbers. Obviating the need for the first two of these alternatives (and the range of choices closely allied to them) is clearly the goal of a semantically-modelled events accounting system, and we have designed aspects of our KMAN prototype to show how we envision this simultaneous support of both accountants and non-accountants occurring.

In Figure 6, we have portrayed the internal data base as divided into an "events" part and a "views and derived data" part which actually correspond to what we called common data files and unique data files in Figure 1. The events data is represented as consisting of REA-modelled elements, but as we develop this prototype further, we hope to integrate this set of base tables with other base enterprise objects (such as an advertising campaign or a distribution channel). These other objects represent fundamental aspects of a corporate world to non-accounting decision makers, but they are most useful when they are portrayed in integrated fashion with related accounting entities such as sales or purchases. The views and derived data consist of elements such as our general ledger accounts which are predefined aggregations. The difference between views and derivations relates only to the periodicity of their update operations [McCarthy, 1982].

4.3. Example KMAN Operations

In Figure 6, a decision maker is portrayed engaging in the intelligence, design, and choice activities discussed earlier. Our KMAN prototype assumes again that this person is seeking support for these processes from an events-structured data base, and in that sense, our example DSS uses thus far have tended toward the "data-oriented" end of Alter's [1980] action implication spectrum. This is probably the most natural range of applications to be supported with an accounting data base, but as we proceed with development further, we expect to show some model-oriented use as well.

Also illustrated in Figure 6 is the variety of presentation methods KMAN allows for retrieval and use of relational data. These methods include presenting data in tables, presenting data as spreadsheets, presenting data in graphical terms (such as pie charts or scatter graphs), and presenting data within prespecified forms. As intimated previously, we have found this wide variety of presentation and extraction methods to be a very appealing feature of an integrated DSS support package. In our events implementation, we have tried to use our base of accounting data as a foundation upon which certain decision support activities could rely. We are, at present, still developing many support scenarios which place a hypothetical manager in decision-making settings similar to ones in which we would envision managers of our manufacturing object system finding themselves. The actual KMAN procedures and operations for some of the support scenarios which we have developed are illustrated in Appendix 4 of [Denna and McCarthy, 1985].

For presentation purposes in this present paper, we can outline some of our procedures and operations in abstract form for
a DSS example used by Sprague and Carlson: the analysis of
bad debts [Sprague and Carlson, 1982]. We assume that the
decision maker in this case works in a company similar to that
specified in our conceptual model (partially illustrated in
Figure 4), that the decision maker has access to an events data
base through an integrated DSS processor like KMAN, and that the
decision maker is interested in a wide variety of customer and
credit policies. More specifics concerning our examples in this
case can be found in Buckley and Lightner [1973], Shapiro and
Kirpalani [1984], and Kotler [1984].

1. Relational retrieval. If a manager was interested in viewing a list of customers with bad credit histories, he or
   she could be provided with such data in tabular form by
   having a relational processor (such as KMAN) join and select
   data from the tables representing customers, sales, sales
   returns and allowances, and cash receipts. A particular
   manager could apply any definition to the bad credit subset
   of customers, and that manager could also look at a wide
   variety of other customer and transaction attributes. Bad
   credit customers could also be subtyped by salesperson or
   product classes. Any manager could be given an individualized
   view of the disaggregate transaction data, and different
   concurrent views could be supported without one affecting
   the other. Tables such as these would be useful in both the
   intelligence and design phases of bad debt analysis.

2. Spreadsheet population and use. Similar to the instantiation
   of the derived tables above, disaggregate data could be used
   from an events data base to populate a spreadsheet according
   to the cell definitions of a particular manager. That particular manager could then experiment with different assumptions about credit-granting within a certain limit for overall bad debt expense. The rows and columns under such a
   scenario could represent items such as customers (grouped
   by credit risk category), aging categories for receivables

(derived from records of sales and cash receipts), or product groupings (derived from relationships linking sales to inventory). Again, such data would be most useful in the design stages of credit decisions.

3. Graphical output. Two graphical representations proposed by Sprague and Carlson [1982, p. 102] for use in the design and choice phases of bad debt analysis can be produced readily from an events data base with a DSS processor like KMAN. These representations are: (a) "A scatterplot of customers by two attributes associated with bad debts used to partition customers into risk groups" and (b) "A pie chart of percent-age of loans by customer risk groups used to evaluate the partition." The customer attributes mentioned are surrogates for the customers' character and capacity to pay obligations, and these would be available as columns in the customer relation. The pie charts would actually track receivables (rather than loans) in our example enterprise, but the DSS principles would be the same. As mentioned above, receivables are obtainable from relations representing customers and the various economic events of customers.

5. CONCLUSION

Although we are only partially done with the construction of our events accounting prototype, we feel confident that the rest of this project will demonstrate clearly the benefits of an events basis for DSS construction and use. Knowledge Manager's abilities to perform a wide variety of aggregation and analysis tasks while simultaneously handling a full range of relational data base operations make it an excellent tool for our project, and we hope to enhance those capabilities even further with development of more complete and realistic cases.

In our future work, we intend to concentrate on the develop-ment of a general model base which will allow a decision maker to do extrapolation and forecasting on the basis of economic event sets. The computational methods for such generation tech-niques are straightforward, and it only remains to make their use simple for decision makers. We also would like to try to integrate our internal data bases with some outside data and to store the results in views for possible DSS use. And finally, we would like to build up our set of base tables further and to see if the ideas of events accounting can be more fully integrated with models and data from the areas of manufacturing, marketing, and distribution.

REFERENCES

Alter, S. (1980). <u>Decision Support Systems: Current Practice and Continuing Challenges</u>, Addison-Wesley.

American Accounting Association (1969). "Report of Committee on Managerial Decision Models," <u>The Accounting Review</u> (Supplement 1969), pp. 43-76.

American Accounting Association (1971). "Report of the Committee on Non-Financial Measures of Effectiveness," <u>The Accounting Review</u> (Supplement 1971), pp. 164-211.

Armitage, H.M. (1983). "Toward an Improved Distribution Accounting Information System Through an Entity-Relationship Modeling Approach," Ph.D. Dissertation, Michigan State University.

Atzeni, P., Batini, C., Lenzerini, M. and Villanelli, F. (1983). "INCOD: A System for Conceptual Design of Data and Transactions in the Entity-Relationship Model," in <u>Entity-Relationship Approach to Information Modeling and Analysis</u>, P. Chen (ed.), North-Holland, pp. 379-414.

Bonczek, R., Holsapple, C.W. and Whinston, A.B. (1981). <u>Foundations of Decision Support Systems</u>, Academic Press.

Borgida, A., Mylopoulos, J. and Wong, H.K.T. (1984). "Generalization/Specialization as a Basis for Software Specification," in <u>On Conceptual Modelling</u>, M. Brodie, J. Mylopoulos and J. Schmidt (eds.), Springer-Verlag, pp. 87-114.

Brodie, M.L., Mylopoulos, J. and Schmidt, J.W. (eds.) (1984). <u>On Conceptual Modelling</u>, Springer-Verlag.

Buckley, J.W. and Lightner, K.M. (1973). <u>Accounting: An Information Systems Approach</u>, Dickenson Publishing.

Chen, P.P. (1976). "The Entity-Relationship Model -- Toward a Unified View of Data," <u>ACM Transactions on Database Systems</u>, March, pp. 9-36.

Davis, G.B. and Olson, M. (1985). <u>Management Information Systems</u>, McGraw-Hill, Inc.

Date, C.J. (1981). _An Introduction to Database Systems_, 3rd ed., Addison-Wesley.

Demarco, T. (1979). _Structured Analysis and System Specification_, Prentice-Hall.

Denna, E.L. and McCarthy, W.E. (1985). "An Events Accounting Foundation for DSS Implementation," Working Paper, Department of Accounting, Michigan State University.

Eswaran, K.P. (1976). "Aspects of a Trigger Subsystem in an Integrated Database System," _Proceedings of Second International Conference on Software Engineering_, IEEE, pp. 243-250.

Financial Accounting Standards Board (1980). _Statement of Financial Accounting Concepts No. 3: Elements of Financial Statements of Business Enterprises_, FASB.

Gal, G. and McCarthy, W.E. (1983). "Declarative and Procedural Features of a CODASYL Accounting System," in _Entity-Relationship Approach to Information Modeling and Analysis_, P. Chen (ed.), North-Holland, pp. 197-213.

Gal, G. and McCarthy, W.E. (1985a). "Operation of a Relational Accounting System," _Advances in Accounting_, forthcoming.

Gal, G. and McCarthy, W.E. (1985b). "Specification of Internal Accounting Controls in a Database Environment," _Computers and Security_, March, pp. 23-32.

Gal, G. and McCarthy, W.E. (1985c). "An Artificial Intelligence Framework for Conceptual Specification and Evaluation of Internal Control," Paper presented at National TIMS-ORSA Meeting, April.

Hammer, M. and McLeod, D. (1981). "Database Description with SDM: A Semantic Database Model," _ACM Transactions of Database Systems_, September, pp. 351-386.

Holsapple, C.W. and Whinston, A.B. (eds.) (1983). _Data Base Management: Theory and Applications_, D. Reidel Publishing Company.

Holsapple, C.W. and Whinston, A.B. (1984). "Building Blocks for Decision Support Systems," _Proceedings of the NYU Symposium: New Directions for Database Systems_, New York, NY, pp. 121-164.

Howe, D.R. (1983). _Data Analysis for Data Base Design_, Edward Arnold.

Ijiri, Y. (1975). _Theory of Accounting Measurement_, American Accounting Association.

Keen, P.G.W. (1976). "'Interactive' Computer Systems for Managers: A Modest Proposal," _Sloan Management Review_, Fall.

Kent, W. (1978). Data and Reality, North-Holland.

Kotler, P. (1984). Marketing Management: Analysis, Planning and Control, Fifth Edition, Prentice-Hall.

Lerch, F.J. and Mantei, M. (1983). "A Framework for Computer Support in Managerial Decision Making," in Proceedings of the Fifth Conference on Information Systems, L. Maggi, J. King and K. Kraemer (eds.), ICIS, pp. 129-139.

Lum, V., Ghosh, S., Schkolnick, M., Jefferson, D., Su, S., Fry, J., Teorey, T. and Yao, B. (1979). "1978 New Orleans Data Base Design Workshop Report," Research Report RJ2554, IBM Research Laboratories, San Jose.

Martin, J. (1982). Strategic Data-Planning Methodologies, Prentice-Hall.

Martin, J. (1983). Managing the Data-Base Environment, Prentice-Hall.

Mattessich, R. (1964). Accounting and Analytical Methods, Richard D. Irwin.

McCarthy, W.E. (1979). "An Entity-Relationship View of Accounting Models," The Accounting Review, October, pp. 667-686.

McCarthy, W.E. (1981). "Multidimensional and Disaggregate Accounting Systems: A Review of the 'Events' Accounting Literature," MAS Communication, July, pp. 7-13.

McCarthy, W.E. (1982). "The REA Accounting Model: A Generalized Framework for Accounting Systems in a Shared Data Environment," The Accounting Review, July, pp. 554-578.

McCarthy, W.E. (1984). "Materialization of Account Balances in the REA Accounting Model," Invited Presentation to the British Accounting Association, Norwich, England, April.

Shapiro, S. and Kirpalani, V. (1984). Marketing Effectiveness: Insights from Accounting and Finance, Allyn and Bacon, Inc.

Simon, H.A. (1960). The New Science of Management Decision, Harper and Brothers.

Smith, J.M. and Smith, D.C.P. (1977). "Database Abstractions: Aggregation and Generalization," ACM Transactions on Database Systems, June, pp. 105-133.

Sorter, G.H. (1969). "An 'Events' Approach to Basic Accounting Theory," The Accounting Review, January, pp. 12-19.

Sowa, J.F. (1984). Conceptual Structures: Information Processing in Mind and Machine, Addison-Wesley.

263

Sprague, R. and Carlson, E. (1982). <u>Building Effective Decision Support Systems</u>, Prentice-Hall.

Tsichritzis, D.C. and Lochovsky, F.H. (1982). <u>Data Models</u>, Prentice-Hall.

Winograd, T. (1975). "Frame Representations and the Declarative-Procedural Controversy," in <u>Representation and Understanding</u>, D.G. Bobrow and A. Collins (eds.), Academic Press.

10. AUDITING, ARTIFICIAL INTELLIGENCE AND EXPERT SYSTEMS*

Andrew D. Bailey, Jr.
Academic Faculty of Accounting
and Management Information Systems
The Ohio State University
Columbus, Ohio 43210-1399, U.S.A.

Rayman D. Meservy
Accounting and Information Systems
Carnegie-Mellon University
Pittsburgh, PA 15213, U.S.A.

Gordon L. Duke, Paul E. Johnson and William Thompson
University of Minnesota
Minneapolis, Minnesota 55455, U.S.A.

1. INTRODUCTION

This paper will provide the reader with an introduction to the field of financial auditing and the applicability of Decision Support Systems (DSS), Artificial Intelligence (AI), and Expert Systems (ES) to that field of endeavor. The paper will also discuss a continuing research project concerning the application of DSS/AI/ES techniques to the evaluation of internal accounting controls. The reader will find that the evaluation of internal accounting controls is a critical step in every financial audit and that it is an area in which the auditor exhibits substantial expertise. It is thus an area of work particularly suited to the application of expert systems technology.

The current research group members each bring special and necessary inputs to the project and in some sense represent our attitude toward work in these areas. We have representatives from the functional areas of accounting and auditing, psychology and computer science. We believe that this interdisciplinary approach is the only way to assure that relevant questions are addressed within the context of the most current research and practice results from the underlying disciplines.

---

* We would like to thank the public accounting firm of Peat, Marwick, Mitchell & Co., the McKnight Foundation, and the Artificial Intelligence Research Center of the University of Minnesota for their support. The paper represents the authors' beliefs and not those of the organizations noted above.

The specific issue addressed by the current research concerns the auditors' evaluation of internal accounting controls. Part of the current research team has been involved with the question for some time. An earlier project reported at an earlier NATO conference worked under the acronym, TICOM, or The Internal COntrol Model. TICOM is a computer supported description and evaluation system for accounting internal controls. While TICOM is based on AI concepts, it does not act as an ES, but rather as a DSS, providing basic information about the internal controls, but leaving all judgements to the auditor [Bailey et al., 1983].

The current research concentrates on the complete process of developing an expert system, but focuses most heavily on the cognitive science issues. Various methods of assessing the auditors' judgement processes are used in order to build the knowledge base. An expert system shell known as GALEN is used to build a computational model of the resulting process. GALEN was developed at the University of Minnesota by two of the authors [Moen, 1984]. The resulting computational model will then be validated using several validation approaches. While this research is a direct outgrowth of the previous TICOM project, TICOM does not form an integral part of this study, as this study concentrates on the cognitive aspects of the auditors' expertise. TICOM will be introduced at a later date as part of the knowledge base of the resulting computational model when the project enters its field development stage.

Our results to date are very encouraging. We are confident that the auditors do exhibit the necessary expertise in making internal control judgements and that that expertise can be represented in a computational model. This paper will present the nature of our research effort, the resulting model structure and the results obtained to date. A complete computational model is not yet available.

The rest of this paper is composed of five sections. Section 2 presents the structure of the financial auditing function and the potential aspects in which DSS/AI/ES techniques may contribute to that function. Section 3 discusses the extant research relevant in extending the expert systems work to auditing and

accounting. Section 4 details the current research effort
in understanding the auditors' judgements processes in evaluating
internal accounting controls for auditing purposes and in building a computational model of that process. Section 5 presents
the preliminary results of that effort and Section 6 concludes
with suggestions for future research efforts in auditing and
expert systems.

2. THE AUDITING FUNCTION AND THE APPLICABILITY OF DSS/AI/ES

This section will introduce the reader to the basic definitions, objectives and structure of the financial audit. We assume
a low level of specific knowledge about the audit process when
making this presentation. For those readers familiar with the
topic, we ask your patience. We believe that to appreciate the
need for DSS/AI/ES techniques in the auditing context and more
particularly to understand the importance of the internal accounting controls issues, the reader must have a sense of the
full audit context. We will attempt to point out likely application areas for DSS/AI/ES techniques as we present this material,
but will expand on these points in the next section.

While accounting and auditing are related, they are distinctly
different activities. "The primary purpose [of accounting] is
'to provide quantitative information primarily financial in
nature, about economic entities that is intended to be useful in
making economic decisions.' As an information system it captures,
processes, and disseminates both externally and internally, economic information about the organization to an assortment of individuals...." Internal control issues are of significance to
accountants in order to assure the accuracy, reliability and
timeliness of the resulting reports and to conform to existing
legal requirements such as specified by the Foreign Corrupt Practices Act (FCPA) of 1977. Internal controls are intended in this
context to provide for the keeping of books, records and accounts,
which in reasonable detail, accurately and fairly reflect the
transactions of the assets of the organization. This is accomplished by devising and maintaining a system of internal control
sufficient to provide reasonable assurance that: (a) transactions

are executed in accordance with management's general and specific
authorizations; (b) transactions are recorded as necessary to
permit preparation of financial statements in conformity with
generally accepted accounting principles or other criteria applicable to such statements, and to maintain accountability for
assets; (c) access to assets is permitted only in accordance with
management's general or specific authorization; and, (d) the
recorded accountability for assets is compared with existing
assets at reasonable intervals and appropriate action is taken
with respect to differences [American Institute of Certified
Public Accountants, 1972]. In summary, accounting is involved
with the maintenance of a system capable of preparing accurate,
reliable and timely financial reports.

Auditing is a systematic process of objectively obtaining and
evaluating evidence regarding assertions about economic actions
and events to ascertain the degree of correspondence between
those assertions and established criteria and communicating the
results to interested users. This definition clearly distinguishes the accounting responsibility for the design and maintenance of systems of accounting from the function of an auditor.
The auditor in this context attempts to obtain evidence in support of the appropriateness of the design, maintenance and resulting reports produced by the accountants system. The financial audit is generally considered to be an attestation audit
designed to communicate a statement of opinion (judgement),
based upon convincing evidence, by an independent, competent,
authoritative person, concerning the degree of correspondence
in all material respects of accounting information communicated
by an entity (individual, firm, or governmental unit) with
established criteria.

The problem of established criteria is not a trivial one for
either accountants or auditors. The criteria for the financial
reports are established by the Financial Accounting Standards
Board (FASB) subject to oversight by the Securities and Exchange
Commission (SEC), the Court system and established practice. The
established criteria for the system designed to produce these
reports is less well established. In general, accepted practice

augmented by limited analysis has been the audit criteria. The
Statements on Auditing Standards provide broad guidelines for the
implementation of control systems. The following categories of
concerns are enumerated:

1. Establishment and supervision of internal accounting con-
    trol systems is a management responsibility.
2. Absolute assurance of effectiveness is probably not cost
    effective; thus, reasonable assurance is acceptable.
3. Concepts of internal control are independent of the data
    processing mechanism. (This applies to computer process-
    ing as well as manual processing of transactions.)
4. Any system of control may be compromised by error, collu-
    sion, management override, or deterioration in compliance.
5. Competent personnel of high integrity are essential to
    good internal control.
6. Segregation of functions implies that those in a position
    to perpetrate "error" should not also perform functions
    enabling them to conceal those "errors." For instance,
    those who control assets should not also control the
    accounting for assets.
7. There is a need to generate independent evidence support-
    ing valid authorization, approval, and performance of
    actions.
8. Proper documentation, recording, authorization, and
    approval of transactions must be maintained.
9. Access to assets must be limited to authorized personnel.
10. Periodic comparisons of recorded amounts to actual assets
    and follow up on deviations are essential to good internal
    control.

Based on broad guidelines of this nature as to the system
designed to capture, process and manipulate economic data for
the preparation of financial reports consistent with generally
accepted accounting principles of reporting, auditors attempt to
gather evidence about managements reports.

The evidence gathering process itself can be organized for
descriptive purposes into four basic phases as illustrated in
Figure 1: Planning and Design of the Audit Approach; Tests of

GATHERING AUDIT EVIDENCE

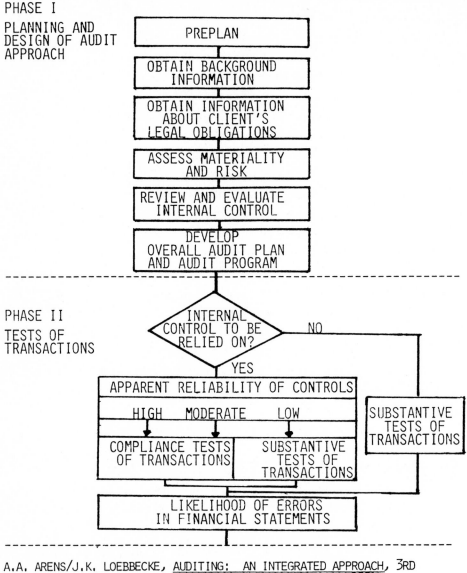

PHASE I
PLANNING AND
DESIGN OF AUDIT
APPROACH

PREPLAN

OBTAIN BACKGROUND
INFORMATION

OBTAIN INFORMATION
ABOUT CLIENT'S
LEGAL OBLIGATIONS

ASSESS MATERIALITY
AND RISK

REVIEW AND EVALUATE
INTERNAL CONTROL

DEVELOP
OVERALL AUDIT PLAN
AND AUDIT PROGRAM

PHASE II
TESTS OF
TRANSACTIONS

INTERNAL
CONTROL TO BE
RELIED ON?

NO

YES

APPARENT RELIABILITY OF CONTROLS

HIGH   MODERATE   LOW

COMPLIANCE TESTS
OF TRANSACTIONS

SUBSTANTIVE
TESTS OF
TRANSACTIONS

SUBSTANTIVE
TESTS OF
TRANSACTIONS

LIKELIHOOD OF ERRORS
IN FINANCIAL STATEMENTS

A.A. ARENS/J.K. LOEBBECKE, AUDITING: AN INTEGRATED APPROACH, 3RD
ED., PRENTICE-HALL., ENGLEWOOD CLIFFS, N.J., COPYRIGHT 1984.
ADAPTED FROM MATERIAL BY TOUCHE ROSS & CO., COPYRIGHT 1978.
REPRINTED BY PERMISSION.

Figure 1

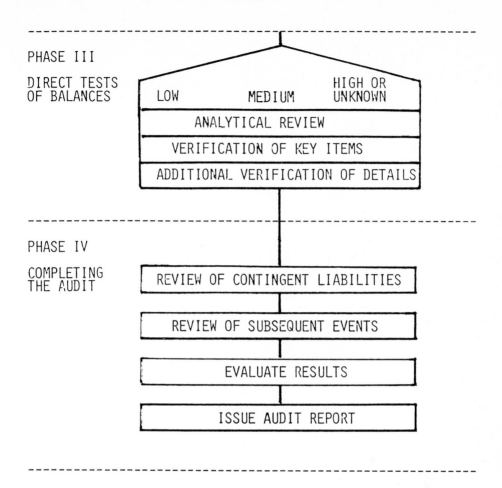

PHASE III

DIRECT TESTS
OF BALANCES

PHASE IV

COMPLETING
THE AUDIT

A.A. ARENS/J.K. LOEBBECKE, <u>AUDITING: AN INTEGRATED APPROACH</u>, 3RD
ED., PRENTICE-HALL., ENGLEWOOD CLIFFS, N.J., COPYRIGHT 1984.
ADAPTED FROM MATERIAL BY TOUCHE ROSS & CO., COPYRIGHT 1978.
REPRINTED BY PERMISSION.

Figure 1 (cont.)

Transactions; Direct Tests of Balances; and, Completing the Audit
[American Institute of Certified Public Accountants, 1972].

Within each of the basic four phases are substantially more
detailed sets of activities and judgements necessary to operationalize the process. We also recognize that this simple linear
scheme is convenient for exposition, but that the process in fact
proceeds in a much less obvious progression of events. To provide
some sense of the increasing complexity of the process consider
the "Assess materiality and risk" box with the Planning Phase of
the audit. Figures 2 and 3 are suggestive of the estimates and
judgements necessary. Both of these processes are critical to
the audit planning and implementation process and are reputed to
involve substantial auditor expertise in their evaluation. Little
objective data is available as to how auditors make these assessments or how they subsequently incorporate them into the subsequent phases of the audit.

Both of the above assessments are related to the evaluation
of internal controls, which involves substantive judgements as
suggested by Figure 4, part of the Planning process, and by
Figure 5, part of the Tests of Transactions process.

These figures allude to the complexity of the audit task,
both in terms of the number of judgements necessary and the lack
of objective, normative criteria for specifying either the judgement itself or its relationship to other parts of the audit.

The applicability of DSS/AI/ES concepts in the auditing
environment is self-evident. Audits are complex decision-making
problems well beyond the capacity of analytic solution even if
many of the judgement aspects of the audit could be reduced to
simple quantitative relationships [Bailey et al., 1981]. At
numerous points in an audit the auditor is called upon to exercise what can only be called expertise: assessing materiality
and risk for a specific client; evaluating internal control;
planning an audit based on the assessment of risk, materiality,
and other inputs; revising the plan based on results obtained
during the audit; and, choosing a final opinion.

273

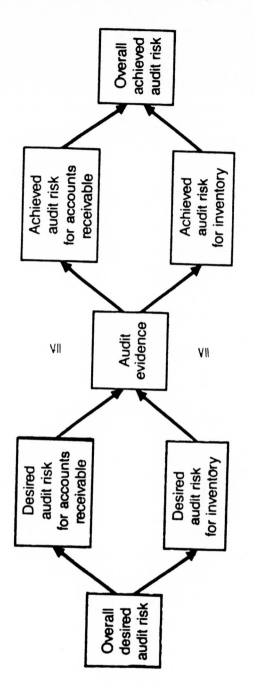

VII

VII

A.A. ARENS/J.K. LOEBBECKE, AUDITING: AN INTEGRATED APPROACH,
3RD ED., PRENTICE-HALL, INC., ENGLEWOOD CLIFFS, N.J. COPYRIGHT
1984. REPRESENTED BY PERMISSION.

Figure 2

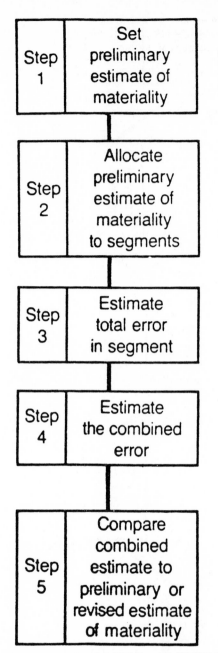

Step 1	Set preliminary estimate of materiality
Step 2	Allocate preliminary estimate of materiality to segments
Step 3	Estimate total error in segment
Step 4	Estimate the combined error
Step 5	Compare combined estimate to preliminary or revised estimate of materiality

Figure 3

275

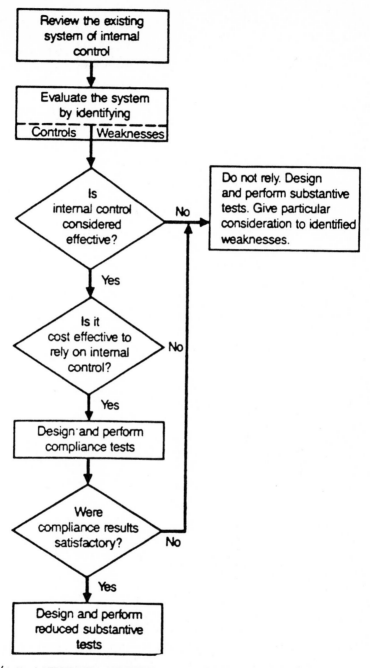

A.A. ARENS/J.K. LOEBBECKE, AUDITING: AN INTEGRATED APPROACH, 3RD ED., PRENTICE-HALL, INC., ENGLEWOOD CLIFFS, N.J. COPYRIGHT 1984. REPRESENTED BY PERMISSION.

Figure 4

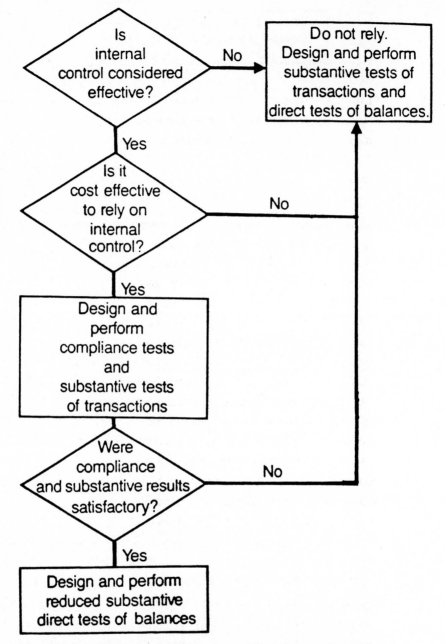

A.A. ARENS/J.K. LOEBBECKE, AUDITING: AN INTEGRATED APPROACH
3RD ED., PRENTICE-HALL, INC., ENGLEWOOD CLIFFS, N.J. COPYRIGHT
1984. REPRESENTED BY PERMISSION.

Figure 5

3. EXTANT AUDITING DSS/AI/ES APPLICATIONS

Interest in DSS/AI/ES and other computer-based decision tools
is epidemic among accountants and auditors. The Symposia on
Decision Support Systems for Auditing and Accounting at the University of Southern California attests to this fact. This section
briefly reviews the existing literature in auditing as it relates
to DSS/AI/ES.

There are many views about what should be included as DSS and
their relationship to AI and ES. While no definitive statement
of definitions and characteristics for DSS exist, the following
are indicative of many of the lists of such characteristics.

1. Computer Based -- It's possible to implement a DSS without
    a computer (certainly paper-based systems do exist), how-
    ever, it is the processing power of computer technology
    that makes most DSS practical. All of the DSS discussed
    in this paper are computer-based systems.

2. Interactive -- Interactive computer usage means that the
    computer may interrupt processing to query the user for
    input. At the same time, the computer may provide infor-
    mation on the results of processing thus far. Another
    form of interaction includes a query by the user request-
    ing additional feedback or data.

3. Data Retrieval and Manipulation -- DSS commonly support
    information access to large data banks. Information
    access may include the abilities to selectively retrieve,
    summarize and classify. In some DSS applications, such
    as data base management systems, data retrieval and
    manipulation is the main function.

4. Decision Model -- Many DSS applications have as their
    main function the implementation of a decision model. A
    decision model combines data and decision rules to sug-
    gest a course of action. A decision rule is a logical
    inequality that evaluates to either true or false or
    into some vector of results with attendant probability
    assignments.

In this paper, we use the term Decision Support Systems or

DSS in a broad sense to refer to any interactive computer application that helps a decision maker by providing access to large data banks or by implementing a decision model or both.

Artificial Intelligence (AI) has been defined by Barr and Feigenbaum [1981] as "the part of computer science concerned with designing intelligent computer systems, that is, systems that exhibit the characteristics we associate with intelligence in human behavior -- understanding language, learning, reasoning, solving problems, and so on." AI systems may use normative or optimal modelling techniques or they may mimic human decision-making processes. Furthermore, they may or may not be designed as an aid for decision makers. A sub-classification of AI is ES. Like AI, expert systems may use optimal modelling techniques or mimic human decision-making processes, and may or may not be designed as aids for decision makers. However, most ES tend to mimic the heuristics of experts.

Expert systems have been defined by Stefik et al. [1982] as "...problem-solving programs that solve substantial problems generally conceded as being difficult and requiring expertise. They are called knowledge based because their performance depends critically on the use of facts and heuristics used by experts." Feigenbaum [1978] says, "we must hypothesize from our experience to date that the problem solving power exhibited in an intelligent agent's performance is primarily a consequence of the specialist's knowledge employed by the agent, and only very secondarily related to the generality and power of the inference method employed. Our agents must be knowledge rich, even if they are methods poor." Thus, expert systems attempt to capture specific knowledge from an acknowledged expert concerning a specific problem domain and replicate the decision inference process used by this expert. In this paper, expert systems is used in a narrow sense to refer to interactive computer applications that help a decision maker by simulating the specific knowledge and inference processes used by experts in their limited domain of expertise.

Alter [1977] proposed a taxonomy of decision support systems that covers a range from data oriented to model oriented systems. We propose a three way taxonomy based on the nature of the DSS in

Auditing Applications. We arbitrarily divide the nature of the DSS into Decision Aids, Non-Expert DSS, and Expert Systems. A system was considered a decision aid for our purposes when it was insufficiently interactive to be classified as a Non-Expert DSS or ES, i.e., level of interaction was the distinguishing characteristic. At the other extreme an ES was distinguished from a Non-Expert DSS on the basis of the degree to which the DSS attempted to emulate the expert's decision processes rather than providing model based solutions to problems. This characterization, like each of the others, is flawed, but will serve our purposes in reviewing the auditing literature to date.

3.1. A Review of Auditing Decision Support Systems

Auditors have long been involved with DSS, long before the computer made its practical debut. Auditing firms are an assembly of independent professionals. In order to attain a common level of professional performance and to train new professionals in the field, auditing firms found that training programs and field decision aids could contribute substantially to improved professional judgement. The issue of measuring the improvement from an auditing context is not settled and perhaps cannot be in any definitive manner. Unlike the medical diagnosis areas where the use of ES first took hold with MYCIN [Shortliffe, 1976] or in the chemical compounds area represented by DENDRAL [Lindsay et al., 1980], in many areas of auditing there is no practical and definitive means of ascertaining the correctness of a professional judgement. In theory, an exhaustive search of the clients' records might permit an accurate assessment, but practical economics precludes such a process except very rarely. Thus the measures of success have tended to focus on professional consensus.

The development of organized methods of collecting, organizing and scoring data collected on audits was a long established practice before the computer. However, the advent of inexpensive computing has opened new horizons. As a result, virtually all of the manual aids previously used by auditors have or are being converted to computer support systems. These include the systems prepared by the major Public Accounting firms, as well as private software houses catering to the Public and Internal Auditing communities. Most of these systems concentrate on data collection from client systems, organization, analysis based on descriptive and normative models, statistical sampling methods, and workpaper control. They are, in most cases, Decision Aids, lacking the characteristics necessary to be a Non-Expert DSS. The list of such systems is an alphabet soup of acronyms including: ASK, AUDITAID, BASE, CARS, PROBE and numerous others [Weber, 1982].

These Decision Aids are computer based, but provide little interactive support, relying on the auditor to select from among the available models for data collective, organization and manipulation. Many of the Decision Aids come equipped with normative models for data analysis purposes, but do not provide a direct recommendation to the auditor or direct the auditor along new paths of inquiry.

In the last several years auditing firms have become very active in extending the capabilities of Decision Aids by adding menu-driven, interactive components to support the various audit functions. Peat, Marwick and Mitchell's SEACAS system is perhaps the earliest and best developed of these systems. Other Non-Expert Decision support systems work in auditing includes the Balachandran and Zoltners [1981] staff scheduling model, the Mock and Vertinsky [1984] risk assessment program, and several efforts in providing training systems in Bayesian revision for auditors. These systems appear to be true Non-Expert DSS, possessing the characteristics noted above, but without effective query capability and no expert analysis potential at this time.

Non-Expert DSS are part of a new wave of technological innovation in the field of auditing. Auditors accept both the technology and the potential. Within the next several years we will see numerous such systems coming on line.

AI related research in auditing starts with the work of Bailey, Gerlach and Whinston and the TICOM II project. TICOM is the acronym for the Internal Control Model. TICOM I was not based on artificial intelligence concepts, but rather on a data based model. TICOM III [Bailey et al., 1985] is the prototype operating systems of TICOM II. TICOM III is a Non-Expert DSS in that, while it employs many artificial intelligence-like analysis methods, it does not provide for an expert judgement by the system itself. This is still left to the auditor. Nevertheless, in concept TICOM differs from the previous DSS efforts in its explicit attempt to provide an intelligent analysis of a system of internal control based on the auditors' criteria and supported by a query system closely approximating the natural query processes used by auditors.

In the last few years, numerous projects have been started that attempt to apply expert systems techniques, a sub-category of AI concepts, in the development of expert systems for auditors. These include the development of TAXMAN and TAX ADVISOR [Michaelson, 1982] to provide legal tax advice. TAX ADVISOR is based on the EMYCIN [van Melle et al., 1981] shell. AUDITOR [Dungan and Chandler, 1980] is an expert system for the evaluation of the adequacy of the client's allowance for bad debts. Systems under development include ones by Braun and Chandler [1982] to aid auditors in Analytic Review, by Wright at the University of Minnesota to provide an evaluation of the bank loan credit assessments, by Hansen and Messier [1982] model for evaluating EDP Controls, and by Bailey, Duke, Johnson, Meservy and Thompson [1984] for internal control evaluation. The Peat, Marwick, Mitchell Foundation, through its Research Opportunities in Auditing (PMM/ROA) program funded several additional projects in its most recent round of awards [Peat, Marwick, Mitchell & Co., 1976].

The interest and acceleration of current activity in building DSS in auditing provides a clear indication that research and development of such systems is about to explode. The above brief discussion of systems in auditing represent only the tip of the iceberg of current interest and activity. Further, this discussion ignores the many studies necessary to the final implementation of such systems. Studies such as that of Biggs [1984] on the Going Concern judgement process, Mutchler [1984] on the issues of Subject To opinions, and numerous others facilitate the future development of DSS for auditors.

From the discussion in Section 2, it should be clear that

numerous expert judgements are necessary in an auditing context. Each of these judgements must be studied in order to gain an understanding of the auditor's judgement processes and then placed within the context of an appropriate computational model, one that uses an analysis methodology analogous to the auditor's. Fundamental research issues must be addressed in many of these areas before the development of expert systems or other DSS can be considered. Significant behavioral issues remain unresolved. In addition, new developments in artificial intelligence will be needed if the richness of the auditing situation is to be embedded in expert systems that are more than small fragments of the audit.

The rest of this section presents a short history of the development of our current research effort in this area. It covers a part of the TICOM research and an ongoing study.

3.2. The Internal Control Model-TICOM

TICOM is a computer-based analytic tool that aids the auditor to first model the internal control system and then to query the model in order to aid the auditor in evaluating the internal control system. In the context of our previous discussion, it is a Non-Expert Decision Support System. However, TICOM is based on concepts in artificial intelligence such as knowledge representation and graph simplification. It was developed to aid auditors in the design of new systems or the description of existing internal accounting control systems and to allow the auditor to query the description. The artificial intelligence properties of TICOM permit a limited analysis and evaluation of the system in response to the auditor's query.

TICOM is composed of two sets of interrelated programs, the Internal Control Description Language (ICDL) compiler and the query processor. TICOM is the first auditor decision support system designed to permit auditors to perform their traditional tasks of internal control description and evaluation while using the power of the computer in an artificial intelligence like mode. The ICDL allows the auditor to develop internal accounting control descriptions at any level of detail or aggregation, maintaining information on agents, objects, repositories and commands necessary for the description.

Agents are the actors in the system who perform a task. Individual agents or groups of agents manipulate the objects within the system. Repositories represent storage locations for objects, such as file cabinets, magnetic tapes, buildings, etc. Agents' tasks are described using one or more commands. The command list is reasonably short including: ASSIGN, MODIFY, DESTROY, TRANSFER, WAIT-FOR, PUT, GET, COPY, END-TASK, REVIEW, and the boolean IF-THEN-ELSE.

The internal representation of a TICOM system description is in the form of a bilogic directed graph showing both control and data flows. A partial ordering of the ICDL description is explicitly encoded in the internal representation. As a result, analytic procedures can operate directly on the internal representation. Analysis makes use of the concepts of contraction and simplification in order to respond to a user query.

In developing our current project, we initially intended to simply extend TICOM by adding appropriate evaluation functions based on the results of the query process. While this may seem like a natural extension to an expert system, we again encountered a difficulty which we had earlier put aside. We, in fact, did not know how the auditor arrived at an evaluation based on the results of querying the system of internal control. As a result our current efforts are directed to the cognitive aspects of the auditor's decision process in an attempt to derive the auditor employed heuristics.

TICOM is not used directly in this study. Completion of this study will, however, lead to the incorporation of TICOM as a part of the static knowledge base of any expert system dealing with the identification of internal control evaluation activity.

4. AUDITING INTERNAL CONTROLS: A COMPUTATIONAL MODEL

Researchers, as well as teachers and practitioners, are interested in the processes that experts use when making judgements and decisions. While expertise in such fields as medicine, physics, and chess have been studied intensely during the past twenty years (e.g., Kleinmutz [1968], Einhorn [1970], Elstein et al. [1978], Johnson et al. [1982]), comparatively little research has been done in the fields of business and management. Particularly in the field of auditing there is a lot of interest in how auditors make judgements.

Expertise has been defined as the "knowledge about a particular domain, understanding of domain problems, and skill about solving some of these problems" [Hayes-Roth et al., 1983]. Davis has proposed that the nature of expertise includes the ability to: (1) solve the problem; (2) explain the result; (3) learn; (4) restructure knowledge; (5) break rules; (6) determine relevance; and (7) degrade gracefully [Davis, 1982].

An expert's knowledge consists of both public and private information. Public knowledge includes the facts, theories and definitions as found in the texts and journals referenced by those studying in the domain. However, human experts also possess private information that is not found in any of the public literature. Much of this private knowledge is in the form of rules of thumb which we will refer to as heuristics. Heuristics allow experts to "make educated guesses when necessary, to recognize promising approaches to problems, and to deal effectively with errorful or incomplete data" [Hayes-Roth, 1983]. Knowledge engineers, who are concerned with the acquisition and representation of knowledge, concentrate much of their effort on the elucidation and reproduction of such "rules of expertise." Human expertise in problem solving is largely the recognition and use of heuristics. Feigenbaum emphasizes that "experience has taught us that much of this knowledge is private to the expert, not because he is unwilling to share publicly how he performs, but because he is unable. He knows more than he is aware of knowing" [Feigenbaum, 1978].

Experts hypothesize possible solutions early in the problem solving process whenever possible. In medical diagnoses, for example, it has been shown that many errors are the result of a failure to include the correct diagnoses in the early hypotheses considered. The medical profession has commonly encouraged med-

ical workup sheets, which serve to increase the number of hypotheses considered and help to avoid premature closure. Accounting firms have similarly used generalized control questionnaires
and standard audit planning worksheets to help auditors analyze
various types of exposures that may occur.

Auditors may be considered experts in performing certain
tasks. The objective of this study is to determine the processes
that auditors use in a specific audit task, formalize and implement those processes as a computational model, and then test the
model.

4.1. Auditing Internal Accounting Controls

The American Institute of Certified Public Accountants (1979)
defines internal controls as "the plan of organization and all
the coordinate methods and measures adopted within a business to
safeguard its assets, check the accuracy and reliability of its
accounting data, promote operational efficiency, and encourage
adherence to prescribed managerial policies..." (Section 320.09)
[AICPA, 1972]. Mair, Wood, and Davis in their book "Computer
Control and Audit" present the definition: "Controls act upon
things that can go wrong which, in turn, leads to the reduction
of exposure" [Mair et al., 1978]. Although all public accounting
firms evaluate controls and general guidelines have been suggested
by several different researchers [Mautz & Winjum, 1981], auditors
still have difficulty evaluating the quality of internal control
systems. Because the extent of audit work to be performed by
external auditors is determined in large part by an evaluation
of internal controls, there is a need for a more rigorous framework of internal control evaluation. Further, the Foreign
Corrupt Practices Act (1977) places particular emphasis on the
existence of, and the auditor's evaluation of internal controls.

The evaluation of internal controls has typically used such
decision support aids as flowcharts, questionnaires, and narratives concerning the client's accounting systems. After studying
the flowcharts and questionnaires, the auditor makes a judgement
as to the relative strengths and weaknesses of the internal control system. The judgement process of evaluating problems in the

system of internal controls from flowcharts and narratives is still a "subjective art" at best. Although experts can provide a novice with some logically sound methods of processing the available data, they cannot tell the novice how to evaluate the strength of an internal control system. In fact, experts themselves sometimes do not agree on what constitutes adequate control. Recently, much research has focused on judgemental consensus among auditors [Joyce and Libby, 1982 and Libby, 1981].

The weaknesses inherent in these traditional techniques have been recognized for some time by accountants and accounting firms. The last several years have witnessed the introduction of a number of new approaches intended to regularize the data collection and evaluation process. Previously referenced research suggests a greater likelihood of success on the collection side than on the evaluation side. Nevertheless, public accounting firms hope that these new approaches will lead to greater consensus in evaluating internal controls among their field auditors.

Libby has suggested that "fault trees could be constructed to indicate important potential errors and the controls designed to detect them. These trees would highlight the key controls and also focus on their interrelationships" [Libby, 1981]. The concept of a fault tree is similar to, but a naive version of, hierarchically ordered production-rules as used in current expert systems.

4.1.1. The Audit Task

The study and evaluation of internal accounting controls is a problem involving the expertise of well-trained auditors. The task of determining the presence (or absence) of accounting controls is a requirement of each and every audit performed by CPAs. The following discussion elaborates on the auditor's task in auditing internal controls. The discussions also attempt to sketch out auditor strategies in order to suggest the means by which a model of the auditor's expertise might be constructed.

The general objective in studying accounting internal controls is to satisfy the auditor's second standard of field work: "There is to be a proper study and evaluation of the existing internal control as a basis for reliance thereon and for the determination of the resultant extent of the tests to which auditing procedures are to be restricted" [AICPA, 1972]. Thus the PRIMARY purpose is to determine whether the accounting controls are strong enough to be relied upon to produce reliable financial information. If the internal controls are determined to be strong, then the scope of other audit procedures may be more restricted than when the internal controls are determined to be weak. A second objective is to provide the auditor with a basis for constructive suggestions on how to improve the client's internal accounting controls [Loebbecke and Zuber, 1980].

4.1.2. Task Expertise

The strengths and weaknesses of an internal accounting control system are evaluated by determining control objectives, identifying controls and faults from a description of the system, and then combining the controls and faults into an overall evaluation of the sufficiency with which each control objective has been met.

Controls and faults are conceptual objects that can be identified by particular recognizable patterns of data embedded within the statements describing the accounting information system. Controls are patterns of data that prevent, correct, or detect system exposures to loss or misrepresentation. These patterns may be of various sizes. Faults, however, act as "red flags" triggering auditor concerns. The identification of a fault does not necessarily indicate a system weakness as there may be offsetting controls, but the identification of a fault generally results in a search for compensating controls.

Auditor associations between specific system designs and the resulting strength of internal controls, are learned through formal education, case examples, and by performing many similar auditing tasks. These associations permit chains of deductive reasoning to be constructed connecting the structural design of the accounting system and the likely functional strengths and weaknesses of the system. This approach is called prototypic reasoning. Based on the pervasiveness of prototypic reasoning among experts and the manner in which auditing expertise is acquired, we will proceed on the assumption that auditors use prototypic reasoning [see Figures 6 through 13].

The result of the internal control evaluation task consists of: (1) a suggested list of controls for the compliance testing phase; and (2) a list of control weaknesses. The list of control weaknesses indicates significant problems discovered during the evaluation process and the resulting exposures that could occur. The auditor uses this list in establishing subsequent compensating audit steps and for interaction with management. The specific weaknesses identified are combined with the controls to determine sufficiency for each control objective, which in turn results in the auditor expanding some of the substantive tests performed later in the audit.

4.1.3. Task Difficulty

The overall system evaluation of internal accounting controls is difficult. There is no unique set of acceptable controls that is considered normative. Rather, the accounting system may be configured with numerous acceptable combinations of controls. Also, experts are unable to describe each step in the evaluation process, rather the process is normally taught by having students solve numerous case problems and provide ex post rationalizations of the analysis process followed. Behavioral studies clearly indicate that the ex post explanation often does not match the process actually followed by the expert [Nesbett and Wilson, 1977].

4.2. The Research Project

The objective of this study is to formulate and test a model of the processes employed by audit managers and partners in reviewing and evaluating internal accounting controls. Development of the model will be based on: (1) interviews with a small sample of practicing auditors; and (2) observations of these same auditors performing the internal control evaluation review task. The resulting model will be implemented as a computational model and tuned to one expert. The model output will consist of two lists: (1) recommendations for specific controls to be compliance tested; and (2) a list of control weaknesses. The model will then

CONCEPTUALIZATION

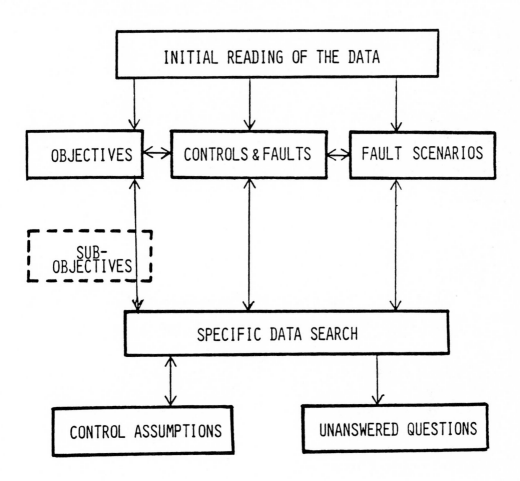

Figure 6

S C E N A R I O S

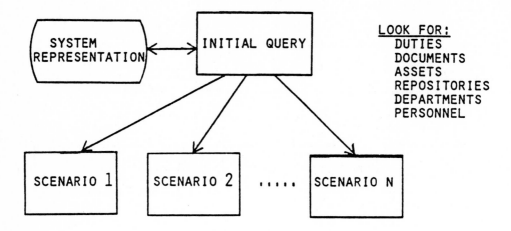

```
SYSTEM              INITIAL QUERY        LOOK FOR:
REPRESENTATION                              DUTIES
                                            DOCUMENTS
                                            ASSETS
                                            REPOSITORIES
                                            DEPARTMENTS
                                            PERSONNEL

SCENARIO 1    SCENARIO 2  .....  SCENARIO N
```

A SCENARIO IS

    A HIGH LEVEL EXPECTATION OF WHAT DOES/MAY
    HAPPEN WITHIN SOME ACCOUNTING ROUTINE.

THIS SUGGESTS LIKELY

    1. EXPOSURES
    2. CONTROL OBJECTIVES

Figure 7

CONTROL OBJECTIVES

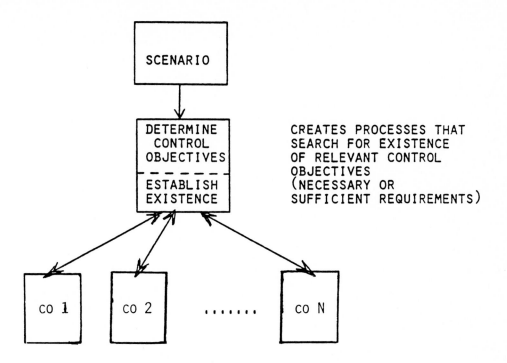

A CONTROL OBJECTIVE IS

    A HIGH LEVEL ABSTRACTION OF WHAT PROTECTIVE/DETECTIVE
DEVICES SHOULD BE USED.

CONTROL OBJECTIVES MAY BE BROKEN INTO CONTROL OBJECTIVE
    SUBGOALS.

Figure 8

CONTROL PROCEDURES

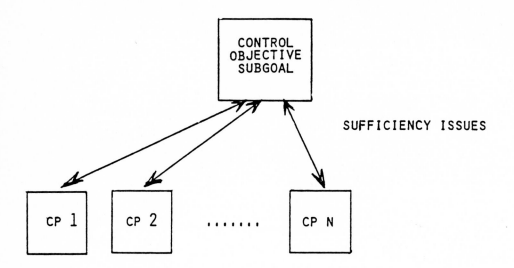

SUFFICIENCY ISSUES

CONTROL PROCEDURES

    1. LOOK FOR AN IMPLEMENTATION (A MATCHING PATTERN)

    2. ARE THE LOWEST LEVEL OF CONTROL KNOWLEDGE.

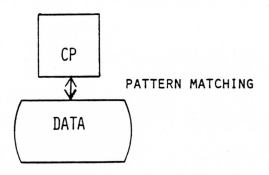

PATTERN MATCHING

Figure 9

CONTROL EXAMPLE

CONTROL OBJECTIVE: CONTROL SHOULD BE ESTABLISHED OVER
GOODS AND SERVICES AS A BASIS FOR:
1. DETERMINING AND RECORDING LIABILITY FOR
GOODS AND SERVICES RECEIVED BUT NOT RECORDED.
2. POSTING ITEM TO DETAILED INVENTORY RECORDS.

CONTROL OBJECTIVE SUBGOAL: RECEIVING REPORTS SHOULD BE
CONTROLLED IN SUCH A WAY THAT IT CAN BE ESTABLISHED
THAT ALL RELATED TRANSACTIONS HAVE BEEN ACCOUNTED
FOR WITH RESPECT TO GOODS.

.

.

.

CONTROL PROCEDURE: [ESTABLISH THAT ALL RECEIVING REPORTS
HAVE BEEN ACCOUNTED FOR.]

Figure 10

CONCEPTUALIZATION OVERVIEW

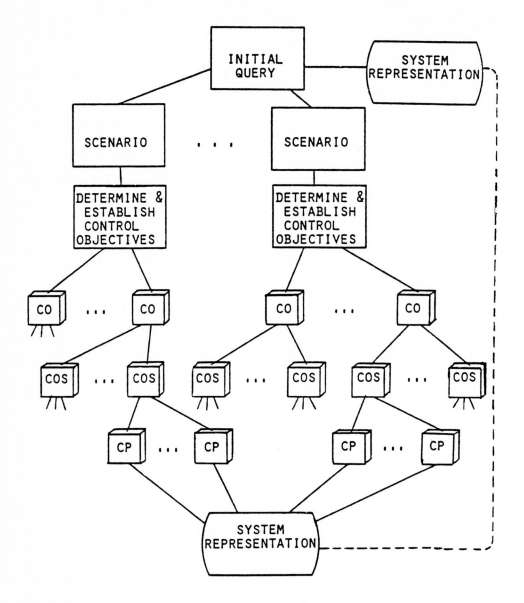

* NOT NECESSARILY A TREE (OVERLAP)

Figure 11

S T R U C T U R E

OBJECTS: REPRESENT FACTS AND CONJECTURES ABOUT THE PROBLEM

PATTERNS: OBJECTS THAT DESCRIBE FEATURES OF OTHER OBJECTS (CONTROLS & FAULTS)

HYPOTHESES: OBJECTS THAT REPRESENT HYPOTHETICAL PROTO-TYPE SITUATIONS (OBJECTIVES, SUBOBJECTIVES, & FAULT SCENARIOS)

ACTIONS: EXECUTABLE PROCEDURES THAT SPECIFY CHANGES TO THE HYPOTHESES

RULES: ASSOCIATIONS BETWEEN PATTERNS AND ACTIONS

Figure 12

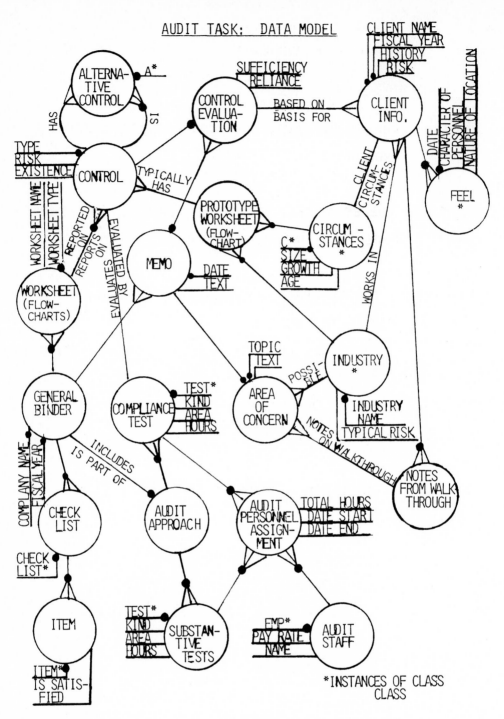

Figure 13

be tested using new cases (same task) and cross-validated against the performance of additional auditors performing the task.

4.2.1. Limitations

The initial model will be limited to evaluating controls commonly found in Purchases, Payables and Cash Disbursement systems. This is consistent with generally accepted auditing standards (Section 320), which emphasizes an ordered approach to considering classes of transactions as follows:

A. Sales, Receivables and Cash Receipts;

B. Purchases, Payables and Cash Disbursements;

C. Inventories and Production;

D. Personnel and Payroll;

E. Property, Plant and Equipment.

In addition, the initial computational model will not be expected to handle novel (uncommonly different) accounting systems.

4.3. Project Phases

The objectives for the research program are summarized in three phases: (1) model development, (2) model implementation and tuning, and (3) model evaluation. (See Figure 14 with discussion below.)

4.3.1. Phase I-Model Development

Preliminary representations of expertise, including key concepts and relationships, have been developed from interviews and experimental task data using experts both as collaborators and as subject-informants. These descriptions consist of problem solving steps and heuristics that represent auditor judgement in (a) identifying internal accounting control objectives, (b) identifying controls and faults in the accounting system, and (c) evaluating the system controls, weaknesses, and sufficiency of documentation.

4.3.1.1. Knowledge acquisition

Research at the University of Minnesota by Johnson [1983] has isolated general principles of eliciting expert knowledge that

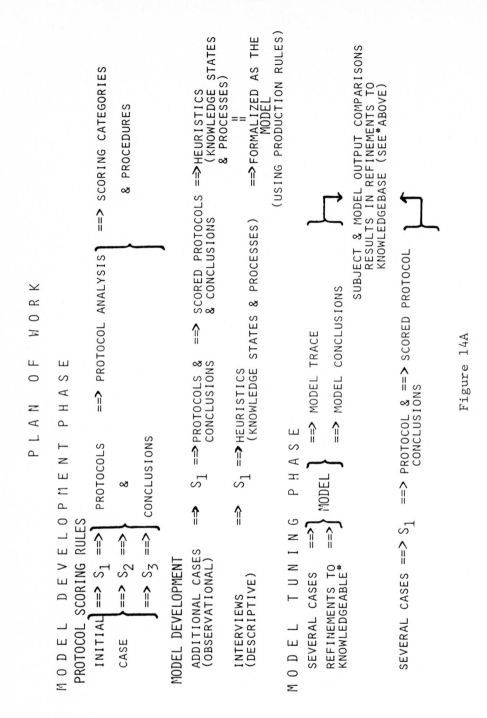

Figure 14A

P L A N   O F   W O R K   (CONTINUED)

M O D E L   V E R I F I C A T I O N   P H A S E

GENERAL DATA

THREE CASES:
1 TYPICAL
2 ATYPICAL

MODEL == 3 TRACES
3 SETS OF CONCLUSIONS*

S_1 (PRIMARY)
S_4, S_5, S_6

==> 9 PROTOCOLS ==> RATER$_1$ / RATER$_2$ ==> SCORED PROTOCOLS (HYPOTHESES CATEGORIES & REASONING PROCESSES)

==> 9 SETS OF CONCLUSIONS* ==> TYPED CONCLUSIONS

PEER JUDGMENT

3 MODEL TRACES
3 SETS OF MODEL CONCLUSIONS*

12 SCORED SUBJECT PROTOCOLS
12 SETS OF SUBJECT CONCLUSIONS(TYPED)*

==> S_7 ==> 45 OUTCOME RATINGS BY:
(A) COMPLETENESS

S_8 ==> (B) EFFECTIVENESS

==> S_9 ==> (C) AGREEMENT WITH CONCLUSIONS

*CONCLUSIONS CONSIST OF:
(1) LISTS OF CONTROLS TO BE COMPLIANCE TESTED
(2) LISTS OF CONTROL WEAKNESSES

Figure 14B

may apply in a variety of settings. This research continues to develop and use these approaches to elicit knowledge from our expert auditors. The multi-method approach is summarized here in three parts.

4.3.1.2. Observational methods

The observational approach adopted for this study is to collect "thinking-aloud protocols" which attempt to probe the problem solving mechanisms being used by experts. These protocols provide information about the organization of the expert's knowledge base, the actual knowledge it contains, and what control structures are used to apply the knowledge. A major difficulty with observational methods is that the very techniques used to determine the reasoning processes may distort those processes [Nesbett and Wilson, 1977]. That is, the line of reasoning chosen by the auditor when asked to relate each thought in the process while solving the problem may be different from the one used when that same auditor solves the problem under more natural conditions [Johnson, 1983a]. In this study, subjects are asked to solve several cases using "thinking-aloud protocols." The protocols are then transcribed and analyzed to determine what processes are being used. The resulting data is formalized as a set of rules. This initial protocol phase of research is followed by a refinement phase in which experts are asked to comment on the preliminary models developed from the protocols.

4.3.1.3. Descriptive methods

Using this method, assessing expertise is essentially a formalization process in which portions of the knowledge of an expert are transformed into an explicit representation. One method of accomplishing this is through interviews with auditors in which they attempt to characterize their knowledge and skill in the given task situation. The type of questions that are asked include the following:

1. "What objectives h do you think of when you see problem data about c?"
2. "What other evidence makes you start thinking about ob-

jective h?"

3. "What do you do immediately after thinking about objective h?"

4. "What evidence (controls or sub-objectives) makes you more certain that objective h is satisfied?"

5. "What do you do when you see evidence that supports objective h?"

6. "What evidence makes you conclude that objective h is satisfied?"

7. "What do you do once you know that objective h is satisfied?"

8. "What evidence makes you less certain that objective h is satisfied?"

9. "What do you do when you see faults in the data that contradict objective h?" (What compensating controls do you look for?)

10. "What makes you conclude that objective h cannot be satisfied?"

11. "What do you do once you know that objective h cannot be satisfied?"

12. "What evidence makes you conclude that you have sufficiently solved the problem?"

13. "What evidence makes you conclude that you cannot solve the problem?"

14. "What do you do when you've seen all the problem data and are still unable to solve the problem?" [Moen, 1984, p. 51].

A second, more formalized means is through the creation of a precise "language" in which the expert describes his/her expertise. The structure of the language is determined by the architecture of the knowledge base. In this case an auditor describes his/her lines of reasoning by means of production rules, if-then statements. Most existing methods of assessing expertise rely heavily on descriptive methods. The major limitation with the descriptive method is that the more competent an expert becomes, the less able he is to describe his problem solving knowledge [Johnson, 1983]. Several books have been written on the objectives, rules and procedures for evaluating internal controls [Johnson and Jaenicke, 1980]. Using descriptive methods, expertise has previously been captured in the questionnaires and workpapers of the large accounting firms. Although these books provide a reference for basic internal control production rules, this study will emphasize those rules elicited directly from the experts rather than from the literature. To the extent rules identified in the literature can be confirmed by auditor performance, such rules may be used.

4.3.1.4. Intuitive methods

Intuitive methods for capturing knowledge exist in two forms. In one case, a knowledge researcher interacts with both the auditor and the literature of the field in order to become familiar with its major problem solving methods. Acting in this capacity, the researcher develops a representation of auditing expertise which is then checked against the opinion of other auditors and eventually incorporated into our computer program. A second intuitive method of knowledge capturing is where a researcher, who is an expert in the area, attempts to describe the basis for his own knowledge and skill. Intuitive methods are less constrained by notation structures than the descriptive analysis techniques which utilize separate auditors and researchers. However, they still suffer from the fact that dependence on intuition as a means of recovering one's own knowledge is subjective and may not be adequate [Johnson, 1983]. Intuitive methods will be used in the model building process to supplement the above described observational and descriptive methods when necessary.

4.3.1.5. Subjects

Practicing CPAs in middle-managment of a large auditing firm are serving as subjects in the project. The local office of an international auditing firm has provided time from busy manager and partner schedules to participate in both the model building and the cross-validation. The model is being built largely with the help of one auditor, who will also assist in model validation. In addition, six other auditors will assist in validating the model.

4.3.1.6. Knowledge acquisition summary

The study began with the creation of a "zero-order" model of auditor processes. The model is then being developed as follows:

1. Interviews (descriptive methods) are being conducted with subjects to gather information and resources for the development of specific task materials and to develop preliminary descriptions of expertise. Experts are used as both collaborators and subject-informants.

2. Experimental tasks are employed to assess expertise (observational methods). Subjects in these tasks attempt to generate relevant internal accounting control objectives and evaluate working papers while "thinking aloud." Transcripts are made of problem solving sessions and these are being analyzed in detail following procedures developed by Erickson and Simon [1984], Johnson at Minnesota [Johnson, 1983], and refined as part of the research.

3. A model of auditor expertise is then being formalized as a set of rules (see the knowledge representation discussion below) and further refined using descriptive methods.

The products of the knowledge acquisition portion of the research includes the representations of auditor expertise in (a) the identification of specific internal accounting control objectives; (b) the evaluation and review processes, identifying which controls should be further tested for reliance thereon; and (c) the type of processes used in recognizing controls and weaknesses.

4.3.1.7. Knowledge representation

We have chosen to represent the expert knowledge of an auditor by the use of production rules. We make no claim for the universal applicability of such a representation, but rather rely on the demonstrated utility of rule-based systems with characteristics similar to those encountered in analyzing internal controls. Rule-based representations (also referred to as situation --> action rules or IF --> THEN rules) allow easy modification and explanation, both considered essential for building and then

tuning such computational models. Basically, each rule must capture a "chunk" of the domain knowledge, meaningful in and of
itself to the domain specialist [Feigenbaum, 1978]. The triggering conditions are normally referred to as the antecedents. The
context is the "scratchpad" or working space describing the current state of the problem being solved. If the antecedents are
matched against the context, then the consequences are enacted.

The rules are normally associated with "lines of reasoning"
and "episodes" that are comprehensible to the domain expert
[Feigenbaum, 1978]. Lines of reasoning involve the system analysis
methodologies employed by the subject. Episodes involve proposing tentative goals and/or subgoals (hypotheses) and trying to
either substantiate or disprove the goal. Such a generate-and-
test framework has been identified in behavioral studies by
Biggs and Mock [1981] and others when studying audit settings.
The formulation and maintenance of lines of reasoning and episodes
often requires the integration of many different "chunks" of
knowledge. It is important that the implemented system be able
to explain its use of knowledge to the domain expert for both
refinement and validation purposes.

The knowledge representation portion of the model development
involves encoding the specific expertise identified (part one)
into production rules along with additional domain knowledge.
Each production rule represents a meaningful "chunk" of either
specific expertise and/or of general domain knowledge.

4.3.2. Phase II-Model Implementation and Tuning

The preliminary model developed in Phase I is being implemented as a computational model by adapting a modelling tool, Galen,
developed at the University of Minnesota [Thompson et al., 1983].
Galen's architecture reflects its development in modelling cognitive processes. Galen's inference engine has the ability to partition the knowledge base, the ability to search for a hierarchical set of goals, apply forward and backward chaining, and can
interact with a LISP representation of the audit working papers.
While demonstrating the generality of Galen, we find that the
adaptation of an already proven tool enhances our productivity.

Combined with the rules developed in Phase I, the product will be the shell of our computational model.

After the knowledge from Phase I is mapped into GALEN's representational framework, the system will be "tuned." Tuning involves running several prototype accounting information systems through the evaluation process and, in collaboration with our expert, checking the lines of reasoning and episodes for reasonableness and making adjustments in the rules.

4.3.3. Phase III-Model Evaluation

Phase III experiments will focus upon comparisons between the control evaluation strategies of the model and the processes employed by auditors. The framework we propose to use to evaluate the model performance has two major features: (1) tests of sufficiency or adequacy of model outcomes; and (2) tests of the quality of model processes and of cue usage. [See Figure 14]

Researchers have not been able to formulate any single critical experiment to which validation of similar models are susceptible. Furthermore, due to the small sample size, statistical evaluations of experimental results are generally not available and researchers are constrained to rely on graphical techniques. The approach used in this study will include several empirical tests. The empirical tests address different types of data, each of which speaks to a different aspect of the model behavior.

The computational model will be fine-tuned around the expertise of one individual auditor (the primary subject). The computational model will initially be validated against this individual using three cases which were not part of the model development phase. In addition, the model will be cross-validated against three additional auditors using the three new cases.

For each case, the primary subject and three other auditors will be asked to read aloud the pertinent data and give "thinking-aloud" protocols while reviewing and evaluating the workpapers prepared by an in-charge auditor. As part of the task, the subjects will be asked to write out a list of: (1) recommendations for specific controls to be compliance tested; and (2) weaknesses identified from the system description. At the conclusion of each case, subjects will be asked to fill out a participant background questionnaire. The complete problem solving session for each subject will be tape recorded and transcribed. The computational model will also receive each case and make similar evaluations. The output of the model will include: (a) recommendations for specific controls to be compliance tested; (b) weaknesses identified from the system description; and (c) a trace of all data analyzed and rules fired.

4.3.3.1. Tests of adequacy of model outcomes

The first type of analysis, for sufficiency or adequacy of model outcomes, is to establish that the computational model can identify and evaluate internal accounting controls. Outcomes to be examined include the lists described above. The model's and all four subjects' outcomes will be retyped and given to another three subjects to judge. For each task, the three subjects will rate the (a) model's and four subjects' evaluations lists, (b) subjects' scored protocols, and (c) model's trace. These outcomes will each be rated on three seven point scales: (1) completeness of review; (2) effectiveness of compliance tests selected; and (3) agreement with review conclusions. These ratings will then be analyzed to determine how well the model performs in relation to the person it is modelled after and in relation to the other auditors.

4.3.3.2. Tests of quality of model processes and cue usage

A second type of analysis involves establishing the quality of the evaluation processes employed by the model and the usage of critical cues. To establish quality of evaluation processes, the inferences made must not only be "legal", but be the type of inferences that experts would make. Determining that a sample of model behavior constitutes adequate auditing behavior is not a simple matter. In games, such as chess, it is fairly easy to determine if the model is performing the requisite behavior because the rules used to determine whether a given move is "legal" are well-defined. By contrast, in environments such as fault diagnosis and internal control evaluation, it is not clear what constitutes a "legal move." Furthermore, as in a game, though all reasoning steps are explainable by logic or rules, some "lines of reasoning" (smaller sets of steps or moves) must be made according to a criterion of quality in order for the task to be well done. In medical diagnosis, for example, there is typically present a small set of cues that if interpreted properly will lead to a correct diagnosis. Experts may differ in their interpretations of other pieces of information, but they tend to agree more on the interpretation of these critical cues and use additional cues to mitigate between competing hypotheses [Johnson et al., 1982].

The model evaluation framework adopted requires that the model's rules for performing the evaluation be found in the heuristics of expert behavior. The judgement as to whether the model is performing the task is then based upon a comparison between the specific acts of model behavior on the task and by the behavior of the expert auditors. The comparisons focus upon (1) the identification and use of specific goals and objectives which direct the search and confirmation processes, and (2) knowledge states, and the cognitive processes that link them. The model quality will be evaluated by transcribing, scoring, and analyzing each model trace and verbal protocol selected. Protocols provide a depth of understanding about judgement and decision making unavailable using other methods. However, as in other methods, the data must be reduced to a structured, objective image of the processes that auditors are using. The analysis is developed by synthesizing the results of two analytical methods: a top-down, global analysis and a bottom-up, knowledge state/cognitive process analysis.

The top-down analysis identifies single problem solving goals from the protocols. Proposed categories are developed through functional analysis of the review task, formalized descriptions of evaluation processes generally, and model fragments found in the auditing literature. An example may be the representation or mental picture of the segregation of duties within the purchasing/cash distribution function. The identification of problem solving goals establishes the boundaries within which the more detailed state and process analysis is performed [Melone, 1984].

The bottom-up analysis focuses on knowledge states, the basic set of facts, concepts and hypotheses generated by the subject, and an associated set of reasoning processes called cognitive processes (e.g., reading, requesting information, searching for information). Scoring protocol for reasoning processes permits an understanding of how auditors use old knowledge states, generate new knowledge states, and the type of processes that link the knowledge states together. This analysis provides a "picture" of the path taken by the auditor through his representation of the task. It differs from the top-down analysis primarily by being more elementary and in finer detail [Melone, 1984]. An example of an operator would be the "comparing" of two items. By associating knowledge states and reasoning processes, a "problem behavior graph" will be developed [Newell and Simon, 1972].

A third, more general type of analysis, "lines of reasoning", will then be determined by analyzing the "problem behavior graphs" and the sequence of problem solving goals. Lines of reasoning involve the methods employed by the subjects to solve the task. Examples would be systemic search and directed search strategies which have been identified in previous auditing research [Biggs and Mock, 1981].

4.3.3.3. Validity and consistency

The transcribed protocols and trace will be scored by two independent raters, trained in the rules for coding these protocols. The coded protocols from each coder will be compared, and the proportion of agreement between the lists developed by each rater for two protocols rated will be computed. Cohen's K [Cohen, 1960], an inter-rater reliability coefficient, will be employed to adjust for agreement due to chance. Traces generated by the computational model will be scored by the same methods used to score subject protocols.

5. PRELIMINARY RESULTS

Discussion of subject's decision processes includes several levels of analysis: (1) systemic or directed strategy; (2) episodes; (3) views or frames of reference; and (4) cognitive processes. From previous experience in cognitive modelling, we have found that the decision-making behavior of experts cannot be adequately understood by analyzing cognitive processes alone, rather several higher, controlling levels of analysis are important to the modelling of expertise. The preliminary results from the protocol analysis of our first three subjects can be summarized in the above four categories. The categories range from the more general decision strategy of the subjects, to very specific types of cognitive processes which allow the auditor to progress from one knowledge state to another.

5.1. Decision Strategy

Each of the original three subjects used a very systematic breadth-first strategy for their analysis of the working papers and decision making. This has been categorized as a systemic strategy. They first identified all controls and then specified audit procedures and sample sizes. Systemic search contrasts with a more directed or depth-first approach where decisions about controls to test, including sample sizes, are made prior to the complete analysis of the working papers. This finding is consistent with studies by Biggs and Mock [1983] and Biggs, Messier, and Hansen [1985]. In each of those studies, two auditors used the systemic strategy and one auditor used the directed strategy. They observed that in both studies, the "experienced subjects used a systemic strategy" [Biggs et al., 1985].

The finding that expert auditors doing internal control evaluations and reviews use a systemic decision-making strategy rather than a directed strategy may be surprising to some researchers studying expertise. We hypothesize that this may be due to the nature of the particular task. Besides identifying controls, deciding which controls to compliance test, and choosing sample sizes, auditors feel that they examine the entire workpapers in order to catch any serious faults that may exist.

Also, many of the controls and possible compliance tests are interrelated, requiring an understanding of the complete system and correlation of tests to maximize efficiency and effectiveness. Therefore, a systemic strategy may be the most effective.

5.2. Episodic Categories

The next macro level of analysis consists of identifying the larger episodes used by the auditor in the decision-making process. As defined earlier, episodes involve proposing tentative goals and/or subgoals appropriate for the task, and then doing the analysis necessary to either substantiate or disprove the goals. The major episodic categories are presented as a graph in Figure 15. The macro goal categories for the task are: (1) Decide on the likely inherent risk category of client and the most probable overall audit approach to expect. Such firm categorization is based on understanding the macro environment within which the firm operates, firm size, growth, industry, and general management characteristics. (2) Decide if there are significant processing controls which can be relied on and the appropriate compliance tests. (3) Choose which boundary controls for accounts payable to rely on and the appropriate compliance tests. (4) Choose which controls over disbursements can be relied on and the appropriate compliance tests. (5) Evaluate the effectiveness of general computer controls and other firm environment factors when appropriate. (6) Draw conclusions on overall audit approach, controls to be relied upon, and appropriate audit procedures. The above episodic categories are closely related to manner in which the firm-specific workpapers have been organized.

We have chosen to graph these episodic categories by dividing each transcribed auditor protocol into a hundred equal units and then classifying each unit in the appropriate category. As can be seen from the partial protocol graph in Figure 15, the episodes are sustained goal-seeking categories. However, these episodes are somewhat interdependent and must sometimes be suspended until other decisions have been reached. An example is where specific processing controls depend on the computer; before conclusions about the specific tests of computer processing con-

GRAPH OF PROTOCOL ANALYSIS

TASK STAGE

SUBJECT #1   CASE #1

EPISODES:
INHERENT RISK...........: 0 1 2 3 4 5 6 7 8 9 0
PROCESSING CONTROLS...;.: 0 1 2 3 4 5 6 7 8 9 0
A/P ADDITIONS.(BOUNDARY) : *********************
DISBURSEMENTS.(BOUNDARY) : 0 1 2 3 4 5 6 7 8 9 0
GENERAL EDP CONTROLS.....: 0 1 2 3 4 5 6 7 8 9 0
CONCLUSIONS ....: 0 1 2 3 4 5 6 7 8 9 *

VIEWS OR FRAMES OF REFERENCE
PROCESSING:.(PO)........: 0 1 2 3 4 5 6 7 8 9 0
COMMITMENTS (PO)........: 0 1 2 3 4 5 6 7 8 9 0
RECEIPT OF GOODS & SERV(RR) 0 1 2 3 4 5 6 7 8 9 0
GOODS RET & CLAIMS ON SUPL 0 1 2 3 4 5 6 7 8 9 0
A/P ADDITIONS (INV).....: 0 1 2 3 4 5 6 7 8 9 0
DISBURSEMENTS (CKS).....: 0 1 2 3 4 5 6 7 8 9 0
INVENTORIES.............: 0 1 2 3 4 5 6 7 8 9 *

SEGREGATION OF DUTIES:...: 0 1 2 3 4 5 6 7 8 9 *
EDP FACTORS.............: 0 1 2 3 4 5 6 7 8 9 0
ADEQUACY OF WORKING PAPERS ***** 1 2 3 4 5 6 7 8 9 0

WRITTEN RESULTS:
CONTROLS TO TEST........: 1 2 3 4 5
WEAKNESSES AND PROBLEMS ..: 1 2 3 4 5

C1S1 WRITTEN RESPONSES

CONTROLS:
1. PROGRAMMED COMPARISON OF RECEIVING REPORT WITH POS ON FILE.
2. A/P COMPENSATING PROCEDURE: IF LIMITED SUPPLIERS, CONFIRM A/P AT YEAR END.
3. DO A "PROOF OF CASH" FOR A FEW MONTHS.

WEAKNESSES:
1. POS: NO AUTHORIZATIONS WITH REGARDS TO AMOUNTS, ETC.
2. SEGREGATION-PURCHASING AGENT: TOO MANY RESPONSIBILITIES.
3. INADEQUATE CONTROLS OVER BLANK CHECKS.
4. QUESTION: ABILITY TO SET UP A.P FOR GOODS RECEIVED, BUT NO INVOICE RECEIVED.
5. SEGREGATION-A/P CLERK: INITIATES PAYMENT AND RESPONSIBLE FOR RECEIVING GOODS.

Figure 15

trols can be determined the auditor first determines the effectiveness of the general computer controls and extent that they
can be relied upon. The graph allows us to relate how the episodes unfold and their relationship with other activities scored
for in the protocols.

5.3. Views or Frames of Reference

Auditors appear to have major frames of reference through
which they view the data. Such frames of reference allow them to
organize and evaluate various aspects of the data cues. The
views or frames of reference identified from the auditor protocols are: (1) processing, i.e., the flow of documents and goods
through various processing tasks and controls within the firm;
(2) segregation of duties, i.e., the determination of incompatible
duties, access, or management override and its effect on controls; (3) electronic data processing (EDP) factors, i.e., the
importance of the computer to the processing and control of data,
and relating how the lack of specific general computer controls
will affect the various application programs; and (4) the adequacy
of the working papers, i.e., how well those preparing the workpapers have captured and documented all relevant aspects of the
client's accounting system in order to draw control conclusions.

The data cues are analyzed from each of the above perspectives, but then must be integrated in deciding which controls may
be effective, which controls should be compliance tested, and
what type of compliance tests should be performed and how large
of a sample would be sufficient. Our primary subject has reported flipping from one view to another in his mind as he analyzes the data and how a change in one view affects his other
views of the data. Much of this "flipping from one view to
another" shows up in the protocol. The graph in Figure 15
illustrates that there may be mention of more than one reference
frame in any of the protocol units. Also note that the primary
frame of reference is processing, which enjoys more sustained
attention. It should be noted that the working papers are organized more from this frame of reference.

5.4. Cognitive Processes

Cognitive process decision operators provide the links between individual knowledge states at the micro level. Scoring the protocol for cognitive processes allows the determination of which operators are used by auditors in their evaluation of internal controls. Figure 16 provides a list of operators scored.

The use of the data search operator is consistent with our previous observation that auditors perform a comprehensive review of all working papers available. In addition, we find that auditors deal with uncertainty by raising questions, building conjectures, making assumptions, and proposing numerous tentative evaluations. This use of discrete assumed outcomes rather than probabilistic assessments of uncertainty is consistent with Biggs et al. [1985] and Doyle's [1983a,b] "reasoning by assumption." No probabilistic remark, such as "I'm 75 percent positive that invoices are adequately accounted for," was found in any of the protocols.

The micro analysis, scoring of the cognitive processes, helped most in the model building process when scored for within the bounds of the specific goals and objectives that direct the search and confirmation processes. The macro analysis of the protocol provided the control structure around which the model was built.

5.5. Conclusions from the Research

A primary contribution of this study arises from our limited understanding of the processes auditors use in reviewing and evaluating internal accounting controls. Analyzing and modelling the knowledge states and related reasoning processes that managers and partners use help to describe what it takes to have expertise in auditing. The research facilitates transmission, reproduction, consensus, enhancement, automation of the routine aspects of the expert's task, and help experts and novices better solve problems [Hayes-Roth, Waterman and Lenat, 1983].

COGNITIVE PROCESSES

==

OPERATORS	NOTATION	BRIEF DESCRIPTION

==

I. DATA ACQUISITION

1. READ	R	ASSIGNED WHEN SUBJECT READS OR REPEATS TASK STATEMENT.
2. DATA SEARCH	DS	ASSIGNED WHEN THE SUBJECT SEARCHES THE CASE FOR SPECIFIC PIECES OF DATA.
3. DATA RETRIEVAL	DR	ASSIGNED WHEN THE SUBJECT RETRIEVES A PIECE OF INFORMATION STORED PREVIOUSLY IN EXTERNAL (I.E., NOTES) OR INTERNAL MEMORY

II. PLAN

| 4. PLAN | P | ASSIGNED WHEN SUBJECT EVALUATES HIS CURRENT REASONING STRATEGY OR SPECIFIES A GOAL OR SUBGOAL |

III. ANALYTICAL

5. ASSUMPTION	A	ASSIGNED WHEN SUBJECT GENERATES AN ARBITRARY FACT ABOUT THE CASE.
6. CONJECTURE	C	ASSIGNED WHEN SUBJECT MAKES AN IF-THEN, SCENARIO, OR HYPOTHETICAL STATEMENT.
7. EVALUATION	E	ASSIGNED WHEN SUBJECT MAKES A TELEOLOGICAL (PURPOSEFUL) JUDGMENT ABOUT THE TASK BASED ON SOME EXPLICIT OR IMPLICIT CRITERION.
8. QUESTION	Q	ASSIGNED WHEN SUBJECT WOULD LIKE FURTHER INFORMATION ABOUT THE CLIENT THAN IS CONTAINED IN THE WORK PAPERS.
9. INFERENCE	I	ASSIGNED WHEN SUBJECT INFERS A CONCLUSION OR MAKES A PREDICTION BASED ON EXPLICIT PREMISES OR CUES.

IV. ACTION

10. GENERATE ALTERNATIVE	GA	ASSIGNED WHEN SUBJECT STATES, IN A TENTATIVE FORM, AN ALTERNATIVE CONTROL, AUDIT PROCEDURE, SAMPLE SIZE, OR OTHER TASK RELATED ACTION.
11. DECISION RULE	R	ASSIGNED WHEN THE SUBJECT SPECIFIED A METHOD (INCLUDING HEURISTICS) FOR MAKING AN AUDIT JUDGMENT.
12. AUDIT DECISION	AD	ASSIGNED WHEN THE SUBJECT MAKES A FINAL DECISION ABOUT A CONTROL, WEAKNESS, OR AUDIT PROCEDURE.
13. OTHER DECISION	OD	ASSIGNED WHEN THE SUBJECT RECOMMENDS OTHER ACTIONS TO BE TAKEN.

(See Malone [1984] and Biggs et al. [1985].)

Figure 16

6. CONCLUSIONS AND SUGGESTIONS FOR FUTURE RESEARCH

The objective of this research is to formulate and test a model of the processes employed by expert auditors in reviewing and evaluating internal accounting controls. The purpose of the research is to describe in greater detail the processes that are used in auditor judgements. The computational model provides a means of testing the understanding.

A primary contribution of this study arises from our limited understanding of the processes auditors use in reviewing and evaluating internal accounting controls. Analyzing and modelling the knowledge states and related reasoning processes that managers and partners use helps to describe what it takes to have expertise in auditing. This research facilitates transmission, reproduction, consensus, enhancement, automation of the routine aspects of the expert's task, and help experts and novices better solve problems [Hayes-Roth, Waterman and Lenat, 1983].

In future research extensions, we plan to join the TICOM modelling, querying, and evaluation techniques under the control of an expert system decision model. Such a marriage could allow the resulting system to query the user for appropriate modelling information, represent the client's system as a TICOM model, then deciding what questions would be interesting to ask, query the model and combine the results into a recommendation of controls to test and a report on control weaknesses. The resulting system would allow both individual companies and auditors to make effective and efficient evaluations of internal controls.

Other research extensions of the current research include extending the cognitive simulation approach developed in this model to other auditing tasks. The possibilities are numerous. Examples of such tasks include combining the results of the compliance tests into a final evaluation of internal control and then planning which substantive test to perform.

Future research will also include such sophistication in auditing as to allow one computer system to analyze another computer's data base system and automatically pick and help evaluate audit samples. There is no lack of interesting research issues involving the use of DSS/AI/ES systems in auditing.

REFERENCES

Alter, S. (1977). "A Taxonomy of Decision Support Systems," Sloan Management Review, 19, 1, Fall, pp. 39-56.

Arens, A.A. and Loebbecke, J.K. (1984). Auditing: An Integrated Approach, 3rd Edition, Prentice-Hall, Inc., Englewood Cliffs, N.J.

American Institute of Certified Public Accountants (1972). Statement on Auditing Standards, AU Section 320, November.

Barr, A, and Feigenbaum, E.A. (1981). The Handbook of Artificial Intelligence, 1, HeurisTech Press.

Bailey, A.D. Jr., Duke, G.L., Johnson, P.E., Meservy, R.D. and Thompson, W. (1984). "Auditing Internal Controls: A Computational Model of the Review Process," research proposal, University of Minnesota.

Bailey, A.D. Jr., Duke, G.L., Gerlach, J., Ko, C., Meservy, R.D. and Whinston, A.B. (1985). "TICOM and the Analysis of Internal Controls," The Accounting Review, April.

Bailey, A.D. Jr., Gerlach, J.H., McAffee, R.P. and Whinston, A.B. (1981). "An Application of Complexity Theory to the Analysis of Internal Control Systems," Auditing: A Journal of Practice and Theory, Summer.

Bailey, A.D. Jr., Gerlach, J.H., McAfee, R.P., Whinston, A.B. and Watson, D.J.H. (1983). "OIS Technology and Accounting: Partners in Conflict," in Data Base Management: Theory and Applications, C. Holsapple and A. Whinston (eds.), NATO Advanced Study Institute Series, D. Reidel Publishing Co., London.

Balachandran, B.V. and Zoltners, A.A. (1981). "An Interactive Audit-Staff Scheduling Decision Support System," The Accounting Review, October.

Biggs, S.F. (1984). "Empirical Analysis and Expert System Development for Auditors Going-Concern Judgment," Symposium on Decision Support Systems in Auditing, University of Southern California.

Biggs, S.F., Messier, W.F. Jr. and Hansen, J.V. (1985). "A Study of the Predecisional Behavior of Computer Audit Specialists in Advanced EDP Environments," ARC Working Paper No. 84-1.

Biggs, S.F. and Mock, T.J. (1983). "An Investigation of Auditor Decision Processes in the Evaluation of Internal Controls and Audit Scope Decisions," Journal of Accounting Research, Spring.

Braun, H.M. and Chandler, J.S. (1982). "Development of an Expert System to Assist Auditors in the Investigation of Analytical Review Fluctuations," research proposal, University of Illinois.

Cohen, J. (1960). "A Coefficient of Agreement for Nominal Scales," Educational and Psychological Measurement, 26, pp. 37-46.

Davis, R. (1982). "Expert Systems: Where Are We? And Where Do We Go From Here?," The AI Magazine, Spring.

Doyle, J. (1983b). "Some Theories of Reasoned Assumptions: An Essay in Rational Psychology," Working Paper CS-83-125, Computer Science Department, Carnegie-Mellon University, May.

Dungan, C. and Chandler, J. (1980). "Development of Knowledge-Based Expert Systems to Model Auditors' Decision Processes," unpublished paper, University of Illinois.

Einhorn, H.J. (1980). "Learning From Experience and Suboptimal Rules in Decision Making," in Cognitive Processes in Choice and Decision Behavior, T.S. Wallsten (ed.), Erlbaum, Hillsdale, N.J.

Elstein, A.S., Shulman, A.S. and Sprafka, S.M. (1978). Medical Problem Solving: An Analysis of Clinical Reasoning, Harvard University Press, Cambridge, MA.

Ericsson, K.A. and Simon, H.A. (1984). Protocol Analysis: Verbal Reports as Data, The MIT Press, Cambridge, MA.

Feigenbaum, E.A. (1978). "The Art of Artificial Intelligence -- Themes and Case Studies of Knowledge Engineering," Proceedings of the National Computer Conference.

Hansen, J.V. and Messier, W.F. (1982). "Expert Systems for Decision Support in EDP Auditing," International Journal of Computer and Information Sciences, October.

Hayes-Roth, F., Waterman, D.A. and Lenat, D.B. (1983). Building Expert Systems, Addison-Wesley.

Johnson, K.P. and Jaenicke, H.R. (1980). Evaluating Internal Control, John Wiley & Sons.

Johnson, P.E. (1983). "The Expert Mind: A New Challenge for the Information Scientist."

Johnson, P.E. (1983). "What Kind of Expert Should a System Be?," The Journal of Medicine and Philosophy, pp. 77-97.

Johnson, P.E., Hassebrock, F., Duran, A.S. and Mollar, J. (1982). "Multimethod Study of Clinical Judgment," Organizational Behavior and Human Performance, 30, pp. 201-230.

Joyce, E.J. and Libby, R. (1982). "Behavioral Studies of Audit Decision Making," Journal of Accounting Literature.

Kleinmuntz, B. (1968). "The Process of Clinical Information by Man and Machine," in Formal Representations of Human Judgment, B. Kleinmuntz (ed.), John Wiley and Sons, New York.

Libby, R. (1981). Accounting and Human Information Processing: Theory and Applications, Prentice-Hall.

Lindsay, R.K., Buchanan, B.G., Feigenbaum, E.A. and Lederberg, J. (1980). "Applications of Artificial Intelligence for Organic Chemistry: The DENDRAL Project," McGraw-Hill.

Loebbecke, J.K. and Zuber, G.R. (1980). "Evaluating Internal Controls," The Journal of Accountancy, February.

Mair, W.C., Wood, D.R. and Davis, K.W. (1978). Computer Control & Audit, The Institute of Internal Auditors, Touche Ross & Co., Florida, p. 34.

Mautz, R. and Winjum, J. (1981). "Criteria for Management Control Systems," Financial Executive Research Institute.

Melone, N.P. (1984). "A Strategy for Knowledge-Based Decision Support: Decision Making Expertise in Corporate Acquisitions," Unpublished Ph.D. Dissertation Proposal, University of Minnesota.

McCarty (1977). "Reflexions on Taxman: An Experiment in Artificial Intelligence and Legal Reasoning," Harvard Law Review, March, pp. 837-893.

Michaelson, R.H. (1982). "An Expert System for Federal Tax Planning," Working Paper, University of Nebraska.

Mock, T. and Vertinsky, I. (1984). "DSS-RAA: Design Highlights," Symposium on Decision Support Systems for Auditing, University of Southern California.

Moen, James B. (1984). "Algorithms and Data Structures in Galen," Working Paper, University of Minnesota.

Mutchler, J.F. (1984). "Auditors' Perceptions of the Going Concern Opinion Decision," Auditing: A Journal of Practice and Theory, Spring, pp. 17-30.

Nesbett, R.E. and Wilson, T.D. (1977). "Telling More Than We Can Know: Verbal Reports On Mental Processes," Psychological Review, May.

Newell, A. and Simon, H.A. (1972). Human Problem Solving, Prentice-Hall.

Peat, Marwick, Mitchell & Co. (1986). Research Opportunities in Auditing, New York.

Shortliffe, E.H. (1976). "Computer-Based Medical Consultations: MYCIN," North-Holland.

Stefik, M., Aikins, J., Balzer, R., Benoit, J., Birnbaum, L., Hayes-Roth, F. and Sacerdoti, E. (1982). The Organization of Expert Systems: A Prescriptive Tutorial, Xerox Palo Alto Research Centers.

Thompson, W.B., Johnson, P.E. and Moen, J.B. (1983). "Recognition-Based Diagnostic Reasoning," IJCAI Proceedings,

van Melle, W., Shortliffe, E.H., and Buchanan, B.G. (1981). "EMYCIN: A Domain-Independent System that Aids in Constructing Knowledge-Based Consultation Programs," Machine Intelligence, Infotech State of the Art Report, 9, 3.

Weber, R. (1982). EDP Auditing: Conceptual Foundations and Practice, McGraw-Hill, New York.

11. SOME PRELIMINARY NOTES ON THE DEVELOPMENT OF A GENERAL DSS FOR AUDITORS

James H. Gerlach
Management Information Systems
University of Colorado at Denver
Denver, Colorado   80202, U.S.A.

1. INTRODUCTION

Since most accounting systems are computer based, the review of accounting data during an external audit is commonly supported with the use of computers, making it feasible to analyze large pools of accounting data. Early computer support tools such as the Audit Command Language (ACL) developed by Will [1981] supplied the auditor with a set of audit specific primitives for processing sequential files. The list of primitives included instructions for performing statistical analyses as well as basic data and file manipulations. More recent innovations utilize data base management concepts enabling the system to handle more advanced data structures and powerful data manipulation languages for specifying custom audit procedures.

Current work in the area of Decision Support Systems (DSSs) for auditors is focusing on the potential use of expert systems technology in areas of auditing that are qualitative and subjective, particularly internal control evaluation [Bailey et al., 1985b]. A related research project by Bailey et al. [1985a] developed a DSS for internal control review. Though the system did not possess audit expertise for reviewing internal controls, the system did provide the auditor with computer-assisted means for documenting the internal control system and a query processing system for logically identifying control points regulating accounting events deemed critical by the auditor, e.g., the preparation of a voucher.

These DSSs for auditors can be categorized according to whether they provide general or specific audit support. Audit tools like ACL for analyzing a client's accounting data provide general support in that the development and selection of audit procedures is the sole responsibility of the auditor. There is

NATO ASI Series, Vol. F31
Decision Support Systems: Theory and Application
Edited by C. W. Holsapple and A. B. Whinston
© Springer-Verlag Berlin Heidelberg 1987

nothing in the system that encourages the use of one system function over another based upon previous analytical results. Such systems can serve a wide range of applications since they do not impose a particular audit philosophy or approach on the auditor. Expert-based systems support judgemental tasks by directing the decision-making process. In so doing, they provide the auditor with a higher level of support, but at the cost of restricting the problem domain for which it is useful and its field of acceptance. For example, an expert system for reviewing the internal controls governing payroll is restricted to payroll applications that satisfy the expert's notions as to what constitutes a payroll system. If the payroll system under review contains new or substitute components not anticipated by the expert, then decision support is hindered until the expert system can be modified to handle this unusual case. Furthermore, the expert system is only useful to those audit firms which are willing to regard the expert as such.

It appears reasonable to assume that every auditing firm has its own expertise upon which they rely heavily. This is evidenced by differences in audit approaches and procedures. Different audit firms have different means for documenting internal control systems, have different questionnaires for evaluating the controls, and place varying degrees of reliance on analytical review of account balances versus statistical review, for example. These individual differences make it impossible to develop a DSS that is applicable to all auditors and audit engagements. A more practical approach would be to construct a DSS environment which is rich in general audit capabilities which can be easily customized to reflect the expertise of the audit firm and any unique properties of the audit engagement, e.g., industry factors.

In this paper, a framework for constructing a DSS environment for auditors is proposed that recognizes the uniqueness of the audit staff and the audit engagement, while providing a strong basis of general support. The end product is not intended to be a DSS but the shell of a DSS that can be customized to satisfy individual needs. The key component of such a system is a knowledge representation that can be used to represent most, if not all, audits. A number of paradigms exist, each of which is useful for explaining and understanding the audit process. However, they were primarily developed as a guide to the audit process and require human interpretation especially in light of exceptional circumstances. What is required is not a new definition of the audit process, but a theoretically complete definition that supports the professionally accepted view of the audit process. The remainder of this paper attempts to develop the basis of such a representation.

2. THE AUDIT PROCESS

Although specific audit procedures are adapted for each specific engagement, the fundamental steps underlying the audit process are essentially the same for every case. These fundamental steps are (SAS No. 1, Section 320):

1. Internal control documentation and review.
2. Internal control compliance testing.
3. Substantive testing of transactions and account balances; and analytical review.
4. Issue an opinion.

A primary purpose for studying the client's system of internal controls relates to the problem of comparing accounting records with empirical reality. Since confirmation of all accounting records is not feasible due to cost and time restrictions, the auditor is forced to employ statistical sampling techniques and analytical review methods in order to obtain persuasive evidence (rather than convincing evidence, SAS No. 31) to arrive at an opinion on the fairness of the financial statements. The amount of substantive testing required is inversely proportional to the effectiveness of the internal controls governing the accounting system. The stronger the controls, the more reliable the accounting information is perceived.

Analytical review procedures are "substantive tests of financial information made by a study and comparison of relationships among data" (SAS No. 23). Analytical review tests vary in degrees of persuasiveness. For example, an auditor may reason that an increase in annual sales was caused by an increase in advertising over last year's expenditure. An example of a more persuasive test is provided by Akresh and Wallace [1985] where they successfully used regression and ARIMA to investigate a utility company. A typical test that they performed related company reported gas revenue to temperature statistics, the Consumer Price Index, and the number of gas customers.

Conceptually, the audit tests should be designed to verify five major management assertions (SAS No. 31): (1) assets or liabilities actually exist at the date reported and nominal accounts represent transactions that occurred during the accounting period; (2) all assets, liabilities, and nominal accounts are reported; (3) that assets and liabilities properly represent ownership rights and obligations of the firm; (4) that all reported accounts are valued according to generally accepted account principles; and (5) that accounts are properly classified, represented and disclosed.

2.1. Audit Risk

Since audit tests are somewhat inconclusive, auditors face the risk of drawing erroneous conclusions that lead to the material misrepresentation of the financial statements. That is to say, the result of an audit test may support an incorrect hypothesis or reject a correct one. In statistical sampling, they are respectively referred to as the Beta Risk and the Alpha Risk and apply both to compliance and substantive testing. In addition to the Alpha and Beta risks, the auditor runs the risk of incorrectly applying the test to an inappropriate situation or improperly executing it. Furthermore, certain accounting transactions or account balances are inherently riskier to audit. For example, there is less risk associated with rent expense than with warranty expense since rent expense is based on actual transactions whereas warranty expense is based on estimates of future transactions [Miller's GAAS Guide, 1984].

3. AN ABSTRACT VIEW OF THE AUDIT PROCESS

From the preceding discussion, which typifies presentations

commonly found in auditing textbooks, the audit process is a
straightforward, sequential process. In fact, the audit process
is generally less structured and more dynamic than the model
depicts. If the review of internal controls reveals a weak
system, then internal control compliance testing is meaningless
and is skipped with a stronger reliance placed on substantive
testing. Guided by the strengths and weaknesses in the internal
control structure, the auditor must decide upon the mix of
analytical tests and statistical tests to be applied while satisfying time and cost constraints.

In the process of conducting these examinations, new problems may be discovered and inconsistent test findings may arise
due to Alpha and Beta errors; which may force the auditor to
extend previously conducted tests and perform additional tests
in order to resolve the discrepancies. In anticipation of these
types of complications, it is common practice to use analytical
review techniques during the audit planning phase to detect and
plan for problem accounts [Miller's GAAS Guide, 1984, p. 8.47].
In fact, the GAAS guide further recommends that analytical
review procedures should be applied throughout the audit process
on a continuous basis. Furthermore, a test of compliance might
very well be related to a substantive test and can therefore
be performed more economically together.

In an attempt to better represent the dynamic and unstructured nature of the audit process, an alternative model is proposed and described below. The proposed model is based upon
previous research conducted by other researchers which is
assembled here into a more complete model. The model is necessarily abstract in order to be applicable to a wide range of
audit situations; an important consideration justified earlier
in the introduction of this paper.

In the proposed model, the audit environment is depicted as
a set of assertions provided by management of the firm being
audited which they claim fairly describes the financial status
of the firm. This set of assertions includes a description of
the internal control system and its assessment, the accounting
data base showing transactions and account balances, and other

information relevant to the audit such as legal documents. The
audit staff is represented by a set of audit tests (procedures)
which accepts any number of assertions and/or external information as its primary input and renders an opinion on the validity
of the targeted assertion as its output. Audit tests may be
mechanical, reflect expert knowledge, rely upon the auditor for
direction and analysis, or any combination thereof. The audit
process consists of selecting and applying tests in order to
gather evidence supporting or refuting management's assertions.
Each test also has associated Alpha and Beta risks, preconditions
that must be satisfied before the test can be performed, and a
cost function for estimating the cost of performing the test.
As new test results are known, the prior belief about the accept-
ability of the assertion(s) in question are updated according to
a specified function operating over a certainty continuum. Like
the audit test itself, all associated predicates and functions
may be fully or partially mechanical and rely upon the auditor
for judgement. Thus in no way does the view to provide the
auditor with computer support diminish the control the auditor
has over the audit. Rather, the computer is able to provide
decision support to the extent that the various components of
the audit process can be formalized.

3.1. An Illustration

Let X represent a management assertion that is to be tested
using an audit procedure designed by the symbol "-->". Furthermore, assume that the audit procedure uses evidence E to either
support or refute the fairness of X. Then, E-->X represents
that the audit test supports the fairness of X and E-->$\sim$X denotes
that the audit test does not support the fairness of X. Evidence E may be composed of management assertions or external
data provided by another source. If we allow F to stand for
fair and NF for not fair, then the Alpha and Beta risks can be
expressed as follows as well as the strengths of the test.

Incorrect Decisions	Correct Decisions
$P(E\text{-->}\sim X \mid X \text{ is } F)$ = Alpha risk	$P(E\text{-->}X \mid X \text{ is } F)$ = 1 - Alpha risk
$P(E\text{-->}X \mid X \text{ is } NF)$ = Beta risk	$P(E\text{-->}\sim X \mid X \text{ is } NF)$ = 1 - Beta risk

The conditional probabilities are based on the assumption that the datums comprising E satisfy the assumptions (preconditions) of the test. Thus, the probabilities P(E is R) and P(E is NR) measure the likelihood that E is reliable evidence. Finally, if P(X is F) and P(X is NF) represent the prior belief that X is fairly or unfairly stated, then the prior belief concerning X can be updated as follows given the result of the audit test.

P(X is F|E-->X) =

    P(E is R)

$$* \frac{P(X \text{ is } F) * P(E\text{-->}X|X \text{ is } F)}{P(X \text{ is } F)*P(E\text{-->}X|X \text{ is } F) + P(X \text{ is } NF)*P(E\text{-->}X|X \text{ is } NF)}$$

    + P(E is NR) * P(X is F)

In the above formulation it is assumed that the test resulted in supporting the fairness of X. It then follows that if E is reliable then the prior probability regarding the fairness of X is updated according to Bayes theorem; otherwise, if E is unreliable then the results of the test are meaningless and we are left with our prior belief concerning the fairness of X. In a similar fashion, the appropriate conditional probabilities can be calculated in the event the test refutes the fairness of X.

The use of Bayes theorem in auditing to update prior beliefs regarding the fairness of an assertion based upon test results was previously proposed by Bailey and Jensen [1977]. Their formulation is somewhat different in that they constructed a two step operation for relating a given test result to the belief about the fairness of the assertion being tested. Their approach first relates the test result to compliance and then relates compliance to fairness. Also, they do not consider the possibility that the evidence the test uses might be misleading. If in the above formulation the P(E is R) is set to unity, then the two formulations can be shown to produce the same result.

The fact that there are alternative methods for revising prior beliefs concerning the fairness of assertions does not cause a loss in generality. All the model requires is a function for updating prior expectations and a continuum for measuring degrees of fairness; it is left to the discretion of the audit

staff to specify the function and the standard unit of measurement. The proposed system will then use them to assist in the
selection of audit tests and incorporate the results as demonstrated by the following examples employing the Bayesian formulation that was developed above.

3.2. An Example of Two Confirming Audit Tests

Figure 1 shows the case of two independent audit tests which
result in consistent findings for determining the fairness of
assertion X. Given the result of the first test, the prior
expectation of X can be directly calculated from Figure 1.
Using this revised probability assessment for X

$$P(X \text{ is } F | E_1 \text{-->} X) = .7 * \frac{.5(.95)}{.5(.95) + .5(.1)} + .3(.5) = .78$$

as its new prior probability assessment, the result of the second
test can be used to further update the certainty factor for X.

$$P(X \text{ is } F | E_2 \text{-->} X) = .8 * \frac{.78(.9)}{.78(.9) + .22(.16)} + .2(.78) = .92$$

$$P(E_1 \text{ is } R) = .7 \qquad P(X \text{ is } F) = .5 \qquad P(E_2 \text{ is } R) = .8$$

$$E_1 \qquad\qquad X \qquad\qquad E_2$$

$$E_1 \text{-->} X \qquad\qquad E_2 \text{-->} X$$

Alpha Risk = .05   Alpha Risk = .1
Beta Risk = .1   Beta Risk = .16

Figure 1. An Example of Two Consistent Test Results

3.3. An Example of Two Conflicting Audit Tests

Figure 2 once again shows the process of auditing X using
two audit tests; however, in this case the test results are conflicting. The revision to the belief about the fairness of X
is calculated similarly

$$P(X \text{ is } F | E_1 \text{-->} \sim X) = .7 * \frac{.5(.05)}{.5(.05) + .5(.9)} + .3(.5) = .19$$

yielding a .49 probability assessment. Thus, we have two conflicting tests whose results offset one another. The probability

$$P(X \text{ is } F|E_2 \text{-->} X) = .8 * \frac{.19(.9)}{.19(.9) + .81(.16)} + .2(.19) = .49$$

that test 1 produced an incorrect result is given by the probability that an Alpha error occurred or that E_1 is not reliable.
Likewise, the probability

$$P(Alpha_1 \text{ error OR } E_1 \text{ is NR}) = .05 + .3 - .3(.05) = .34$$

$$P(Beta_2 \text{ error OR } E_2 \text{ is NR}) = .16 + .2 - .2(.16) = .33$$

that the result of test 2 should be discounted can be calculated.
Hence, for this example the likelihood of producing inconsistent
test results is significant. The auditor is now faced with the
problem of resolving the conflict by either extending one or
both of the tests or conducting a third test. An alternative
action would be to try to match X with other assertions in place
of a third test. This is demonstrated next.

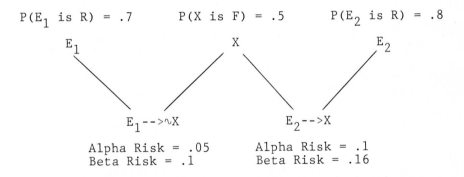

Figure 2. An Example of Two Inconsistent Test Results

3.4. An Example of System Review

The task of resolving the conflicting signals regarding X
might be inexpensively expedited if the audit is approached from
a system perspective. The concept of a system approach to
auditing is not new. The basic equations of double entry accounting that govern financial statements is a simple form of
system review. A more extensive application of this concept
might model an entire firm from an operational perspective.

Consider a manufacturing firm, purchases of raw materials affect raw materials inventory; raw materials inventory, labor and factory overhead limit the production of finished goods, which ultimately has implications for finished goods inventory and sales. These functional relationships constitute asset/ liability and revenue/expense flows. By understanding these interrelationships, certainty regarding the fairness of one flow can be related to other flows. For instance, the basic accounting equations dictate that ending raw materials inventory is equal to beginning inventory + purchases - withdrawals for production. Last year's audit gives the beginning inventory balance and ending inventory is directly observable, e.g., via sampling. If further knowledge can be acquired regarding either purchases or withdrawals, then the other is directly determined. If tests were applied to all of the account balances in the equation, then the equation could be used to determine if the findings were consistent. The more interrelationships known, the more effective the cross-checks would become. For example, if industry standards for unit cost production were known as well as factory capacity, then it might be advantageous to use this information to see if reported production was feasible by comparing it analytically to factory capacity and labor, raw materials and overhead standards.

Kaplan [1979] suggested that the audit might be better effected if the organization was modelled as a large system of equations, the simultaneous solution of which is the fair representation of the financial status of the firm. The problem with this approach is that there is no complete theory of the firm for developing a complete set of equations. Furthermore, the process of specifying the equations is prone to error, creating a higher order verification problem. By regarding an equation as an audit test, the organizational model can be reduced to those aspects deemed most critical by the audit staff. Also, the test will have associated Alpha and Beta risks that are necessary for taking into account the inexactness of the test. Tests that represent the basic accounting equations would obviously have Alpha and Beta risk values of zero.

Figure 3 shows the situation in which assertions X and Y
are interrelated; that is, there is a test which uses Y to ascertain X. The test assumes that Y is reliable if it is fair. The
result of performing the test is that Y supports X. Given that
Y is already reasonably known, it is possible to better determine the fairness of X. This can be done by substituting the
known values into the probability revision equation, deriving
a .82 probability assessment for X.

$$P(X \text{ is } F|Y\text{-->}X) = .9 * \frac{.49(.95)}{.49(.95) + .51(.16)} + .1(.49) = .82$$

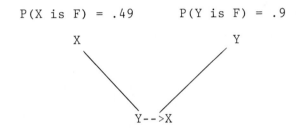

$$P(X \text{ is } F) = .49 \qquad P(Y \text{ is } F) = .9$$

Alpha Risk = .05
Beta Risk = .16

Figure 3. An Example of Using a Known Assertion as Evidence

3.5. Summary

In this manner, assertion X can be directly tested and evaluated for consistent findings with other interrelated assertions.
This particular approach should be useful for detecting occurrences of Alpha and Beta errors. For this last example, the
evidence collected from the three tests supports the notion that
the first test should be ignored since either E_1 is not reliable
or an Alpha error occurred. Again, by applying the rules of
probability, the likelihood of each event can be calculated.

4. CONCLUSIONS

In this paper, a view of the audit process has been presented
that is believed to be useful towards the development of a general DSS for auditors. Essential to this view is the proposition
that the audit process is principally a series of audit tests

conducted in order to gain knowledge concerning the fairness of the assertions made by management. Development of the audit procedures is seen to be an audit staff responsibility; hence, a language for specifying audit procedures needs to be provided. The language must also provide a standard protocol for audit test specification that makes known to the DSS the preconditions for performing the test, the type of assertions to which the procedure may be applied, the means for calculating the test's Alpha and Beta risks, and the result of the test. The DSS, equipped with an audit staff supplied procedure for revising prior fairness assessments, would be able to update and maintain the level of certainty regarding the fairness of each assertion.

What is of most interest to the author are the future developments that hopefully will spring from this framework. One such use was illustrated in the last example of this paper: the assessment of interrelated test findings in order to detect and correct inconsistent findings. Another related use concerns the development of a series of tests to be conducted as a part of the audit plan. Based upon the assertions to be confirmed and descriptions of the available audit procedures, complete with functions for estimating the cost of applying the test, it might be possible to help formulate an economical audit plan. The plan would consist of interrelated tests designed to be self-correcting and meet the level of certainty regarding the fairness of the financial statements as demanded by the audit staff.

At the very least, a DSS developed along these lines ought to provide several practical advantages. Formalized descriptions of the audit procedures should result in efficiency gains through automation and effectiveness gains through the consistent and proper application of audit procedures. The audit process would be virtually self-documenting and would be reuseable from year to year.

REFERENCES

Akresh, A.D. and Wallace, W.A. (1985). "The Application of Regression Analysis for Limited Review and Audit Planning," Working Paper, University of Rochester.

Bailey, A.D. Jr., Duke, G.L., Gerlach, J.H., Ko, C., Meservy, R.D. and Whinston, A.B. (1985a). "TICOM and the Analysis of Internal Controls," The Accounting Review, April.

Bailey, A.D. Jr., Duke, G.L., Johnson, P.E., Meservy, R.D. and Thompson, W. (1985b). "Auditing, Artificial Intelligence and Expert Systems," Proceedings of NATO A.S.I. on Decision Support Systems, Acquafredda di Maratea, Italy, June.

Bailey, A.D. Jr. and Jensen, D.L. (1977). "A Note on the Interface Between Compliance and Substantive Tests," The Journal of Accounting Research, Autumn.

Kaplan, R.S. (1979). "Developing a Financial Planning Model for an Analytical Review: A Feasibility Study," Symposium on Auditing Research III, University of Illinois.

Miller, M.A. and Bailey, L.P. (1984). GAAS Guide, Harcourt Brace Jovanovich, New York.

Statements on Auditing Standards (1972). American Institute of Certified Public Accountants, November.

Will, H.J. (1981). ACL (Audit Command Language): User Manual, University of British Columbua.

12. ON KNOWLEDGE-BASED DECISION SUPPORT SYSTEMS FOR FINANCIAL DIAGNOSTICS

Leif B. Methlie
Norwegian School of Economics and Business Administration
Bergen, Norway

ABSTRACT

This paper consists of two parts. In the first part a conceptual framework of knowledge-based DSS for financial decision making is discussed. Characteristics of the DSS technology and the expert system technology are described. Subsequently, as financial decision making to a large extent is diagnostic decision making, a diagnostic reasoning process is described in terms of conceptual structure, tasks, reasoning strategy and classification. Finally, a conceptual framework of a knowledge-based DSS supporting financial diagnostic tasks is described focusing on functional capabilities and systems architecture.

The second part describes an experimental expert system, BANKER, for bank loan evaluations. A systems overview is given and some aspects of the design tool EMYCIN, in which BANKER is implemented, is discussed. BANKER is currently being reprogrammed in PROLOG to be able to experiment with alternative search strategies.

PART 1: A CONCEPTUAL FRAMEWORK ON KNOWLEDGE-BASED DSS

1. <u>DECISION SUPPORT SYSTEMS AND EXPERT SYSTEMS TECHNOLOGIES</u>

Decision Support Systems (DSS) originated as a systems concept from MIT in the beginning of the 1970s. It emerged out of the many failures of applying computers to problems of managerial decision making, in particular, ill-structured problems for which it is difficult to prescribe an algorithmic solution. A shift in focus took place. Instead of the traditional operation research approach, focusing on solution optimization given a fixed set of alternatives, the process of decision making was now emphasized. The DSS technology, therefore, is directed towards finding computer support for this decision-making process. Studies of organizational decision making at

Carnegie Institute of Technology in the 1960s became seminal
work for the definition of this concept (see e.g., Newell and Simon
[1972], Simon [1977]). Support is the key issue in DSS. A man-
machine system should be designed to increase the decision making
effectiveness by a division of tasks between the computer and
the human being in such a way that the comparative advantages
of the two are utilized.

Thus, a computer's processing speed and storage capacity
are used to perform numerical calculations and store and retrieve
data. On the other hand, human intuition and judgement, and
processing of unformalized information is regarded as superior
to computer processing. However, the sharing of information
processing tasks between the two is a matter of advances in
computer systems technology. As we shall see later the expert
system technology can move the balance point of the DSSs of
today towards more "intelligent" computer processing tasks. In
the tradition of quantitative modelling, which was taken as a
basis for much of the early DSS development, analytical models
and formatted data were the basic components of the computer
system. Sprague [1980] formulated a conceptual framework where
he depicted a DSS as consisting of three components (Exhibit 1):
  - model base
  - data base
  - software component for managing models, data and
    dialogue
Due to the ill-structureness of the problem solving task to be
supported by a DSS, and the sharing of information processing
between man and computer, the man-machine interface is of key
importance to a successful design.

A typical DSS consists of analytical models and numeric data
with problem solving methods defined prior to model solving.
Its analytical capabilities comprise functions for: scenario-
building (what if), means-ends analysis (goal seeking), sensitivity analysis, risk analysis, and optimization.

Tools for easy and flexible building and modification of a
DSS, so-called DSS-generators, have been developed. They are
typically built around the following technology: a modelling

language to set up two-dimensional models of the equation type, a data management function to handle primarily data arrays (usually time-series of data), and command- or menu-driven dialogues. The spreadsheet technology opens for table-driven DSSs, and the business graphics technology allows diagrammatic output which conceptually is a shift from state values-representations towards trends-representations.

Recently, another systems concept has emerged in the public arena, namely expert systems. Actually, expert systems have been a research topic for more than 15 years, or about as long as the DSS-concept. It emerged from the product-oriented research in artificial intelligence (AI). The expert system concept was a paradigmatic change in AI research. Most artificial intelligence research prior to this change was concerned with generalized strategies of problem solving. However, it was recognized that human beings develop expertise not because they have learned a problem solving method, but because they have acquired domain specific knowledge. Therefore, to develop computer systems that could handle real-world, complex problems requiring an expert's interpretation, the computer system must contain a knowledge base where the domain specific knowledge can be represented, as well as reasoning models.

The term expert system connotes replacement of human expertise with computer systems. It is

"loaded with a great deal more implied intelligence than is warranted by their actual level of sophistication. The popular use of the term ... tends to give people the impression that an expert system is equivalent to a human expert in a given field" [Schank, 1984].

To avoid this rigorous interpretation the term "knowledge-based system" is sometimes used. In this paper we shall use the terms knowledge-based system and expert system interchangeably. Furthermore, instead of replacing human experts, these systems are used to amplify expertise. In many applications, e.g., in medicine, expert systems are used in a consultation mode by domain-specialists to amplify their expertise in certain tasks. We shall later on develop some characteristics of knowledge-

based decision support systems where problem solving support
again will be emphasized. Despite the debate about the label
"expert system" they are indeed developed on a technology which
can contribute to more effective decision-making aids for management. Going back to the description of DSSs we are now at a
point where more intelligent tasks can be taken over by the
computer by this technology.

The basic components of an expert system, as depicted in
Exhibit 2, are:
  - knowledge base
  - data base
  - reasoning system

In some descriptions of expert systems we find the data base,
representing factual information, as part of the knowledge base.
The most common representation mechanism for knowledge is production rules. Data are represented as associative triplets;
objects, attributes and values. The reasoning system, or inference engine as it sometimes is called, reasons about a problem
by applying rules on the data either stored in a data base or
provided during a consultation with the user.

In 1975 Allen Newell and Herbert Simon received the "Turing
Award". In their lecture they emphasized the two concepts
"symbol" and "search" as fundamental in intelligent problem
solving. A typical expert system is concerned with symbolic
inference. It reasons about a problem by searching a solution
space for a solution which can be discriminated by logical rules
or constraints, sometimes also increasing reasoning effectiveness by heuristic methods. It exhibits intelligent behavior by
applying knowledge (rules) in a a context- (problem-) dependent
manner.

Its functional capabilities can be classified into consulting and explanation. The consultation facility recommend solutions to a problem while the explanation facility can describe
what the system is doing. A broad generic framework of application categories comprises problems of interpretation, prediction, diagnosis, design, planning, etc. (see Hayes-Roth et al.
[1983] for more detail). We shall be particularly concerned with

diagnostic problem solving.

Tools for building expert systems, so-called shells or design tools, have been developed. We shall look at one such, EMYCIN, in discussing the BANKER system. These tools are typically built around the following technology:
- a representation language for production rules
- a control structure for reasoning (forward or backward chaining)
- host programming language (LISP, PROLOG, FORTRAN, PASCAL, etc.)
- systems controlled dialogue (Question/Answer-type)
- natural language interface.

2. THE PROBLEM OF FINANCIAL EVALUATION

In this section we shall use an example from the financial area to demonstrate the shortcomings of traditional decision support systems and illustrate what we think can be accomplished by merging the DSS-technology with the expert system technology in the area of financial decision making.

Konstans [1982] has described a model that can assist an analyst in identifying financial problems in business organizations. The model is based on ratio analysis of financial statements, a target area of many financial DSS applications. The advantage of ratio analysis is its computational ease. Numeric models define the ratios and by providing numeric data these ratios are computed. Konstans' model takes these computations one step further by grouping ratios (evidences) which can identify certain problems. Exhibit 3 shows the results of applying this model on financial data for a specific company. It is a table of data where rows represent variables and columns time periods.

For a person without any knowledge of finance this table is nothing more than a collection of figures. With some knowledge we may be able to interpret what each individual figure means, e.g., what it means that the ratio "net income/net sales" is .7%. It requires even more knowledge to make meaningful comparisons, e.g., that a figure for the firm is less than the industry average. And how can we relate figures to each other, since the table does not explicitly describe any relationships, e.g., "inventory/current assets" and "Days sales in inventory"?

Here is an expert's conclusion of the financial analysis of this firm:

"The company is undercapitalized, and its management of receivables and inventory is questionable. Its operations are inefficient, or it is operating below break even point, thus dissipating the owners' investment. Assets are being diverted from uses productive of revenue. These factors all result in a liquidity problem and a general decline in the company's financial condition" [Konstans, 1982].

How do we get from the table of data shown in Exhibit 3 to the conclusions shown above? In the traditional DSS-approach the computer system performs the computations and the analyst performs the evaluation of these data in order to reach a conclusion. This evaluation, also called diagnostic reasoning, is the target area of expert systems. This will be discussed subsequently.

We can distinguish three tasks in financial analysis (slightly modified from Methlie [1984]):

1. Intelligence, where information relevant to the problem domain is collected and interpreted.
2. Quantitative analysis where income statements and balance sheets are processed into key-variables, a set of standard ratios.
3. Qualitative reasoning, where the figures are dealt with in qualitative terms based on logical rules and constraints.

By providing the computer system with knowledge on how to interpret the figures, it can employ a process of symbolic reasoning in addition to computing the figures. The task of judging the financial position of a company has much in common to evaluating the health of a patient. It involves diagnosis: the identification of a problem and its causes on the basis of observable symptoms.

3. DIAGNOSTIC REASONING

Diagnostic computer programs have been available for more than two decades, particularly in medicine. Applications range from supporting tasks of diagnostics to making complete diagnoses. Most programs up to mid-70s were based on the normative models of statistical decision theory. However, these programs have had little impact on the practice of medicine [Pople, 1982]. Feinstein [1977] argues that the reason that physicians have not adopted computer-based decision aids is that these are not based on the way the judgements are actually performed. Furthermore, he argues [Feinstein, 1974] that identifying a disease name, which is typically the output of a diagnostic system, is not a goal in itself but only a vehicle for choosing an appropriate therapy.

In this section we shall look at some aspects of the diagnostic reasoning process. We shall start by defining a conceptual structure, a terminological framework, of a diagnostic system. We shall look at a goal-subgoal structure in the problem set. Subsequently, we shall define the diagnostic tasks and discuss reasoning strategies, the control structure of the process. Finally, a typical model of diagnostic reasoning, called the classification model, is presented.

3.1. Conceptual Structure

Diagnostic systems

"advise their user on a "problem" of some sort and they might make an attempt to isolate the "cause" of that problem. Some systems are also recommending a "repair" that would rectify this problem and suggesting additional "test" that might verify the hypothesized problem and its cause" [Bennett, 1985].

The conceptual structure of the diagnostic reasoning task is a set of abstract categories and inference steps that link these categories together, e.g., evidences to problems -- the relationships between observable symptoms and the possible inferences they support (Exhibit 6).

The evidence set consists of symptoms, that is observable facts. In the case of financial diagnostics this will be the collection of financial data as found in the income statements, balance sheets, etc. The evidence set may be preprocessed in two steps: first, an interpretation of these data should be done in order to validate the data. Second, the validated data should be processed through analytical models to compute other information, e.g., ratios.

The problem set consists of descriptors of the real system to be diagnosed. In the case of a medical system, this set consists of diseases. In the case of a financial system, financial descriptors are such as profit, liquidity, capital-structure, and solvency.

"A key aspect of a problem detection is the identification of what constitutes an indicative, characteristic "symptom" [Bouwman, 1983].

Pople [1982] has suggested that the problem of medical diagnosis is ill-structured, using Simon's [1973] work as basis. Ill-structured diagnostic tasks arise due to a problem set which is not a differential set, i.e., a fixed set of alternatives, or that mappings from evidences to problems are not unique, or that incomplete knowledge of the problems exists. There are evidences to believe that financial diagnostics is ill-structured, among other things because financial problems are intertwined, that is, profitability, liquidity, capital-structure, etc., are not mutually exclusive problems. We shall not elaborate on this topic any further, only notice that diagnostic reasoning is likely to be ill-structured, and that problems to be supported by a DSS are characterized by ill-structureness. The expert systems of today do mainly operate on differential problem sets and employ a classification model (see below). Therefore, we may expect that in future systems the DSS technology may contribute to better diagnostic systems.

3.2. Causes

Causes are a set of operators which usually will be drawn from the evidence set (as indicated by the link in Exhibit 6).

Links between "causes" and "problems" represent significant findings in the evidence set, findings which determine the causes and
thus explain the problem.

3.2.1. Action Set

After having determined the causes of the problems, appropriate actions can be recommended. The link between "causes"
and "actions" represents the therapy-part of the diagnosis if
the causes have been completely determined, or it can represent
recommendations to collect additional evidences.

In Exhibit 6 instances of the various categories are presented.
The evidences given by the two ratios of the firm compared with
the industry average, determine a low profit which can be explained by high selling and administrative costs. Recommended
action is cost reduction.

3.3. Hierarchical Set Structures

If the problem set can be hierarchically structured into an
inference tree (sometimes called a goal structure) and evidences
associated with subcategories, the reasoning process will be more
efficient. In the case of BANKER which we shall return to later,
the problem set consists of two goal elements: accept or reject
a loan application. The goal structure may represent empirical
as well as causal knowledge. BANKER's inference tree is shown
in Exhibit 14. This hierarchical structure can be used to guide
the evidence collection, so that only relevant data are collected.

3.4. Diagnostic Tasks

Within this conceptual structure we can identify the tasks
of the diagnostic reasoning process:
  - detect problems
  - determine causes
  - recommend actions
  - determine tests to produce additional evidences
  - predict observations
  - evaluate evidences

3.5. Control Structure

The control structure determines the reasoning strategy of
the diagnostic process. There are generally two basic strategies
to control this process:
- goal directed (backward chaining)
- evidence (data) driven (forward chaining)

In a goal directed search the diagnosis starts by hypothe-
sizing a problem (a goal) and seeks evidences to verify this
hypothesis. In the evidence driven strategy the diagnosis starts
with evidences, and looks for significant findings which can
detect problems.

Pople has in some length discussed the nature of the diagnostic reasoning process in medicine.

> "The question of what it is that distinguishes the
> expertise of an accomplished clinician has been inves-
> tigated by a variety of techniques both in our labora-
> tory and elsewhere. One nearly universal finding is
> that the physician responds to cues in the clinical
> data by conceptualizing one or more diagnostic tasks
> which then play an important role in the subsequent
> decision of additional data and the range of alter-
> natives considered in the eventual diagnostic decision
> making process. One mark of an expert is his ability
> to formulate particularly appropriate differential
> diagnostic tasks on the basis of sometimes subtle
> hints in the patient record" [Pople, 1982].

Also Elstein et al. [1978] have studied medical problem
solving and state:

> "Diagnostic problems are solved through a process of
> hypothesis generation and verification".

Bouwman [1983] has described a general model of diagnosis
which he has applied to financial analysis. It consists of the
following steps:
- selection of financial data to be examined
- test if examination is "significant"
- formulate problem hypotheses

- decision on further search or formulation of final
  evaluation

It seems that these descriptions of the nature of diagnostic
processes all employ a combination of goal directed and evidence
driven reasoning strategies. An evidence driven strategy is
performed to generate a hypothesis and a goal driven process is
executed to verify this hypothesis. Bouwman's process-descrip-
tion, however, is predominantly evidence driven. Most of the
expert systems developed for diagnostics, e.g., MYCIN, apply goal
directed, backward chaining control structures. The BANKER-
system, implemented in EMYCIN, employs a backward chaining
reasoning system. It starts with the hypothesis to accept the
loan application and seeks evidences among financial, management
and bank internal data to verify this hypothesis. If not verified the loan application is rejected.

3.6. Classification Models

Most expert systems designed for diagnostic consultations
(e.g., MYCIN, PUFF, CASNET) apply a classification model for
the reasoning process. This model views the diagnostic task
as one of "differential diagnosis" [Pople, 1982]. The term
"differential diagnosis" refers to a type of task wherein the
decision maker is confronted with a fixed set of diagnostic
alternatives in the problem set. His job is to determine whether
sufficient data are available to make a decision among elements
of this set and if not, to obtain whatever additional data may
be required to make a decision.

The classification model is a suitable framework in which
production rules can be used, as shown in Exhibit 7.

4. KNOWLEDGE-BASED DECISION SUPPORT SYSTEMS

Expert systems and DSSs are two different approaches to
support of managerial problem solving. An expert system simulates expert human reasoning by means of a knowledge base containing inference knowledge. A DSS amplifies the manager's
decision-making capabilities by providing data and analytical
models. Furthermore, a DSS accommodates learning through its

open man-machine interaction. Merging these two concepts seems
to be a promising approach in application areas involving quantitative analysis as well as qualitative, symbolic reasoning.
We have already shown that this is the case in financial diagnostics.

4.1. Functional Capabilities of a Knowledge-Based DSS

First of all, we want our system to be supportive to managerial decision making. Expert systems aiming at replacing expert
knowledge focus on solutions, that is, they find a solution to a
given problem. DSSs aiming at amplifying decision making effectiveness focus on the process. Given the ill-structured problem
domains of our target systems we shall focus on problem solving
support. Problem solving in this context consists of the diagnostic tasks described above. However, these tasks are carried
out in the context of man-machine interactions. We can define
the following supportive roles of a knowledge-based DSS:
- consultative
- explanation
- understanding
- learning

Consultative means using the system to obtain specialists'
advice or other means of help in accomplishing a task. The
system amplifies the decision maker's expertise in a given domain,
and can sometimes replace the need for expert help in the decision process. For instance, a manager may rely on financial
analysts to evaluate the company's financial position. This
expertise may be replaced by an expert system. Most expert
systems of today, including our own BANKER, are designed for this
role. Basden [1983] lists some benefits of this role:
- greater reliability
- increased consistency
- increased accessibility
- greater efficiency
- duplication of expertise.

Furthermore, Basden discusses the sharing of tasks between
a consultative-role expert system and the user:

"the human still have the advantage of being able to
take apparently extraneous factors into account (such
as economic or political factors), and to recognize
which factors are relevant" [Basden, 1983].

4.1.1. Explanation

The ability to explain reasoning is considered an important
rule of any expert system. There are, however, several levels
of explanations. On the surface level the system should be able
to explain what it is doing in terms of what knowledge it is
currently using or have been using in the reasoning process. In
BANKER a consultation is run by backchaining through the applicable rules, asking the user for data when necessary. (Using
BANKER to examplify here, means actually EMYCIN, since the
reasoning system of BANKER is that of the design tool used.)
WHY is used to ask the system why a specific question is asked,
and BANKER returns the rule currently invoked. HOW is used to
descend the inference structure explaining how sub-goals can be
achieved. The system responds with a list of rule numbers.
There is also a command EXPLAIN that can be used to explain the
results of the consultation. Exhibit 18 shows a sample of
BANKER's explanations.

There are several limitations to this level of explanation.
First, BANKER explains entirely in terms of what it is doing
(you ask why it is doing what it does and how it does it). Any
system that can explain the inference steps it has gone through
understands at a level of "making sense". At the level of

"cognitive understanding the program must be able to
explain why it came to the conclusions it did, what
conclusions or lines of reasoning it rejected and why
it rejected them, and how previous experiences influ-
enced its response. The machine must be able to answer
the question How do you know? at the level of understanding that a schoolteacher would reasonably expect
from his students" [Schank, 1983, p. 61].

Cognitive understanding requires deeper knowledge than we
find in most current systems. For instance, to answer the

question "why is profit low" causal knowledge is required. This
question can be made even more complicated by asking "why is
profit decreasing" which in addition to a causal network of knowledge requires time relationships represented. Explanations of
this kind are developed in the ROME-project [Kosy and Dhar, 1983].
The explanation system of NEOMYCIN [Hasling et al., 1984] can
explain on an abstract level, explaining general principles,
as well as on a concrete level, referring to aspects of the
current problem situation.

4.1.2. Understanding and Learning

Understanding is here used in the sense that the system can
support the user to understand a particular problem, for
instance, understanding conceptually the problem. This may require a dictionary as well as a causal network. The system may
also help the user to understand the effect of certain actions,
e.g., do I really understand how these parameters interact?,
and to classify problems as conceptual vs. procedural problems,
i.e., what is the real problem and how it can be solved? Understanding is also a question of:
  - "what if X happens?"
  - why happens X?
  - how can X be prevented?

Learning is the matter of how to refine the domain knowledge
of the system through use. Learning can be accomplished by
better understanding. Learning implies the dynamic aspects of
the knowledge base. Future expert systems will have better
understanding capabilities as well as learning capabilities.

4.2. System Architecture

Exhibit 9 presents an architecture of a knowledge-based system
performing quantitative analysis, qualitative reasoning and
information retrieval, tasks that are necessary to perform
financial diagnostics. The architecture is designed taking
elements from the DSS technology and the expert system technology
together. Some of these aspects have been discussed already.
Here, we shall briefly discuss some other aspects of this

architecture.

4.2.1. Symbolic Reasoning and Numeric Calculations

Inferential knowledge is the kind of knowledge that enables an expert system to do symbolic reasoning and analytical models enables a DSS to do quantitative analysis and simulation. The reasoning system uses inferential knowledge on factual knowledge represented in the data base, and the calculation/simulation system uses analytical models on this same data base. We need systems with good interfaces between these two kinds of reasoning so that data can be easily processed through analytical procedures before being used in the inferential logic of the reasoning system.

4.2.2. Empirical versus Causal Knowledge

Many of the early expert systems employed inferential knowledge consisting of a collection of rules that captured empirical associations about their problem domain. The BANKER system, for example, arises from an assembly of rules that encode the experiences of loan officers in American banks captured by an empirical study. These rules are justified on purely empirical grounds, they associate financial evidences with the decision of granting or rejecting a loan. Inferential knowledge of this type is sometimes called shallow knowledge.

Recently, interest has grown in the development of expert systems that reason from an understanding of more fundamental relationships, the causal relationships. Causal relationships can be modelled into a causal network describing how states and variables that characterize our real system, influence each other.

One of the first known medical expert systems employing a causal model is CASNET [Weiss and Kulikowski, 1984]. Davis [1983] explores the use of causal models in troubleshooting digital electronics. Finally, Bouwman [1983] in his discussion of a financial diagnostic system employs a causal model, called an "internal model of the firm", to characterize operations of business, such as how demand, units sold, and production capacities influence each other.

Exhibit 11 illustrates a typical empirical association represented as a production rule as well as an extension of this
association into deeper knowledge.

The causal knowledge can be used for:
- better (deeper) explanations
- generate problem-hypotheses [Bouwman, 1983]
- deduce the most likely cause of a problem [Weiss and Kulikowski, 1984]
- aggregating elements in diagnosis and thereby reducing number
  of alternatives to be considered [Pople, 1982]
- establishing milestones to simplify the diagnosis
- indicate further tests (evidences to be collected).

In the financial area we can see two types of causal networks,
one representing arithmetic relationships and one representing
logical (qualitative) relationships. The first kind is represented as part of the analytical model. The latter is part of
the inferential knowledge. Thus, we have established the knowledge base to consist of:
- empirical associations
- causal relationships
- factual knowledge
- analytical relationships.

Since we have little experience of reasoning from causal
knowledge in expert systems, to have all these kinds of knowledge
working together is still an area of research.

4.2.3. Man-Machine Interaction and Systems Interface

Man-machine interaction is a well-known research topic in the
DSS field. Because of the required flexibility in model building
and model execution, emphasis is put in the dialogue design of a
DSS. The system should be controlled at every point by the user.
Therefore, menu or command driven dialogues are most frequently
used. The spreadsheet concept has also been highly adopted.

In expert systems we find two characteristics of the man-
machine interface: first, a question/answer-dialogue controlled

by the system is used; second, an approximation to natural language input/output-form is employed. We should bear in mind that there are numerous DSSs in real use today, while the number of expert systems in real use is rather low. We should therefore, capitalize on experiences we have and build financial expert systems with interface-facilities that take advantage of the experiences gained in the two fields.

Also, most expert systems are self-contained, and therefore lack good interfaces to other programs (of any language) or data bases. A question in designing a design tool for financial expert systems arises as to what extent the system architecture as described in Exhibit 9 should be supported by one software module, or rather, build our system as modules utilizing software technology which is best suited for the various tasks and designing good module-interfaces to ensure an integrated system.

PART II: BANKER - AN EXPERIMENTAL EXPERT SYSTEM*

1. BACKGROUND

BANKER is an experimental model of an expert system for bank loan application analysis. It has been developed as part of a larger project to apply the expert system concept to financial decision making and to develop financial expert systems for banks, insurance companies and management consultants. The objective of this project is to develop methods and design tools for financial diagnostic systems. This includes financial analysis as well as financial advising.

The project started late 1983 and BANKER is the first milestone of this project. BANKER is implemented in EMYCIN [van Melle et al., 1981], an expert system design tool. The goal of building BANKER has been to develop a working system without going through a lengthy apprenticeship in AI methods and techniques and thereby gain practical knowledge and experience in a relatively short time. Furthermore, we wanted to apply EMYCIN on a financial application to observe its strengths and weaknesses for financial decision making.

* This part is an excerption of a working paper written on BANKER [Ribe, 1985].

Bank procedures for analyzing business loan applications is a typical expert task. Loan officers have developed expertise in diagnosing an applicant's financial position, its management, and short and long terms benefits for the bank of having the applicant as a customer. To acquire this human expert knowledge requires cognitive modelling of experts' problem solving processes. A separate project to acquire loan officers' expert knowledge is currently in process. However, to shortcut the development time, BANKER's knowledge base is built from a 20-year old empirical study of procedures for analyzing loan applications in American banks [Cohen et al., 1966]. The result of this study was a deterministic simulation model based on a set of decision tables. We have converted the knowledge stored in these tables into production rules, although to some extent modified.

Banker's knowledge base consists of one context type (the loan applicant), 36 parameters and 114 rules. The problem set of BANKER has been hierarchically structured into goals and subgoals until it links with evidences. This goal structure, here called an inference tree, is shown in Exhibit 14.

2. SYSTEMS OVERVIEW

BANKER collects relevant information about the loan applicant (e.g., loan type, 3-year average net profits, management competence, etc.) by conducting an interactive dialogue with the user. It asks some basic questions first (e.g., the name of the applicant). The information entered by the user in response to these questions is used by the rules to advise on whether to accept or reject a loan application. If, during this process, further information is required, the system will either try to infer it from the data it already has or it will ask the user for it.

The rules are frequently of a tentative kind, indicating, for example, that certain symptoms imply a conclusion only to some level of certainty (inexact reasoning). This uncertainty, which is particularly present in empirical associations, is either associated with evidences or with the domain knowledge (the rules).

BANKER's reasoning system is determined by EMYCIN's reasoning mechanism which employs a goal directed backward chaining search procedure. The search starts at the top of the inference tree and descends this tree in an exhaustive, depth-first search, i.e., the system generates a hypothesis and search for evidences to verify this. Evidences are found at the leaf nodes of the tree. These evidences are collected by asking the user during a consultation. However, the system can do default reasoning, that is, if the data the system is asking for cannot be provided by the user, default knowledge may exist in the knowledge base. This is similar to how human experts solve problems. An expert can draw conclusions even if complete information does not exist. The conclusion may be more uncertain, but still a solution is reached. In the same way BANKER is able to proceed even if not all the desired information exists. At each node of the tree, BANKER tries to reach a conclusion. It searches the knowledge base for rules which conclude about a parameter at this point, for instance the Bank's own credit rating (see Exhibit 14).

If BANKER were trying to infer on the bank's credit rating, one of the rules invoked would be RULE 048 (Exhibit 15). In this case the premise is the conjunction of three conditions. If all evidences (parameters) had already been traced, the premise could be concluded to be either true or false. In the former case this rule concludes that the credit rating is high. However, if the value of some parameter referenced is not available, a further search is executed. This might involve a similar process in which other rules are executed, for instance, to find profitability rating, or a question is asked the user, for instance, about the loan type.

Backward chaining ensures a coherent line of reasoning. The aim is to ask as few questions as possible by asking for information only when needed. This implies that the search to a conclusion may differ from one consultation to another and the sequence of questions will also vary. In this respect, BANKER exhibits a kind of intelligent behavior. Examples of consultations are shown in Exhibits 16 and 17.

3. FUTURE DEVELOPMENTS OF BANKER

BANKER has so far not been evaluated or used by real loan
officers. In so far as the model developed by Cohen et al.
[1966] can be used in real loan application evaluations, BANKER
should also be a practical tool. However, as already stated
the objective of this study has been to build an experimental
system to make a shortcut into the world of expert systems technology in general, and EMYCIN in particular. For a review on
MYCIN and EMYCIN the reader is referred to Cendrowska and Bramer
[1984]. Using an existing design tool like EMYCIN puts several
constraints on the structure of the system to be designed. For
instance, the search strategies employed in EMYCIN must be used
in BANKER. We are, therefore, currently in the process of repro-
gramming BANKER in PROLOG to be able to experiment with different
search strategies. Also the need for better analytical tools
is present which is another reason to depart for EMYCIN.

REFERENCES

Basden, A. (1983). "On the Application of Expert Systems,"
    Int. J. Man-Machine Studies, 19.

Bennett, J.S. (1985). "ROGET: A Knowledge-Based System for
    Acquiring the Conceptual Structure of a Diagnostic Expert
    System," J. Automated Reasoning, 1.

Bouwman, M.J. (1983). "Human Diagnostic Reasoning by Computer:
    An Illustration from Financial Analysis," Management Science,
    29, 6, June.

Cendrowska, J. and Bramer, M.A. (1984). "A Rational Reconstruc-
    tion of the MYCIN Consultation System," Int. J. Man-Machine
    Studies, 20.

Cohen, K.J., Gilmore, T.G. and Singer, F.A. (1966). "Bank
    Procedures for Analyzing Business Loan Applications," in
    Analytical Methods in Banking, Hammer (ed.).

Davis, R. (1983). "Reasoning from First Principles in Electronic
    Troubleshooting," Int. J. Man-Machine Studies, 19.

Elstein, A.S., Shulman, L.A. and Sprafka, S.A. (1978). "Medical
    Problem Solving: An Analysis of Clinical Reasoning,"
    Harvard University Press, Cambridge, Mass.

Feinstein, A.R. (1974). "An Analysis of Diagnostic Reasoning: The Construction of Clinical Algorithms," Yale J. Biology and Medicine, 1.

Feinstein, A.R. (1977). "Clinical Biostatistics XXXIX," Clinical Pharmacology and Therapeutics, 21, 4, April.

Hayes-Roth, F., Waterman, D.A. and Lenat, D.B. (eds.) (1983). Building Expert Systems, Addison-Wesley.

Hasling, D.W., Clancey, W.J. and Rennels, G. (1984). "Strategic Explanations for a Diagnostic Consultation System," Int. J. Man-Machine Studies, 20.

Konstans, C. (1982). "Financial Analysis for Small Businesses," Business, 34, April-June.

Kosy, D.W. and Dhar, V. (1983). "Knowledge-Based Support Systems for Long Range Planning," CMU-RI-TR-83-21, Carnegie-Mellon University.

Methlie, L.B. (1984). "Knowledge Based DSS for Financial Diagnostics," Working Paper A-84.005, Norwegian School of Economic and Business Administration, Bergen.

Newell, A. and Simon, H.A. (1972). Human Problem Solving, Prentice-Hall, Englewood Cliffs, N.J.

Pople, H.E., Jr. (1982). "The Structuring of Medical Diagnosis," in Artificial Intelligence in Medicine, P. Szolovits (ed.), Westview Press, Boulder.

Ribe, H. (1985). "BANKER - An Experimental Model of an Expert System for Credit Evaluation Implemented in EMYCIN" (in Norwegian), Working Paper No. 5/1985, SAF, Norwegian School of Economic and Business Administration, Bergen.

Schank, R.C. (1984). The Cognitive Computer, Addison-Wesley.

Simon, H.A. (1973). "The Structure of Ill-Structured Problems," Artificial Intelligence, 4.

Simon, H.A. (1977). The New Science of Management Decision (revised edition), Prentice-Hall, Englewood Cliffs, N.J.

Sprague, R.H., Jr. (1980). "A Framework for the Development of Decision Support Systems," MIS Quarterly, December.

van Melle, Scott and Pairs, Bennett (1981). "The EMYCIN Manual," Computer Science Dept., Stanford University.

Weiss, S.M. and Kulikowski, C.A. (1984). Designing Expert Systems, Rowman & Allanheld, N.J.

SOME ASPECTS OF THE DSS TECHNOLOGY

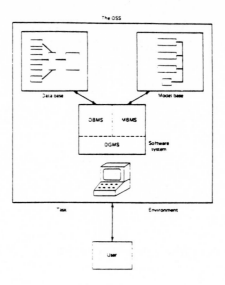

SPRAGUE's FRAMEWORK OF A DSS

FUNCTIONAL ORIENTATION

- ILL-STRUCTURED DECISIONS
- PROBLEM SOLVING PROCESS SUPPORT

FUNCTIONAL CAPABILITIES

- NUMERIC MODELS / CALCULATIONS
  (SCENARIO-BUILDING (WHAT IF), MEANS-ENDS
  ANALYSIS (GOAL SEEKING), SENSITIVITIY ANALYSIS,
  RISK ANALYSIS, OPTIMIZATION)
- NUMERIC DATA

DSS-TECHNOLOGY

- MODELING LANGUAGE
- DATA ARRAY -/ MATRIX-HANDLING
- COMMAND -/ MENUE-DIALOGUES
- SPREAD SHEET DRIVEN DIALOGUE
- BUSINESS GRAPHICS

Exhibit 1

SOME ASPECTS OF THE EXPERT SYSTEM TECHNOLOGY

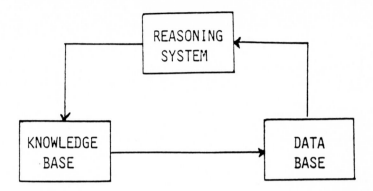

BASIC BUILDING BLOCKS OF EXPERT SYSTEMS

FUNCTIONAL ORIENTATION

      - EXPERT PROBLEM SOLVING
        (PARTICULARLY DIAGNOSTIC PROBLEMS)

FUNCTIONAL CAPABILITIES

      - SYMBOLIC MANIPULATION
        CONSULTATIONS (RECOMMEND SOLUTIONS)
        EXPLANATIONS (DESCRIBE BEHAVIOR)

EXPERT SYSTEMS

        - KNOWLEDGE REPRESENTATION LANGUAGE (RULES)
        - CONTROL STRUCTURE
        - HOST PROGRAMMING LANGUAGE
        - SYSTEM CONTROLLED DIALOGUE
        - NATURAL LANGUAGE INTERFACE

Exhibit 2

FINANCIAL ANALYSIS

1. MODEL - RESULTS

	1968		1969		Year 1970	
Ratio	Firm	Industry	Firm	Industry	Firm	Industry
Margin:						
1. Net income/net sales*	7%	3.0%	loss	2.3%	loss	2.7%
2. Gross profit/net sales	20.0	22.0	22.0%	22.0	21.0%	20.0
Turnover:						
3. Average collection period* (in days)	69.0	36.0	75.0	38.0	82.0	41.0
4. Days sales in inventory*	71.0	35.0	72.0	34.0	79.0	22.0
5. Net sales/stockholders' equity* (times per year)	7.9	5.3	6.8	5.0	6.4	4.9
6. Net sales/total assets* (times per year)	2.2	3.7	2.0	3.6	1.8	3.6
7. Net sales/net fixed assets (times per year)	19.0	21.1	13.4	22.0	14.1	20.0
8. Net sales/net working capital (times per year)	17.5	7.2	25.7	6.8	28.8	6.2
Balance:						
9. Fixed assets/stockholders' equity plus long-term liabilities*	41.0%	9.1%	51.0%	9.2%	45%	9.4%
10. Current plus fixed assets/total assets*	96.0	96.0	93.0	95.0	90.0	96.0
11. Current assets/total assets	84.0	85.8	78.5	86.3	78.0	85.7
12. Current liabilities/total liabilities	99.0	44.0	99.6	47.8	99.5	47.3
13. Total liabilities/stockholders' equity	257.0	134.0	244.0	152.0	250.0	166.0
14. Accounts receivable/current assets	45.0	45.0	48.0	46.5	48	46.9
15. Inventory/current assets	52.0	41.0	51.0	40.0	51.0	37.0
Liquidity:						
16. Current assets/current liabilities	1.2:1	1.6:1	1.1:1	1.5:1	1.1:1	1.5:1
17. Acid test	.6:1	1:1	.5:1	.9:1	.5:1	.9:1
Solvency:'						

*Denotes a primary ratio
'Ratios could not be derived from the data provided.

2. A FINANCIAL ANALYST's CONCLUSIONS:

THE COMPANY IS UNDERCAPITALIZED, AND ITS MANAGEMENT OF RECEIVABLES AND INVENTORY IS QUESTIONABLE. ITS OPERATIONS ARE INEFFICIENT, OR IT IS OPERATING BELOW THE BREAKEVEN POINT, THUS DISSIPATING THE OWNERS' INVESTMENT. ASSETS ARE BEING DIVERTED FROM USES PRODUCTIVE OF REVENUE. THESE FACTORS ALL RESULT IN A LIQUIDITY PROBLEM AND A GENERAL DECLINE IN THE COMPANY'S FINANCIAL CONDITION.

Exhibit 3

JUDGING THE FINANCIAL POSITION

OF A COMPANY

1. INTELLIGENCE

2. QUANTITATIVE ANALYSIS

3. QUALITATIVE REASONING

Exhibit 4

THE DIAGNOSTIC REASONING PROCESS

- CONCEPTUAL STRUCTURE

- HIERARCHICAL STRUCTURE OF CATEGORIES

- DIAGNOSTIC TASKS

- CONTROL STRUCTURES

- THE CLASSIFICATION MODEL

Exhibit 5

THE DIAGNOSTIC REASONING PROCESS

- A CONCEPTUAL STRUCTURE -

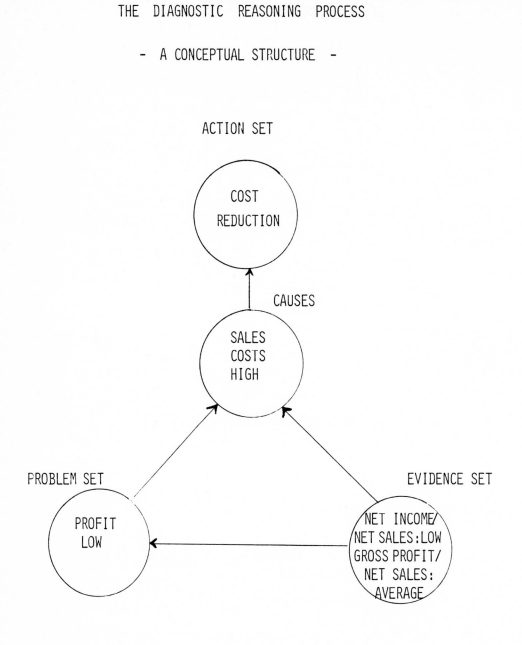

Exhibit 6

THE CLASSIFICATION MODEL

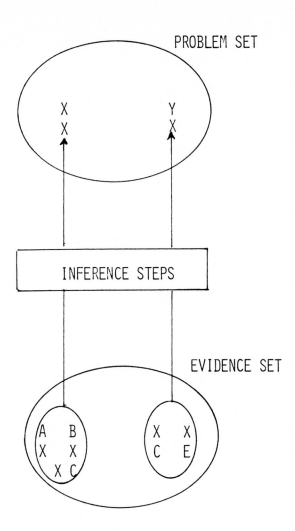

INFERENCE KNOWLEDGE EXPRESSED AS PRODUCTION RULES:

    IF   A IS TRUE, AND
          B IS TRUE, AND
          C IS FALSE,
    THEN CONCLUDE X

Exhibit 7

KNOWLEDGE BASED DSS

FUNCTIONAL CAPABILITIES:

- CONSULTATIVE

- EXPLANATION

- UNDERSTANDING

- LEARNING

Exhibit 8

KNOWLEDGE BASED DSS SYSTEMS ARCHITECTURE

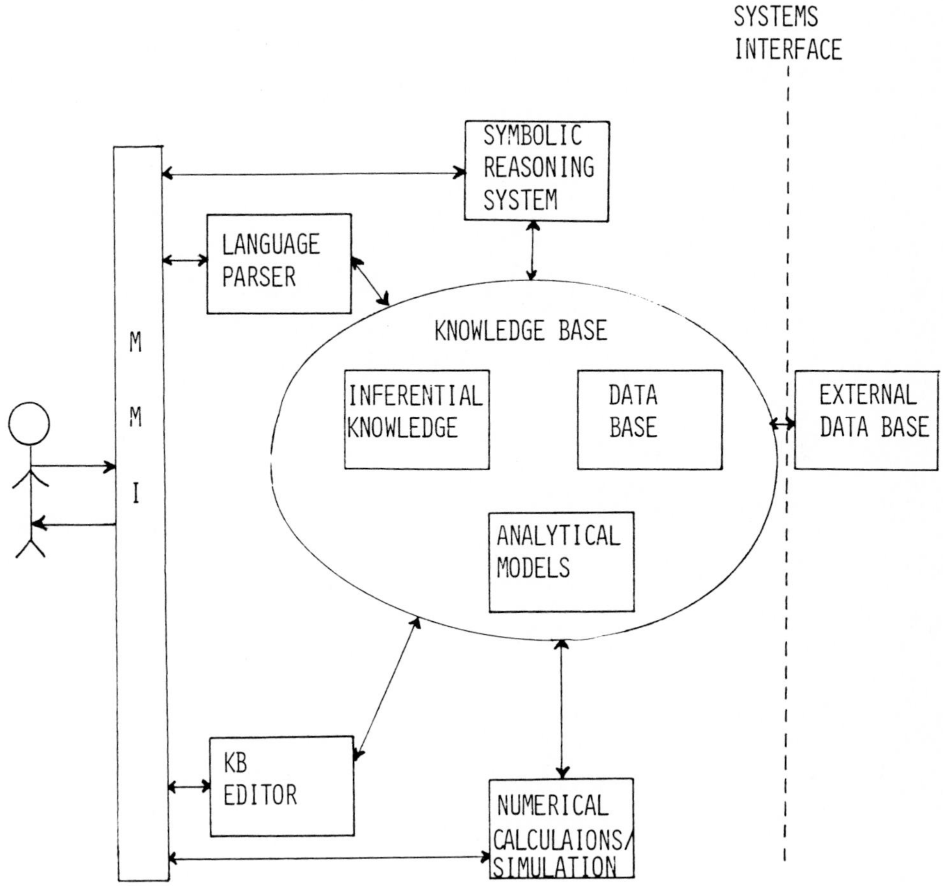

Exhibit 9

SYSTEMS ARCHITECTURE

IMPORTANT ISSUES TO BE ADDRESSED:

- SYMBOLIC MANIPULATIONS AND NUMERIC CALCULATIONS

- EMPIRICAL VERSUS CAUSAL INFERENCE KNOWLEDGE

- MAN-MACHINE-INTERACTION

- SYSTEMS INTERFACES

Exhibit 10

INFERENTIAL KNOWLEDGE

1.   EMPIRICAL ASSOCIATIONS

    IF CURRENT RATIO IS LESS THAN 2, AND
       ACID RATIO IS LESS THAN 1,
  THEN   LIQUIDITY IS BAD

2.   CAUSAL NETWORK (PART OF)

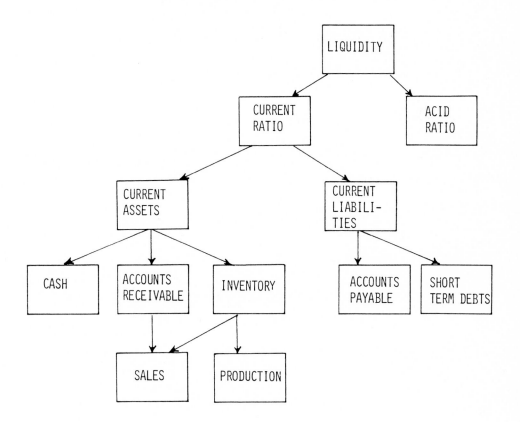

Exhibit 11

CAUSAL KNOWLEDGE CAN BE USED FOR:

- BETTER EXPLANATIONS

- GENERATE PROBLEM-HYPOTHESES

- FIND PROBLEM CAUSE

- AGGREGATE ELEMENTS OF THE INFERENCE STRUCTURE

- ETABLISH MILESTONES

- INDICATE FURTHER TESTS

Exhibit 12

B A N K E R

AN EXPERIMENTAL EXPERT SYSTEM FOR BANK
ANALYSIS OF BUSINESS LOAN APPLICATIONS.

DESIGN TOOL: E M Y C I N

KNOWLEDGE BASE: 1 CONTEXT
36 PARAMETERS
114 RULES

Exhibit 13

INFERENCE TREE

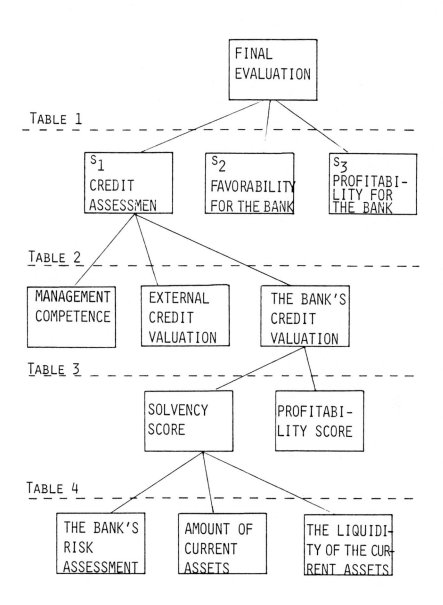

Exhibit 14

RULE048

This rule is tried in order to find out about bank's own credit
rating of the loan-applicant.

If: 1) The loantype applied for by the loan-applicant is seasonal,

      2) A rating of how profitable the loan-applicant is high,
         and

      3) A rating of the solvency of the loan-applicant is high

Then: It is definite (1.0) that bank's own credit rating of the
      loan-applicant is high.

PREMISE: (AND (SAME CNTXT LOANTYPE SEASONAL)
                  (SAME CNTXT PROFITABILITY HIGH)
                  (SAME CNTXT SOLVENCY HIGH))
ACTION: (CONCLUDE CNTXT F3 HIGH TALLY 1000)

Exhibit 15

369

This is a banking consultant offering advice on a
loan-applicant's credit-worthiness and attractiveness
as a customer. It is based on rules developed by
Cohen, Gilmore and Singer (Analytical Methods in Banking,
Homewood 1966).

To run the consultants you have to answer a number of
questions.

-------LOAN-APPLICANT-1-------

1) What is the name of the loan-applicant?
** HIGH-TECH
2) What is the average balance of deposits expected
   to be made by High-tech?
** 200000
3) What is, based on pro forma balance sheet, the net
   working capital of High-tech?
** 800000
4) What is the ratio of cash to total current liabilities
   (based on pro-forma balance sheet) for High-tech?
** 1
5) What is the 3-year average net profits of High-tech?
** 0
6) What loantype is the loanapplication by High-tech for?
** TERM

Decision regarding loan-application from High-tech is as
follows:
    REJECT.
THE SUM 4 (S1) + 3 (S2) + 3 (S3) is as follows:
    0.

Exhibit 16

```
---------LOAN-APPLICANT-2----------
```

1) What is the name of the loan-applicant?
** HIGH-TECH
2) What is the average balance of deposits expected to be
    made by High-tech?
** 500000
3) What is, based on pro forma balance sheet, the net
    working capital of High-tech?
** 1500000
4) What is the ratio of cash to total current liabilities
    (based on pro-forma balance sheet) for High-tech?
** .8
5) What is the 3-year average net profits of High-tech?
** 2000000
6) What loantype is the loanapplication by High-tech for?
** TERM
7) What is the percentile in industry of the ratio of
    pro-forma pre-tax profits to total tangible assets of
    High-tech?
** .8
8) What is the percentile in industry of the ratio of
    pro-forma net profits to tangible net worth for High-tech?
** .6
9) How do you rate the competence of the management of
    High-tech?
** HIGH
10) What is the percentile value of current ratio of
    High-tech, based on pro-forma balance sheet?
** .75
11) What is the median current ratio of industry of High-tech?
** 1.3
12) What is the bank's profit-factor for deposits made by
    High-tech?
** .1

Decision regarding loan-application from High-tech is as
follows:
        GRANTED.
THE SUM 4 (S1) + 3 (S2) + 3 (S3) is as follows:
        14.

                        Exhibit 17

Enter Debug/review phase, or other option (? for help): EXPLanation
Do you wish to continue with the regular QA module? ** YES

Type HELP for the list of question options.

** EQ 10 11 12 13
    Question 10 was asked in order to find out percentile in
        industry: ratio of pro-forma pre-tax profits to total
        tangible assets for A/s Autobil in an effort to execute
        RULE085.
    Question 11 was asked in order to find out percentile in
        industry of ratio of pro-forma net profits to tangible
        net worth of A/s Autobil in an effort to execute RULE085.
    Question 12 was asked in order to find out the competence of
        the management of A/s Autobil in an effort to execute
        RULE046.
    Question 13 was asked in order to find out external credit
        rating of A/s Autobil in an effort to execute RULE037.

** TYPE RULE 037

RULE037

This rule is tried in order to find out about final credit rating
    of the loan-applicant
    If: 1) The competence of the management of the loan-applicant
            is average,
         2) External credit rating of the loan-applicant is fair, and
         3) Bank's own credit rating of the loan-applicant is marginal
    Then: It is definite (1.0) that final credit rating of the
            loan-applicant is 0

** HOW DID YOU FIND F3?

The following rules use:
        bank's own credit rating of the loan-applicant

16, 17, 20, 21, 22, 23, 24, 25, 26, 27, 28, 29, 30, 31, 32, 33, 34,
    35, 36, 37, 38, 39, 40, 41, 42, 43, 44, 45, 46

The parameter most frequently concluded by these rules is:
        final credit rating of the loan-applicant

Would you like a summary of ALL the parameters concluded by these
rules?
** NO
...

Which of the rules do you wish to see?
        **

Exhibit 18

13. DECISION SUPPORT SYSTEMS FOR RESOURCE ALLOCATION

James Gantt
Army Institute for Research in Management
Information and Computer Sciences (AIRMICS)
Advanced Concepts and Technology Integration Division
Georgia Institute of Technology
Atlanta, Georgia

Donovan Young
School of Industrial and Systems Engineering
Georgia Institute of Technology
Atlanta, Georgia

1. INTRODUCTION

In 1978 AIRMICS started a research project dealing with Decision Support Systems (DSSs). When this project was started the concept of a DSS was almost unknown in the US Army. Even though DSSs are not found everywhere in the Army today, the concepts are being applied with greater frequency.

This paper reviews three DSSs that deal with resource allocation. The first system, the Automated Project Management System (APMS), is an AIRMICS funded project with the School of Industrial and Systems Engineering of the Georgia Institute of Technology serving as the contractor. The second, a location-allocation system was accomplished by Army officer graduate students and Georgia Institute of Technology faculty, with administrative support from AIRMICS. The Mobilization DSS (MDSS) is an AIRMICS funded project with Information Systems and Networks, Inc. (ISN) serving as the contractor. All of these systems assist planners in the allocation of resources. APMS assists project managers, the location-allocation systems assist Army division staff, and MDSS guides mobilization planners.

2. THE AUTOMATED PROJECT MANAGEMENT SYSTEM

A project is organized into a set of separate mutually exclusive and exhaustive tasks or _activities_. Activities have precedence relationships: certain activities must be completed before their successor activities can begin. Activities can consume various _resources_, and for purposes of summing and comparing

NATO ASI Series, Vol. F31
Decision Support Systems: Theory and Application
Edited by C. W. Holsapple and A. B. Whinston
© Springer-Verlag Berlin Heidelberg 1987

resource consumptions over time intervals less than the full duration of an activity, its consumption rate is assumed level.

CPM techniques aim at finding a best schedule -- one that best
balances time and resource considerations, assuming accuracy of
duration and consumption estimates. CPM planning ends with a
schedule that is accepted as a plan. PERT analysis begins with
the plan and aims at estimating the probability distributions of
actual results that may be obtained when the project is executed
according to the plan. Traditionally, PERT planning investigates
the consequences of variability of activity durations.

2.1. Interactive CPM Scheduling with Multiple Constrained Resources

Scheduling of activities with multiple constrained resources
and resource-time tradeoffs is mathematically intractable (the
best procedure reported to find a guaranteed-shortest feasible
schedule can handle only ten activities, three resources, and
three possible durations per activity [Talbot, 1982]). This suggests
either the use of heuristics in lieu of optimal algorithms, or
the use of a system to facilitate interactive evaluation (to
"evaluate" is to report consequences of a putative solution) in
lieu of optimization, or both. APMS does both: it allows a
user to input or modify a schedule interactively and immediately
view the time and resource consequences, and it also computes and
reports suggested heuristic schedules that can be compared to
those generated by the user or used as trial schedules to be
modified or accepted by the user.

Given a system that interactively evaluates rather than
optimizes, many modelling opportunities arise. Optimization
models must maintain mathematical tractability while trying to
fit reality, but evaluative models concede the tractability
requirement and hence are free to be generalized in any consistent
way that will better fit reality and remain comprehensible to the
user.

Talbot [1982] treats "a general class of nonpreemptive (mul-
tiple-) resource-constrained project scheduling problems in
which the duration of each job is a function of the resources
committed to it." Each resource may be given a limit on its total

consumption by all activities either per period ("renewable") or over the life of the project ("cumulative"). Each activity consumes resources at uniform rates throughout its duration and can have precedence relationships whereby one activity (a successor) cannot start until all of a list of predecessor activities have finished. The object of Talbot's algorithm is to minimize some objective function while not violating any resource limits, by possibly delaying start times of some activities beyond their CPM early-start times and possibly choosing durations of some activities longer than their minimum durations. "Typical of the objective functions permitted are minimize project duration, minimize project cost given performance payments and penalties, and minimize the consumption of a critical resource" [Talbot, 1982].

2.2. The APMS Model

The APMS model may be viewed as this model with several generalizations and extensions, which may be grouped as global extensions, resource extensions and activity extensions.

Global extensions of APMS are provided through allowing a tree-structured hierarchy of separate networks along the lines suggested by Leila DeFloriani [1978], except that APMS allows arbitrary network decomposition into subnetworks whose activities may have precedence relationships with those in other networks. Milestones in APMS are actually global events: an event in one network can act as a predecessor or successor of activities in other networks. This allows for decomposition of a large project into subprojects that do have some interaction but can be managed essentially separately. The hierarchical tree structure can also be used for purposes other than decomposing a large project into separately manageable subprojects: a single activity in any network can be elaborated into a subnetwork in order to perform a more detailed estimate of its resource consumptions at various durations, or a project can be organized into macroprojects that summarize its details for high-level management, or several projects can be scheduled together sharing some common resources. These global extensions provide a convenient structure for PERT simulation of groups of resource-sharing projects, something that has not been done before.

Resource extensions in APMS allow modelling advances. First, availabilities of resources can be limited in an entirely general way; the maximum amount allowed to be used in one period is not necessarily the same as that allowed for another period, and cumulative limits may be set for consumption in time intervals of any length, again with the amount in one interval not necessarily the same as that in another interval. This allows for "resource profiling" as a generalization of resource leveling, where the schedule can be adjusted to use resources more heavily when they have greater availabilities. APMS provides also for weighted averages of resources to be represented separately, and for an overall "cost" resource that can express a wide range of objectives including penalties and progress payments. These extensions provide a convenient structure for PERT simulation to include variation of how much of each resource turns out actually to be available in various periods or intervals, and for a single criterion of value (the "cost" resource) to be reported for each simulation experiment.

A particularly powerful modelling extension in APMS is that of a hyperbolic interpolation of resource consumptions. As an activity varies in its scheduled duration, its estimated consumptions vary. The user can specify up to three "key" durations for which consumptions are explicitly input, but the possible durations tried for the activity in a search for a good schedule are not confined to the "key" durations; intermediate durations can be tried for which the user has not given consumptions explicitly, and APMS will estimate the consumptions on the basis of a hyperbolic interpolation function. This extension provides a convenient structure for PERT simulation of the corresponding resource consumptions when activity durations are simulated.

Activity extensions in APMS include dependent-duration-activities (DDAs), offset precedences, and generalized criticality. A DDA, often representing such functions as management, inspection, or utility service, starts and finishes along with the earliest and latest start and finish times of the activities on which its duration depends. In a PERT simulation, its duration can be simulated accordingly. Offset precedences allow part of a successor activity to start before a predecessor finishes, and part of a predecessor to remain unfinished when a successor can begin.

In APMS, activities are scheduled at their early-start times unless the user "fixes" them to start at some other time. These "fixes" are the method by which a resource-feasible schedule is attained. The process of fixing activities may be viewed as substituting time constraints for resource constraints. Recall that a critical activity in CPM and PERT is one that, if its start were delayed, either the project completion time would be delayed or precedences would be violated. In APMS, the fixed points are considered analogous to the project completion time, so that an activity is critical if a delay in its start would cause either a delay in project completion or violation of precedences or of fixed points. In PERT simulation, this generalized concept of criticality allows statistical representation of the probability that a given activity will violate fixed points (and thus perhaps cause resource conflict), with project completion time being one of the fixed points.

2.3. PERT Simulation

Many techniques have been proposed to solve task-event networks, with CPM and PERT being the most widely used. Both methods are relatively simple and easily applied to a wide range of problems. CPM is applicable to projects where little uncertainty exists for activity durations. This usually occurs when tasks are familiar to the individual producing the estimates for activity durations and the sequence of activities is known. This is usually referred to as a deterministic situation. APMS adds the requirement for the definition of the relationship between time and resources. In this deterministic world a schedule is developed to allocate resources.

PERT was developed for projects which contain tasks that exhibit varying amounts of uncertainty with respect to activity duration times which are random variables. This is usually referred to as a stochastic situation. Even though this is more realistic, certain assumptions are made to improve computational ease, introducing inaccuracy. PERT analytical methods (now supplanted by simulation), replaced random activity durations with deterministic equivalents (optimistic, pessimistic and most likely activity duration) from the Beta family of distributions. Hartley and Wortham [1966] point out weaknesses in using these estimates to obtain a unique and fixed critical path by summing expected completion times to produce the maximum path length. MacCrimmon and Ryavec [1964] have reported inaccuracies and biases that result from using analytical methods that assume the distribution of project duration to be the same as the distribution of the fixed critical path. PERT calculated means will always be biased optimistically, and PERT calculated standard deviations may be biased in either direction. Because of these limitations, modern PERT analysis is accomplished via simulation, allowing various probabilistic descriptions of activity durations and avoiding the equating of the distribution of project duration with that of a single path.

Another factor which produces bias in PERT or CPM is the introduction of resource constraints into the problem. Shortages of resources tend to delay the start of activities and this changes the expected completion time of the network. APMS addresses this situation in a CPM environment, and (with user interaction) responds to any increases in project completion time. Davis [1975] has pointed out that the imposition of resource constraints often produces increased project durations. Bentley [1978] says that "resource allocation becomes increasingly complex as the number of activities and resources increases." The bias identified by Davis and Bentley -- that a PERT analysis is biased optimistically whenever resource restrictions can cause -- is applicable equally to analytical or simulation approaches to PERT.

Simulation of PERT networks has replaced PERT analytical methods. "Using statistical PERT ... with Monte Carlo simulation, if required, unbiased estimates of the mean and variance of the completion time may be found as well as its cumulative distribution function" [Ringer, 1971]. Van Slyke [1963] was the first to suggest using Monte Carlo simulation to find the cumulative distribution function (cdf) of PERT network completion times. He also allowed

durations to have non-Beta duration distributions. Douglas [1978]
has pointed out that traditional PERT addresses the activities
and variables that deal with the critical path, often ignoring
other activities and paths which are not critical but which in
a real project requires managerial consideration. Douglas [1978]
says that "the most promising approach to solving this problem
appears to be simulation." PERT simulation systems commercially
available use the Van Slyke approach and avoid these biases
[Moder and Phillips, 1970].

2.4. Extensions

The following is a description of the extensions planned as
part of future research. The user inputs, besides the deterministic APMS data used to develop an initial schedule, stochastic
data on activities, consumptions and availabilities for a given
schedule. Figure 1 shows the stochastic variables that are
allowed under this system. The APMS extension of hyperbolic
interpolation allows for PERT simulation of the corresponding
resource consumptions when activity durations are simulated. The
simulation reports and displays probable variations of executed
progress from scheduled progress, based on aggregation of simulation experiments.

Activity Duration
Activity Start
Activity Finish
Amount of Resource in Interval
Number of Intervals Resource is Available
Resource Consumption
Time of Exogenous Events
Cost Factors
Start of Project

Figure 1. Stochastic Variables

Each simulation experiment will result from generating
availabilities of each resource for each time interval of availability constraint, generating durations of each activity, gen-

erating consumptions of each resource by each activity, and calculating the resulting start times, project duration, resource infeasibilities, cost and other outcomes. The cost resource provides a single criterion of value to be reported for each simulation experiment. The estimated probability distributions of these outcomes, obtained from runs of many simulation experiments, is the output that is reported and displayed.

When an activity is planned to start but not all resources are available, there are several possible reactions: (1) extend activity duration enough to stay within availabilities, (2) delay activity start times until availabilities become sufficient, (3) reschedule, or (4) substitute resources or obtain more of critical resources. Since these managerial reactions would occur in the real world and would have the effect of mitigating the effects of shortages, the simulations must approximate those reactions; otherwise, the simulations would magnify the effects of shortages, because the simulated solution would be equivalent to going ahead with an inappropriate schedule after conditions have changed.

APMS aids a user in selecting start times and durations of activities, given deterministic data on duration-dependent resource consumptions by activities and on resource availabilities, so that the scheduled consumptions will be feasible; the system also aids a user in comparing actual progress with scheduled progress [Young and Rardin, 1985]. The user interactively works toward a solution and is an integral part of the system. A heavy reliance is placed on graphics and the user gets immediate feedback for each action he takes.

The overall plan for interactive PERT simulation management will be as follows: Let the computer run simulations of the project and continually display the cumulative results. Rules for automatic reaction to anticipated contingencies are set in advance, but when a situation is met for which an automatic reaction was not specified, the system halts and seeks user intervention in the particular experiment at hand. At this time the user can input an ad hoc reaction or change the rules. Previous individual experiments can also be reviewed and corrected or discarded. When a sufficient number of valid experiments were

complete, the simulation will halt or be halted. Figure 2 shows
the interface structure of the current APMS and the PERT simulation capability that has been added.

The main aim of our current experimentation with PERT in the
APMS system is to reduce the occurrence of situations in which
the user must intervene. This is being done in two ways: First,
we are trying to identify situations in which ad hoc user intervention actually turns out to follow rules that are feasible to
program in advance; we hope to substitute the appropriate artificial intelligence logic for these interruptions. Second, we
are trying to develop a reliable method of identifying when a
difficult decision's resolution nevertheless cannot significantly
alter the aggregate outcome of a simulation run; when such cases
are identified the system will choose a decision at random, save
the conditions for later reporting, and proceed without interruption.

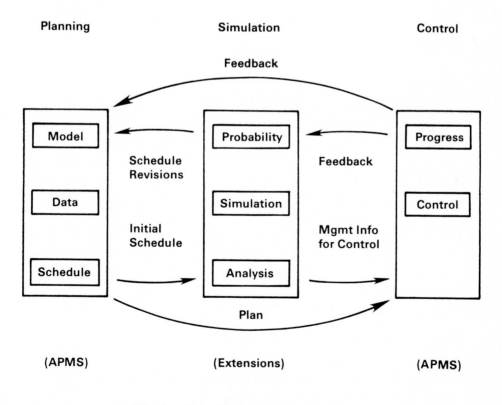

Figure 2. APMS and Extensions

3. THE LOCATION-ALLOCATION DECISION SUPPORT SYSTEM

A decision support system for location of military water
points was developed by Captain Monty J. Anderson [1980] (U.S.
Army Engineer) at Georgia Institute of Technology with administrative support from AIRMICS, and was the basis for a system for
selection of ammunition transfer points developed subsequently
by Captain Patrick Link [1982] (U.S. Army Artillery).

3.1. The Location-Allocation Problem

The location-allocation problem is a relatively intractable
integer programming problem for which exact solutions require
unacceptably high completion costs [McGinnis, 1977], yet the
available heuristic methods are well suited for interactive implementation [Khumawala and Whybark, 1971]. It is a commonly arising
model: given a flow network with known supplies, demands, and
supply capacity limitations at various nodes, known costs per
visit flow to traverse various arcs, and known fixed costs for
"opening" various nodes for supply (letting them have nonzero
flow), the location-allocation problem is that of deciding which
set of supply nodes to open so that the total cost of meeting
all the demands with flow from open supply nodes is minimized.

Given a set of open nodes, the subproblem of finding the cost-
minimizing supply plan (routes and amounts) is the relatively
trivial one known in the literature as the ("Hitchcock") transportation problem.

3.2. Interactive Optimization Approach

A straight-forward approach to the location-allocation problem
is to set up an interactive optimization cycle in which (1) the
user selects a set of open nodes, (2) the computer computes and
reports the best plan and total cost for this set of open nodes
and also displays a picture of the solution and sensitivity analysis information, and the cycle repeats until the user is satisfied the solution is the best that can be attained.

In implementations, many sensitivity-analysis reports (best-
served and worst-served nodes, incremental costs for opening or

closing nodes or adding or subtracting flow in or out of various
nodes, etc.) are made available, not all of which fit on one
screen, so the user may call interactively for several reports
and displays before choosing a new set of open nodes. Reports
and displays are given in application terms (gallons, boxes,
miles, trucks, map displays, etc.) not in terms of the mathematical model.

There are two advantages of the interactive optimization
approach over that of heuristic computer codes. First, since the
user can exercise flexibility, judgement and pattern recognition,
the final solution is more likely to be the optimal one than if
a "blind" heuristic is used. Second, with the interactive approach one can consider factors outside the purview of a location-
allocation model, such as the desirability of moving, concentrating, or dispersing assets for defendability.

3.3. Army Applications

In an Army division, the Division Engineer is responsible for
providing potable water, including identifying potential sites,
selecting them, developing them as necessary to insure access by
the supported units' 400-gallon water trailers, which must make
round trips towed by 2½-ton trucks. The entire division of 15,000
men requires about 35 or 40 trips daily, and a reasonable formal
optimization aim is to minimize total travel distance.

This water-point decision support system was designed for
this problem. The ammunition transfer point decision support
system was designed for a very similar problem involving resupply
of artillery ammunition instead of water.

3.4. Implementation

Both DSSs were implemented on a Chromatics CG series (512x512
pixel resolution color graphics system) stand-alone microcomputer
system similar to the MICROFIX or Zenith Z-120 systems now beginning to be widely distributed to military units. A facility is
included for tracing a road map as input data; this procedure
defines nodes and arcs and automatically gives distances along
arcs, which can be used as the cost matrix, if desired. All

data, including costs, can be entered or changed by direct batch
or interactive procedures. Final output is in the form of a set
of highlighted networks each showing what routes are to be followed between a given unit location and its one or more sources of
supply, and how much supply is to be picked up at each source.
Hard copies of these would become part of each units tactical
orders. It is also possible to display or print highlighted networks each showing what routes are to be followed by one or more
units being served by a given source.

Program design is modular, to allow relatively easy conversion
when, for example, digitized terrain maps might become available
from the Corps of Engineers. The current MICROFIX arrangement
whereby digitized maps can be overlayed on the screen (but without
the map data being directly accessible to the running program) is
compatible with the design of these two systems. Eventually, if
maps evolve to contain data such as road distances in computer-
readable form, the changes necessary to take advantage of such
data would be confined to a single module of the program.

3.5. Extensions and Use

Limited user tests under simulated conditions [Anderson, 1980;
Link, 1982] have confirmed that the prototypes both do a good job
of supporting the logistics decisions without demanding excessive
computer resources. Truely practical use would require automated
travel-distance input from a general source. It would not make
sense to manually trace out the travel distances in a decision
area for the sole purpose of placing water points or ammunition
transfer points; once the travel distances are in the computer,
they would be useful for many other purposes. It would make
sense to develop a single location-allocation system that could
be used for general logistics purposes in a division area, fed
by travel distance data supplied as a general "utility" by the
Corps of Engineers.

Further, it would make sense to develop a general-purpose
terrain data and display system along similar lines to that of
the long-defunct IBM system GADS (Geo-data Analysis and Display
System) [Young and Rardin, 1985]. Such a system would provide a

consistent data base and interface for such functions as line-of-sight analysis, troop movement, target analysis, and mine field control, in addition to location-allocation analysis. Such systems have heretofore been developed in piecemeal fashion, although they all involve maintaining a data base with respect to maps at tactical scales, displaying data superimposed on tactical maps, collecting location-specific user input of the kind best collected through screen-touch protocols (mouse, light pen, joystick, arrow-keys, etc.), and supporting location-specific decision problems.

Even without such integration, there is a clear tendency to use tools such as the location-allocation DSSs to perform tasks that transcend the travel-minimizing optimization model on which they are based. The water-point location DSS, for example, inevitably becomes viewed by its user as simply a means for developing a temporary distribution plan for fresh water. Potential users indicated that what might be uppermost in their minds while using the system might be site survivability or anticipation of the next troop movement. Users did not see achievement of a lowest-cost solution as the primary "closure" in using the system; instead, they viewed the primary closure as the printing of the route networks that would be given to each unit to show it where to pick up water and which roads to use.

4. THE MOBILIZATION DECISION SUPPORT SYSTEM

The Mobilization Decision Support System (MDSS) is a joint project of AIRMICS and the U.S. Army Forces Command (FORSCOM). This research project is designed to look at new methods and approaches to mobilization planning. Users accepted the MDSS because it was developed rapidly and allowed them the freedom to change requirements. The users at the initial site have actively sought to "market" the system to other potential users.

4.1. Background

This DSS has been implemented at Ft. Stewart, Georgia and it is designed as an aid for post level mobilization planners. Previously, a planner at the post level had no automated support. This system provides microcomputer support for planning and

actual use in case of mobilization. One of the major objectives
is to provide the planner with the capability to examine alternatives and to determine the shortcomings of current resource
allocation plans. After problem areas have been identified the
planner can then use the system to explore potential alternative
allocations of resources. A key factor in this process is time.
The examination of alternatives has been prohibitive because of
time. With this system questions are being asked and answered
that were not even asked in the past.

4.2. Hardware/Software

MDSS is implemented on an IBM/PC that has 256K of main memory.
A light pen was used for much of the initial user interaction
but was removed in the later stages due to security considerations. The PC also has a floppy disk, a 10 megabyte hard disk,
and a color monitor. Color is used to encode information as an
aid to the decision maker (color was also removed for security
reasons). A digitizing tablet and companion software was used
to create maps of Ft. Stewart. All software is written in BASIC
or dBase II. Commercial software has been used as much as
possible to speed up development.

4.3. Functions

The most unique function in the system is the use of maps for
selection of areas of interest and encoding of information. One
application is the assignment of units to eating, housing, and
administrative buildings. The planner can touch a portion of
the Fort Stewart map and it will be enlarged until he can see
individual buildings. The buildings are color coded to show
the type of building (mess hall, etc.) and its availability.
By touching the building shown on the map the planner can get
written information and can make assignments of units to specific
buildings. The current use of this feature is for planning and
resource evaluation, but this capability could be used during mobilization or day-to-day decision making. The most heavily used
feature of the system is the ad hoc reporting feature of the system. After only a few months of operation, users are getting

answers to questions that would have been impractical to address
in the manual mode. Some standard reports have been identified
and are available to the user. The standard reports include
summaries of ammunition, fuel, and transportation needs. The
reporting is done using dBase II with BASIC menu drivers.

Another function is a weapons range scheduler. This function
allows the planner to schedule ranges, get fixed reports, and
check on the availability of ranges by time period. Additional
applications will be added as this project proceeds. One of the
major needs that is under development is in the area of scheduling. Scheduling will include both training and convoy movement.

4.4. Research Objective

AIRMICS used this project to validate a DSS development strategy for use in a government environment. Previous research had
identified a variety of methods for the development of DSSs.
This project selected a particular approach, the Iterative Staged
Development, for the development of MDSS. The procedure differs
from those employed in typical MISs. Selected applications are
chosen and implemented in a cyclical or iterative fashion, but
there are distinct stages that the process follows. The results
are frequent enhancements to the system and a substantial reliance on user feedback to direct the next stages of development.
In less than a year the hardware was purchased and three itera-
tions of the software delivered to the user. The user is currently using the system about an hour and a half per day. The project
was completed in November of 1984.

5. CONCLUSIONS

APMS, the location-allocation DSSs, and the MDSS all assist
managers in the allocation of resources. APMS allows any type
of resource associated with a project to be allocated and in the
future it will allow simulations of the allocation process. The
location-allocation DSSs allow selection of locations for distribution points. Even though the MDSS has a military flavor many
similar resource allocation problems exist in other environments.
Any allocation problem that has a spatial representation could

benefit from the lessons learned in the MDSS project and the
location-allocation projects.

REFERENCES

Anderson, Monty J. (1980). "A Prototype Decision Support System
for the Location of Military Water Points," Master's Thesis,
Georgia Institute of Technology, June.

Barbosa, L.C. and Hirko, R.G. (1980). "Integration of Algorithmic Aids into Decision Support Systems," MIS Quarterly,
March.

Bentley, T. (1978). "Project Planning and Control," Management
Accounting, 55, 9, October, pp. 404-406.

Davis, E.W. (1975). "Project Network Summary Measures for Con-
strained-Resources Scheduling," AIIE Transactions, 7, 2,
June, pp. 132-142.

DeFloriani, L. (1978). "A Method for Organizing a Project Network into a Tree Structure," Third Symposium on Operations
Research, Mannheim University, Tagungsbericht, September.

Douglas, D. (1978). "PERT and Simulation," 1978 Winter Simulation Conference, pp. 89-98.

Gantt, J. and Young, D. (1985). "Interactive PERT Simulation
Modeling For Resource-Constrained Project Scheduling," 18th
Annual Simulation Symposium, Tampa, Florida, March.

Gowens, John (1982). "Analysis and Evaluation of Decision
Support Systems in an Army Functional Application,"
AIRMICS.

Gowens, John (1983). "Decision Support Systems -- Development
and Test," AIRMICS.

Hartley, H.O. and Wortham, A.W. (1966). "A Statistical Theory
for PERT Critical Path Analysis," Management Science, 12,
10, June, pp. B-469 - B-481.

Khumawala, B.M. and Whybark, D.C. (1971). "A Comparison of Some
Recent Warehouse Location Techniques," The Logistics Review,
7, 31.

Link, Patrick (1982). "A Prototype Decision Support System for
the Selection of Ammunition Transfer Points," Master's
Thesis, Georgia Institute of Technology, August.

MacCrimmon, K.R. and Ryavec, C.A. (1964). "An Analytical Study
of the PERT Assumptions," Operations Research, 12, 1, pp.
16-37.

McGinnis, L.F. (1977). "A Survey of Recent Results for a Class of Facilities Location Problems," AIIE Transactions, 9.

Moder, J.J. and Phillips, C.R. (1970). Project Management with PERT/CPM, Van Nostrand Reinhold Company, New York.

Ringer, L.J. (1971). "A Statistical Theory for PERT In Which Completion Times Of Activities are Inter-Dependent," Management Science, 17, 11, July, pp. 717-723.

Talbot, F.B. (1982). "Resource-Constrained Project Scheduling With Time-Resource Tradeoffs: The Nonpreemptive Case," Management Science, 28, 10, October, pp. 1197-1210.

Underwood, W.E., Siegmann, P.J. and Gehl, J. (1984). "Analysis of Existing Decision Support Systems to Provide a Current Baseline of Applications, Implementation Methodologies, Problem Areas, Hardware, and Communication Complexities," AIRMICS.

Van Slyke, R.M. (1963). "Monte Carlo Methods and the PERT Problem," Operations Research, 11, 5, pp. 839-860.

Young, D. and Rardin, R. (1985). "GITPASE: An Interactive Planning Aid for Project Scheduling With Time-Resource Tradeoffs," to be published in Computer Augmentation of Human Decision Making, Wayne Zachary and Julie Hopson (eds.), Laurance E. Earlbaum, Hillsdale, N.J.

14. DECISION SUPPORT SYSTEMS - A CASE STUDY IN THE USE OF DBMS TECHNOLOGY IN ENERGY MANAGEMENT

Norman Revell
Centre for Business Systems Analysis
City University
London, United Kingdom

ABSTRACT

With the ever increasing costs of energy worldwide, the importance of conservation has come to the fore. Many organizations have recognized this fact and have appointed executives at corporate level whose sole responsibility is energy management.

In terms of information management their job is complex - they are faced with a multi-faceted problem domain, some of the more important ones being:
- Many different buildings with different operating characteristics.
- Different fuels and equipment at those premises.
- A wide choice and variation of tariffs from the energy supply utilities.
- Variations in meteorological data both seasonal and geographic.

The energy manager is concerned primarily with decision making in three areas:
- The day to day monitoring of energy consumption against projected targets.
- Tariff optimization at both the building and corporate level.
- Investment in new plant and energy conservation measures.

This paper describes a computer-based decision support system that has been developed in order to meet the needs of the energy manager for both operational and strategic data on which to base his decisions. The conclusions drawn from the case are presented in the form of a review of the role of data base technology in the decision support area.

NATO ASI Series, Vol. F31
Decision Support Systems: Theory and Application
Edited by C. W. Holsapple and A. B. Whinston
© Springer-Verlag Berlin Heidelberg 1987

1. INTRODUCTION

For a very small organization with only a handful of premises, or indeed for the domestic householder the task of energy management is a comparitively simple one. By reading energy meters or analyzing suppliers bills it is possible to make a calculation of potential savings that could be derived from adopting conservation measures, fuel substitution, etc. The degrees of freedom and resultant complexity of the situation described above are not applicable to the small organization. In a large organization it is virtually impossible for the energy manager to have the degree of operational control over the energy consumption that the individual householder or small business has. To date manual methods of recording and control have been used with three practical disadvantages:

a) that they are labor intensive and therefore expensive to operate
b) that the time taken to prepare a graph or table is too long to present an up-to-date view and
c) a variety of output is not available.

The area is ideally suited to a computer-based DSS in that all of the above problems can be overcome. In designing such a system a choice must be made from a variety of modelling techniques available. The problem domain is characterized by the following data characteristics:

a) a large variety of data inputs from such things as meter readings thru to engineering and climatic data.
b) a complex data structure to support the above.
c) a variety of outputs covering graphs, standard reports and ad hoc reports.

Reasons for the data base approach: A data modelling exercise produced the structure diagram shown as Appendix I. This would certainly point to a data base solution owing to the complexity of the structure and also the fact that most transaction types would involve access to several entities via their interrelationships. Standard file management techniques would be extremely cumbersome and would involve complex accessing programs. There are many cases where the choice between file management and data base management is fairly marginal, though in this case the need for a data base solution was self-evident.

The question was then one of which type of DBMS? The fact that recursive relationships and many-to-many relationships are involved restricted the choice to either a full network system, or a relational system.

System selection: The size of the application measured some tens of thousands of records, which therefore suggested a micro-computer-based solution.

A first approximation of sizing the data base is given by:

Size = (No of premises) * (Mean no of fuels per premises)
        * (No of readings stored per fuel per premises) * 10

This formula assumes that individual readings will be the dominant factor.

As an example suppose we have 100 premises and two fuels on average and 3 years of weekly readings the size becomes:

100 * 2 * 150 * 10 = 300K characters.

To this of course must be added the storage and structure over-heads of any DBMS chosen. The historic data held of 3 years worth of readings was considered by the end users to be suffi-cient for relevant management. Even with 1000 premises we are well within the storage capabilities of a typical business micro-computer though this latter figure would cover most large organ-izations.

In terms of data volumes the weekly keying load to enter the reading data would be within the capabilities of a single opera-tor.

It was decided therefore to design the system around an IBM personal computer (PC), this being the most universal system of its type, thus ensuring a high degree of portability and upgrade potential to meet the needs of the larger user.

2. SYSTEM SPECIFICATION

In this section we shall examine in more detail the input and output requirements of the system and hence lead onto the software design.

2.1. System Inputs

The prime input is the energy meter reading taken for each fuel at each premise. Professional experience has shown that weekly readings are most appropriate from both the technical and managerial point of view. Most of the management reports and analyses are monthly but nevertheless it is necessary to go into finer detail than this for some of the calculations involved in the presentation of such data.

Other inputs are required to maintain the standing data on the system such as premises details, climatic data, etc. These would normally only be entered on an annual or ad hoc basis such as when a building is modified. Meteorological data is stored in units of "degree days" which is a measure of temperature variation from an assumed mean ambient temperature of 19 degrees Celsius. In the UK this is available by geographical region in two forms, the first being a 20 year average and the second being actual recorded data that is current. Thus any system for targetting energy consumption will base itself on the 20 year data for predictive purposes but use current data for monitoring and analysis.

2.2. System Outputs

The system needs to be able to provide output at four different levels.

Level 1 is concerned with the operation of the energy management system itself. A typical example of this would be error reporting on missing meter readings. This not only ensures the consistency of stored data but is also a management control, since premises that are not submitting their reading reports on time are also less likely to be applying other routine energy conservation measures.

Level 2 is concerned with single premises reporting at the management level, typically actual consumptions versus projected. It is desirable here to be able to present the information both graphically and in a tabular form on printed reports.

Level 3 is concerned with corporate level reporting, the performance of whole departments are compared either historically or with each other. Also total energy costs are reported on here. Individual premises are reported on only on an exception basis.

Level 4 concerns ad hoc analysis and reporting. Given the complexity of the data structure there are virtually an infinite number of possible information requests that can be made. In the non-computer based environment these would nearly always be in response to a problem identified at one of the above levels of reporting. For example a typical query might take the form "Give me a list of the premises whose consumption is more than 10% over target year to date and whose boilers are more than 6 months overdue for a service." The particular problem here is that the requests cannot be anticipated and therefore a query language needs to be used.

2.3. System Volumes

As indicated in the previous section the upper limit of number of premises was set at approximately 1000. The user requirement was also that there should be no arbitrary limit on the amount of past data stored that is software determined, the only limit being that of hardware capacity. Thus there should be calendar data stored along with readings to give them a unique identifier.

Although readings are recorded weekly it was decided to enter them monthly so that for a given premise there would be four or five readings each month to be entered. Even for a large system this is well within the capabilities of a single operator.

2.4. User Interface

The entire system had to be designed for a non-procedural
end user based on menu selections and full screen form-filling
for data input and display. Also for graphical output the full
screen color graphics capabilities of the IBM PC were to be used.

3. SYSTEM DESIGN

An earlier abortive attempt to produce the system using conventional file management techniques and a high level programming
language had been attempted by the user. This had been abandoned
for the following reasons: firstly that the complexity of the
data structure meant that most of the code written was in fact
emulating the features of a standard DBMS rather than being applications oriented, and secondly that it was not possible to provide for the variety of input and output requirements at a
reasonable level of coding cost.

It was decided therefore to build the system around the
following standard software tools:
a) A DBMS to mirror the natural data structures as closely as
    possible.
b) A screen I/O management package.
c) A high level procedure definition language for output reports.
d) A query language.
e) A business graphics package.

In choosing the packages a high level of functional integration was also desirable to permit easy transitions between the
different parts of the end user system.

In choosing a DBMS a network data structure was preferred to
a relational one for the following reasons:
a) The complexity of the data structure meant that for many
    standard transactions and output requirements several time-
    consuming "joins" would be required.
b) The maximum potential size of the data base.

The main criticism of the network structure is that of lack
of flexibility to change and add new entities and relationships
dynamically was not a problem here in that the data structures

were very accurately defined and unlikely to change. What was
likely to change was the output requirement.

It was for this reason that MDBS III [1981] was chosen since
it had the modelling capabilities to handle N:M data structures
and also recursive relationships. Thus it was possible to construct an MDBS III schema (shown as Appendix II) which was a
one-for-one translation of the data model. Further, the query
system QRS would meet the needs for Level 4 type queries. The
recently announced Knowledge Manager interface to MDBS III meant
that this latter package could be used for output reports and
graphs thus providing a totally integrated applications development environment. To manage the screen handling, the Screen
Master package was chosen since this is highly integrated with
the MDBS III data base.

In this environment the only code that actually needed to
be written was application dependent. For the data input modules
of the system all of this code was written in "C" whereas for the
reports and graphs it was written in KMAN [KnowledgeMan User
Manual, 1983]. This latter choice was made, even though KMAN,
being an interpreted language, is much slower than "C". The
ease of modification was the prime reason for the choice.

4. SYSTEM IMPLEMENTATION

The system was initially implemented for a London Borough
with some 200 premises approximately. These range from very
small premises no larger than individual dwelling houses up to
offices, buildings and schools. To cater for the larger premises
the facility to have several meters for each fuel type was
built into the design (see Appendix I). Thus individual energy
users within a premise could have their use recorded and monitored.

The application itself presents as an entirely menu driven
structure. Once the user has signed on with an appropriate
code the main menu is presented which gives access to the main
functional areas of the system. Typically there are 3 levels
beneath this down to individual data entry or retrieval screens.

Movement down the structure is controlled by menu choices whereas to go up the structure to the higher menu it is only necessary
to use the "ESC" key. Because of this structure it is possible
to control user access entirely on function. Each menu choice
calls a program for which the user must have permitted access
(see Appendix II) before it can be executed. Since these authorizations are built into the data base itself the operation of
the user access controls is similar to that of IBM's System R
concept, now implemented in DB2 [DB2 Concepts and Facilities
Manual], namely that at the start of operations one privileged
user is able to grant and remove "privileges" for other users
entirely dynamically. The weakness of this scheme is that any-
one who has direct access to the data base (such as a query user
via QRS) is able to short circuit it. This is not as serious
as it sounds though since the data contained on the data base
is not intrinsically sensitive; the purpose of the controls are
essentially to maintain a high level of data base integrity. A
QRS user opens the data base for read-only access and thus the
integrity of the data base is not at risk even if it is not
properly closed.

5. SYSTEM OUTPUTS

As described in the previous section, the system was required
to provide for the four categories of output to support the
management functions required of it.

Level 1 outputs comprise:
a) An error report on missing readings, abnormal values, etc.
b) A meter reading record report.
c) A computer generated input form of projected consumption,
comprising a graph with upper and lower bounds.
d) A dump of premises data and related records, e.g., targets.

Level 2 outputs comprise:
a) A graph of historic versus projected consumption for a specified premise for a specified fuel. (Shown as Appendix III.)
b) A report containing the same information in tabular form.

Level 3 outputs comprise:
a) A historic analysis of departmental performance compared with previous years.
b) A financial comparison of energy costs by departments.
c) A performance summary showing for a given department the actual to projected consumption for all of the premises in that department.

The above are the principal standard outputs provided by the system. In arriving at their specification the approach taken was to model the energy consultants role in a non-computer environment. Thus the operational and some Level 2 outputs were arrived at. Level 3 and Level 4 outputs were then developed from these. As previously mentioned, the Level 4 requirements have been met by the use of QRS - the MDBS III query system. This has been applied mainly to the engineering part of the schema where there is only a more limited need for standard reports and a much greater need for ad hoc reporting.

6. SOME OBSERVATIONS FROM THE CASE

The role of the expert system in this environment is worth exploring here. Whilst not constructed internally as an expert system, i.e., being designed and implemented using conventional data base and system design techniques, to the end user it presents as an expert system in that it is being used as a substitute for the energy consultant. The knowledge on which he bases his job has been captured both into the data base structure and the procedures used to derive the outputs from that structure. There is very little conventional data processing in the use of the system. Therefore viewed externally the system can be regarded as an expert system component of a DSS supporting the energy manager. The important principle being that expert systems may be developed using different tools from the classical PROLOG/LISP type of environment. Knowledge representation is handled by the structure of the data base and the functionality of the system so that the end user has a high level non-procedural interface. Where an expert system in the strict internal sense could be applied is in the Level 4 reporting, especially in the engineering area. Knowledge in the form of stored production rules could be used to analyze a particular part of the data base which would have first been identified by the procedural routines built into the system. Thus the expert systems component would integrate with the other software components of the system.

Another area worth exploring here is the evolving data base environment. A paper by the author [Revell, 1981] has described the external environment of the data base and the nature of problems encountered in its implementation. The system as described has integrated a network and a relational DBMS plus a number of other software components. The exclusivity of data base to be either relational or network has already been challenged by CULLINET [IDMS R Manual] with their relational interface to IDMS and also by MDBS with the interface to MDBS III used in this application. A typical mixed system scenario which has emerged from the experience of this case might be as follows:

"From a data model of a known problem domain identify the most stable entities and relationships and construct a network schema from them. For less stable entities and uncertain relationships construct relational tables. As the data base evolves convert tables which have become stable in time to the network schema and vice versa entities which have lost their initial stability should be converted to tables."

It would be possible for this migration to be assisted or even made an automatic feature of the DBMS. This "dynamic" data base environment may then be a "back end" to a variety of different interfaces depending on the user requirements from purely conventional programmed systems through query languages to AI components such as natural language and expert systems interfaces. This principle has recently been defined in a paper by Whinston et al. [1985] as "Synergistic integration" where a number of diverse software components such as those in the system described are tightly integrated.

401

7. CONCLUDING COMMENTS

In the context of the decision support environment this case has several particular areas of practical importance. Firstly it demonstrates the validity of using personal computers for complex data base applications which would traditionally have required a mini or mainframe solution. Secondly it presents an integration of a number of software tools including both a relational and a network DBMS. Thirdly it demonstrates how an expert system may be constructed by using data base and functional programs as a knowledge base rather than the more traditional approach.

REFERENCES

DB2 Concepts and Facilities Manual, IBM.

IDMS R Manual, Cullinet Corporation, Wellesley, MA, USA.

KMAN User Manual, MDBS Inc., Lafayette, IN, USA.

MDBS III User Manual (1981). MDBS Inc., Lafayette, IN, USA.

Revell, N. (1981). "Managing the Development of Database Systems," IAG Journal, 4, 4.

Whinston, A.B., et al. (1985). "The Use of Synergistic Integration," Working Paper, Purdue University, West Lafayette, IN, USA.

APPENDIX I

Energy Monitoring Schema (Simplified)

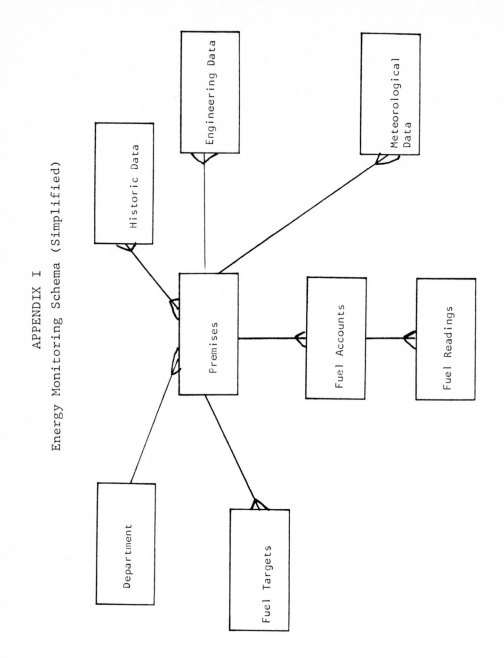

APPENDIX II

Simplified Data Base Schema

```
/********************************************************************/
/*    SCHEMA DEFINITION FOR THE                                     */
/*    ENERGY MONITORING AND TARGETING SYSTEM                        */
/********************************************************************/



/********************************************************************/
/*                DATABASE IDENTIFICATION SECTION                   */
/********************************************************************/


database name is RICHMOND
    file name is "RICHMOND.DB"
    size is 4090 pages
    page size is 1024 bytes
    title is "RICHMOND ENERGY MONITORING AND TARGETING SYSTEM"



/********************************************************************/
/*                USER AND PASSWORD SECTION                         */
/********************************************************************/

user is CHRIS with BUIST


/********************************************************************/
/*                RECORD       SECTION                              */
/********************************************************************/

record name is PREMISES
    item name is ITMPRM1                                UNSIGNED 2
        title is "PREMISES CODE"
    item name is ITMPRM2                                CHAR 25
        title is "PREMISES NAME"
    item name is ITMPRM3                                UNSIGNED 4
        title is "PREMISES AREA"
record name is DEPTMENT
    item name is ITMDEPT1                               UNSIGNED 2
        title is "DEPARTMENT CODE"
    item name is ITMDEPT2                               CHAR 25
        title is "DEPARTMENT NAME"

record name is REGION
    item name is ITMREG1                                UNSIGNED 2
        title is "REGION CODE"
    item name is ITMREG2                                CHAR 20
        title is "REGION NAME"

record name is PUMPS
    item name is ITMPMP1                                UNSIGNED 2

        title is "PUMP NUMBER"
    item name is ITMPMP2                                CHAR 20
        title is "MANUFACTURER"
```

Other engineering record types follow here

```
record name is COST
    item name is ITMCOST1                              UNSIGNED 2
        title is "DATE FROM"
    item name is ITMCOST2                              UNSIGNED 2
        title is "DATE TO"
    item name is ITMCOST3                              REAL 8
        title is "ELECTRICITY COST"
    item name is ITMCOST4                              REAL 8
        title is "GAS COST"
    item name is ITMCOST5                              REAL 8
        title is "OIL COST"

record name is REFGAS
    item name is ITMREFG1                              UNSIGNED 4
        title is "FIRST QUARTER"
    item name is ITMREFG2                              UNSIGNED 4
        title is "SECOND QUARTER"
    item name is ITMREFG3                              UNSIGNED 4
        title is "THIRD QUARTER"
    item name is ITMREFG4                              UNSIGNED 4
        title is "FOURTH QUARTER"
    item name is ITMREFG5                              UNSIGNED 4
        title is "TOTAL"


records for the other fuels follow here

record name is GASTRGT
    item name is GASITM1                               REAL 8
        title is "TARGET HEATING CONSUMPTION"
    item name is GASITM2                               UNSIGNED 2
        title is "EQUIVALENT DEGREE DAYS"
    item name is GASITM3                               REAL 8
        title is "TARGET 12 MONTH DHW BASE-LOAD"
    item name is GASITM4                               REAL 8
        title is "TARGET HEATING BASE LOAD"
    item name is GASITM5                               REAL 8
        title is "TARGET MISCELLANEOUS BASE-LOAD"

records for the other fuels follow here

record name is YEAR20DD
    title is "20 YEAR DEGRÉE DATA"
    item name is ITM20FRM                              UNSIGNED 2
        title is "YEAR FROM"
    item name is ITM20TO                               UNSIGNED 2
        title is "YEAR TO"
    item name is ITM20APR                              UNSIGNED 2
        title is "APRIL"

record name is YEARACDD
    title is "ACTUAL DEGREE DATA"
    item name is ITMACFRM                              UNSIGNED 2
        title is "YEAR FROM"
    item name is ITMACTO                               UNSIGNED 2
        title is "YEAR TO"

record name is WEEKSMTH
    title is "WEEKS IN A MONTH"
    item name is ITMWKFRM                              UNSIGNED 2
```

```
record name is GASACCT
    item name is ITMGASAC                            CHAR 12
        title is "GAS ACCOUNT"

record name is GASMETR
    item name is ITMGASM1                            CHAR 8
        title is "GAS METER ID"


record name is WORKDAYS
    item name is WORKITM1                            UNSIGNED 2
        title is "YEAR FROM"
    item name is WORKITM2                            UNSIGNED 2
        title is "MONTH"
    item name is WORKITM3                            UNSIGNED 2
        title is "YEAR TO"
    item name is WORKITM4                            UNSIGNED 2
        title is "WORKING DAYS"

record name is GASRDNG
    item name is GARDITM1                            UNSIGNED 2
        title is "YEAR FROM"
    item name is GARDITM2                            UNSIGNED 2
        title is "MONTH"
    item name is GARDITM3                            UNSIGNED 2
        title is "YEAR TO"
    item name is GARDITM4                            UNSIGNED 2
        title is "WORKING DAYS"
    item name is GARDITM5                            CHAR 8
        title is "WEEK 1 READING"
    item name is GARDITM6                            CHAR 8
        title is "WEEK 2 READING"
    item name is GARDITM7                            CHAR 8
        title is "WEEK 3 READING"
    item name is GARDITM8                            CHAR 8
        title is "WEEK 4 READING"
    item name is GARDITM9                            CHAR 8
        title is "WEEK 5 READING"
```

The above definitions are all repeated for the other fuel types

```
record name is USERID
    item name is NAMEUSER                            CHAR 12
    item name is NAMEPASS                            CHAR 16

record name is PROGRAM
    item name is PROGID                              UNSIGNED 2
    item name is PROGNAME                            CHAR 8
    item name is PROGDESC                            CHAR 50

record name is SPARE1
    item name is ITMSPA11                            CHAR 10
    item name is ITMSPA12                            CHAR 10

record name is SPARE2
    item name is ITMSPA21                            CHAR 10
    item name is ITMSPA22                            CHAR 10
```

```
/**********************************************************************/
/*                    SET          SECTION                          */
/**********************************************************************/
```

Note that all the System owned sets have been omitted for reasons
of clarity

Where set relationships exist for different fuels they are just
shown here for gas

```
set name is DEPTPREM
    type is 1:N
     retention is OPTIONAL
       owner is DEPTMENT
          insertion is MANUAL
       member is PREMISES
          insertion is MANUAL
          order is SORTED by ASCENDING(ITMPRM1)
          duplicates are NOT allowed

set name is PRGASREF
    type is 1:N
     retention is OPTIONAL
       owner is PREMISES
          insertion is MANUAL
       member is REFGAS
          insertion is MANUAL
          order is IMMATERIAL

set name is REGPREM
    type is 1:N
     retention is OPTIONAL
       owner is REGION
          insertion is MANUAL
       member is PREMISES
          insertion is manual
          order is SORTED by ASCENDING(ITMPRM1)
          duplicates are NOT allowed



set name is PREMCONT
    type is 1:N
     retention is OPTIONAL
       owner is PREMISES
          insertion is MANUAL
       member is CONTROLS
          insertion is MANUAL
          order is SORTED by ASCENDING(ITMCTRL1)
```

Other premises related sets connecting premises to engineering
plant follow here

```
set name is PREMWORK
    type is 1:N
     retention is OPTIONAL
       owner is PREMISES
          insertion is MANUAL
       member is WORKDAYS
          insertion is MANUAL
          order is SORTED by ASCENDING(WORKITM1,WORKITM2)
          duplicates are NOT allowed
```

```
set name is REGCOST
    type is 1:N
     retention is OPTIONAL
        owner is REGION
            insertion is MANUAL
        member is COST
            insertion is MANUAL
            order is SORTED by ASCENDING(ITMCOST1)
            duplicates are NOT allowed

set name is REGACTUA
    type is 1:N
     retention is OPTIONAL
        owner is REGION
            insertion is MANUAL
        member is YEARACDD
            insertion is MANUAL
            order is SORTED by ASCENDING(ITMACFRM)
            duplicates are NOT allowed

set name is REG20YR
    type is 1:N
     retention is OPTIONAL
        owner is REGION
            insertion is MANUAL
        member is YEAR20DD
            insertion is MANUAL
            order is SORTED by ASCENDING(ITM20FRM)
            duplicates are NOT allowed


set name is PREMGAS
    type is 1:N
    retention is OPTIONAL
        owner is PREMISES
            insertion is MANUAL
        member is GASACCT
            insertion is MANUAL
            order is SORTED by ASCENDING(ITMGASAC)
            duplicates are NOT allowed

set name is ACCTGAS
    type is 1:N
    retention is OPTIONAL
        owner is GASACCT
            insertion is MANUAL
        member is GASMETR
            insertion is MANUAL
            order is SORTED by ASCENDING(ITMGASM1)
            duplicates are NOT allowed

set name is GASRDGS
    type is 1:N
    retention is OPTIONAL
        owner is GASMETR
            insertion is MANUAL
        member is GASRDNG
            insertion is MANUAL
            order is SORTED by ASCENDING(GARDITM1,GARDITM2)
            duplicates are NOT allowed
```

```
set name is PREMGTGT
    type is 1:N
    retention is OPTIONAL
        owner is PREMISES
            insertion is MANUAL
        member is GASTRGT
            insertion is MANUAL
            order is FIFO

end
```

APPENDIX III
Sample Output

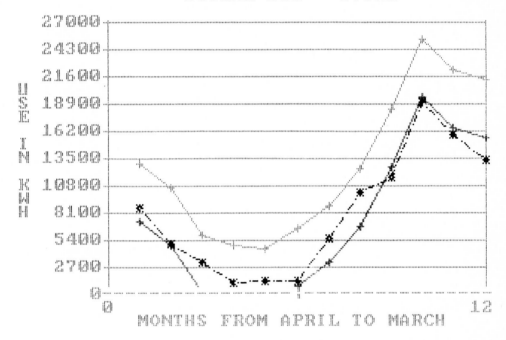

KEY: +   MAX AND MIN TARGETS
        *   ACTUAL USE TO DATE

DEPARTMENT   :   AMENITIES

PREMISES NUMBER: 605

PREMISES NAME   :   TEDDINGTON LIBRARY

PATAMS   -   SYSTEMSTAR

15. DEVELOPMENT, USE, AND VERIFICATION OF EXPERT SYSTEMS IN MODELLING MICROECONOMIC SYSTEMS

Elizabeth Hoffman, Varghese S. Jacob and Andrew B. Whinston
Krannert Graduate School of Management
Purdue University
West Lafayette, IN 47907, USA

and

James R. Marsden
Department of Economics
University of Kentucky
Lexington, KY 40506, USA

1. INTRODUCTION

Decision Support Systems (DSS) and Expert Systems (ES) have
potential application in widely diverse arenas. In the present
paper, we consider their application and testing in the field
of economics. We begin by outlining the structure of a microeconomic system following Smith [1982]. It is readily apparent
that the rule and information flow structures of such microeconomic systems are excellent candidates for expert system
modelling. Taking the framework one step further, we argue that
the ES approach also fits well for modelling the behavior of
economic agents or "experts" who repeatedly face similar decisions problems. We detail the suggested approach by outlining
an example of an auction bidding mechanism and of the participating economic agents or "bidders."

Formulation of the presentation, however, is but the first
step in attaining an acceptable ES. The second, and critical
step involves testing the appropriateness and accuracy of the
ES. To date, this second stage has received but scant attention
and has not been the focus of formal scientific inquiry common
in the physical, biological, and various social sciences. Depending on the outcome of testing, the ES may be accepted for
the stated purposes or additional steps in development and representation may be required. If, however, scientific testing
is ignored, the ES researcher is put in the position of accepting
and operating a system on "faith," on "belief," or on some attitude toward the professionalism of those that developed it.

NATO ASI Series, Vol. F31
Decision Support Systems: Theory and Application
Edited by C. W. Holsapple and A. B. Whinston
© Springer-Verlag Berlin Heidelberg 1987

Realizing the common importance of qualitative as well as quantitative information variables, we suggest approaching the testing issue from two perspectives, making use of the long history of statistical testing and recent suggested approaches from psychology (see Tversky [1977]) in the area of similarity testing. The latter emphasizes the use of qualitative information variables and provides guidelines for the development of testing strategies and techniques. Our present goal is to raise the testing issue and suggest a variety of alternatives rather than to provide an exact testing methodology.[1]

2. MODELLING MICROECONOMIC SYSTEMS USING AN EXPERT SYSTEM FRAMEWORK

Smith [1982] provides a general characterization of microeconomic systems (S) utilizing two major components, an environment (e), and an institution (I), or S = (e,I). In what follows we outline Smith's representation, highlighting the key fact that the system is represented in a rule-based framework and is thus directly amenable to our intended expert system representation.

Smith defines the microeconomic environment by:

$$e = (e^1, e^2, \ldots, e^n)$$

where e^i represents the characteristics of each agent i. The ith agent is characterized by the vector

$$e^i = (u^i, T^i, w^i)$$

where u^i is the agent's utility function, T^i is the technology or knowledge endowment, and w^i is the commodity endowment. Each is defined on the k dimensional commodity space R^k. The environment, therefore, specifies the set of initial characteristics.

The institution (I) specifies the rules of private property under which agents may communicate and exchange or transform commodities for modifying initial endowments in accordance with private tastes and knowledge. The microeconomic institution is

---

[1]This latter formulation, the detailing of specific testing procedures is the subject of a present on-going research project involving OCS offshore oil lease auction bidding processes.

defined by the collection of individual property right characteristics, where $I = (I^1, I^2, \ldots, I^n)$. Each agent's property
rights are defined by:

$I^i = (M^i, h^i(m), c^i(m), g^i(t_0, t, T))$ where M^i is the set
of messages sent by i;

$H = (h^1(m), h^2(m), \ldots, h^n(m))$ is the set of allocation rules;

$h^i(m) \in H$ is the allocation rule, which states the final
commodity allocation to i as a function of the messages
m sent by all agents, and $m = (m^1, m^2, \ldots, m^n)$, $m^i \in M^i$;

$C = (c^1(m), c^2(m), \ldots, c^n(m))$ is the set of cost computation
rules;

$c^i(m) \in C$, is the rule which states the payment to be made
by agent i as a function of the messages sent by all
agents;

$G = (g^1(t^0, t, T), \ldots, g^n(t^0, t, T))$ is the set of adjustment
process rules consisting of a starting rule specifying
the initial conditions, transition rules governing the
sequencing and exchange of messages, and a stopping
rule, under which the exchange of messages is terminated.

Given the above characterization of a microeconomic environment, the outcome behavior of agent i in a static description
of the economy is defined by a function $B^i(e^i|I)$ which yields
the allocation determining message m^i sent by agent i with
characteristics e^i given the property rights of all agents
defined by I.

In a dynamic description of the economy, agent i's response
behavior can be defined by $m^i(t) = F^i(m(t-1)|e^i, I)$ which gives
message response m^i at point t to earlier messages m(t-1) by
all agents. This response behavior could follow an optimal
decision rule or a rule of thumb.

This rule-based form of Smith's characterization of microeconomic systems provides us with the direct link to pursuing
our suggestion of representing such systems as expert systems.
The problem of determining outcome behavior in a microeconomic
system closely parallels the medical diagnosis problem where

expert systems have begun to play helpful roles (e.g., MYCIN [Shortliffe, 1976], PUFF [Aikins et al., 1984]).

A typical diagnostic problem involves determining a diagnosis given certain observed symptoms, the diagnosis being based on knowledge about diseases and their effects. In other words, the diagnosis is based on the rules which govern normal bodily functions and rules about diseases and their effects. This can then be represented as $D(SY|K)$, i.e., the diagnosis based on the symptoms (SY) given the knowledge required for diagnosis (K).

In a microeconomic system, the problem one is faced with is similar, in that the object of interest is the outcome behavior which is based on environmental features given the institutional rules under which the individual functions, i.e., $B^i(e^i|I)$. This implies that the knowledge base would need to have the set of rules which characterize the institution, i.e., the allocation rules, cost computation rules, and process adjustment rules. In addition to this, the knowledge base should have details about the choices which are possible under various environmental conditions. The knowledge base could also contain information about such aspects of behavior as minimizing cost or maximizing utility and the process for computing each.

There is an additional reason why ESs provide an attractive economic modelling technique. One of the continuing major problems facing economic policy analysis is the limited nature of historical (naturally-occurring) data. Such data typically possess limited range and are commonly flawed by severe multicollinearity. Variable values of current interest may be in a range far outside that of historically occurring values. Policy analysis focuses on "what if" considerations rather than being limited to a choice set that merely repeats previous occurrences. As an alternative to relying upon estimation results calculated from historically occurring values (data sets), several recent authors (Griffin [1972, 1977], Marsden et al. [1974b], Bever et al. [1982a,b]) have suggested the development and utilization of mathematical process modelling as a data generating technique. In production modelling, policy concerns involve the possible introduction of untried input combinations and the implementation of feasible, but hitherto uneconomical, technologies. For example, in assessing the oil price leaps of 1974-1975, policy makers had to consider a myriad of new implementations of feasible but unutilized technologies. Many of these previously unused technologies have become commonplace today, but sound economic analysis in 1974-1975 required their consideration prior to their appearance and thus prior to the generation of any real world or historical data. To accomplish this, analysts used process models to generate the necessary data for economic analysis.

We argue here that ESs can play a similar role as data generators. In selecting economic institutions (e.g., auction bidding processes and procurement procedures) policy makers can better estimate their impact in that they can study how the institutions perform for given sets of experts. For example, if the policy makers know little of the characteristics of the experts they will be dealing with, then they may wish to choose an economic institution which is insensitive to the expert's behavior, i.e., one which yields acceptable and predictable results. On the other hand, if the policy maker knows that the experts that will interact with the economic institution are risk lovers (or risk averse), then the appropriate institution would be that one which performs best (e.g., yields highest auction returns) for risk loving (risk averse) economic agents. In each case, the generated individual bidder behavior provides information for studying the performance of institutions of interest and for making an appropriate choice from among the set of feasible institutional alternatives. We return to this point at the end of the next section, suggesting such a data generating use of the ES model of auction bidding institutions.

3. THE ENGLISH AUCTION - A RULE-BASED ES MODEL

One example of a micro-economic system is the English auction, where each economic agent (bidder) may bid after each and every bid taken or accepted by the auctioneer, with the auction ending when no new bid is forthcoming or recognized by the auctioneer. Modelling the institution for such a bidding process requires transition rules in addition to the usual cost and allocation rules. For the straightforward English auction form, the process proceeds as follows:

i)   process initiated by call for opening bid which becomes the accepted and announced bid;

ii) accepted and announced bid remains the standing bid until it is displaced by an accepted and announced higher bid;

iii) the process stops when no higher bid ("overbid") is forth-coming from the economic agents; the object is awarded to the agent who bid last at a price equal to that last bid.

For the case of two bidders (a_1 and a_2), one seller (S), and a single object (OB) being auctioned, the initial state could be characterized as follows:

1)   S has OB;
2)   S calls for opening bid;
3) a_1 has endowment V_1;
4) a_2 has endowment V_2;
5)   standing bid (SB) = 0.

Since the auction process is dynamic by nature, there could be several intermediate stages (i.e., new bids recognized) prior to reaching the goal stage where I is sold. A typical such intermediate stage could be represented as follows:

1)   call for new bid that must exceed SB;
2) a_1 has endowment V_1;
3) a_2 has endowment V_2;
4)   bid X_i made, X_i > SB; X_i becomes new SB (i corresponds to agent i).

When no bid greater than the prevailing SB is either forthcoming or recognized, the process has reached the goal state which may be characterized as:

a)   SB = X_i;
b)   no satisfactory response (i.e., X_j > SB) to call for new bid;
c)   OB awarded to a_i at price equal to SB = X_i;
d) a_i's endowment reduced from V_i to $V_i - X_i$;

e) a_j's endowment remains V_j (no payment from loser, i.e., underbidder).

The following four rules provide a means for modelling the English auction process just described:

RULE 1 - IF [object OB is to be auctioned] THEN [call for bid]

RULE 2 - IF [SB = X_i] AND [new bid offered of X_j] and [$X_j > X_i$] THEN [SB = X_j] AND [call for new bid]

RULE 3 - IF [SB = X_i] AND [call for new bid unanswered or $X_j < X_i$] THEN [award OB to a_i]

RULE 4 - IF [a_i awarded OB] THEN [reduce V_i to V_i - (SB = X_i)].

The bidding process using these rules can be summarized in the following manner. Initially the global data base contains information about the object being auctioned and the endowments of the two agents. RULE 1 is now activated and the data base is updated to depict the call. If there is a response, i.e., a bid is tendered, then RULE 2 models the transition between the intermediate states. RULE 3 models the transition from an intermediate state to the goal state. RULE 4 completes the transition by computing the changes in the endowments.

Suppose that there are several auction bidding institutions under consideration for utilization in offshore oil lease sales.[2] With each of the institutions modelled as outlined above -- that is using rule-based expert systems in conjunction with Smith's structuring -- policy makers could investigate and compare the performance of the various alternatives without the expense and difficulty of actually implementing them in specific auction sales. Further, the bid generating ES mechanisms could be for-mulated based upon what, if anything, the policy maker knows about the economic agents likely to participate in future auc-tions. Consider two cases, one where the policy maker knows little about the likely behavior of the agents and another where,

---

[2] Such a set would include those auction forms meeting all legal specifications such as highest bidder wins, collusion not permitted, etc.

from past experience perhaps, the policy maker knows quite a
bit about the economic agents' behavior, including their attitudes toward risk.

In the first case, the performance of the institutions would
be studied over a bid set generated by using a wide variety of
economic bidding agent models. With little known about the
actual bidder the policy maker might opt for selecting an institution which performs acceptably well for a variety of bidder
types rather than one which performs best if the bidding agents
display risk averseness but perform poorly if they do not.
Through sufficient data generation and analysis of the institutional performances under various data sets, the policy maker
can study the tradeoffs in performance against the uncertainty
(or variability in performance) introduced by a potential lack
of knowledge of individual bidding agents.

In the second case, where the policy maker is knowledgeable
about certain characteristics of the likely economic bidding
agents, these characteristics can be introduced directly into
the ES model of bid generation. For example, the policy maker
may know that the bidding agents are risk neutral and that certain of them have "bidding quirks," e.g., agent i bids on no
more than 10 lease sites, agent j never bids on adjoining plots,
agent s bids only on adjoining plots, etc. Such knowledge can
be directly incorporated into the bid generation ES. These ESs
then would be used to provide the bid data for input into the
analysis of the auction institutions' performance for the
restricted economic agent set. The more that is known about
the economic bidding agents, the more accurately the bid generating ES should be able to track their bidding behavior and the
more optimal should be the bidding institution selection process.
But, as indicated in our first case scenario, even where little
is known of the economic agents with regard to their attitude
toward risk or individual characteristics, ES bid generating
models can still be utilized to provide the data input for analyzing institutional performance.

An approach similar to that just outlined may prove useful
in individual bidding agents' choice of bidding strategy. In

this case, the simulation would analyze the performance of varying bidding strategies under differing institutional settings and bidding competitor characteristics. Here, the institution or likely changes in the institution would be known to the individual bidder.

4. VERIFICATION - TESTING ES REPRESENTATIONS

To date, little of the ES literature has directly focused on testing whether or not ESs are accurate representations of the human processes for which they are intended to act as substitutes. In some cases, the purpose of the ES is to improve upon the human expert's performance, while in others it is to replicate the human performance. In either case, there is the question of whether the ES should be accepted as being an accurate representation of the structure being modelled. In what follows, we take the position that ESs represent scientific modelling and should be judged using scientific methods and testing procedures.

Karl Popper, the oft-cited philosopher of science, suggests the "demarcation criterion" that divides science from non-science. Blaug [1983, p. 10-11] provides the following summary of Popper's approach:

> ... In short, you can never demonstrate that anything is materially true but you can demonstrate that some things are materially false, a statement which we may take to be the first commandment of scientific methodology. Popper exploits this fundamental asymmetry in formulating his demarcation criterion: science is that body of synthetic propositions about the real world that can, at least in principle, be falsified by empirical observations because, in effect, they rule out certain events from occurring. Thus, science is characterized by its method of formulating and testing propositions, not by its subject matter or by its claim to certainty of knowledge; whatever certainty science provides is instead certainty of ignorance.
> The line that is hereby drawn between science and non-science is, however, not absolute: both falsification and testability are matters of degrees [Popper, 1965, p. 113; 1972b, p. 257; 1976, p. 42].

If ES research is to qualify for the label of scientific endeavor, then it is time to subject its performance to testing. In Popper's terms, the conditions under which any particular

ES is to be rejected (i.e., falsified) should be fully specified. He recognized that any particular theory can be maintained in the face of contrary evidence through the utilization
of "immunizing stratagems" (Popper [1972a, 1976], Blaug [1980]),
but argued that methodological limits must be put on the use of
such stratagems. Testing involves the specification of a non-
empty set of conditions under which the theory, in our case the
ES, will be rejected as not satisfactory. Up to the present,
there is little evidence of the study of individual ES performance. There appear to be no general principles for testing
or falsification of ES representations.

In the context of using ES to represent microeconomic
systems, specifying the role for falsification conditions will
differ with the nature and purpose of the particular ES system.
More specifically, consider the examples outlined earlier where
ESs were suggested for use in 1) modelling alternative economic
institutions; 2a) modelling individual economic agent behavior
(in our examples -- bid generation) where much information is
available concerning individual economic agent characteristics;
and 2b) modelling individual economic agent behavior where little
is known about individual economic agent characteristics. In
the first two cases, specific criterion can be set forth under
which relevant ESs would be falsified, i.e., rejected as in-
sufficient mirrors of either the economic institution or economic
agent behavior being modelled. The tests might even be set out
as a joint test where the ES models of the auction institution
and bid generation mechanism are considered together.

One way to test for possible falsification of ESs is to
design a laboratory experiment in which human experts are asked
to accomplish the same decision -- making task as the ES,
using the same information the ES uses. As part of the testing
procedure, we can test whether ES generated results are similar
to those generated by human experts (see Hoffman, Marsden and
Whinston [1985]).

For the third category, denoted as 2b) above, falsification
of the ES is not relevant for there is no standard for comparison. The purpose here is the generation of a wide variety of

alternative behavior forms since very little is known about the
actual individual economic agents. The ES is used not to mirror
any specific individual, but to enable data generation for a
broad cross-section of _possible_ agents for use in the study of
the performance of various auction institutions. In such cases
the ES is actually a simulation tool rather than a human expert
substitute.

Thus narrowing our consideration of falsification to the
two categories of ES utilization, we still face the problem of
structuring criterion to be used as the basis in our tests. We
suggest approaching the problem using two complementary avenues:
1) statistical comparison testing and 2) operationalization
of similarity testing (see Tversky [1977]) from psychology.
The first of these, statistical testing, provides a set of
straightforward, often applied techniques. But these techniques
are not necessarily applicable to every verification problem we
face. The use of a large number of 0,1 (presence-absence) variables is common in expert systems and such use carries with it
the likelihood of severe multicollinearity problems. Similarly,
the use of qualitative variables entails the problem of determining a meaningful quantitative scale if statistical techniques
are to be applied satisfactorily. In each of these situations,
the attractiveness of techniques such as similarity testing is
enhanced. But there remains the problem in this area of oper-
ationalizing the analysis suggested in Tversky's foundation
outline [1977]. Briefly we expand on each of the two suggested
approaches for ES verification, pointing out the usefulness as
well as the limitations and difficulties in properly employing
each.

a. _Statistical Analysis Utilizing Random Coefficient Modelling_

The random coefficient model [Swamy, 1971] provides an
attractive statistical framework for our desired estimation and
testing. In certain circumstances we would have three sets of
data for estimation and comparison purposes. This would occur
when the auction mechanism and the expert modelled by our ESs
parallel real world events, (i.e., when we possess a naturally-

occurring or historical data set generated by the modelled
agents interacting within the modelled auction institution
modelled) and <u>when experimental economic results have been
generated</u>. Our three data sets -- historical (empirical), experimentally generated, and ES generated -- would present three
information sources for comparison and analysis. The random
coefficient model enables somewhat homogeneous data sets to be
integrated into one data set for estimation and analysis purposes. Since we would have three different data sources we
would expect some heterogeneity, with interest focusing on
whether such heterogeneity was "acceptable" or not, a term of
the art that must be defined within each specific setting. More
formally, the general Swamy formulation of the random coefficient
model takes the form:

$$Y_i = x_i'\beta_i + \varepsilon_i$$

$$x_i(\beta + \delta_i) + \varepsilon_i, \quad i = 1,\ldots,n$$

$$E(\delta_i) = 0, \quad E(\delta_i\delta_i') = \Delta$$

$$E(\delta_i\delta_j') = 0 \quad \forall \, i \neq j$$

$$E(\varepsilon_i\varepsilon_j') = \begin{bmatrix} \sigma_{11} & 0 & \cdots & 0 \\ 0 & \sigma_{22} & & \\ \vdots & & & \\ 0 & & & \sigma_{nn} \end{bmatrix}$$

$$x_i' = [x_{i1},\ldots,x_{ik}]$$

$$\beta_i' = [\beta_{i1},\ldots,\beta_{ik}]$$

Where Y_i represents the ith outcome (e.g., ith expert's bid
on ith ES bid generated); X_i is the associated vector of information and characteristic values, δ_i the random components of the
β_i coefficient set (with variance-covariance matrix Δ), and ε_i
the usual stochastic term.

Under standard (though not necessarily trouble free) assumptions, Swamy [1971] presents a detailed variety of statistical testing procedures in the random coefficient model framework. With regard to our present framework, the specific areas of interest are those that provide means for testing whether heterogeneity is evidenced by the three data forms. More specifically, the tests would include those directed at analyzing the similarity values across the three subgroups, (an "intergroup cohesiveness" test, see Hoffman et al. [1984]), and other tests directed at analyzing and comparing the variances of the coefficients for heterogeneity characteristics (see Hoffman et al. [1984]).

Though the random coefficient model provides an attractive flexible form for our analysis, it nevertheless suffers from potential difficulties alluded to earlier. In our framework, the most significant of such difficulties involves 0,1 (presence-absence) and qualitative variables. A variety of possibilities for dealing with dummy variables and for determining mappings from qualitative forms to quantitative values are available, but none completely overcomes the problems or provides a reliable statistical tool.

b. <u>Similarity Testing</u>

Tversky [1977] dealt with the problem of similarity between objects and suggested the use of feature matching. The approach is set - theoretic rather than metric, though the mapping from the feature mapping to a similarity scale is at the heart of the usefulness of Tversky's suggested approach. Much of Tversky's pioneering work is directed at setting forth the conditions for the existence of such a similarity scale, termed S.

In our context, the focus is on decisions rather than objects. The set of features referred to by Tversky would be replaced by a set of characteristics of the decisions reached. More formally, using Tversky's contrast model form [1977, pp. 331-332]:

Let D = [a,b,c,...] be the set of decisions the expert system makes and let A,B,C,... be the set of dimensions associated with decision a,b,c... respectively. Let

D' = [a',b',c',...] be the corresponding decisions by the
expert, and A',B',C'... the dimension associated with
a',b',c'... Then

$$S(D,D') = S(a,a') + S(b,b') + \ldots$$
$$= \theta_1 f(A \cap A') - \alpha_1 f(A-A') - \beta_1 f(A'-A) + \theta_2 f(B \cap B')$$
$$- \alpha_2 f(B-B') - \beta_2 f(B'-A) + \ldots$$

where S(D,D') is the similarity scale measure between D and
D' represented as a linear function of the similarity scale
between the individual decision characteristics of decision
set D and decision set D'. This in turn is represented as
parametric (θ's, α's, β's) functions of the grouped characteristics A of decision a, A' of decision a', B of deci-
sion b, B' of decision b', etc. (A∩A' is the set of characteristics common to decision a and a'; A-A' is the set of
characteristics present in decision a but not in a'; A'-A
is the set of characteristics present in decision a' but
not in decision a, and so on.)

Though the similarity scale approach provides an interesting
alternative for our analysis, its fruitfulness rests on the
determination of the similarity scale S and non-negative scale
f. Tversky [1977] demonstrated the existence of appropriate S
and f under five assumptions he termed matching, monotonicity,
solvability, independence, and invariance (for exact specification see Tversky [1977], pp. 330-332). Although the operationalization is application specific, Tversky does provide an
illustration using perceived similarities among transportation
vehicles.

In a paper evaluating the performance of MYCIN, Yu et al.
(including E. H. Shortliffe) [1979] make several comments that
are consistent with our suggested use of similarity testing in
the ES setting. The authors' division of the decision parallels
the use of decision characteristics in similarity testing.
Indeed, the following quotation's two forms of disagreement
might be classified as "similar decisions" and "dis-similar
decisions":

Because of the complexity of the task, there is often no single 'correct' conclusion to be made about a patient. Experts may disagree among themselves in two important respects. First, experts may select a <u>slightly different approach</u> to diagnosis or therapy <u>from among a group of generally acceptable alternatives</u>. Thus we allowed them to indicate that an alternative decision is acceptable, even if not identical with their own. Second, experts sometimes disagree over conclusions that, for them, <u>have no acceptable alternatives</u>, for example, whether an infected patient requires coverage for an 'Escherichia coli', even if none has actually been isolated from any cultures (emphasis added - single quotes indicate itali-cized portions in original article).

In their comparison between MYCIN and human experts' diagnoses, the authors present "the percentage of instances in which the program's conclusions were <u>either identical to an expert's or were acceptable alternatives</u>." Substituting "sufficiently similar" for "acceptable alternative" highlights the applica-bility of similarity testing suggested above.

As noted earlier, evaluating the similarity between ES decisions, the human expert's decision and the third data source, experimentally generated decisions, will involve determining the dimensions of the decisions that are relevant for each appli-cation. A key role of the researcher is to differentiate between dimensions or characteristics in such a way that simplic-ity and completeness are balanced. Excluding irrelevant infor-mation simplifies the procedure; excluding relevant information makes the process incomplete and likely to be in error.

5. SUMMARY

We have directed this paper at a consideration of two impor-tant issues in ES research: 1) the potential for expanded use of ESs, and 2) the need to develop testing procedures for analyzing the accuracy of DSS decisions. Using the area of economic analysis, we have outlined how ESs can be utilized to model microeconomic systems. Smith's [1982] general character-ization of a microeconomic system was utilized to indicate the direct applicability of rule-based ESs to the representation of microeconomic institutions and decision processes. An example of the use of ESs was then presented for the single

object English auction. It was suggested that a variety of
simulations could prove helpful for policy makers attempting to
evaluate various economic institutions under differing assumptions about the known characteristics of participating human
experts.

But representation of the expert mechanism is but the first
part of the ES development process. We have argued that the ES
must be tested in a scientific manner and have suggested a
falsification approach along the lines set forth by Karl Popper.
Moving beyond a simple comparison of actual human expert v. ES
decisions, we have posited the use of random coefficient modelling and similarity testing for analyzing the applicability of
the ES for the desired tasks. We have outlined means for incorporating three data sets -- historical or naturally occurring,
experimental economics generated, and ES generated -- into the
testing and analysis structures. The procedures suggested here
are not presented in fully operational form, a task that is the
focus of the authors' current research. Our intention is to
raise the testing and verification issue and to suggest avenues
of approach.

ESs provide an extraordinary new research tool for many
disciplines, including economics. But before they can play a
fruitful rather than confusing role in any area, ESs must be
subject to verification testing. Simple replication of historical decision making is not sufficient, since it is unlikely
that future decision problems will be identical in range, scope,
and complexity to those of the past. ES selection processes
that incorporate the ability of the ES to perform unanticipated
as well as anticipated decision tasks provide another dimension
of safety and reliability for the policy maker.

REFERENCES

Aikins, Janice S., Kunz, J.C., Shortliffe, E.H. and Fallat,
    R.J. (1984). "PUFF: An Expert System for Interpretation
    of Pulmonary Function Data," in Readings in Medical Arti-
    ficial Intelligence, W.J. Clancey and E.H. Shortliffe (eds.),
    Addison-Wesley Pub. Co., Reading, Mass., pp. 444-462.

Bever, Robert C., Marsden, J.R., Salas-Fumas, V. and Whinston, A.B. (1982a). "Verifying the Usefulness of Process Models Applied to Forecasting," Electric Power Research Institute, Final Project Report EA-2441, Palo Alto, Calif.

Bever, Robert C., Marsden, J.R., Salas-Fumas, V. and Whinston, A.B. (1982b). "Aggregate Summary Functions: Heterogeneity and the Use of Random Coefficient Models," Advances in Applied Microeconomics, II, pp. 38-60.

Blaug, Mark (1980). The Methodology of Economics, Cambridge University Press, Cambridge.

Blaug, Mark (1983). The Methodology of Economics, Cambridge University Press, Cambridge.

Griffin, James M. (1972). "The Process Analysis Alternative to Statistical Cost Functions," American Economic Review, 62, pp. 46-56.

Griffin, James M. (1977). "Long-Run Production Modelling with Pseudo-Data: Electric Power Generation," Bell Journal of Economics, 8, 1, pp. 112-127.

Hoffman, E., Marsden, J.R. and Whinston, A.B. (1984). "Efficient Use of Economic Data," zerox.

Hoffman, E., Marsden, J.R. and Whinston, A.B. (1985). "Laboratory Experiments and Computer Simulation: An Introduction to the Use of Experimental and Process Model Data in Economic Analysis," zerox and forthcoming in Advances in Behavioral Economics.

Marsden, J.R., Pingry, D.E. and Whinston, A.B. (1974a). "Engineering Foundations of the Production Function," Journal of Economic Theory, 9, pp. 124-140.

Marsden, J.R., Pingry, D.E. and Whinston, A.B. (1974b). "The Process Analysis Alternative to Statistical Cost Functions: Comment," American Economic Review, 64, pp. 773-776.

Popper, K. (1965). The Logic and Scientific Discovery, Harper Torchbooks, New York.

Popper, K. (1972a). Objective Knowledge. An Evolutionary Approach, Oxford University Press, London.

Popper, K. (1972b). Conjectures and Refutation. The Growth of Scientific Knowledge, Routledge and Kegan Paul, London.

Popper, K. (1976). The Unended Quest, Fontana, London.

Shortliffe, E.H. (1976). Computer Based Medical Consultations: MYCIN, North Holland, New York.

Smith, Vernon L. (1982). "Microeconomic Systems as an Experimental Science," American Economic Review, 72, pp. 923-955.

Swamy, P.A.V.B. (1971). Statistical Inference in Random Coefficient Models, Springer Verlag Co., Berlin.

Tversky, A. (1977). "Features of Similarity," Psychological Review, 84, pp. 327-352.

Yu, V.L., Buchanan, B.G., Shortliffe, E.H., Wraith, S.M., Davis, R., Scott, A.C. and Cohen, S.N. (1979). "Evaluating the Performance of a Computer-Based Consultant, Computer Programs in Biomedicine, 9, pp. 95-102.

16. STRATEGY PLANNING: IMPLICATIONS FOR THE DESIGN OF DSS*

Vicente Salas Fumás
Departamento de Economia
de la Empresa
Facultad de Empresariales
Universidad de Zaragoza
Spain

Strategic planning is one of the elements in the overall corporate planning process of a firm or any complex organization. The main purpose of strategic planning is to formulate, revise and update the strategy of the firm, the master plan which establishes the major objectives and courses of action which will guide the activities of the firm in a long term perspective. Strategy is closely related to the relationship of the organization with its environment. More rapid and challenging changes in the environment are forcing firms to adopt a combination of anticipatory decision making with flexible and real time decision making. Therefore strategy formulation is no longer a quasi-independent part on the overall managerial process of the firm, but more often is difficult to separate strategic from operational problems and decisions. The implications of this evolution for the design of DSS are easy to anticipate.

A second distinct feature of recent trends in strategy planning is the importance of industry and market data in the analysis and decision of the competitive strategy of the firm. Business strategists are realizing that not all the business environment is equally relevant for the success and failure of their firms. In the early days of corporate strategy environment was associated with "nature", that is with uncertainties and unpredictable changes common to most firms and organizations. Today, the industry and market segment where the firm competes are considered the key element of the environment. The exogenous, non-controllable, variables which influence the performance of a given firm are not random variables, but the strategic variables controlled by the rival firms. From the game against nature which firms seemed to be playing when strategy came about,

* Research partly financed by the CAICYT. Project No. 3354-83.

the notion of strategy has evolved toward a competitive game among rational actors. The challenge for DSS is now to provide models of imperfect competition which can help decision makers to select a winning strategy.

Basic Features of Strategic Planning. -- Probably the most fortunate definition of planning is problem solving in the abstract. When we plan we are modelling the real world, abstracting from details and trying to find the best way to achieve our objectives. The modelling and search process are relevant whenever we are facing a new objective or constraint for which no previous solution has been learned and memorized before. Once the plan of action is decided, the execution and problem solving in the real world will be guided by such a plan. Therefore, plan and action are clearly interrelated, although conceptually separated.

The distinct feature of strategic planning comes from the nature of the problem that is intended to solve. Among the different classifications of problems in general, and business problems in particular, strategic problems are unstructured, with many variables and constraints, with difficulties for balancing conflicting objectives and with broad spectrum of consequences inside the organization. Moreover, the substance of the problem deals with aspects which condition the survival of the organization and very often involve organizational changes which require to gain cooperation and overcome resistances to change, from groups of people inside the organization.

Resolution of the strategic problem implies identifying strategic objectives (those whose achievement conditions the long term survival of the firm) and finding strategies, (ways and means) for reaching them. The abstraction and modelization which takes place in planning implies that information is the main "raw material" employed in the process. The nature of the strategic problem will also influence the kind of information which is often found in strategic planning. Keen and Scott-Morton [1978] summarize the characteristics of the information used in strategic planning in the table that follows.

Task Variables	Strategic Planning	Management Control	Operational Control
Accuracy	Low	-----	High
Level of Detail	Aggregate	-----	Detailed
Time Horizon	Future	-----	Recent
Frequency of Use	Infrequent	-----	Frequent
Source of Information	External	-----	Internal
Scope of Information	Wide	-----	Narrow
Type of Information	Qualitative	-----	Quantitative
Age of Information	Older	-----	Current

As we will show later, this view of the difference between the information for strategic and for operational planning is more adequate for a traditional view of strategic planning where this process is separated from operational decision making. Under the traditional perspective it would be considered "ridiculous" or a "useless exercise", [Keen and Scott-Morton, 1978, p. 84] to provide fast access to current data for strategic planning. The reason was that strategic planning was not viewed as a real time decision-making process, but a process throughout which the organization was preparing the grounds for future decisions or deciding on something whose execution and implementation would occur later on in the future. Since there are still many instances where the traditional view of planning is followed, we will present a review of both, periodic and real time planning.

Structure and Process of Strategic Planning: Traditional View. -- It would be too long and impractical to review the extensive literature on strategic planning. Instead we have tried to summarize the most relevant features along two dimensions, the process of planning and the levels of the organizational hierarchy where it takes place. The summary is presented in Figure 1, where each entry of the table includes the main types of variables and models which are present at that point of the process and at that level of the hierarchy.

Figure 1 implies that there is not a single strategy for the firm but a combination of strategies organized along the lines of the organizational structure. At the highest level we find

Process of Planning Strategy Level	Internal Audit	Environment Analysis	Company Objectives	Strategic Problem	Proposal of Alternative Strategies	Evaluation and Choice	Programming and Execution
Societal (Company President and Board)	-Social Audit -Contribution of the Firm to Social Welfare	-Political, Cultural and Social Trends	-Corporate Culture -Corporate Social Responsibility -Business Ethics	-Past and Future Trends of the Social Strategy -Patterns of Reference in Social Attitudes Towards Private Firms	-Own and Other Companies Expe -Models of Power Influence and Legitimation	-Combination of Firm's Social Preferences Environmental Trends and Constraints (Multiattribute Utility Theory)	-Concern for Company's Culture -Integration of Employees and Managers -Influence on Corporate Strategy
Corporate (General Manager; Top Management)	-Business Portfolio -Synergies (B.C.G., McKenzie)	-Economic Turbulence -Macroeconomic Data and Trends -Technological Change	-Value Creation -Control of Bankruptcy Risk -Concern for Positive Synergies	-Trends in Future Portfolio Evolution -Internal Consistency and Sustainable Growth	-Models of Internal Resource Allocation -Models for Evaluation of Mergers -Diversification Models	-Maximum Long Term Value of the Firm	-Business Objectives -Distribution of Resources among Business
Business (Divisional Manager)	-Physical, Technical Human, Organizational Resources -Business and Financial Risk	-Business Attraction -Industry and Market Data -Life Cycle -Market Share	-Profitability, Growth, Risk -Flexibility and Stability	-Cost, Profit, Investment -Market Share Trends -Strengths and Weaknesses	-Competitive Variables at the Firm Level: Price, Advertising, R&D; Long-term Perspective	-Optimization Models -Game Theory and Imperfect Competition	-Program Budgeting -Functional Policies -Operating Decisions

Figure 1.   Structure and Process in Strategic Planning:
Data and Models Involved in the Process

what Ansoff calls the "Societal Strategy", that is the strategy
which integrates the firm with its environment in the broadest
sense. The importance of this strategy for the private enterprise comes from the growing conflict between the private and the
public interest in fields such as environment protection, distribution of income, minority interest, scarcity of energy and other
basic resources. At the same time this level of the strategy is
the main theme for public enterprises and not for profit organizations which often appear to substitute and compensate the
activities of private initiatives in fields of social concern.

At the second level of the hierarchy we find the corporate
strategy which is particularly involved with the relations which
the firm has established with the economic segment of its environment. For most of the private companies, the economy, the
market, the cost of inputs and the evolution of technology are
the main areas of concern. If at the same time the firm is
organized around several businesses (distinct product/market combinations), the corporate strategy, under the responsibility
of the general manager of the firm, has the role of integrating
into a common objective and direction each business strategy.

The management of individual business inside the corporation
justifies the creation of multidivisional structures where each
division, and divisional manager, is in charge of managing one
of the businesses. At the business level the strategy establishes
how the firm is going to compete in the business and therefore
the strategy formulation changes from unaccustomed and unfamiliar
sources, including foreign technologies and competitors. At the
same time, the speed at which such changes have developed has
been increasing to a point where the periodic system of decision
making may no longer be capable of perceiving and responding to
them fast enough. Strategic response in real time is therefore
the reflection of a new strategic decision-making system which
has to respond to unfamiliar and surprising changes in a very
short time (in an unplanned manner).

Although there may be different real time decision systems,
we focus on what Ansoff calls planned management behavior where
response to change is a combination of extrapolative forecasting

augmented by threat/opportunity searching environmental surveillance. The extrapolative accounting-based information system of
the past is extended into a comprehensive environmental surveillance system which receives information, filters it and diagnoses
the existence or not of threats and opportunities. The distinct
features of this system will now be analyzed.

Planned management behavior in real time may be considered
a problem solving process which tries to build into the organization the patterns of behavior which are described in the cognitive theory of human psychology and conduct [Simon, 1960].

Strategic problem in this context is defined by the existence
of a positive difference between the organization's strategic
objectives and the most reliable forecast on the situation of the
firm when the current strategy is projected into the future.
This difference is named planning gap, and from the gap analysis
it should be possible to make a diagnosis about the basic reasons
behind the poor anticipated performance of the organization. The
computation of the planning gap, and in order to make a diagnosis
about which is the strategic problem behind the poor anticipated
performance, requires specific information about what is the forecast for future environment and what is the current status on the
organization's capabilities and resources available for competition. The internal audit and the environmental analysis of the
periodic planning cycle are intended to obtain such complementary
information in a permanent and systematic manner. In a real time
decision-making perspective, however, another solution is needed
based upon the perceptive recognition of strategic issues in the
flow of information which is continuously capturing the surveillance system.

The operation of the surveillance system involves three main
parts, forecasting, modelling and impact estimation. The main
techniques involved in each of the parts and their degree of
application according to the status of the environment are
summarized in Figure 2. The operation of the system may be
viewed as an intelligence system which has to filter the information from the environment and pass it into the organization.
Once the first filter is passed, the information reaches the

	Type of Environment		
	Extrapolative	Life Cycle	Discontinuities
* Forecasting External Environment (Economic Social, Cultural, Political)			
- Extrapolation	X		
- Scenarios	X		
- Competitive Analysis	X	X	X
- Experts Opinion	X	X	X
* Modelling of the Environment/Organization Relation			
- Input-Output	X		
- Econometric Models	X	X	
- Mathematical Programming Models	X		
- Cybernetic	X	X	X
* Estimation of Impact			
- Impact Analysis			X
- Cross Impact Analysis			X
- Deductive Analysis		X	

Figure 2.   Parts and Techniques of the Environment Surveillance System

Adapted from Ansoff [1984, p. 327]

decision-making units which have to either accept or reject the
received signal. The acceptance or rejection will be dependent
on their education, past experience, attitudes ..., that is on
their perception about the relevance of the data they are provided
with. From the perspective of the cognitive theory of behavior,
the surveillance system of the organization is the link between
the strategic image of the organization and the changing external
environment. This image is described as the knowledge base of
the organization or collection of information that the organization has on itself and on its relevant environment. The process
of interaction between the image and the internal or external
environment through the surveillance system may be interpreted
in two ways, according to the planning model adopted. In the
periodic planning model the interaction is a way of updating the
knowledge base of the organization. From the real time decision-
making perspective, on the other hand, is a way of detecting
strategic issues, that is events occurring outside or inside the
organization and which are perceived to be relevant for its
success or failure.

The steady state equilibrium of the organization may then be
described as a situation where current or learned action plans
are perceived as the actual ways of achieving the strategic objectives (no gap or problem is detected). When the image, knowledge and reference models, captures a signal which modifies
current equilibrium, the system enters into an emergency situation
which in turn starts the solution process. The first step in the
process is a memory search for a solution which may have been
detected to be useful in the past under similar circumstances.
Whenever the perturbation of the image is sufficiently strong
and new, the memory search for learned solutions may end up
with a failure and a creative process of new learning has to take
place. Additional internal and external information may be
gathered, at the same time that all available information may be
logically interrelated into a model of the organization and its
environment. The model may be useful to help to identify new
courses of action and to stimulate and orient the search for alternative strategies. Among them a final decision will have to
be made on what to choose to be implemented. This choice will

respond to given preferences, risk attitudes and overall goals
and objectives of the organization which may also be considered
part of the knowledge base.

Finally, the selected strategy has to be translated into
operating plans which will become the instructions guiding the
future actions at all levels of the organizational hierarchy.

The summary of the basic elements of the cognoscitive model
for real time strategic planning may be represented as follows

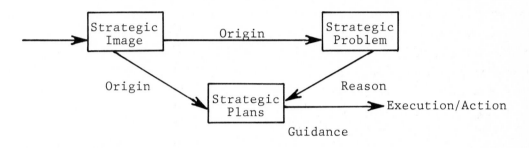

Observing this picture we clearly understand the basic role
of the organizational image in the overall planning process.
The image filters the external signal sensing presence or not of
a problem, and is the source of the proposed solutions (plans)
for trying to solve such problems.

Strategic Issues. -- The input which brings into action the
strategic planning system described above is called by Ansoff
strategic issue, forthcoming development, either inside or outside of the organization, which is likely to have an impact on
the ability of the organization to meet its objectives. The
real time strategic planning system is in charge of detecting
the occurrence of such issues, analyzing them and sending instructions to those who are responsible for immediate action. This is
done generally outside or even in substitution of the formal
period planning cycle. Two main considerations are made to justify
the opportunity of this distinction. One is the fact that some
organizations, especially small ones, cannot afford or do not
need, the rigid and expensive process of annual strategic planning. The other circumstance is related to the turbulent nature
of the environment for some organizations. There are however

situations where both, the periodic planning cycle and the management of strategic issues may be implemented together, each of them
devoted to one purpose complementary to the other: periodic planning is concerned with determining the basic objectives and
policies of the organization and the strategic issue management
is addressed to deal with deviations from these thrusts which may
occur as a result of new threats and/or opportunities.

The operation of a strategic issue management system is
based on two main attributes, early identification and fast response. Early identification is assured by a "real time", permanent attention to internal and external developments. This may
imply a monthly review and update of a list with strategic issues.
A summary of what may be an example of this list is shown in
Figure 3.

Fast response on the other hand requires that the management
of the system is under the responsibility of the senior management group, with power and resources to take immediate action
when it is needed. Sometimes this may even require cutting
across normal hierarchical lines, organize project teams and
look for expert individuals.

The strategic issue management system may also have a permanent structure inside the organization. This structure will
divide responsibilities among the groups involved in the system.
A staff group, for example, may be in charge of detecting and
evaluating strategic issues, alerting decision managers of any
unpredicted important occurrence. In another situation the staff
group is unnecessary and the general management has direct responsibilities for detecting and assessing the importance of the issues. The third potential element of the structure is the project team, in charge of resolving the issues with proper actions.

Together with a formal structure, and the permanent list of
issues, the management system includes a methodology for evaluating the urgency of the issue.

Mathematical Modelling in Strategic Planning. -- The lack of
a formal, well-defined, theory of corporate strategy has seriously
limited the application of mathematical modelling to strategic

Environmental Trends	Internal Trends
Trends in the global marketplace	Size
Growth of government as a customer	Complexity
Monetary trends	Structure
Inflationary trends	Communications
Competitive importance of technology	Centralization/decentralization
Emergence of new industries	Capital intensity
Consumer pressures	Technological intensity
Union pressures	Work force competence
Competition from developing countries	Management competence
Strategic resource shortages	Product diversification
Changing work attitudes	Market diversification
Redistribution of power within the firm	Values and norms

Objectives

Profitability

Growth

Cyclical stability

Flexibility

Vulnerability

Solvency

Market share

External social responsiveness

Responsiveness to aspirations of internal constituencies

Work satisfaction

Figure 3. Illustrative List of Strategic Issues

plant location problems to production planning, optimal pricing
and advertising effort, etc. However models, including features
which have been traditionally considered important in the business
strategy literature, market share, learning, and life cycle are
scarce. Probably the best of them is still the STRATPORT for a
single business unit reported by Larreche and Srinivasan [1982].

Modelling of Competition. -- Mathematical modelling is a growing field in corporate strategy. New developments in the theory
and conceptualization of strategic planning are progressively
incorporated into a more comprehensive and useful mathematical
model. There is, however, a particular orientation in the
development of the literature on strategy which is worth mention-
ing for its implications in the future of corporate models. The
new orientation comes from the critics to the traditional view
of business strategy for ignoring the role of industry and market
competition in explaining the performance of a given firm. The
critics point out that traditional strategic planning concepts
do not provide a comprehensive approach to understanding industry attractiveness. At the same time they have ignored in-depth
treatment of competitor's reactions and initiatives. To remedy
this situation some authors, Porter [1980] propose a new conceptual framework for strategic planning, defined competitive strategy, which is built upon the basic models of industrial economics
and oligopoly theory.

To model this new orientation in the strategy field corporate
planners will need instruments which take into account the competitive situation of the firm in the market. Game theory, in
the branch of competitive games, or even cooperative games if
collusion is also contemplated, will have to be the starting
point of conceptual and mathematical modelling in the strategy
field. The basic concepts underlying the theory of games are:
the rules of the game (the environment), the players (competitors), the pay-offs, moves, choices, alternatives, information
and strategies. These elements lead naturally to the operational
definitions of concepts such as viability, vulnerability, com-
mitment, deference ... which offer intriguing insights into
making moves and countermoves.

The future mathematical models in the field of competitive strategy will probably evolve from current management games, which are mostly used for executive training and education. However the new models will have to include mathematical relations describing _real_ industries and markets, instead of the simulated situations which are part of the management game. Before real models become available, further steps will have to be taken to complete data bases including firm and industry information on the main competitive variables. The PIMS (Profit Impact of Market Strategy) program of the Strategic Planning Institute is an initiative in that direction. The program utilizes a data base of strategic information on over two thousand product-line businesses and its objective is to find statistical regularities on type of market environment, competitive strategy and business performance. The participants in the project receive from PIMS a certain number of reports, including a report on what is the normal return for business similar to the company business; reports on the future prospects of a given strategy; and reports on the evolution of their future portfolio of businesses.

It is unlikely that a firm will be able to collect this type of detailed information about its immediate competitors in order to build its own mathematical model of the industry. However, repeated interaction with the PIMS data base may provide sufficient insights to be able to incorporate competitors and industry data into the game's theoretical model of competition. From another perspective the model included in the decision support system of the firm may be designed to accept the industry data and mathematical relations of the PIMS data base as the relevant model of the competitive arena with which the company is playing the competitive game.

Figure 4 shows an example of a hypothetical decision tree in a competitive situation between two firms. Player one represents a firm who has to decide whether or not to enter into a new market which is currently under control of a dominant firm, player two. The new entrant realizes that competition will be hard in any case, but his chances of success depend critically on the financial reserves which the incumbent firm will have at its disposal

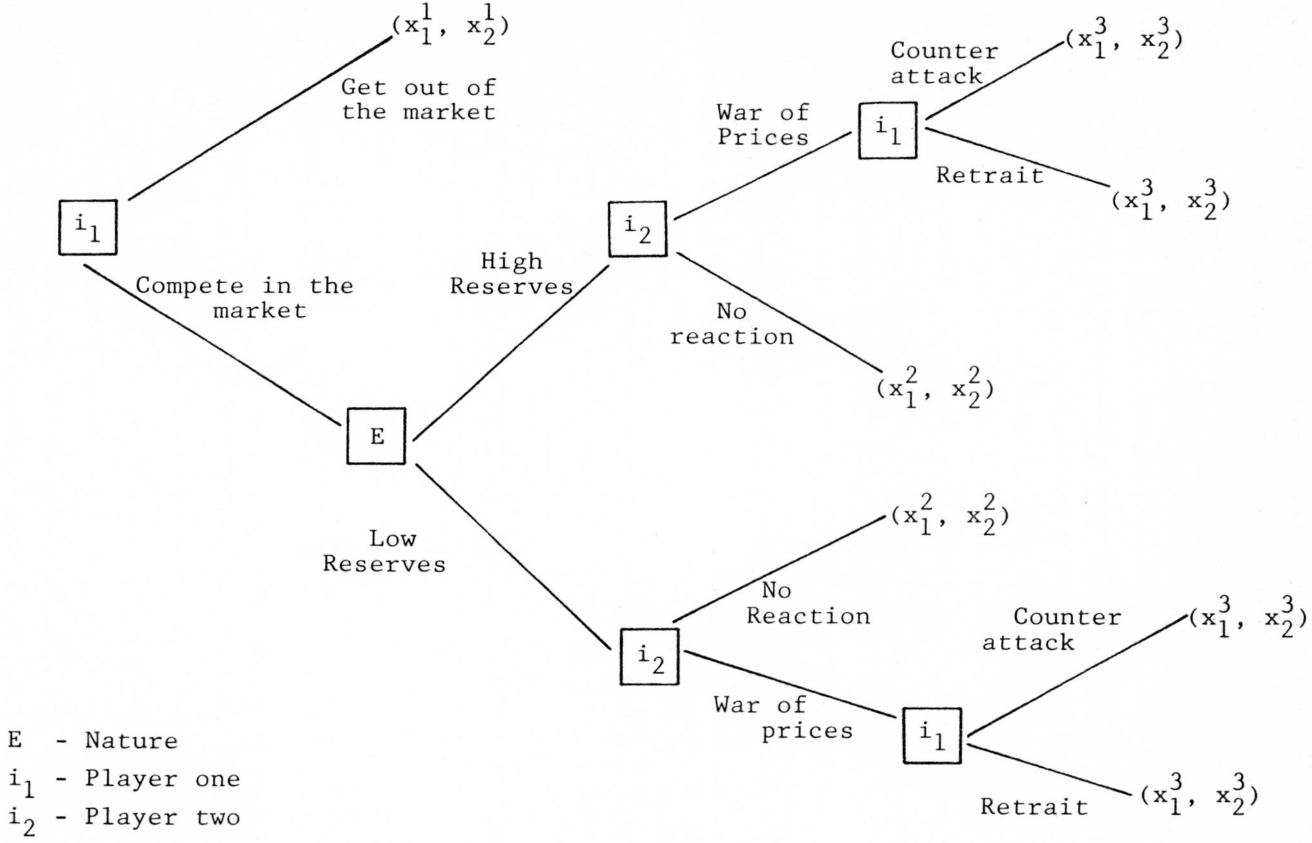
(x_1^1, x_2^1)
Get out of the market
Compete in the market
i_1
E
High Reserves
Low Reserves
i_2
War of Prices
No reaction
i_1
Counter attack
Retrait
(x_1^3, x_2^3)
(x_1^3, x_2^3)
(x_1^2, x_2^2)
i_2
No Reaction
War of prices
(x_1^2, x_2^2)
i_1
Counter attack
Retrait
(x_1^3, x_2^3)
(x_1^3, x_2^3)
E - Nature
i_1 - Player one
i_2 - Player two

Figure 4. Example of a Decision Tree in a Competitive Game Ponssard [1977, p. 69]

to start a price war. Since the existing firm is a division of a multi-business conglomerate, it is difficult to forecast how the parent company is going to react in the issue of financial reserves. From the point of view of the entrant the uncertainty on the financial reserves may be contemplated as a play against nature. On the other hand, the price war may be analyzed as a rational move and countermove of the incumbent firm. The pairs (x_1^t, x_2^t) indicate the payoffs of the players at move t in their competitive war. To solve for the best competitive strategy some additional information is needed on subjective probabilities of each player about the other player's reaction to his competitive moves. The complete formulation and solution of this game may be found in Ponssard [1977].

Implications for the Design of Decision Support Systems. -- This paper is not on DSS, but rather tries to bring into the attention of those involved in the design of DSS new developments and decision-making problems in the field of organizational planning and strategy. We now specifically address the issue of how the developments in the strategy field affect the future of DSS.

From our perspective, a DSS is a combination of logical, software, and physical, hardware, resources to improve the human's capabilities for solving complex problems which appear in the context of personal or organizational decision making. In this context they are recognized to be the synthesis of related fields such as Management Information Systems, Operations Research, Language Theory, brought together for the purpose of helping humans to make better decisions.

Computers have been present in planning and decision making for a long time, especially in data processing and operations research applications. The functions traditionally performed by computers in these situations were access to data bases, resolution of mathematical problems and management of data bases. Our review of planning and strategy does not suggest that these traditional uses of computers will no longer be important in the future. However, we agree with those who point to DSS as the most adequate combination of logical and physical computation technology to improve decision making at the level of strategic planning. As Keen and Morton [1978] point out, DSSs have distinct features such as assisting managers in supporting their decisions instead of replacing them, recognizing the ill-defined and un-structured nature of strategy formulation, and being oriented towards improving effectiveness rather than efficiency of the decision. These are features which are demanded by those involved in strategic planning. Bonczek, Holsapple and Whinston [1980], on the other hand, indicate that DSS may be viewed as the culmination of an evolution in the field of corporate modelling, from an early stage characterized by a long communication chain between the decision maker and the computer, primitive data handling methods and concentration in problems of operational control, to a recent stage where the importance of incorporating extensive data handling capabilities and models into a single system with which the decision maker can directly communicate, is widely recognized [p. 338].

The concept of DSS, the basic features and orientations, are therefore well established. Our points will be made only on what should be the actual content of a DSS from a strategic planning perspective. We start with the general comments on what is demanded in future DSS, to finish with the two main points raised in this paper. A set of representative generalities may be summarized from Naylor [1981].

Modular. -- The second generation of DSS for strategic planning were characterized by an attempt to incorporate as many planning and modelling features as possible into a single computer system. It seems likely that many of the existing planning and modelling software systems will adopt a modularized approach. That is, the user will be able to purchase the parts of the system which respond to his problem needs and qualifications, without having to purchase sophisticated modules of econometric modelling or risk analysis. As his familiarity with the system improves he will acquire additional modules as they are needed.

Interfaces. -- Third generation decision support systems will reflect and exploit the complementarity of corporate simulation models, analytical portfolio models, and optimization portfolio models. The DSS being built will have to incorporate the required linkages among them.

Graphics. -- Future DSS will have to maintain or even increase their graphical output capabilities.

Mini-Computers. -- The extension of DSS for strategic planning to be implementable in mini-computers will be demanded by small companies interested in performing strategic planning.

Ease of Use. -- There are clear indications that future generations of planning and modelling languages will become even easier to use than in the past.

Together with these general trends in the future developments of DSS we believe that the real challenges will come from the progress of strategic decision making in real time and the incorporation of competitive gaming among the mathematical models of competitive strategy. The design, review and update of the strategic issues list will require important data management capabilities. The operation of environmental surveillance systems to detect strategic issues, evaluate their impact and transmit the alarm and need for action to the persons affected in the organization, will demand pattern recognition and artificial intelligence capabilities. The experience in management games may help in constructing the oligopoly models of industries and markets which will help organizations in selecting their optimal competitive strategy. However more research is needed to build realistic models of industries and markets where firms compete. Until a more comprehensive solution is found, DSS will have to be adapted to the actual conditions of competition. In this perspective, Scott Morton [1982] suggests the following specialization: If the firm is competing in a market which is just emerging, DSS should help managers in making their first move, in a similar way as the opening move of the

chess game. In more mature markets, with experience enough to
estimate and operate mathematical models, simulation and "what
if" capabilities of the DSS will be especially important. Finally, when markets decline and a few competitors are left in the
market, the DSS should help management in playing the "end game"
providing complete and detailed winning strategies.

REFERENCES

Abel, D. and Hammond, J. (1979). Strategic Market Planning,
    Prentice-Hall.

Ansoff, J. (1984). Implanting Strategic Management, Prentice-
    Hall.

Bonczek, R., Holsapple, C. and Whinston, A. (1980). "The Evolv-
    ing Role of Models in Decision Support Systems," Decision
    Sciences, April.

Davis, B., Caccappolo, G. and Chandry, M. (1973). "An Econometric
    Planning Model for AT&T Company," Bell Journal of Economics,
    Spring.

Hamilton, W. and Moses, M. (1974). "A Computer-Based Corporate
    Planning System," Management Science, October.

Hofer, C. and Schendel, D. (1978). Strategy Formulation: Analyt-
    ical Concepts, West Publishing.

Keen, P. and Scott Morton, M. (1978). Decision Support Systems,
    Addison-Wesley.

Larreche, J. and Srinivasan, V. (1982). "STRATPORT: A Model
    for the Evaluation and Formulation of Business Portfolio
    Strategies," Management Science, September.

Lorange, P. and Vancil, R. (1977). Strategic Planning Systems,
    Prentice-Hall.

Naylor, T. (ed.) (1982). Corporate Strategy, North-Holland.

Naylor, T. and Thomas, C. (eds.) (1984). Optimization Models
    for Strategic Planning, North-Holland.

Ponssard, J. (1977). Logique de la Negotiation et Théorique
    des Jeux, Les Editions d'Organization.

Porter, M. (1980). Competitive Strategy, Free Press.

Scott Morton, M. (1982). "The Role of Decision Support Systems
    in Corporate Strategy," in Corporate Strategy, T. Naylor
    (ed.), North-Holland, p. 97.

Seaberg, R. and Seaberg, C. (1974). "Computer Based Decision System in Xerox Corporate Planning," <u>Management Science</u>, April.

Simon, H. (1960). <u>The New Science of Management Decision</u>, Harper & Row.

17. COMPUTER-ASSISTED STRATEGIC PLANNING

Prof. Dr. Peter Mertens
Universität Erlangen-Nürnberg
Lange Gasse 20
D-8500 Nürnberg, West Germany

1. INTRODUCTION

Many companies have traditional systems to assist corporate planning by edp. Examples are systems of equations to simulate the consequences of different investments, policies of depreciation or profit distribution on earnings, taxes, cash flow, and balance sheet of the next years. Other applications are risk analysis or models to estimate the influences of changes in sales on the usage of the production capacities.

In recent years, strategic planning has gained more importance. So it seems worthwhile to ask whether computer assistance may be used for these purposes too.

On the one hand we are at the very beginning, on the other hand there already exist some interesting ideas and pilot projects.

In the first part of my paper I'll describe some possibilities for using modern information technology to improve the strategic position of the company, whereas in the second part we'll see how these techniques may help to make better decisions (Figure 1).

2. IT AND STRATEGIC POSITION

Let's take some examples:

1) A large insurance company in Nuremberg, my home town, offers personal computer software which helps people in banks to advise clients how to invest their savings, or tax advisors to calculate alternatives. In certain cases the computer program would ask whether the clients have enough insurance protection and give the advice to reflect signing new insurance plans. No wonder that the Nuremberg insurance company's own special plans, by the way, are also demonstrated.

2) A manufacturer of hospital equipment has implemented special

NATO ASI Series, Vol. F31
Decision Support Systems: Theory and Application
Edited by C. W. Holsapple and A. B. Whinston
© Springer-Verlag Berlin Heidelberg 1987

Figure 1. Information Technique (IT) and Strategic Planning

terminals in his wholesalers' offices. Using these terminals
they can efficiently send their orders to the manufacturer.

3) A large credit card organization has implemented machines
    where travelers can get new traveler's checks just by put-
    ting in a plastic card and a password in the lobby of first
    class hotels [Canning, 1984].

4) A manufacturer of air conditioners gives personal computers
    including software packages to plumbers or architects. When
    designing a new air conditioning system these people can use
    the pc's, but sometimes the result of the calculations will
    be such that the system must be built using the components
    of our manufacturer.

5) Foremost McKesson is a drugstore distributor which showed a
    mediocre performance in the past [Rockart and Scott Morton,
    1985]. A new management shifted attention to information
    technology. Each step in the value-added chain was examined
    to find ways to use IT as efficiently as possible (Figure 2).

    In purchasing, more accurate forecasts for demand were
kept. In receiving, checking all items against invoices
was supported by IT. The result of these two measures was

that the employees could handle more items and the inventory was reduced.

In the next step terminals were installed in the drugstores. The customers could order directly and the company guaranteed delivery within a specified time. The advantage for the drugstore distributor was that the customer was now doing the order-entry job, for the drugstore the advantage was that they could reduce inventory because of the guaranteed delivery time.

The real strategic payoff of this use of IT was achieved by strengthening the close link to the drugstores because the personnel were familiar with the installed terminals. Information about products ordered by the customers but currently not in the program helped the company to add those items to the product line.

In the next step the company offered its customers the service of collecting the payments from the insurance companies for the products sold. This use of information technology gave the company not only a link to a new customer (the insurance company) but opened up a totally new business: claims processing and collection.

My examples stem from quite different areas, but they have one feature in common: the company which offers such computer-assistance first has a strategic advantage, for the tax advisor

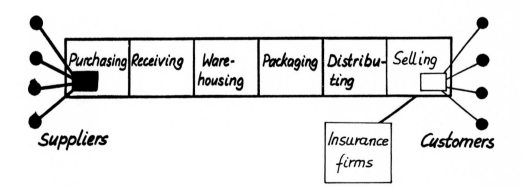

Figure 2. Value-added Chain of a Drugstore Distributor

will never use the hardware and software of more than one insurance company, the wholesaler of hospital equipment will not
install a battery of terminals for the single manufacturers in
his office, the hotel management may give room only for one
machine to print traveler's checks remotely and the drugstore
does not want to bother with more than one terminal and software.

3.   IT AND STRATEGIC DECISIONS

   We can find three possibilities to assist strategic decision-
making by modern information techniques (Figure 3):
1)   Systems to collect information
2)   Decision support systems to model strategic problems
3)   Systems to improve the communication between the decision-
     makers.

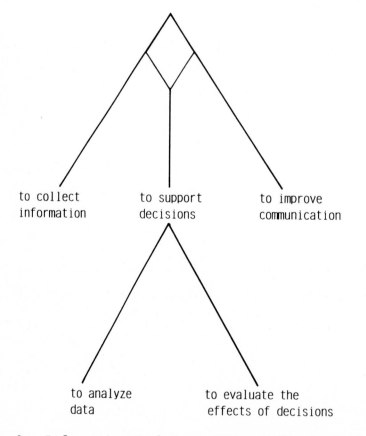

Figure 3.   Information Technique (IT) and Strategic Decisions

3.1. Systems to Collect Information

3.1.1. Know-how Data Bases

FESTO is a manufacturer of pneumatic and electronic control
equipment [Matschke et al., 1984]. Its business is worldwide.
Consider the following case: a sales engineer in Canada is working with a Canadian dairy on how to improve the movement of milk
buckets. Some weeks later the sales representative of the firm
in South Africa has a similar problem. How does he know that
the engineer in Canada has made an offer and written a system
design including drawings, etc.? So we built a so-called know-
how data base: all documents on bids, technical proposals, etc.
are sent to the corporate headquarters and abstracts are stored
in a data base. Using a special information-retrieval system,
interested employees can find solutions for special industries,
certain technical purposes, those who make use of special components, etc. (Figure 4).

In the first phase the system will work offline, but in a
few years it will be connected to the international electronic
mail system of FESTO which is based on Hewlett Packard computers
(series 3000).

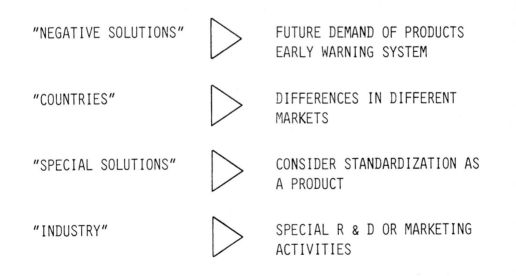

Figure 4.   Usage of a Know-How-Data-Base for Strategic Planning

This picture is a summary of information retrieval in a data base where messages from readily available publications are stored (Figure 6). It shows large government projects in several countries; e.g., projects to build new power plants. As MAN's sales and profits are heavily dependent on such projects it turned out that it was very important to search intensively in these information bases when preparing strategic decisions.

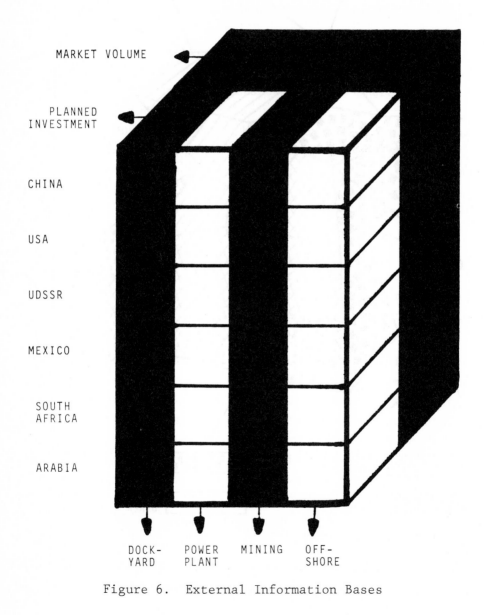

Figure 6.   External Information Bases

In a variation of the retrieval process we see in which large industrial projects our main competitors are participating (Figure 7).

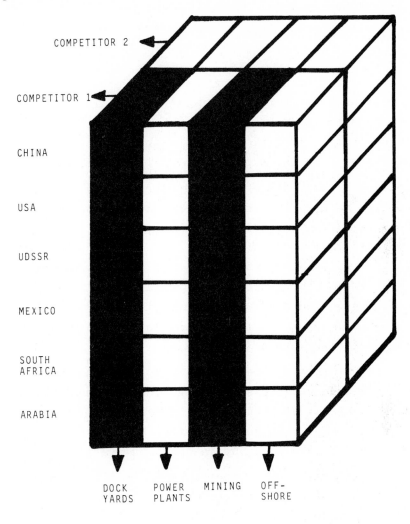

Figure 7.   External Information Bases

Let me finish this part of my paper by giving one more general hint: According to our experience it was a problem that when discussing the results of our data base queries with managers of MAN there were always new ideas how to modify the questions or how to group the information in a different way. So it might be worthwhile to download an extract of the host's data

base and store it in our own computer, maybe a microcomputer.
Then we can make a relaunch of the retrieval procedure. But
pay attention to the copyright problems!

3.2. Decision Support Systems

3.2.1. STRATPORT

STRATPORT is a special corporate model for the analysis of
strategic alternatives [Larreche and Srinivasan, 1981]. Its
basic philosophy follows the ideas of John D.C. Little's famous
paper on the so-called decision calculus [Little, 1970]. The
next figure shows this basic philosophy (Figure 8).

The manager begins with a basic hypothesis; e.g., that the
reaction of the market share on an advertising campaign will
have an S-shape. Then the computer asks some questions in order
to gain information on the parameters of the S-shaped function.
For example, it will ask at what level the market would be satu-
rated so that any further advertising would be useless, or what
level could be defended without any advertising, or which
market share would result if the company raised its advertising
to 150% of the current state (Figure 9).

Using this information the computer program constructs the
function by non-linear regression. Then the dialogue between man
and computer continues with the computer asking for some input
data for a simulation. The question might be: How much advertising money do you plan to spend in the next six months?

The machine then simulates the development of the market
share using the model it built itself after the initial dialogue
with the human planner.

Now comes an important step: when the program has calculated
the new market share it asks the user whether he has the opinion
that the market share is plausible. Pay attention that the
question is not whether the market share is correctly calculated
because such a question wouldn't make sense. If the resulting
market share seems plausible the user might gain confidence and
work with the model in practice. In the other case he might try
with some other data sets or come back to the initial dialogue to

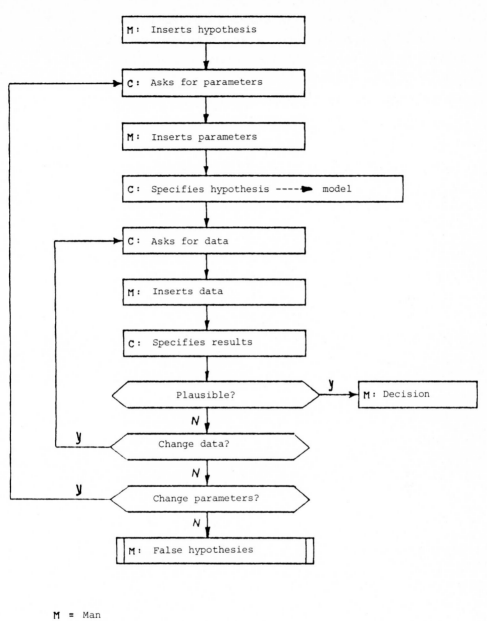

Figure 8.   Procedure of the Decision Calculus (Simplified)

modify the parameters of the S-shape or even try with quite
another model; e.g., one with a progressive function. This is
an important item of decision calculus too because the work with
the system showed the manager that he might have had wrong ideas
on how the market reacts to advertising.

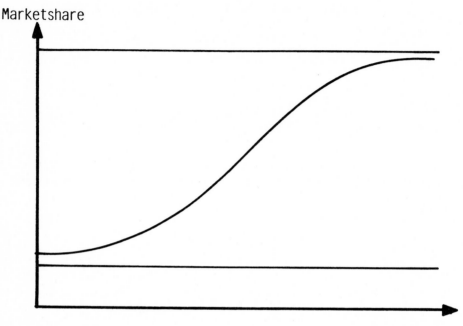

Marketshare

Advertising

Figure 9. Marketshare as a Function of Advertising

Now after this brief introduction into the decision calculus
philosophy let's come back to the special decision calculus model
called STRATPORT.

The next figure shows the structure of STRATPORT (Figure 10).

Investments in strategic business units afford costs; e.g.,
for advertising. Hopefully, market share and sales will grow.
On the other hand, we need additional production capacity and
so we have to spend money again. Moreover additional sales and
additional production will be accompanied by higher inventories
which means more storage costs such as interest. Then the additional earnings and the additional costs are summarized to see
whether the investment would increase profits.

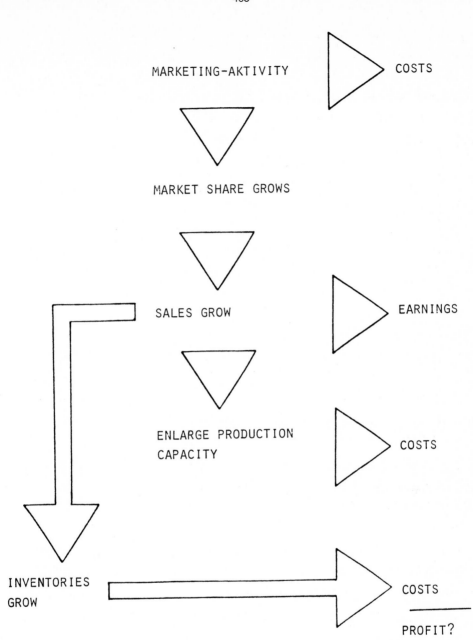

Figure 10.   Chain of Effects in STRATPORT

Some functions used in STRATPORT are:
1)   investment in marketing - market share
2)   investment to defend market share - market share
3)   investment in production capacity - capacity
4)   working capital - sales
5)   cost per unit - cumulative production
6)   price - cumulative production

For the relation between advertising and market share we suppose the mentioned S-shape curve.

The next function shows which costs have to be spent to defend our market share. The assumption is that it is more difficult to defend a big market share than a small one because competitors use to attack the big share first.

The investments to enlarge our production capacity depend on whether it is possible to grow in our present factory or whether we have to look for a new one, maybe in another city (then the investment costs jump).

The working capital may grow exponentially with additional sales because of the growing inventories. If you work in the field of PPS-systems you know this phenomenon.

The production costs per piece often fall with the production volume because of the learning curve. The next figure shows an example from the large German airframe manufacturer MBB (Figure 11).

Now if we suppose that price is strongly related to costs we can make the assumption that the prices also fall exponentially with cumulative production.

Working with DC models like STRATPORT has advantages and disadvantages: According to the experience of colleagues, practitioners in German firms, and ourselves, the advantage is that planners and managers have to make up their minds how the markets work when experimenting with the dialogue model. The disadvantage is that there are so many parameters that you can hardly control and explain the consequences of changing some of them in combination. You would need complicated experimental

465

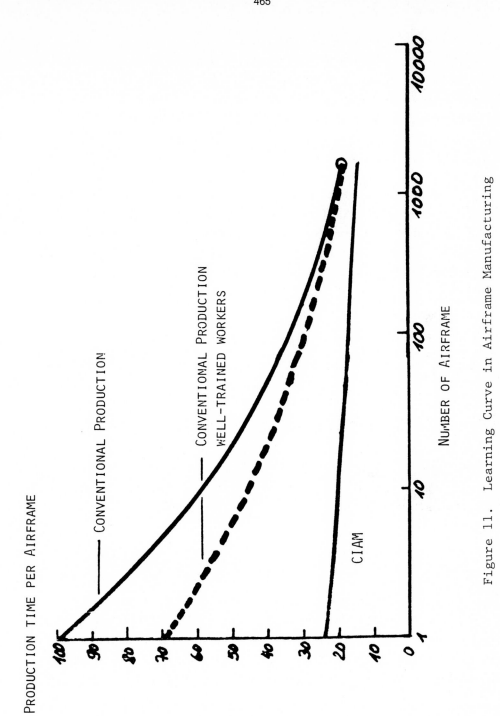

Figure 11. Learning Curve in Airframe Manufacturing

design techniques which are far from being user-friendly.

3.2.2. Scenario Writing Using Cross-Impact Analysis

It is of utmost importance for strategic planning to gain
some information on future developments of the environment of
the company. Very often strategic planners try to build scenarios.

We shall ask whether it might be possible to produce these
scenarios by computer. One idea is cross-impact analysis. We
shall describe in short the system called INTERAX of the
University of Southern California, but in a very simplified manner [Enzer, 1979].

Here we have a matrix with estimates of experts concerning
important future developments including probability estimates
about the time when these events might occur (Table 1).

In the next table we find the so-called cross-impact factors (Table 2).

Let's suppose that government decrees a speed limit. Then
the probability rises that OPEC will collapse because much less
gasoline will be needed. So the factor is greater than one.

On the other hand, if OPEC crashes first, the probability
that government will decree the speed limit falls because in
this case enough gasoline will be available at a reasonable
price.

Now the computer program proceeds similar to the well-known
risk analysis which was first described by Hertz [1964]: Using
random numbers the computer generates a first event. Then it
changes the probabilities of all other events depending on the
factors of the cross-impact table. Then - regarding the new
probabilities - another event is generated, etc. In this way, a
path leading to a certain scenario is written.

Maybe the data of the computer-generated scenario are transferred to other corporate planning models.

Let me say again that my description of the cross-impact
method was a very simplified one.

Table 1. Examples of Events and Their Probabilities

	Probability	Timing in %		
		Until 1988	88-94	94-00
1) OPEC-break down	.200	39.0	37.8	23.2
2) Solar energy	.600	9.3	31.8	58.9
3) Coal-liquesaction	.700	10.4	33.0	56.6
4) More usage of coal	.750	35.5	50.3	14.2
5) Oil slate	.600	6.4	38.3	55.3
6) Nuclear energy forbidden	.175	39.1	32.6	28.3
7) Limitation of gasoline	.400	34.8	40.2	25.0

Table 2. Cross-Impact Factors (Events / Events)

	1	2	3	4	5	6	7
1	1.00	0.90	.90	0.90	0.90	1.50	0.50
2	1.10	1.00	0.80	0.90	0.80	1.20	0.90
3	1.10	0.90	1.00	0.90	1.00	1.05	0.90
4	1.10	0.90	1.00	1.00	1.00	1.10	0.90
5	1.10	0.90	1.00	0.90	1.00	1.05	0.90
6	0.80	1.20	1.20	2.00	1.20	1.00	1.20
7	1.20	1.20	2.00	1.20	2.00	0.80	1.00

As far as I see the method is not well-known in Europe.
One reason may be that the Delphi-method to question the experts
for the estimates is very time-consuming and costly. Maybe
industrial associations will build the cross-impact tables.

3.2.3. Life-cycle Planning

Another idea is to superimpose the life cycle curves of the
main products to attain the total sales curve of the company.
This model is interesting for firms with four or five main products as is the case in the automobile industry [Mertens and
Rackelmann, 1979].

In an analysis with data from the Volkswagen Corporation
we could show that it is possible to predict the life cycle
curve of a car with reasonable accuracy.

In this picture we see the idealized superposition of the
product life cycles (Figure 12). When one product finishes its
cycle and is taken out of the market, the next one is introduced
and ready to become what strategic planners call a "cash cow."
So the whole company shows a healthy growth.

Now assume that one product begins to lose market shares
before its "due date" as was the case with the VW Beetle. And
as we are used to saying in Germany "one accident seldom comes
alone," so we see the Beetle's successor, the Rabbit, is not yet
ripe for introduction into the market, it is a bit behind schedule. The superposition shows that the consequence of these
rather minor effects is a terrible break-down of the company's
total sales.

You can imagine that with a graphic display we can simulate
certain possible developments and use the model as an early
warning system.

It is also possible to link the sales curves with cost
curves in order to gain a forecast of the profit situation. The
cost curves follow the sales curves with a delay. One reason
is that workers cannot be or should not be laid off at the same
time that sales diminish.

470

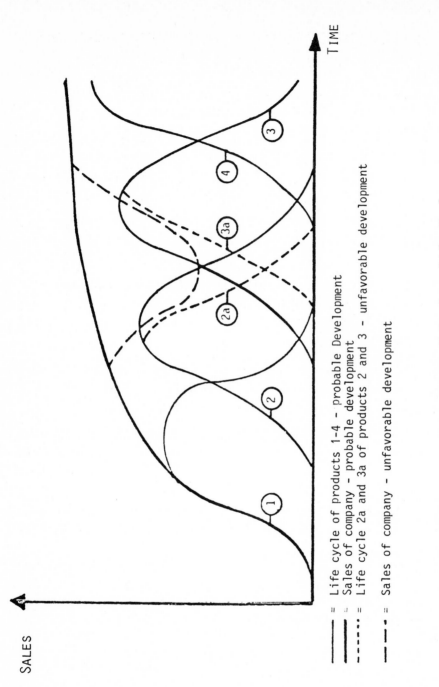

SALES

TIME

——— = Life cycle of products 1-4 - probable Development

····· = Sales of company - probable development

······ = Life cycle 2a and 3a of products 2 and 3 - unfavorable development

— — — = Sales of company - unfavorable development

Figure 12. Superposition of Product Life Cycles

3.3. Improving the Communication between the Decision Makers

3.3.1. Plotting Charts

A main set of tools of the strategic planners consists of matrices like those which the Boston Consulting Group proposed. Let's take as an example the matrix shown in Figure 13.

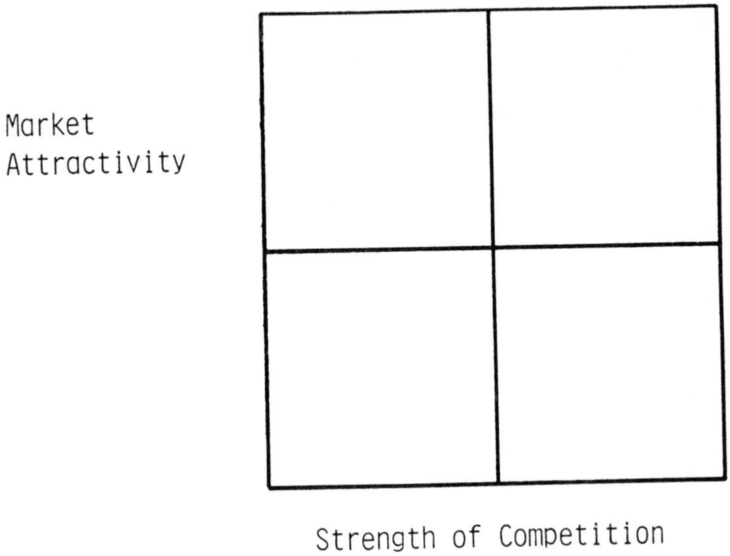

Market
Attractivity

Strength of Competition

Figure 13. Bubble Generator

It shows strength of competition and market attractivity. Both criteria are aggregated from a number of other criteria. For example market attractivity is a function of the market growth, of the attractivity of the technology related to the technological strength of our company, and so on.

At the Siemens Corp. there is a tool called the "Bubble Generator." Its input consists of scores for the single attributes. Using a simple scoring model which includes a weighting procedure the system computes the values of the market attractivity or other aggregated criteria for the single products or product groups and plots them into the matrix. As this procedure needs only seconds, the Siemens people can perform something like a what-if analysis.

Faber-Castell				Datum:	
				Rückgabetermin:	
Projekt-Grobbewertungsbogen				Ideen-Nr.:	
Produktgruppe:		Substitution von:		Bearbeiter:	

Bewerten Sie die einzelnen externen und internen Bewertungskriterien in der dafür vorgesehenen Punkte-spalte im jeweiligen Feld. Sie können pro Zeile die Punktzahl 1, 3 oder 5 vergeben.
Sie gelangen in die einzelnen Felder durch Betätigen der Taste "Springen/Weiter" im rechten Funktionsblock.

Produktidee:

Bewertungskriterien		1	3	5	Punkte
Externe Be-wertungs-kriteren	*Absetzbare Menge (pro Jahr)*	D: I:			
	Ø erzielbarer Händler-EKP	D: I:			
	Produktlebenszeit (in Jahren)				
	Markttrend	rückläufig	stagnierend	expansiv	
	Marktzugang	schwer	leicht zu erlangen	vorhanden	
	Mitbewerbsprodukte	viele	wenige	keine	
	Produktüber-legenheit	keine	normal	groß	
	Marktchance		=	Zwischensumme1	
Interne Be-wertungs-kriterien	*Entw.-kosten in TDM*				
	Investitionen in TDM				
	Herstellkosten in DM				
	Entwicklungs-Know How	schwer zu erlangen	leicht zu erlangen	vorhanden	
	Herstellungs-Know How	schwer zu erlangen	leicht zu erlangen	vorhanden	
	Realisierungspotential		=	Zwischensumme 2	
				Gesamtsumme	

Anmerkungen für Bewerter:

Anmerkungen vom Bewerter:

Figure 16. Project Evaluation Form

The decision makers input their special evaluation and send the form back to the computer.

When all evaluations are available, the computer calculates means, standard deviations and other such measures. Moreover there is a simple graphic display of the results (Figure 17). When a new product is introduced into the market the same electronic mail system is used to plan and control the necessary activities.

3.4. The Corporate Planning System of the ÖIAG

ÖIAG (Österreichische Industrieverwaltungs-Aktiengesellschaft) is the holding company of the government-owned Austrian primary and investment products manufacturing industry with approximately 120000 workers.

The company is continually analyzing and evaluating large industrial projects as well as discussing basic problems of investment, finance, and mergers. For these purposes they built a large model which might be the most sophisticated in the German-speaking area. It is not only used for strategic purposes, but also for these purposes [Mertens and Griese, 1984].

The components of the total system are shown in Figure 18.

The plant models calculate the costs, the development of the revenues, the inventory, the liabilities, and the accounts receivables. These models are rather individual for the specific types of companies within the trust. For process-oriented firms the model simulates the cycles of material and energy using an input-output table. Basic data are the planned production program (product mix) and the prices.

The equipment model computes the influence of investment, disinvestment and depreciation policy on the balance sheet and the profit-and-loss statement.

The fixed asset model has the task to project the consequences of credits and loans on the balance sheets of the following years. It calculates the time series of the credits, expenses for interest, and annuities.

Statistische Auswertung der Projekt-Grobbewertungsbögen

Kriterium	Mittelwert	Minimum	Maximum	Spannweite	Standardabweichung
Absetzbare Menge	3,57	3	5	2	0,9
Ø erzielbarer Händler-EKP	2,43	1	5	4	1,4
Produktlebenszeit	4,43	3	5	2	0,9
Markttrend	4,71	3	5	2	0,7
Marktzugang	1,86	1	3	2	0,99
Mitbewerbsprodukte	1,86	1	3	2	0,99
Produktüberlegenheit	3,57	3	5	2	0,9
Zwischensumme 1	22,43	17	27	10	3,33
Entwicklungskosten		3	5	2	0,7
Investitionen			5	2	0,99
Herst					

Marktchancen- u. Realisierungspotentialbewertung

Marktchance: Min.7, Max.35 Punkte ; Realisierungspotential: Min.5, Max.25 Punkte.

Bewerter	A	B	C	D	E	F	G
Marktchance	25	17	19	27	25	21	23
Realisierungspotential	19	17	17	15	23	19	21

Figure 17. Statistical Analysis of Project Evaluation Form

477

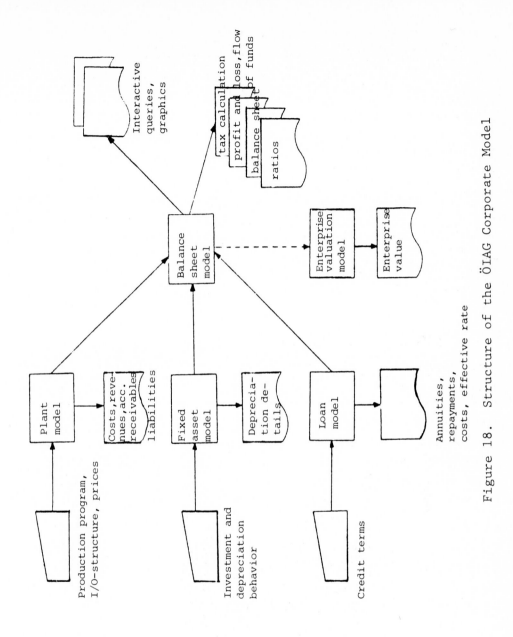

Figure 18. Structure of the ÖIAG Corporate Model

The nucleus of the system is the <u>balance sheet model</u> which
computes the long-term development of the balance sheet, the
cash flow, and certain ratios. This module takes the results of
the other models. So it is possible to simulate the consequences
of different strategies in the individual companies on the holding. These consequences are transferred by the payments between
the companies themselves and between the daughter companies and
the holding.

The <u>valuation model</u> calculates the value of the single firms
and of the trust. So ÖIAG can estimate to which overall value
of the firms or of the trust different strategies lead.

Some problems analyzed with the model and some questions
of the top management answered by the staff using the model are:
1) What growth of the trust is possible, given the financial
   restrictions?
2) What is the investment budget when different possibilities
   of financing it are chosen?
3) In what rhythm should new shares be issued?
4) What are the outcomes of alternative money exchange rates on
   the balance sheet?
5) What are the consequences of different methods of valuating
   the firms and of different depreciation strategies on the
   balance sheet?

The model was developed with a rather small budget in terms
of manpower and computer costs. This was possible because the
little team was extremely motivated and the people in the strategic planning department programmed all their models themselves,
even in a period when this wasn't yet commonplace and when fourth
generation languages were not widespread.

4. <u>SOME IDEAS TO USE EXPERT SYSTEMS FOR STRATEGIC PLANNING</u>

Strategic planning seems to be too soft to use expert systems
for the whole process. But there might be some partial problems.
Such a partial field is portfolio planning. The portfolio model
is a very simple one. So a lot of scientists and consultants
have been trying to extend the method by including more

influencing factors. But now the procedure has become too complicated. Expert systems could allow the consideration of a large
number of influences while the user would not have to see them
all simultaneously in his short-term memory ("brain amplifier")
[Mertens and Plattfaut, 1985].

In this figure we show the factors influencing the market
growth in a tree structure. This hierarchy of conditions could
be made more sophisticated in a real system. In such a system,
soft facts could be considered also (Figure 19).

The usage could be as follows: The expert system would try
to verify a certain hypothesis - in our case the rate of market
growth. It would put questions to the user and check the conditions of the hypothesis by going backward through the tree of
rules. When certain conditions are not fulfilled, branches of
the tree would no longer be considered. When some hypotheses
are verified, the system could propose a so-called "norm-
strategy."

We think that the special advantage of this approach would
be that no factors which once were regarded as important would
be eliminated from the reasoning process. The path leading to
the conclusion would be traced and could be evaluated by other
persons in the company too. New findings in the process of
strategic decision making could be included by additional rules.

As in most expert systems the main problem will be to make
the design for the tree of rules, a task which is often called
"Knowledge engineering." As in many fields it is difficult in
strategic planning to collect the basic information. And a
famous word of Feigenbaum fits: "What the masters really know
is not written in the textbooks of the masters."

REFERENCES

Canning, R.G. (ed.) (1984). "Developing Strategic Information
    Systems," EDP Analyzer, 22, 5.

Enzer, S. (1979). "INTERAX - An Interactive Model for Studying
    Future Business Environments," Working paper No. M35 of the
    Center of Futures Research of the University of Southern
    California at Los Angeles, Los Angeles.

480

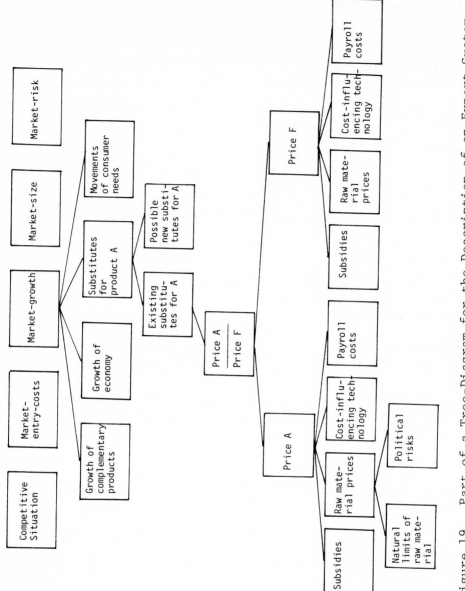

Figure 19. Part of a Tree-Diagram for the Description of an Expert System

Fendt, H. (1983). "Blick in die Zukunft," in Wirtschaftswoche, 37, 29, pp. 40.

Hertz, D.B. (1964). "Risk Analysis in Capital Investment," Harvard Business Review, 42, 1, pp. 95.

Larreche, J.-C. and Srinivasan, V. (1981). "STRATPORT: A Decision Support System for Strategic Planning," Journal of Marketing, 45, 4, pp. 39.

Little, J.D.C. (1970). "Models and Managers: The Concept of a Decision Calculus," Management Science, 16, 8, pp. B466.

Matschke, R., Grosse, W., Mertens, P., Schiller, W., Springer, R. and Zielinski, B. (1984). "Das Konzept einer Know-how-Datenbank im Industriebetrieb," Angewandte Informatik, 26, 11, pp. 471.

Mertens, P. and Griese, J. (1984). Industrielle Datenverarbeitung, Bd. 2, Informations- und Planungssysteme, 4. Aufl., Wiesbaden.

Mertens, P. and Plattfaut, E. (1985). "DV-Unterstützung der Strategischen Unternehmensplanung," Die Betriebswirtschaft, 45, 1, pp. 19.

Mertens, P. and Rackelmann, G. (1979). "Konzept eines Frühwarnsystems auf Basis von Produktlebenszyklen," in Frühwarnsysteme, Ergänzungsheft 2 der Zeitschrift für Betriebswirtschaft, H. Albach, D. Hahn and P. Mertens (eds.), pp. 70.

Rockart, J.F. and Scott Morton, M.S. (1985). "Implications of Changes in Information Technology for Corporate Strategy," Interfaces, 14, 1, pp. 84.

INDEX

Data base (*cont.*)
  evolving, 400
  extensional (EDB), 74, 77
  external, 456
  global, 417
  intensional, 78
  interface, 75
    component of, 75
  internal, 254, 256, 260
  know-how, 455-456
  management, 38, 165, 191,
      193-194, 244, 321, 393
  management of, 445
  multidimensional, 155
  network, 189
  office, 219-220, 231
  patent, 456
  physical, 8
  OPTRANS (OPTRANSDB), 143,
      145-147
  PIMS, 443
  postrelational, 189
  query, 459
  relational, 19-20, 22, 24,
      27-28, 30, 46, 55, 69,
      73, 139-140, 143, 146-
      147, 150-151, 154
    extended, 55
  representation, 129-131
  search, 228
  semantic, 223
  structure, 399
  theory, 96
Data base management systems
    (DBMS), 7, 8, 55-57, 60-
    61, 71, 137, 219, 241,
    243, 277, 391, 393, 396,
    400
  conventional, 57, 60
  deductive (DDBMS), 60-61,
      65, 79-80
    relational, 55
    architecture of, 60-62
  function, 137
  multidimensional, 137
  network, 400-401
  relational, 400-401
Data definition language
    (DDL), 61
Data/knowledge base manage-
    ment system
  architecture, 57, 59
Data manipulation language
    (DML), 61
Data set, 422
  historical, 422

Data set (*cont.*)
  homogeneous, 422
Data types, 57
DB2, 398
DB-queries, 72
DB query language expression
    (DBQLE), 59-60
dBase II, 377
Decision, 423-424
  aid, 279-280
  calculus, 460, 462
    procedure of, 461
  characteristic, 424
  dis-similar, 424
  DSS, 425
  economic, 267
  ES, 425
  human expert, 425
  making, 3, 10, 14, 185,
      225, 228, 436
    anticipatory, 429
    diagnostic, 335
    financial, 335, 339, 351
    organizational, 4, 10
    real time, 429, 431, 434,
      436
    strategic, 447, 454, 479
  process, 3, 425
  set, 424
  similar, 424
  strategic, 454, 458
  support, 208-209, 212-213,
      217-218, 222, 231, 235,
      239, 243, 257, 322, 326,
      401
Decision support systems (DSS),
    3-11, 13, 19, 46, 55, 91,
    95, 108, 128, 137, 139-
    141, 143, 159-175, 177-
    183, 185-187, 191, 193-
    195, 197-199, 208, 212,
    236, 239-241, 254, 256-
    260, 265-266, 277-279, 281-
    282, 322, 332, 335-336,
    339, 342, 345-346, 349-351,
    373, 382, 385, 387, 391,
    399, 411, 430, 440-441,
    443, 445-448, 454, 460
  accessibility, 473
  artificially intelligent,
      185-186, 194, 196, 204,
      206-207, 210, 212
  auditing, 279
  auditor, 282
  bandwagon, 3, 10
  characteristics, 165, 183

NATO ASI Series F

NATO ASI Series F